War, Institutions, and Social Change in the Middle East

v^qy

EDITED BY

Steven Heydemann

UNIVERSITY OF CALIFORNIA PRESS
Berkeley   Los Angeles   London

This volume is the result of a project on war and social change in the Middle East, directed and sponsored by the Social Science Research Council, Joint Committee on the Near and Middle East.

University of California Press
Berkeley and Los Angeles, California
University of California Press, Ltd.
London, England
© 2000 by the Regents of the University of California

Library of Congress Cataloging-in-Publication Data

War, institutions, and social change in the Middle East / edited by Steven Heydemann.
    p.   cm.
    "This volume is the result of a project on war and social change in the Middle East, directed and sponsored by the Social Science Research Council, Joint Committee on the Near and Middle East."
    Includes bibliographical references and index.
    ISBN 0-520-22421-3 (alk. paper).—ISBN 0-520-22422-1 (pbk. : alk paper)
    1. Middle East—History—20th Century.   2. War and society—Middle East.—3. War—Economic aspects—Middle East.   I. Heydemann, Steven.   II. Joint Committee on the Near and Middle East.

DS62.8 W37   2000
956.04—dc21   00-028657

Manufactured in the United States of America

The paper used in this publication meets the minimum requirements of ANSI/NISO Z39.48-1992 (R 1997) (*Permanence of Paper*).

This book is a print-on-demand volume. It is manufactured using toner in place of ink. Type and images may be less sharp than the same material seen in traditionally printed University of California Press editions.

CONTENTS

ACKNOWLEDGMENTS

Editing a volume is often described as the kind of thing everyone should do
. . . once. In this instance, however, it was not the editor who bore the burden of keeping a project on track but the contributors to the volume who
deserve my thanks and gratitude for their willingness to tolerate so good-
naturedly the long delays in the preparation of this manuscript. The project began during my tenure as director of two programs at the Social Science Research Council in New York—the Program on the Near and Middle
East, and the Program on International Peace and Security—and without
the support of the SSRC, both fiscal and administrative, the project would
not have been possible. We were also fortunate to have received the support
of the Ford Foundation through a grant from the Cairo field office that
funded the participation of scholars from the Middle East in a conference
where initial drafts of some of the papers included here were presented.
The conference was held in the wonderful setting of the Institut d'Études
Politiques in Paris, thanks to the intervention of Jean Leca, a former member of the Joint Committee on the Near and Middle East. Although more
papers were presented at the conference than we could reasonably include
within this volume, the ideas contained in them have had a significant impact on the final shape of the project. Within the Council, this enterprise
fell under the purview of the Joint Committee on the Near and Middle East,
whose members were an ongoing source of critical guidance and critical
support. Joel Migdal, chair of the Committee from 1991 to 1996, was centrally involved in the design and conceptualization of this project. He deserves much of the credit for bringing it to completion.

This volume is dedicated to my wife, Gail David, who endured the many
absences imposed on me both by my responsibilities at the SSRC and by the
demands of bringing this long-running project to a close.

War, Institutions, and Social Change in the Middle East

Steven Heydemann

This volume responds to two significant and related gaps in the study of war in the Middle East, one empirical, the other theoretical. The first is a serious deficit in research on war making and war preparation as sources of state and social formation and transformation in the Middle East. With the partial exception of Israel, where the social and institutional effects of persistent conflict have received a measure of attention, the study of war in the Middle East has been shaped much more by military and diplomatic historians, theorists of international relations, and journalists than it has by their counterparts in comparative politics, comparative and historical political economy, sociology, social history, and anthropology.[1] War has been a growth industry for analysts and researchers of conflict resolution, peace keeping, arms control, and negotiation, as well as specialists on foreign policy and strategic studies. Particular disputes are the subject of voluminous literatures: first and foremost the Arab-Israeli conflict, with the Iran-Iraq and Gulf Wars not far behind. Yet we know relatively little about how states and societies in the Middle East have been shaped and reshaped by their intensive and prolonged exposure to and participation in war making and war preparation, often conducted by regimes that have embraced militarization as an everyday tool of governance as much as (if not more than) a means to ensure national security. Despite the now thoroughly noncontroversial observation that war making, state making, and "society making" are mutually interdependent, there have been no more than a handful of studies that have explored how these dynamics interact in the Middle East.[2] Without in any sense disparaging the contributions of the existing literature on war in the Middle East, it remains true that such research has been deficient in its attention to war as a social and political process.

The presence of a gap, however, is not in itself justification for a response. Many topics that go unstudied no doubt deserve their fate. But in this instance, the consequences of this relative neglect are twofold, and they make quite clear its empirical and analytic costs. First, we lack the knowledge base that would permit us to explain the effects of war making and war preparation on current political, economic, and social arrangements in the Middle East. If we take seriously the proposition that war is a social process, then understanding these effects deserves our attention. Second and just as important, we lack an analytical basis for determining whether the experiences of the Middle East might force social scientists to rethink the general assumptions that have defined research on the relationship between war and state formation in other cases. In some respects this latter concern is the more significant. In the absence of efforts to explore rigorously where Middle East cases align with or challenge current theories of the relationship between war and state formation, it will not be possible to construct alternative, more satisfactory, theoretical accounts. Without such accounts, our understanding of dynamics that have been central in shaping the contemporary Middle East will be at best incomplete and at worst distorted.

The contributions to this volume take both empirical and theoretical concerns seriously. They present considerable new material about the social, institutional, and political dynamics of war making and war preparation in the Middle East, and thus add significantly to what we know about these processes in the region. They also frame the material, in most instances, as a critical response to existing theories of how war making, state making, and social processes like the construction of citizenship interact. In many cases they highlight significant points of divergence between available theories and the realities of the Middle East and thus underscore the value of this region to the larger theoretical enterprise of understanding how war shapes patterns of social, institutional, and state formation and transformation.

Considering the scope and scale of war making and war preparation in the Middle East—the sheer intensity of militarization as a persistent and pervasive attribute of everyday life across the region—the paucity of research on war as a social and political process is puzzling, not least because academics typically are far too entrepreneurial to leave a significant phenomenon unstudied. Why then, has such an obvious and important research agenda been left to languish? Answering this question is necessary to help situate the second, theoretical, gap this volume hopes to address: the lack of fit between the experience of war in the Middle East and the research base that shapes theory building in the study of war, the state, and society.

In my view, the absence of research on war and the state in the Middle East has relatively little to do with an inherent lack of interest on the part of Middle East specialists but quite a bit to do with the peculiar genealogy of the research program on war and the state that emerged (or perhaps reemerged) in the United States in the 1970s as a result of the important work of Charles Tilly and the other contributors to his edited book *The Formation of National States in Western Europe*. Tilly's volume helped consolidate a broader renewal of interest in "the state as a conceptual variable," yet over time the research agenda it inspired became embedded within assumptions that gradually undermined its capacity to innovate and adapt.[3] In other words, it is the path-dependent quality of research on war and the state— the extent to which it has become constrained by the conceptual frameworks around which it was originally organized—that explains, at least in part, the puzzling neglect by Middle East specialists of research on war as a social and political process.

This claim deserves elaboration. To an exceptional degree, contemporary research on war and the state has been organized around and shaped by an interest in explaining the macrohistorical dynamics of state formation in Europe.[4] Researchers have focused particular attention on the period from the sixteenth to the nineteenth century and have followed lines of inquiry that are broadly similar to those mapped out by Tilly—according distinctive weight to the role of war in the expansion of state capacities, the emergence of new patterns of human and economic mobilization, the organization of extractive institutions, and, for some, the transition from absolutist to republican forms of government.[5] The coherence of this agenda should not be taken to imply convergence in its findings. Where Tilly and colleagues have explored links between war making and the gradual transition from absolutism to representative forms of rule, Downing argues that "extensive domestic resource mobilization" produced the destruction of representative governance and the rise of autocracy.[6] Nonetheless, among scholars of the contemporary developing world, one response to the hegemonic status of Europe has been to take the generalizability of this larger research program as given and to regard the conceptual assumptions underlying it as unproblematically portable across time and space.[7] Unfortunately, these efforts have tended to confirm for us little more than the fact that the twentieth-century developing world is not like eighteenth-century Europe. That is, the results of these projects tend to show, to take just one example, that war has not been positively correlated with the emergence of strong states and representative forms of governance in postcolonial Africa as it was in the transition from absolutist to republican France.[8] Quelle surprise.

Yet the implications of this response are too troubling to treat dismissively, as many other critiques of the Europeanist impact on the organization of research have already pointed out.[9] They reinforce an impression of the developing world as "non-Europe," a domain in which outcomes (typically negative outcomes) are accounted for by the absence of attributes that explain outcomes that are coded as positive in the European context.[10] Rather than question whether a given research framework offers an appropriate starting point, scholars who adopt approaches to the study of war and the state based on the experience of early modern Europe seem more concerned with figuring out why the contemporary developing world deviates from what is assumed to be the modal historical trajectory established by Germany, France, and England between 1500 and 1900.

Among those interested in explaining trajectories of state and social formation in the Middle East, the more common response to the prominence of early modern Europe in research on war and the state has been to take seriously the vast differences separating it from the contemporary developing world and to look elsewhere, typically inward, for explanations of state institutional formation, the construction of national markets, and the organization of state-society relations. On one level this is an appropriate reaction. Where an existing literature seems to hold little promise for explaining a particular puzzle, it is eminently reasonable to turn elsewhere. And this response also suggests that the gap identified here is less the result of neglect than of a rational decision by scholars of the Middle East reacting to the regional parochialism that has been so evident in research on war and the state. Yet this response also imposes significant costs. It focuses attention on mechanisms other than war in explaining institutional, political, and social outcomes in which war has been implicated in numerous settings, and it obscures the effects of a major, global force driving state and social formation and transformation. With these concerns in mind, a second aim of this volume is to strengthen connections between research on war as a social process and the study of political, social, and institutional change in one part of the contemporary developing world.

What is striking and noteworthy is that the current trajectory of research on war and the state did not become path constrained because the initial findings in this area generated increasing returns to scale theoretically for the scholars who applied them to settings other than Europe. In fact, the authors who helped revive interest in the topic of war and the state were quite cautious about the extent to which early modern Europe might hold out lessons that could be generalized to more recent periods and other regions. Tilly warned, for example, that "our ability to infer the probable events and sequences in contemporary states from an informed reading of European history is close to nil." At the time, he was prepared to speculate only that "some general relationships among the ways of building state power, the forms of relationship between men and government, and the character of the political institutions which emerge from the process of state building which held within the European world still hold today."[11]

Thus, the current analytic hegemony of Europe in research on war and the state represents a consequence that was both anticipated *and* unintended. Why then did it happen? In my view this development reflects in no small measure the dramatic reversal of intellectual fortunes among scholars of the developing world since the late 1960s, as well as the failure of some of their successors to heed the cautions of Tilly and others. It underscores how shifts in the organization of research agendas within comparative politics over the past thirty years have worked, unintentionally, against the emergence of a more broadly grounded set of approaches to the study of war, the state, and society. To establish how this came about, however, requires a brief bit of theoretical archeology, excavating among the ruins of research programs that were buried in the seismic shifts that reconfigured comparative politics when modernization and systems theories crumbled during the 1970s.

For those who study a part of the developing world like the Middle East—whose uncertain standing in the social sciences epitomizes the ambivalent relationship between area studies and the disciplines—there is no small measure of irony in recalling that *The Formation of National States in Western Europe* had its origins in the work of the Social Science Research Council's Committee on Comparative Politics, best known for its sponsorship of a series of influential books on political development in the "developing areas," including the Middle East.[12] In 1969 the committee's members invited Tilly to direct a project on European state formation. The invitation grew out of the committee's interest in using European cases to test and refine systems theories of political development and modernization that were derived from the imposition of organic-functionalist frameworks onto the developing world.[13] Yet the interest in Europe among comparativists was not merely an attempt to make the world safe for systems theory. It also reflected a broader concern that Europe itself was on the verge of becoming marginal to comparative politics. The interest of the Social Science Research Council (SSRC) in European state formation was thus in part an effort to revitalize the study of Europe by incorporating it within (and subjecting it to) the field of political development.[14] While it takes a long memory to recall a moment in American social science when comparativists worried about Europe's marginal role in the advancement of theories that originated in the experience of Africa or the Middle East, Lucian W. Pye, chair of the SSRC committee when the Tilly volume was in preparation, made this argument in his foreword to the book.[15] "One of the purposes of the study reported in this volume," he noted, "was to discover the extent to which a review of state-building in Europe could usefully inform contemporary efforts at advancing both the practice and theories of political development."[16]

Pye and the committee, however, were to be disappointed, a fact he scarcely bothered to conceal in his rather grudging acknowledgment of Tilly's effort. What seemed especially disturbing to Pye, apart from the importance the contributors attached to violence in the process of state formation rather than to the role of the state as dispenser of justice, was the project's failure to find support for the ahistorical and universalizing assumptions of political development as defined by the Parsonian systems theories of Apter, Almond, Coleman, and others. Tilly made this difference of perspective explicit: "The analysis of political development," he claimed, "has had about the same relationship to historical experience as a dog on a long leash to the tree at the other end of the leash. . . . Some political scientists want to break the leash or at least move the tree. The authors of this book want, instead, a leash which is very long but very sure."[17] Given the usual relationship between dog and tree, this analogy speaks volumes about tensions in the collaboration between historians and political scientists that Pye had singled out as one of the most significant benefits the project was expected to generate. I will leave it to the reader, however, to decide whether historians or political scientists were cast in the role of the tree.

Tilly's critical response to the universalizing ambitions of the SSRC committee captured emergent strains in the relationship between history and political science and added one more voice to a growing chorus of criticism being directed against the methodological assumptions underlying the committee's work, both from within and without.[18] By the time *The Formation of National States* was published in 1974 the field of political development was fragmenting, breaking apart under the combined weight of its own totalizing ambitions and the sustained salvos of its critics.[19] The work of Tilly and his collaborators helped, along with many others, to shift the study of state formation from the domain of political development and systems theory to the domain of macrohistorical comparative sociology and comparative-historical political economy. Within the SSRC, the Committee on Comparative Politics was decommissioned in 1972, even before the Tilly volume appeared. After some short-lived and undistinguished follow-on efforts, the SSRC Committee on States and Social Structures was formed in 1983, "bringing the state back in" and signaling in a decisive fashion the transition in analytic and empirical emphasis then under way in the social sciences.[20]

While few mourn the passing of systems theory, what concerns us here is not the reorganization of postmodernization social science in general, but one specific effect: the increasing appeal of state-centered approaches, including a growing interest in American political development and the workings of the capitalist state, contributed to a dramatic inversion of perceptions within political science concerning the analytical relevance of particular regions.[21] Europe and the industrialized West once again secured their position as the analytic metropole, while large parts of the Third World—Africa, South Asia, the Middle East—again became theoretically peripheral. Given this shift it is not surprising that while scholars of the

Middle East found statist theory to be highly productive—even if only as the object of their criticism—the flow of ideas tended to be one way: from the analytic metropole outward to the analytic periphery.[22]

Thus, comparative research on the state in the Middle East, including the very limited work that has been done on war and the state, almost inevitably has been framed as a test of theoretical claims derived from research on Europe against the experience of Middle East cases.[23] Tilly himself, despite his own concern that European history might teach us relatively little about "probable events and sequences" in contemporary states, seemed to endorse precisely this choice of research strategies. He stressed, in a claim that evidences a certain complacency about the rightness of Europe's leading role in the organization of research, that the "European historical experience, for all its special features, is long enough, well-enough documented, and a large enough influence on the rest of the world that any systematic conclusions which did hold up well in light of that experience would almost automatically become plausible working hypotheses to be tried out elsewhere."[24] Tilly has since retreated from this position, recognizing that *The Formation of National States*[25] simply replaced one unilinear model of state formation with another. Yet scholars of the Middle East might nonetheless be forgiven for wondering what distinguishes the length or archival record of Europe's historical experience from that of Egypt, Syria, or Iraq (or the Ottoman, Safavid, or Mughal Empires). The larger concern, however, is that in his earlier work Tilly did not seem either to envision the kinds of distortions that would follow the "automatic" acceptance of European experiences as plausible hypotheses nor perceive of a way in which the rest of the world might influence Europe. And in fact, completing feedback loops—using findings drawn from the experience of Middle East cases to reshape the theoretical assumptions of the "metropole"—has happened only rarely.

My intent in raising (resurrecting?) these issues is not to invoke nostalgia for the era of systems theory—a construct of Rube Goldberg–like complexity and misplaced energy—simply because it provided a vehicle for the inclusion of developing countries at the core of the social sciences. Nor, on the other hand, do I mean to suggest that research that takes Europe as its reference point is somehow complicit in a larger Orientalist project, a position expressed by Said, Mitchell, and Bromley among others.[26] The engagement between Middle East scholarship and European ideas has been far more reflective and self-critical than such an interpretation allows. Rather, my purpose is to underscore how larger trends in the organization of the social sciences have shaped research on war and the state in the Middle East and thus helped to produce the theoretical gap to which this volume is a response. Is there agency lurking somewhere in this sketchy account of institutional developments in the social sciences, a causal mechanism that would make clear how shifts at one level affect outcomes at another? There is, but agency is found largely in the diffuse and often opaque incentives and sanctions that guide individual choices about how to position one's work: which assumptions one accepts as automatically plausible, which frameworks to adopt, which audiences to engage, and which arguments to challenge.

Where then, does this volume fit? *War, Institutions, and Social Change* establishes a starting point for shifting research on war and the state in what we hope will be seen as more productive directions for scholars and students of the developing world. We also hope to establish more clearly where the points of divergence and convergence lie in the comparative study of war, the state, and society and thus strengthen the foundations of cross-regional research in which European experiences are understood as no more and no less idiosyncratic and historically bounded than those of the Middle East. This is not in any sense a rejection of existing frameworks. Our starting point is not the incommensurability of theories that derive from the experience of different regions. Not only would this outlook simply promote multiple parochialisms, but it would obscure the extent to which our concerns overlap with the agenda of those who work on similar processes in different times and places. Like our colleagues who study Europe, we are interested in understanding the origins of distinctive institutional configurations, how state capacities, including extractive capacities, are formed and transformed by war, and how war preparation and war making affect patterns of state-society relations and techniques of governance.

Thus, the contributors to this volume explicitly view their work as theoretically engaged, not regionally constrained. Our aim is to work toward research agendas that more adequately take into account how differences in the social, institutional, political, and economic circumstances of war making and war preparation in the late-developing periphery change the kinds of questions we ask and the kinds of research we design. At the end of the day our cases are different not because they are non-Western but because the conditions in which the dynamics of war making and war preparation have unfolded in the twentieth-century Middle East differ in crucial ways from those of pre-twentieth-century Europe. Moreover, our focus on explaining points of divergence led contributors to adopt an inductive rather than a deductive approach to their chapters. It encouraged caution in asserting the generalizability of claims that emerge from the detailed exploration of the dynamics that link war making, state making, and social change in specific historic instances. The contributions thus exhibit a richness of historical and ethnographic detail—in many cases presenting new archival or interview material—in their effort to establish precise causal mechanisms in specific cases ranging from the relationship between food security and tribal participation in the Arab revolt, to the effect of war on the organization of Israeli labor markets after 1967, to the impact of colonial rule on wartime patterns of popular mobilization in Syria and Lebanon, to the economic and institutional factors that make possible a reliance on repressive forms of war preparation as a strategy of rule in contemporary Syria and Iraq.

Second, the identity of our cases as late-developing peripheral states led us to broaden and treat more flexibly the disciplinary boundaries of research on war and the state. Contributors are drawn largely from the disciplines of political science and history but include the occasional sociologist and anthropologist, as well. Thus, while individual chapters often reflect the theoretical concerns of particular disciplines, they are not constrained by such concerns. More generally, my hope is that the volume reflects the sensibility that Geoff Eley described as "a mobile or eclectic interdisciplinarity, in which discussion of 'the state' is . . . removed from its most familiar political science location . . . [, and reflects a] mobility of context, in which discussion moves freely between a variety of conventional 'levels' of analysis, including not just the usual primary context of the territorial and institutionally bounded nation-state, but also the international state system, and the micropolitical contexts of social relations, locality, and the everyday."[27]

POINTS OF DIVERGENCE AND CONVERGENCE

The basis for my claim that European experiences should not be seen as offering an automatic starting point rests on a sense of how sharply the context of war making and war preparation in the twentieth-century Middle East diverges from that of early modern Europe. Moreover, what is most distinctively different about our context holds not just for the Middle East but for other late-developing regions. Although the following discussion does not begin to exhaust the relevant issues, it identifies some key points of divergence that are taken up by the contributors to this volume. These include war making as an indirect and mediated phenomenon; the transnationalization of war preparation and war making; war and the political economy of resource and social mobilization; and the role of war as a source of domestic social and institutional transformation.

First and most obvious, war has interacted with processes of state and social formation and transformation in ways that differ fundamentally from European experiences.[28] Above all, it is not always the state that makes war. In the Middle East as in other developing regions, war making has been indirect, mediated, and deeply transnationalized. In some respects states in the Middle East can be seen as products of World War I and the postwar collapse of the Ottoman Empire. In some instances (the cases of Israel, Saudi Arabia, and the unified republic of Yemen) war making and state formation are linked more directly. Yet the external imposition of state boundaries and institutions of state management through which the vast majority of Middle East states were created is far removed from the dynamics that link war making and state formation in early modern Europe.[29] It was not until 1948 that states in the Middle East engaged one another directly in war as sovereign political units.[30] Political decolonization was not complete until the early 1960s in North Africa and until the beginning of the 1970s in the Gulf.

For much of the last century, therefore, across large parts of the Middle East, war making was an enterprise that had immediate, often deadly effects and consequences for local populations but was nonetheless *indirect* with respect to local states, driven by the aims and interests of external colonial powers rather than local actors. World Wars I and II brought tremendous institutional, political, and social changes to the region, but these conflicts functioned as intervening or mediating variables, creating new possibilities both for colonial intervention and for bargaining on the part of local political actors. Chapters 2 through 5 in this volume explore the dynamics of war making under conditions of colonial intervention or control. Tariq Tell places the Arab Revolt of 1916 in the dual context of Britain's efforts to undermine Ottoman authority in the Arab provinces, on the one hand, and a highly variable local agrarian economy, on the other. The decisions by individual tribes to participate in the revolt were driven not by a commitment to protonationalism, but by the opportunity war provided to trade participation for British guns and grain. As Ottoman troops retreated north, British resources helped to reconfigure domestic political coalitions in the territory that would later become Transjordan. War making altered the dynamics of local struggles over food security as grain-rich tribes of the north faced new challenges from the more grain-dependent tribes of the arid south, who had allied themselves with the imported political leadership of the al-Hussein, themselves sponsored by the British.

Elizabeth Thompson argues that World War II fundamentally transformed patterns of bargaining between French colonial authorities and local actors in Syria and Lebanon. Prior to the war, a wide range of Syrian and Lebanese social groups mobilized to secure services and benefits from the French mandate even as nationalist elites struggled to achieve independence. French authorities responded to social demands with a paternalistic form of welfarism that nonetheless redefined relations between local societies and the colonial state. Under wartime conditions, however, French authority weakened, local demands expanded, and a more articulated colonial welfare state was put in place, legitimated not on the basis of colonial noblesse oblige but on the rights of citizens to welfare. Yet these processes of state expansion and mass mobilization linked to war also reshaped local political conflicts concerning the identity of the state. They pushed domestic debates over public policy and the role of the state to center stage and brought new prominence to political forces in competition with the largely conservative and dominant nationalist elites, thus inaugurating postwar (and postcolonial) struggles over the organization of the Syrian and Lebanese states. In these cases, therefore, war interacted with colonialism, nationalism, and popular mobilization to produce institutional and social outcomes that figured prominently in postwar and postcolonial political struggles in Syria and Lebanon.

Robert Vitalis and I are similarly concerned with the institutional and social effects of World War II but, in chapter 4, focus on the role of Allied regulatory interventions in Syria and Egypt in shaping durable patterns of state-market relations, and we take a view different from that of Thompson regarding the political economy of the colonial state. While all three of us agree on the importance of the war as a critical juncture for postwar political and developmental trajectories, for Vitalis and I the most important attribute of the British colonial state in Egypt or the French mandatory regime in Syria was the narrow extent to which these states had created the institutional capacities to regulate local economies. Where Thompson perceives a more engaged and interventionist colonial welfare state, Vitalis and I find states whose interventionist capacities were sharply limited. In our account, it was the imperative of responding to war-induced shortages—the result of a near total shipping embargo—that created a new demand for domestic regulatory capacity, a demand that originated not with local actors, but among Western forces operating in the Middle East. To ensure an adequate supply of food and to cope with the effects of wartime inflation, Allied bureaucrats bargained with local politicians to construct a distinctive mix of state regulatory capacities. Acting through a regional organization called the Middle East Supply Centre, these bureaucrats imported into the region new state interventionist norms and administrative practices that then became embedded within dozens of new regulatory institutions—from trade oversight commissions to census bureaus to local supply boards. Allied interventions also helped shift the Syrian and Egyptian economies toward import substitution industrialization, creating the context for postcolonial conflicts over the organization of the political economy in Syria and Egypt—as well as in Lebanon.[31]

In these cases, war making intersected with processes of state institutional change and social transformation but did so more as an intervening variable than as a direct cause of social, political, or institutional change. World Wars I and II produced new patterns of public-demand-making, popular mobilization, and state intervention. They reshaped domestic political arenas and state institutions. Yet throughout the Middle East their effects were mediated by the politics of colonial domination and local resistance, with significant implications for the specific kinds of state capacities and state-society relations war making helped to create. Indirect participation in World War II promoted the deepening of state capacity to regulate trade and agricultural production and supply in Syria and Egypt, but did little to alter the capacity of the state to tax. Considering the centrality of the link between war and the formation of extractive capacities among the states of early modern Europe, this key difference underscores the need to treat skeptically the claim that findings based on European experience represent a set of automatically plausible hypotheses for the rest of the world.

In the post–World War II period—the focus of the six chapters that make up part two of this volume—war preparation and war making were no longer mediated through the experience of colonial rule. Yet even under conditions in which states make war directly—only one of the several forms of war making examined in this volume—war in the contemporary Middle East exhibits attributes and dynamics that suggest important points of divergence between the cases and theoretical assumptions that derive from the literature on early modern Europe.

Most important for the contributors to this volume is the extent to which war in the contemporary Middle East is a transnationalized phenomenon, a reality whose significance Roger Owen stresses in the book's conclusion. In the most basic sense the term *transnationalized* simply emphasizes that war preparation and war making are always, as Eley suggests, multilevel phenomena that are not contained by the boundaries of a territorial state, the political resources of local power holders, or the productive capacity of a domestic economy. Certainly we can interpret the experiences of Middle East states in World Wars I and II in this light, and chapters in this volume do so. Yet the observation holds for the contemporary period as well, in distinctive but no less compelling ways.

For the postindependence states of the Middle East, war preparation and war making—activities typically associated with the aggressive assertion of territoriality—have, ironically, rendered the state highly porous. Moreover, among the states that have been the most engaged participants in Middle East wars—Egypt, Syria, Israel, Jordan, Iraq—the transnationalization of war has been an explicit and conscious strategy of state elites. Preparation for war is funded by foreign military assistance or rents of one form or another, war making is undertaken with imported weapons, global strategic networks and global norms of sovereignty and nonintervention are mobilized to secure local military advantage, and peace settlements are negotiated and guaranteed by external powers. Almost inevitably these circumstances require that we look beyond the demands that war places on domestic institutions, economy, and society to focus on the organization and practices of transnational forms of war making and war preparation, as well as how the transnational and the domestic interact.

The questions that result from broadening our focus in this way have a direct bearing on established agendas of research on war and the state. What remains in such cases of the linkages between war and the extractive capacity of the state, between war and bureaucratization, or between war and technological change? Douglass North, for example, joining scholars from Joseph Schumpter to Goran Therborn to Charles Tilly and his collaborators, argues that a war-driven "fiscal crisis of the state . . . forced rulers to make bargains with constituents . . . the consequence was the development of some form of representation on the part of constituents . . . in return for revenue."[32] Can we therefore account for the absence of representative governments in the Middle East (or assume the legitimacy of authoritarian regimes) by noting that war making has not been accompanied by increased demands for taxation in the Arab world as was typically the case in early modern Europe? How does war making shape patterns of state-society relations when it does little to alter the scope of state autonomy? What are the causal mechanisms through which systemic resources are translated into domestic capacity to mobilize populations or to wage war? In other words, when war making and war preparation become transnationalized, how should we theorize their impact on domestic level processes?

Chapter 5, by Volker Perthes, and chapter 9, by Isam al-Khafaji, take up these questions, among others, for the cases of Syria and Iraq, respectively. In both countries significant state revenues, virtually the entire state budget in the case of Iraq, are secured "externally" through some combination of strategic and oil rents, sources of income that do not require the extraction of resources from domestic populations. Some of the consequences are not hard to anticipate, including the vast expansion of military bureaucracies and huge levels of military expenditure relative to the size of the Syrian or Iraqi populations—and relative to any reasonable assessment of threats. In both cases, the structure of state revenue—the availability of rents—helps explain the capacity of the Iraqi and Syrian (and, one might add, Israeli and Egyptian) regimes to supply military institutions at a level that exceeds what the local economy could support on its own.

The more interesting consequences are found elsewhere. One is the emergence of domestic political economies organized around the regional and international pursuit of strategic rents, a process in which political commitments are mined for their value as productive assets. Contrary to Mann's assertion that the emergence of a capacity to tax domestic populations is so important that the survival of a state often hangs in the balance, in the cases studied here elites have placed much more emphasis on developing a capacity to extract resources from the international system than from their own citizens.[33] As Perthes and al-Khafaji show in considerable detail—findings that call into question Korany's rather suspect distinction between the "warfare state" and the "welfare state" in the Middle East—this mode of resource mobilization is often little more than extortion, has become an end in its own right, and, in the Syrian case, perpetuates an extraordinarily high level of war preparation despite the clear reluctance of the regime over the past thirty years to engage in a full-scale war.[34] This strategy binds the processes of state building, state institutional formation, and the organization of state capacities to the maintenance of a level of threat, or perception of threat, sufficient to permit regimes to extract rents from regional and international alliance networks.

The domestic side of this strategy, moreover, is to strengthen connections between a highly transnationalized political economy of strategic-rent seeking and the use of militarism as a means of domestic social control and social mobilization. Furthermore, such connections complicate in useful ways the notion of a straightforward correlation between the presence of economic rents and state autonomy. Militarism may appear to authoritarian regimes as a highly centralizing and tractable form of mass mobilization. Yet militarism has everywhere been legitimated through ideologies of mass participation, aggressive nationalism, citizenship, and membership in a collective dedicated to the pursuit of a common goal. Even in the authoritarian regimes of the Middle East, recourse to these ideologies creates linkages between states and societies, deepening the accountability of regimes for their performance in war. Reem Saad's ethnography of an Egyptian peasant's memories of war, in chapter 8 of this volume, is a powerful and telling example of this phenomenon.

Although war thus operates as a highly transnationalized phenomenon, the experiences of Syria and Iraq (as well as other states in the region) reaffirm its well-established importance in strengthening the capacity of states to mobilize and repress populations and to articulate especially aggressive forms of nationalist ideology. Yet, as Perthes and al-Khafaji also show, these capacities become embedded in and reproduced through war preparation and war making as routine modes of governance and domination, rather than emerging as responses to the exceptional and temporary exigencies of war.[35] Indeed, it is precisely the normalization of war—the routinization of urgent threats to the nation, the transformation of the extraordinary into the everyday—that reflects the extent to which militarism organizes processes of state formation and state-society relations in a number of Middle East states.

The transnationalization issue is posed most sharply, however, in a case that may be unique to the region—the Palestinian experience of deterritorialized war making as a strategy of state formation, the subject of Yezid Sayigh's chapter 7. As Sayigh argues, "It was war that enabled the [Palestine Liberation Organization] to emerge as the non-territorial equivalent of a state (paradoxical as the notion may be), assert its brand of nationalist discourse and practice, and structure its relations with Palestinian society accordingly[;] . . . war assisted the PLO both to acquire such institutional autonomy as it did and to obtain the resources (whether material, especially financial, or symbolic) that allowed it to occupy a state-like position in relation to its 'domestic' constituents."[36] War making and war preparation (functioning here, too, as independent variables) permitted a group of Palestinian political entrepreneurs to construct the institutional forms of stateness despite their lack of control over territory. "Palestine" thus became visible to and a legitimate participant in an international arena organized as a system of states. It acquired the right to make claims on the attention and resources of that system well before the emergence of Palestine as a territorial entity.

Sayigh also shows how, nonetheless, the absence of a national territory complicated the construction of Palestinian stateness, creating an environment in which consolidating political institutions, centralizing authority, and securing compliance involved tremendously complex, multilayered bargaining among widely dispersed "substate" political factions, multiple state actors, and networks of transnational organizations. To take just one example, political organizations that competed with the PLO for leadership of the Palestinian national movement had autonomous recourse to the means of violence, autonomous sources of revenue, high capacity to exit from central institutions, and independent access to the "domestic constituencies" of diaspora Palestinians. To borrow Tilly's phrase, within the Palestinian community both capital and the means of coercion were characterized by high accumulation but low concentration.[37] Under these conditions the formation of statelike institutions was contingent on the PLO's capacity to define and enforce the terms of legitimate inclusion within the Palestinian national movement, to impose a monopoly on the legitimate use of violence by Palestinians resident in existing Arab states, and to assert its control over revenue flows whether in the form of taxes extracted from Palestinian populations or in the form of foreign aid. The PLO accomplished this task (to the extent that it did) by consolidating its standing as the legitimate representative of an abstraction, .Palestinian stateness— gradually capturing the single most powerful political and symbolic resource of the national movement and wielding it effectively in its relations with competing organizations, Arab states, and the international community.

Issues of stateness, territoriality, transnationalism, and the political economy of militarism play out in very different ways in the case of the 1975–90 Lebanese civil war. In this instance, as Elisabeth Picard illustrates in chapter 10, the collapse of Lebanon's formal political institutions under the strain of intense sectarian violence led to the emergence of a distinctive political formation: the sectarian militia. Lebanon's militias arose initially to protect sectarian communities in the absence of a viable central authority. Yet they rapidly became highly organized mechanisms of predation, taxing the populations they protected and engaging in a wide range of criminal and predatory activities. And they drew not only on local communities of coreligionists but on a range of transnational networks from Lebanese diasporas to state-level and NGO alliance networks that provided both material and financial support. Here too, as in the cases of Syria and Iraq, militias exploited the civil war as a means for extracting resources from diasporas and the international system.

As their activities expanded, militia leaderships appropriated the symbols and practices of stateness and territoriality in an attempt both to legitimate their control over the means of violence and to institutionalize their authority. Nonetheless, despite Lebanon's protracted civil war the state never fully disappeared. It remained a presence in part because its ruins affected the topography of what was built on top of them, but also because of the continued utility of the state for a number of actors, both domestic and external. For the militias the state remained an object of predation, but it also continued to mark a boundary between legality and criminality that the militias could exploit for their own purposes. Thus, the authority of state institutions to sanction certain kinds of activities, to license and authorize, was a significant asset for militia leaders looking to legalize and make systematic what might otherwise appear to be merely the ad hoc pursuit of extortion, smuggling, and theft. Militia economies, moreover, operated within the remnants of a national market, leading, as Picard shows, to extraordinary forms of economic collusion and cooperation among warring militias, whose capacity to maximize the gains from predation forced them to acknowledge the state as an economic space even as they sought to subvert it.[38] The carcass of the state became an ecosystem that helped feed and sustain militia operations internally, while for external actors it provided the only recognizable armature around which interventions and efforts at diplomatic triage could be assembled. Ultimately, Lebanon's militias failed to realize their statist ambitions, and through external intervention Lebanon's state institutions gradually began to assert their authority over local communities. However, the militias and the militia-economies they created between 1975 and 1990 provide an example of microlevel processes of state formation that probably bear closer resemblance to the experiences of early modern Europe than do any of the other cases discussed in this volume, and provide some important clues as to why so many of those experiences ended in failure.

WAR, INSTITUTIONS, AND SOCIAL CHANGE

I've focused thus far on attributes of war preparation and war making in the Middle East that cut across what Eley called "conventional 'levels' of analysis," emphasizing how war as a mediated and transnationalized phenomenon directs our attention to processes that diverge from the local dynamics that figure most prominently in research on war and the state in early modern Europe. However, for virtually all of the contributors to this volume, the most significant effects of war are experienced at the level of local societies and domestic institutions. Almost without exception, the dependent variables in these chapters are domestic-level outcomes of one form or another, from changes in patterns of social mobilization to the rise of new strategies of social control to shifts in modes of economic regulation and levels of state institutional capacity. Since these are also the concerns that have shaped research on war and the state in Europe, our interest in war as a source of domestic transformation would seem to offer especially rich opportunities for the cross-regional and transtemporal flow of ideas and plausible hypotheses. Yet here, too, common ground should not obscure some significant points of divergence, suggesting that cross-regional exchanges of hypotheses will perhaps be more useful in exploring variation than in confirming similarity.

Research findings drawn from European experiences have tended to highlight the centralizing and consolidating effects of war on states. Yet as Joel Migdal in chapter 6, Reem Saad, Elizabeth Picard, and Isam al-Khafaji make clear, war can also sharpen competing identities and affiliations, erode national cohesion, and weaken the position of states that ground their legitimacy in the aggressive pursuit of national security. As demonstrated by the aftermath of the 1967 Arab-Israeli war, even conflicts that end in military victory can reopen the political arena to debates that previously had been viewed as settled. Migdal's chapter offers graphic evidence of how the 1967 war resurrected the question of national boundaries, of statism, and of Israeli identity, transforming and polarizing Israeli society in ways that have decisively influenced local, regional, and international politics ever since. Saad emphasizes the extent to which participation in war on the part of Egyptian peasants redefined their understandings of citizenship, membership in the nation, and relationship to the state, making the state both more immediate but also less imposing. Al-Khafaji stresses the corrosive effects of protracted conflict on Iraqi society, an outcome exacerbated by the Ba'thist regime's cynical manipulation of identity politics as one of the mechanisms it deploys to secure its own survival. Even where war making is less corrosive to the consolidation of states and societies, however, it opens up new arenas of conflict, bargaining, and accommodation, as Thompson's essay illustrates for the cases of Lebanon and Syria in the 1940s.

Rather than assume, therefore, that war advances the consolidation of state institutions and enhances the capacity of states to organize and control societies, the chapters in this volume focus on the capacity of war to turn the structure and roles of the state into highly contested issues of public debate. War makes more transparent the practices by which leaders have sought to construct the state as a set of autonomous institutions and to insulate these institutions from public examination. It calls existing political institutions and practices into question and subjects them to new levels of scrutiny and criticism. In Israel's democratic political system, post-1967 challenges to prewar conventions and practices promoted a sharp political transition from labor to Likud and led to deep and still unresolved conflicts over the core identity of the Israeli state. In the nondemocratic states of the Arab world, war has exposed the fragility of authoritarian regimes and, less frequently, forced a retraction of state power. In these ways, war can create political openings that provide societies under authoritarian rule with moments of exceptional transformational potential.

As we see in much of the research on war and the state in Europe, the transformational capacity of war arises in part from the reciprocal nature of political and social obligations that take shape in the process of preparing for and making war, leading—under certain specific conditions, if we take Downing's argument seriously—to new commitments and new levels of accountability for those who rule. Societies are never simply the objects of state control; they possess a range of mechanisms through which they struggle to impose diverse and conflicting preferences on rulers. These claims and preferences are often reinforced by the tendency of leaders to justify war making in universalist language and categories. The advent of mass conscription, to take just one example, is often accompanied by appeals to the universal equality of citizens and the universally representative character of political institutions that citizens are required to defend. Employing this language however, as Saad shows in the case of Egypt, can give rise to serious conflicts as individuals seek to exercise rights or to reconcile such appeals with existing norms and practices, or as rulers retreat from such claims once external threats recede.

Alternatively, military mobilization can strengthen the political institutions and the authority of political leaders in late-developing contexts as surely as it did in the rise of absolutist states. Theda Skocpol argued that certain forms of radical regimes excel "at conducting humanly costly wars with a special fusion of popular zeal, meritocratic professionalism, and central coordination."[39] Following the 1967 and 1973 Arab-Israeli Wars, and during the long Iran-Iraq War, Syria, Israel, Iraq, and Iran have all experienced exceptionally, perhaps uniquely, high levels of mobilization. Beyond the administrative and financial consequences of managing, supplying, and coordinating sustained mobilization at such levels, whole generations of Arabs, Iranians, and Israelis have been encouraged by state elites to recognize the state and the military as essentially indistinguishable terms. Given the extent of military rule in the Middle East, the lack of distinction between army and state is not surprising. In more subtle ways, however, the self-definition of citizens as members of society is shaped and continually reinforced by participation in the armed forces.

In addition to direct military mobilization, states devote considerable resources to the mobilization of whole societies to support military objectives and to support a notion of the military as a social institution, one whose role in society is defined in explicitly political terms. The military is often consigned a leading role in the process of nation building, as the guarantor of national values and as the agent of "modernization." Military mobilization thus becomes a process of state-directed and society-wide political mobilization organized around the privileging of certain kinds of social and political identities over others. Moreover, the rise of mass armies has significantly widened the social groups that are vulnerable to the incorporating and ordering effects of this mobilization. While the composition of the officer corps in the Arab Middle East is often determined by particularistic, ideological or other nonmeritocratic criteria, the personnel requirements of mass militaries have compelled Arab leaders to recruit from outside of narrow politically reliable constituencies and, as al-Khafaji demonstrates, extend the material and professional benefits of military service to previously excluded social groups. This has the potential, however, to enhance the organizational cohesion of groups who oppose the state and to provide them an arena within the state from which to attack it. As noted by Nigel Young, "War crystalizes the nature of the state more than any other activity, though, despite Bourne's dictum, it is not always healthy for it in the longer term."[40]

Thus, war making generates conflicts regarding not only the nature of citizenship and political authority but also, and perhaps more fundamentally, regarding the definition of society itself. Al-Khafaji and Saad underscore this dimension of war making in Iraq and Egypt, respectively, showing, in the Iraqi case, the tight links between war making and the coercive imposition of new definitions of Iraqi identity that were deployed by the regime as powerful tools of exclusion and repression against Kurds, Jews, and Shi'ites. Beyond these cases, the expulsion of nonresident populations following the Gulf War from states where many of these "nonresidents" were born or had lived for decades—Palestinians and Yemenis in particular—indicates that state-centric notions of citizenship have become much more central to definitions of society than membership in some larger nation or transnational community, such as that of "the Arabs," or the Islamic *umma,* the community of Muslims. The general issue raised by these examples is how war renders more or less flexible the definitions of society and perceptions of its political roles, and how it creates an opening to examine the processes through which both states and state-society relations are defined and transformed.

WHAT DOES WAR EXPLAIN?

These elements of convergence and divergence suggest how a research agenda on war as a source of state and social transformation might usefully incorporate the experience of late-developing states. Can we also use this summary, however, as a starting point for generalizable conclusions about the effects of war preparation and war making on state and social formation, either in the Middle East or more broadly? Do these phenomena help us explain variation in patterns of state and social formation, and in state-society relations, across a range of state forms? Can we use the findings generated by these chapters to develop systematic comparisons about the effects of war on state and social formation in the Middle East and about how Middle East states and societies experience war preparation and war making? I argue that the answer to these questions is a tentative yes, understanding that while the following chapters provide data that make it possible to advance this aim, it was not their explicit intent to do so.

Such an agenda would need to encompass three distinct comparative projects. One is the project around which this introduction has been organized: comparing the experiences of early modern Europe with those of the twentieth-century Middle East, starting with the variables identified as relevant in the literature on early modern Europe. In other words, this comparison would test Tilly's assumption that hypotheses generated out of the European experience represent an automatically plausible set of starting points. The second is an intraregional comparison among contemporary Middle East states to explain the relationship between war preparation and war making, on the one hand, and variation in patterns of state institutional design, state-society relations, and the organization of the political economy within this one region, on the other. The third project is a comparison between experiences of war making and war preparation in the twentieth-century Middle East (meaning the period from World War I to the present) and contemporary experiences of war making and war preparation in other regions, including both the developing world and Europe.

Inevitably, the design of these comparisons will differ, and the material in these chapters lends itself more readily to the first and second than to the third. The following chart sets out points of comparison by highlighting some of the apparent differences in the causal links between war making, war preparation, and state formation in early modern Europe and the Middle East. It is intended not as a comprehensive list but as a starting point that identifies some of the core relationships we need to explore in order to understand how war preparation and war making have shaped states and societies in the Middle East, and the extent to which hypotheses drawn from experiences of early modern Europe can assist us in this task.

	Early Modern Europe	*Contemporary Middle East*
War and state formation	War makes the state: strong correlation between war making and the formation of national states.	States as "compulsory political units": weak correlation between war making and the formation of national states.
Sovereignty as the organizing principle of the international system	Sovereignty as a dependent variable: strong correlation between state consolidation and emergence of sovereignty as organizing principle of international system.	State consolidation as a dependent variable: strong correlation between a robust norm of state sovereignty and consolidation of Middle East states.
War and state survival	Losers disappear: strong correlation between defeat in war and elimination of the defeated political entity.	Losers survive: weak correlation between defeat in war and elimination of the defeated state.
War and state consolidation	The state makes war: strong correlation between war preparation, war making, and development of state extractive capacity.	Weak correlation between war preparation, war making, and state extractive capacity.
War and the transition from absolutism to democracy (Tilly)	No taxation without representation: strong correlation between state extraction, downward accountability, and emergence of representative systems of rule.	Low taxation, low representation: weak correlation between state extraction, downward accountability, and emergence of representative systems of rule.
War and the transition from constitutionalism to autocracy (Downing)	Strong correlation between (1) level of domestic militarization, (2) level of mobilization of domestic economic resources, and (3) rise of autocracy. Fiscal dependence of the state on society linked to rise of autocracy.	Strong correlation between (1) domestic mobilization of human resources (militarization) and (2) consolidation of authoritarian regimes. Strong correlation between fiscal autonomy of the state and consolidation of authoritarianism.

	Early Modern Europe	*Contemporary Middle East*
War making, industrialization, and innovation	Strong correlation between war making, patterns of industrialization, and capacity for technological innovation.	Weak correlation between war making, patterns of industrialization, and capacity for technological innovation.
War and state-society relations	Strong correlation between war preparation and increased capacity for social mobilization.	Strong correlation between war preparation and increased capacity for social mobilization.
War preparation and patterns of social mobilization	Moderate reliance on militarism as basis for social incorporation and control; degree of reliance on militarism shifts in response to changes in the level of threat.	High reliance on militarism as basis for social incorporation and control; degree of reliance on militarism does not shift in response to changes in level of threat.
The fiscal sociology of war making	Strong correlation between capacity of political power holders to wage war and capacity to extract resources from domestic populations.	Weak correlation between capacity of political power holders to wage war and capacity to extract

What does this list tell us, apart from reinforcing the self-evident differences in context and process that separate these two sets of cases? On one level, these stylized comparisons can be seen as confirmation of the causal processes highlighted in the literature on war and the state in early modern Europe. Where key independent variables are absent, and the trajectories of state and social formation differ from those in which they are present, we can have a higher degree of confidence in the positive claims that link particular forms of war preparation and war making to the distinctive patterns of early state formation characteristic of European cases. However, more interesting patterns also emerge from the variation captured in this chart and suggest a number of possibilities for organizing a productive research agenda on the relationships between war, the state, and social change in the contemporary Middle East—that is, for determining what war does and does not explain.

These possibilities include a range of questions that have already been the subject of limited research, including how shifts in the organization of the international system, notably the consolidation of sovereignty as the dominant norm in interstate relations, structures patterns of war making and influences the effects of war on Middle East states. In this regard, Lustick has noted how the defense of sovereignty as a norm by external powers lead to a disconnect between defeat in war and survival of a national state, or between victory in war and territorial expansion, both of which helped to sustain and reproduce the territorial divisions that followed the transition from Ottoman Empire to colonial state in the aftermath of World War I and prevent the emergence of a Middle Eastern great power.[41]

With respect to domestic processes, however—our focus in this volume—the chart underscores at least two key findings that are critical for explaining the effects of war on state and social formation in the post–World War II Middle East. First, *war preparation matters more than war making.* In fact, the intensity of war preparation is only loosely correlated with levels of external threat and with the actual outbreak of war. Moreover, the *intensity* of war preparation—understood as a social process in the broadest sense and not merely as a matter of provisioning or of episodic mass mobilization—is not tightly correlated with a *capacity* to engage in war making. Indeed, as noted here and in the following chapters, for the first half of the twentieth century war making for Middle East states may be most usefully understood as a form of exogenous shock that punctuated existing territorial, political, or social arrangements and helped to structure how those arrangements were reshaped. However, even after national states come to exist as independent political units, war making and war preparation remain only loosely correlated, and it is the latter that carries more weight in accounting for patterns and variation in forms of social mobilization, the dynamics of state-society relations, state fiscal policies, and styles of governance, especially within the dominant-party or single-party regimes that figure prominently in this volume.

Second, and relatedly, *modes of resource extraction explain patterns of war preparation.* Though the data are incomplete, there seems to be a significant correlation between the sources of state revenue, on one hand, and patterns of war preparation, notably the extent to which militarism dominates systems of governance and social mobilization, on the other. This relationship establishes the organization of state revenues as an independent variable and patterns of war preparations as a dependent variable, thus reversing the direction of causality found in at least one set of European cases.[42] Where state elites have access to "external" economic resources—resources such as oil revenues, military grants, or other forms of rent that are generated through means other than extraction from domestic populations—their capacity to institutionalize a militarized system of rule is enhanced, and this capacity increases as the contribution of external resources to state revenue goes up. Therefore, in an explanation of how the Syrian, Iraqi, Egyptian, and to some extent Algerian regimes are able to sustain authoritarian strategies of governance that operate in part through the pervasive militarization of everyday life, the fiscal autonomy of state elites stands out as a critical factor. Indeed, the presence of such external resources, and the interest of Middle East states in securing them, can be seen as necessary conditions for the production of the highly militaristic and authoritarian systems of rule found in the dominant- or single-party regimes of the Middle East. Alternatively, it seems difficult to imagine that the constellation of features associated with radical and militaristic forms of authoritarianism could become (or remain) so deeply consolidated under conditions in which rulers depended on citizens for revenue.

In addition, variation in the level of eternal resources correlates positively with variation in the intensity of militarization and of the authoritarian character of the regime. Precise data are hard to come by, but in general Iraq is characterized by the highest levels of external resources as a percentage of state revenue, the highest levels of militarization—defined as number of armed forces personnel per capita—and the most intensely authoritarian system of rule among the major single-party regimes of the region.[43] Syria occupies a middle ground with respect to all three of these variables. Egypt exhibits lower levels of external resources as a percentage of state revenue, lower militarization, and a less intense form of authoritarian rule.

In making these claims, and in looking for the specific causal mechanisms that support these correlations, a third key finding becomes clear: *regime type matters*. The phenomenon of external resources, high militarization, and authoritarian rule are characteristic principally of the secularist, single-party regimes of Iraq, Syria, and Egypt. For the tribal monarchies, exceptionally high levels of external resources relative to the size of their populations have permitted them to avoid *either* the mobilization of, *or* the need to extract resources from, domestic populations. Instead, war preparation and war making are delegated to more powerful states on a fee-for-service basis.

These hypotheses provide one starting point for a comparative assessment of how war shapes processes of state and social formation and transformation in the Middle East—the intraregional dimension of our comparative framework. But what about the cross-regional dimension, comparing European and Middle Eastern experience? Here, the possibilities seem to lie in using regional variation in the relationship between war and state formation to identify a broader range of trajectories and make clear the causal mechanisms that underlie them. Tilly, for example, argues that in Europe between 990 and 1990, "state structure appeared chiefly as a by product of rulers' efforts to acquire the means of war." My argument reverses this causal relationship. It suggests that the structure of revenues, the export into the region by colonial powers of a more fully articulated model of the national state, and the presence of a consolidated international state system weakened the link between war making and state structure.

This difference appears most vividly with respect to the fiscal sociology of the state, notably the interactions among war preparation, state capacity, levels of taxation, patterns of social mobilization, and possibilities for the emergence of representative government. Here, the possibility for drawing on the experience of the Middle East to shed light on debates among historians of Europe is not as far-fetched as might be assumed. For example, the experience of Middle East states would seem to contradict Downing's claim that the intense mobilization of domestic resources, both human and economic, causes the transition from constitutional to autocratic forms of rule. Instead, Middle East cases suggest that the ability of state elites to *avoid* the intense mobilization of domestic economic resources makes possible the militaristic and authoritarian mobilization of their populations and the consolidation of authoritarian systems of rule. Alternatively, this hypothesis would lead us to expect that as levels of direct taxation increase (largely as a result of economic reform programs), the intensity of militarization and of authoritarian rule would diminish. However, the evidence for this is far from conclusive. In several cases in the Middle East (Tunisia and Egypt in particular), efforts to increase the extractive capacity of the state as part of a larger program of economic liberalization have overlapped with an intensification of authoritarian practices. Thus, while the Middle East does not yet offer much support for the link between taxation and representation, it seems to confirm the negative side of that equation. Low levels of direct taxation have helped state elites in the Middle East avoid moves toward greater representation.

In addition, the experience of the Middle East adds a useful new dimension to debates concerning the relationship between war and the capacity of the state to tax. As Campbell has noted, "Despite their relevance for debates in political sociology about the determinants of state policy in general, we still do not know whether taxes vary with war because citizens grant political elites more leeway, because the structural dependence of the state on capital investment subsides, or because war fundamentally alters the decision-making calculus of political elites."[44] What the experience of the Middle East suggests, however, is that in addition to the factors mentioned by Campbell, the composition of state revenue also plays an important role in shaping the relationship between war, variation in state fiscal policies, and how particular kinds of state capacities are formed.[45] In the cases discussed here, levels of state dependence on private capital are in general low, citizens possess few mechanisms for influencing fiscal policy, and levels of taxation have not varied as a result of war despite protracted episodes of high mobilization. In fact, war preparation often operates as a mechanism

for the downward distribution of state revenue, as suggested in the chapters
by Perthes and al-Khafaji.

CONCLUSION

Even this cursory attempt to use the essays in this book to draw systematic
conclusions about the effects of war preparation on Middle Eastern states
and societies should help to make clear the stakes involved in responding
to the first gap I noted at the outset—the need to expand the knowledge
base about war as a social and political process in the Middle East. War
preparation and war making are so deeply implicated in processes of state
and social formation and transformation in the Middle East that the absence of research on its effects represents a critical shortcoming—one that
this volume can only begin to address. What about the second gap, however, the lack of fit between existing, Eurocentric theoretical frameworks
and the experiences of the twentieth-century Middle East? What conclusions can we draw on this front, however tentative they might be? What this
volume helps to show is that neither of the two positions expressed by Tilly
in his introduction to *The Formation of National States* is correct. We can neither dismiss the experience of early modern Europe as holding out few
clues to the connections between war, the state, and society in the modern
Middle East, nor accept the experience of Europe as leading automatically
to plausible hypotheses for explaining those connections. In this introduction I have stressed the costs associated with an acceptance of Tilly's second
proposition (Europe as the automatic source of plausible hypotheses) and
used the chapters in this volume to illustrate a few of the key points of divergence between existing theories and the experiences of states and societies in the Middle East. At the same time, however, the kinds of outcomes
for which we are trying to account bear more than a passing resemblance to
those that interest our colleagues who work on early modern Europe, including the big questions of how war configures and reconfigures states and
societies and changes the terms of their interaction. These shared concerns
offer one basis for optimism about the benefits of a research agenda in
which early and late developers would be accorded equal weight. Moreover,
this agenda need not be based on a one-way flow of ideas. While research
on war and the state in early modern Europe cannot be anything other than
archival, scholars of the contemporary world are not so constrained. Recourse to a level of data not widely available in 1600 and to methods such
as ethnography and participant observation can point scholars of Europe
toward relevant causal relationships and processes that might otherwise remain elusive, holding out the real possibility for a two-way flow of ideas and
of hypotheses to be tested. If the current volume helps move research on
war and the state in this direction, it will have accomplished a great deal.

NOTES

Several people offered useful comments on this chapter, including Robert Vitalis, Roger Owen, Joel Migdal, Peter Katzenstein, Charles Tilly, Gregory Gause, James Gelvin, and an anonymous reader for the University of California Press.

1. See Lissak, *Israeli Society and Its Defense Establishment: The Social and Political Impact of a Protracted Violent Conflict;* and Ben-Eliezer, *The Making of Israeli Militarism.*

2. Included among this handful are Barnett, *Confronting the Costs of War: Military Power, State, and Society in Egypt and Israel;* Lustick, "The Absence of Middle Eastern Great Powers: Political 'Backwardness' in Historical Perspective," pp. 653–83; Gongora, "War Making and State Power in the Contemporary Middle East," pp. 19–50. In making this claim I distinguish between international relations literature that treats the state as a unit of analysis to explore system-level dynamics, where war or the absence of war is often the dependent variable, and work that is concerned with the domestic effects of war as an independent or intervening variable.

3. Nettl, "The State as a Conceptual Variable," pp. 559–92.

4. The predominance of European cases in the study of war and the state has also been noted by Asian specialists. See Richard Stubbs, "War and Economic Development: Export-Oriented Industrialization in East and Southeast Asia," pp. 337–55.

5. See Tilly, *The Formation of National States in Western Europe;* as well as Tilly, *Coercion, Capital, and European States, AD 900–1990;* Tilly, "War Making and State Making as Organized Crime," pp. 169–91; Parker, *Military Innovation and the Rise of the West, 1500–1800;* Mann, *States, War, and Capitalism;* Gillis, *The Militarization of the Western World;* Downing, *The Military Revolution and Political Change: Origins of Democracy and Autocracy in Early Modern Europe;* Burke, *The Clash of Civilizations: War-Making and State Formation in Europe;* Porter, *War and the Rise of the State;* Eley, "War and the Twentieth-Century State," 155–74; and Rosenthal, "The Political Economy of Absolutism Reconsidered," pp. 64–108. The dominance of European cases in research on war and the state reflects the condition of comparative politics more generally, a fact recently affirmed by Hull, "Comparative Political Science: An Inventory and Assessment since the 1980s," pp. 117–24. Hull found that the "dominant focus for comparativists . . . continues to be Western Europe and North America. Africa and the Middle East have received the least coverage."

6. Downing, *The Military Revolution,* p. 9.

7. This for example was the starting point of articles by Gongora, "War Making and State Power," and by Herbst, "War and the State in Africa," pp. 117–39.

8. Herbst opens his article with the following observation: "Most analyses assume that in Africa, as elsewhere, states will eventually become strong. But this may not be true in Africa, where states are developing in a fundamentally new environment. Lessons drawn from the case of Europe show that war is an important cause of state formation that is missing in Africa today" ("War and the State in Africa," pp. 117–39).

9. It should be emphasized that this volume makes no claims to great originality in observing that categories and concepts that originated in the historical experience of Europe do not always travel well.

10. Simon Bromley also notes the transformation of the Middle East into "non-

Europe" as a result of the kinds of frameworks that are used to study it. See *Rethinking Middle East Politics,* pp. 6–16.

11. Charles Tilly, "Reflections on the History of European State-Making," in *The Formation of National States,* p. 82. Despite this claim, however, Tilly was quite inconsistent in his view of the utility of European experiences as a basis for research, as my subsequent references to this chapter indicate.

12. For some examples of this introspection, see Bill, "The Study of Middle East Politics, 1946–1996: A Stocktaking," pp. 501–12; and Tessler, *Area Studies and Social Science: Strategies for Understanding Middle East Politics.*

13. The initial attempt by the Committee on Comparative Politics to explore European experiences of state formation in terms of political development theory took place through a planning committee organized under the direction of Gabriel Almond.

14. Verba, "Some Dilemmas in Comparative Research," pp. 111–27.

15. In case this view seems skewed, it is worth recalling that Seymour Martin Lipset drew readily on case material from the Middle East, notably Daniel Lerner's *The Passing of Traditional Society: Modernizing the Middle East,* in writing what is arguably one of the most influential studies ever written on the relationship between economic development and democracy, *Political Man: The Social Bases of Politics.* By comparison, several scholars of the contemporary Middle East point out its more recent exclusion from major studies of both democratization and economic reform. See Hudson, "After the Gulf War: Prospects for Democratization in the Arab World," pp. 407–26. This shift on the part of the Middle East from inclusion to exclusion is an interesting and not trivial indicator of how the relationship among subfields has changed in American social science over the past forty years.

16. Lucian W. Pye, foreword to *The Formation of National States in Western Europe,* p. x.

17. Tilly, *The Formation of National States,* p. 3.

18. Among the sharpest, and intellectually most idiosyncratic, of the critiques by scholars who had participated in the work of the committee was that of Leonard Binder. See *Islamic Liberalism: A Critique of Development Ideologies,* pp. 24–84.

19. Among those who made much more sophisticated theoretical use of history in accounting for trajectories of state and social change were Rudolph and Rudolph, *The Modernity of Tradition: Political Development in India;* Ake, "Modernization and Political Instability: A Theoretical Exploration," pp. 576–91; and, perhaps most influential of all in the challenge it posed to Lipset, O'Donnell, *Modernization and Bureaucratic Authoritarianism: Studies in South American Politics.*

20. Following the Committee on Comparative Politics, the SSRC established a Committee on the Comparative Study of Public Policy, but not much came of its work. My thanks to Kent Worcester for his keen grasp of SSRC committee history. One subsequent cohort of political development theorists, in a critical reaction against modernization and systems theory, now turned its attention to relations between state and society. A second cohort, reacting against the culturalist bias of much modernization theory, moved toward microlevel rational choice approaches—finding universality not in the organic functioning of political systems or in the sequencing and phases of development but in the self-interested motiva-

tions underlying human behavior. For the former, see Migdal, *Strong Societies and Weak States: State-Society Relations and State Capabilities in the Third World*. For the latter, see Bates, "Macropolitical Economy in the Field of Development," pp. 31–54.

21. See Ira Katznelson, "The State to the Rescue? Political Science and History Reconnect," pp. 719–37.

22. Among those who made productive use of state theory, Tilly in particular, in the study of the Middle East was Lisa Anderson, *The State and Social Transformation in Tunisia and Libya, 1830–1980*.

23. The Social Science Research Council–American Council of Learned Societies Joint Committee on the Near and Middle East tried to develop an alternative research program for the study of the state in the Middle East around the theme of weak states and strong societies. But following a contentious conference in the mid-1980s, in which it became clear that no consensus approach to the study of the state could be designed, the project was abandoned.

24. Tilly, "Reflections," pp. 13–14.

25. Tilly, *Coercion, Capital, and European States*, p. 14.

26. Bromley, *Rethinking Middle East Politics;* Mitchell, *Colonising Egypt;* and Said, *Orientalism*.

27. Eley, "War and the Twentieth-Century State," p. 156.

28. Note that this is quite different from Herbst's claim, in "War and the State," pp. 117–39, that war was not a significant factor in state formation in Africa. In fact, World War II was no less important in shaping state capacities in parts of Africa than it was in the Middle East.

29. On this point see Dirk Vanderwalle, *Libya since Independence: Oil and State Building*.

30. There were conflicts among what might be called protostates prior to this, however, including in the Hijaz. See Kostiner, *The Making of Saudi Arabia, 1916–1936: From Chieftancy to Monarchical State*.

31. Gates, *The Merchant Republic of Lebanon: Rise of an Open Economy*.

32. North, *Institutions, Institutional Change, and Economic Performance*, p. 113; Goran Therborn, "The Rule of Capital and the Rise of Democracy," *New Left Review* 103 (May-June): 3–41.

33. This finding has very important implications for a wide range of relationships, including processes of state consolidation, the organization of state structures, and the dynamics of state society relations. On the link between taxation and state survival see Mann, "State and Society, 1130–1815: An Analysis of English State Finances," pp. 73–123.

34. See Korany, "The Old/New Middle East," pp. 135–50.

35. See Wedeen, *Ambiguities of Domination: Politics, Rhetoric, and Symbols in Contemporary Syria*.

36. See Sayigh, chapter 7 of this volume.

37. Tilly, *Coercion, Capital, and European States*.

38. This phenomenon is far from unique to Lebanon. David Keen considers these forms of economic exploitation to be a principle function of civil wars in general. However, Keen and Picard occupy very different positions with respect to the role of the state in civil war. In my view, Picard exhibits a more nuanced under-

standing of the tension between the militias' dependence on and subversion of the state, and the continuing centrality of the state as a boundary between legality and criminality. Keen, *The Economic Functions of Violence in Civil Wars.*

39. Theda Skocpol, "Social Revolutions and Mass Military Mobilization."

40. Nigel Young, "War Resistance, State and Society," in *War, State and Society,* pp. 95–116.

41. See Lustick, "The Absence of Middle Eastern Great Powers."

42. In *Coercion, Capital, and European States,* p. 30, Tilly identifies three main patterns in the relationship between coercion and capital, and associates each with a particular trajectory of state formation and of state-society relations: coercion intensive (forced extraction of resources), capital intensive (negotiated extraction of resources), and capitalized coercion (combining force and bargaining in the extraction of resources). All three patterns, however, rest on the need for war makers to extract resources from populations residing within the territories they control.

43. Data on the number of armed forces personnel per capita can be found in Arms Control and Disarmament Agency, *World Military Expenditures and Arms Transfers,* though the data on Iraq are spotty at best. Data on the extent to which governments rely on external resources is trickier, since neither Iraq nor Syria releases information on revenues from the sale of oil, and data on other forms of external rent are also closely held. For partial information see Ishac Diwan and Nick Papandreou, "The Peace Process and Economic Reforms," pp. 227–55.

44. Campbell, "The State and Fiscal Sociology," p. 166.

45. This claim about the relationship between the composition of state revenue and state capacities is also reflected quite centrally in Kiren Chaudhry, *The Price of Wealth: Economies and Institutions in the Middle East.*

PART ONE

War, State, and Markets in the Middle East

The Political Economy of World Wars I and II

2

Guns, Gold, and Grain
War and Food Supply in the Making of Transjordan

Tariq Tell

In 1924, a "commentator on Middle Eastern affairs" who wrote under the pseudonym Xenophon, remarked that "of all the provinces of the vast Turkish empire left disorganized at the end of the World War, there was none so abandoned as that part of Arabia now known as Transjordania." Transjordan had evolved from the wreckage of World War I, conjured up by Churchill and Lawrence in 1921 as part and parcel of the division of the Fertile Crescent between Britain and France. Yet if war, in a literal sense, made modern Jordan, the relationship between war making and state making along the desert marches of southern Syria was quite different from that envisaged by Charles Tilly. Once the "Great Arab Revolt" launched by Hussein ibn 'Ali, the sharif of Mecca, spilled over from the Hijaz in July 1917, tribes as well as states waged war and the power of the Ottoman state receded. By December 1918 the revolt had undermined the Ottoman order and ensured that an upsurge of tribalism, rather than an increase in "stateness," was Transjordan's legacy from the war to end all wars.

If the war years did little to build a Jordanian state, they did much to cement the claims of Hussein and his sons to leadership of the nascent Arab Movement. The Arabist pretensions of the Hashemites have in turn ensured that Jordan's official historians chronicle the transition from Ottoman rule in patriotic terms.[1] Hussein's revolt is seen as the culmination of the Arab Awakening, and its march on Damascus is viewed through a nationalist lens. Typically, it is argued that Transjordanians gave spontaneous and absolute loyalty to the Hashemites, that most of them "actively supported the revolt," and that by enlisting in its ranks in the "thousands" they were "a major factor in the successful outcome of the revolt."[2] The "Arab Movement" is assigned a crucial role in the creation of Transjordan. If the country's borders were fixed by bargaining by the Great Powers after the war, "its national character was preserved by Arab effort."[3]

The aftermath of World War I did much, however, to devalue the claims of Hashemite Arabism. Hussein launched his uprising with British prompting, yet the end of the war saw Britain reneging on the promise of Arab independence held out by Hussein's famous correspondence with MacMahon. Britain's "perfidy" and the accommodation of the sharif's sons 'Abdallah and Faisal to its tutelage after 1921 has cast doubt on the credentials of the revolt. Arab radicals came to condemn its imperial provenance and to see it as a reactionary affair representing narrow and dynastic interests that in practice delivered the Fertile Crescent to colonial rule.[4] Sympathetic historians argue that to give credit to the Transjordanian tribes for the success of the revolt is a "historical blunder." Instead the tribespeople "abided by decisions of their shaykhs, who usually joined hands with the side that offered them the more profitable terms. . . . Neither the ordinary bedouin nor his shaykh were able to appreciate the wider meaning of events and the historical significance of the Arab revolt."[5]

Contending views of the transition from Ottoman rule remain central to ideological politics in contemporary Jordan.[6] Yet neither the Hashemite historians nor their protagonists provide an adequate understanding of Arabism as an ideology, of early Arab nationalism as a social movement, or of how the context of war conditioned the course of Hussein's revolt. The politics of Arabism are portrayed as an affair of notables and nationalists, with a corresponding neglect of non-elites and rural actors.[7] The Arab Movement is imbued with "an immutable and singular identity," wherein Arab nationalism, rather than being reinvented or diversely imagined by different social groups, is spontaneously recovered and diffused among the population at large by the conjuncture of Turkish oppression and Sharifian example.[8] As a result, narratives of the revolt impose an unwarranted coherence on what was always a multilayered and conflictual movement and give scant attention to the motives of the tribesmen who served as its foot soldiers, or to the social and material forces that led them to rally to the Sharifian cause.

This chapter seeks to recover the contingent and contested qualities of the revolt through a microhistorical focus on the local dynamics through which war making shaped the trajectory of Transjordanian state formation. In the account presented here, it is precisely the social and economic conditions of war, local strategies, and material incentives, rather than the high politics of British treachery and Hashemite ambition, that hold center stage. It was, in particular, variation in the extent to which social groups (tribes) were vulnerable to hunger as a result of wartime shortages that shaped patterns of participation in the revolt. Tribes whose food security was at risk were responsive to the material incentives provided by the leaders of the revolt in exchange for their commitment to participate. Where food security was less vulnerable to wartime conditions, and where Ottoman forces controlled the markets on which tribal units depended for their subsistence, tribal leaders displayed a greater reluctance to join forces with the anti-Ottoman campaign of Sharif Hussein and his associates. In other words, it was the material incentives or disincentives associated with a political commitment to the anti-Ottoman campaign of Hussein—not the ideological claims of notables and nationalists—that led tribes to participate in the revolt or withhold their support.

East of the Jordan River, these factors were played out in the context of a revitalized Ottoman administration that had been consolidating its hold on Transjordan since the mid-nineteenth century, co-opting or importing local proxies, and greatly expanding the local presence of the Ottoman state.[9] The contours of this resurgent order were obscured from contemporaries like "Xenophon" by the destructive legacy of the war years and concealed from more recent commentators by an Arabist historiography that for too long dismissed or distorted the significance of four centuries of Ottoman rule.

TRIBE AND STATE IN TRANSJORDAN UNDER THE OTTOMANS

In broad terms, the history of Ottoman Transjordan confirms the veracity of Zeine's comment that "the Arabs up to the reign of Abdul Hamid (1876–1908) suffered not from too much Turkish government but from too little."[10] Until the second half of the nineteenth century, Ottoman intrusion into this dusty corner of Bilad al-Sham did not go beyond ensuring the safe passage of the annual Hajj caravan. Ottoman officials appeared in the country in significant numbers only during the twenty or so days it took the pilgrimage to traverse the distance between southern Syria and the borders of the Hijaz. Such imperial influence as existed at other times was exercised by the local proxies of Ottoman governors or by tax collectors in their intermittent forays from Damascus and other towns of southern Syria.

In the absence of routinized central authority, Transjordan was dominated by a local order, "a social, economic and cultural fusion of nomads and peasants" created by the interaction of bedouin and villager along the frontier of settlement in southeastern Syria.[11] Although southern Syria's location at the periphery of imperial control has thrown a veil of ignorance over many aspects of the local order, tribal histories, anthropological work, and recent writings on the extension of "the frontier of settlement" allow the construction of a provisional picture of a tribalized society that lacked significant urban centers and was dominated by parochial loyalties and the ideology of segmentary kinship.[12]

The population divided broadly into bedouin (literally, dwellers of the steppe, or *badia*) and cultivators, or *fallaheen*. Local sources list the bedouin by tribal affiliation but also refer to them generically as *al-'arab* or *sukkan al-khiyyam*, the tent dwellers. Apart from their mode of residence, the bedouin were a heterogeneous group ranging from camel nomads who drove their flocks eastward to winter in the Wadi Sirhan and Jabal Tubayq, to more sedentary tribes who combined sheepherding with scattered cultivation.[13] The general pattern was for the more mobile camel-herding tribes—various factions of the 'Anayza and the Bani Sakhr in the north and center of Transjordan, the 'Adwan in Balqa, and the Huwaytat in the south—to dominate the more sedentary ones. An annual tribute, *khuwwa* (literally, brotherhood payment), was exacted from the weaker tribes in return for protection against raiding *(ghazuw)*. For the more powerful bedouin tribes, such as the Bani Sakhr and the Ruwalla (or the Harb, Billi, and Bani 'Attiyyah further south and in the Hijaz), this was supplemented by the levying of protection money *(surrah)* from the Ottoman authorities in return for the safe passage of the Hajj caravan, which also formed the main market for the bedouins' camels.

The bedouin also collected *khuwwa* from the *fallaheen*. Until the mid-nineteenth century, the double burden of Ottoman taxation and the exactions of the bedouin restricted sedentary cultivation to the hills of 'Ajlun and the town of al-Salt in al-Balqa. While the cultivators dwelt in stone villages and caves rather than tents, they were everywhere tribal. In 'Ajlun the villagers were organized into subdistricts *(nahiyyats)*, each headed by the locality's most powerful clan: the Shraydah in Kura, the 'Utum and al-Farayhat in 'Ajlun and al-Mi'radh, the Khasawnah and Nusayrat in Bani 'Ubayd, the 'Azzam in al-Wustiyyah, the 'Abaydat in Bani Kananah, the Rusan in al-Saru, and the Zu'bi *tariqah* (Sufi religious order) in Ramtha. The people of al-Salt, al-Saltiyyah, presented a united front to outsiders but divided internally into two major tribal factions: al-Akrad headed by the 'Arabiyyat clan, and al-Harah headed by the 'Awamlah.[14]

Where influential shaykhs or shaykhly clans could harness their tribal followings to gain control of local tax collection or to monopolize the escort of the annual Hajj caravan, chiefdoms emerged—notably under the Shraydah in Kura, the Majali in Karak, the Adwan and Bani Sakhr al-Fayez clan in Balqa—to fill the vacuum left by the absence of effective Ottoman control.[15] However, only the Ruwalla of the great camel-herding tribes of the Syrian Desert passed through Transjordan, and the power of the local chiefs remained limited in comparison to the larger tribal emirates of northern Arabia. As a result the local order in Transjordan remained weak and fragmented, subject to the ebb and flow of actions by contending power centers outside its borders—on the one hand, the Wahhabi and Rashidi emirates in the Arabian interior, and on the other, the Ottoman pashas or quasi-autonomous tax farmers in Damascus, Acre, and Sidon.

It was the second set of influential groups that began to gain the upper hand after the middle of the nineteenth century with the arrival in Transjordan of the centralizing influences of the *tanzimat*. Between 1851 and 1893, a direct Ottoman presence was established in forts and outposts stretching from Irbid to Aqaba, and an armed expedition in 1867 compelled the submission of the Balqa bedouin, collected unpaid taxes, and ended the extraction of *khuwwa* from the villagers. After 1870, Ottoman authority was reinforced by the arrival of settlers loyal to the new order. Caucasian refugees were implanted along the frontiers of settlement in 'Ajlun and the Balqa, and Turcoman villages were established at Lajjun and al-Hummar. As imperial authority consolidated itself, merchants and migrants from Damascus and Palestine flocked to Irbid and al-Salt, and their enterprise turned Circassian villages like Amman and Jarash into significant market towns.

The integration of Transjordan into the grain export trade of the Syrian interior provided the economic foundations of the new order. Consular sources report wheat coming to Jerusalem from beyond the Jordan River as early as 1850, and by 1860 grain farming had led to the emergence of a distinct landowning elite among the Fayez clan of the Bani Sakhr.[16] The upward trend in wheat prices between 1840 and the end of the Crimean war boom, and the dwindling number of pilgrims using the overland route to Mecca, may have been the main forces encouraging the growth of grain farming before the establishment of direct Ottoman control. The return of the Ottoman state provided an additional (if indirect) boost to grain farming. The collection of tax arrears in al-Salt created excess demand for liquidity and, therefore, an opportunity for merchants to accumulate capital through money lending. Merchants and money lenders anxious to integrate grain production and trade invested the proceeds of usury in land, consolidating great estates and thereby cementing the transition to commercial agriculture in the Balqa.

Commercialization brought rapid growth in agricultural production and exports. By 1894 the newly created *sanjaq* of Ma'an (which included the districts of al-Balqa and al-Karak) was exporting some 12 million francs worth of agricultural goods, including wheat, barley, and livestock products such as *samn* (ghee). Further north, 'Ajlun was integrated into the export agriculture of the Hawran. By 1901, there were a million acres under cereal cultivation in the district, and over 3 million bushels were exported from the area. In all, 'Ajlun's production amounted to over one-third of the Hawran's combined grain harvest.[17]

It is possible to document a flow of land transfers in the area north of the Mujib (Moab) valley from the 1880s onward—in particular the communal pastures of the bedouin—from the indigenous tribespeople to merchants and settlers. Moneylenders and bureaucrats acquired large estates in the

Balqa, the Jordan Valley, and the environs of Irbid. However, how much land the indigenous tribespeople lost is unclear. The 1880s also saw the emergence of the "bedouin plantation village"—land registered in the names of influential shaykhs and farmed by Egyptian and Palestinian sharecroppers.[18] Both the Balqa and 'Ajlun witnessed "indigenous" movements of colonization that kept land in tribal hands. Madaba and a number of villages in the environs of al-Salt were settled by local Christians in the 1870s, and a section of the Khasawna clan took possession of al-Nu'ayma after being forced from their homes by the Christians of al-Husn.

On the available evidence it seems that the extension of the Ottoman frontier in northern Transjordan generated a dual system—with commercial estates and settler villages existing uneasily alongside indigenous tribes.[19] The tensions in the system were apparent in tax revolts and in inter- and intratribal feuding that did not die down until the 1880s. However, overt resistance to the new order subsided in the following decades as the infrastructure of Ottoman power in Transjordan was completed with the registration of land and property, and with the building of a communication network that culminated in the passage of the Hijaz Railway through the country in 1906.

TRANSJORDAN BETWEEN OTTOMANISM AND ARABISM

The Ottoman order in north and central Transjordan seemed secure by the first decade of the twentieth century. A permanent Ottoman presence had been established in 'Ajlun and Balqa for two generations or more. It was now buttressed by the construction of the Hijaz Railway, by a dense network of roads and telegraphs, and by merchants and migrants loyal to the Ottoman state. The old tribal order survived at the local and village level, whether in the form of customary land tenures—which persisted despite registration in the Ottoman *tapu*—or an enduring loyalty to tribe and clan.[20] Nevertheless, both the cultivators and bedouin were enmeshed in the grain export economy of southern Syria. The economic surplus this generated funded the Ottoman administration and allowed an embryonic elite to emerge from the bedouin aristocracy and the larger merchant landowners.[21] Whether as members of town councils or as local district officers *(qaimmaqam)*, the new tribal landlords acted as proxies for Ottoman rule.

South of the Mujib, direct Ottoman rule was both more recent and less secure. The Ottomans had to maintain the *surrah* to prevent the bedouin from attacking the Hijaz Railway.[22] With the exception of a small Turcoman presence at Lajjun and the temporary inflow of Damascenes into Ma'an during the construction of the railway, Ottoman rule lacked the reliable auxiliaries available further north in settlements such as Amman or Jarash. Except on the Karak plateau, the agricultural surplus was meagre, and even here it was used to supply the surrounding bedouin rather than for export. The town's merchants—for the most part migrants from Damascus and Hebron—were little more than shopkeepers and never attained the wealth or status of their counterparts in al-Salt.

Therefore the local order was largely intact in southern Transjordan when the accession of the Young Turks in 1908 brought new efforts to centralize the Ottoman state. Having subjugated the Jabal Druze in the summer and fall of 1910, an Ottoman force under Sami Pasha al-Faruqi moved south to impose conscription and disarm the population in 'Ajlun. While al-Faruqi's troops faced little resistance north of the Mujib line, attempts to impose the same measures in Karak brought protests, pleas, and petitions from the local shaykhs. When these failed to move the authorities, a bloody uprising broke out in Karak that spread to Tafila and led to bedouin attacks on some of the stations on the Hijaz Railway. The revolt was led by the Majali, whose paramount shaykh, Qadr, fed the Karakis' fears of conscription and disarmament and played on rumors that the Young Turk–led Committee of Union and Progress (CUP) intended to suspend payments to the bedouin along the Hijaz Railway.

The Karak revolt was eventually suppressed and its ringleaders imprisoned. However, al-Karak's cause was taken up by the Arabist press in Damascus and in the Ottoman parliament, where Arab feeling was on the rise in reaction to the Turkifying policies of the CUP and where Tawfiq al-Majali, the town's deputy to the Ottoman *mab'uthan* (Ottoman parliament), moved in nationalist circles. Together with the participation of the surrounding tribes in sympathetic attacks on the railway, this has led some historians to interpret the Karak revolt in nationalist terms or to see in it a precursor of the Great Arab Revolt of 1916.[23] However, contemporary Arabists were for the most part separated by a considerable social and political gulf from the rebels of al-Karak. While the former were urban nationalists who sought a larger share in the Ottoman polity, the Karakis seemed wholly opposed to it. Their victims during the uprising were the town's merchants, the hapless census teams, and such representatives of the Ottoman order as failed to find sanctuary in Karak's citadel.[24]

The Karak revolt is better seen as the dying spasm of the local order, a doomed attempt of a tribal system to defend itself against an encroaching state. The Ottoman hold on the district was rapidly reestablished, and the Karakis for the most part remained loyal Ottomanists throughout the subsequent years of war and revolt. At least at the grassroots level, a similar antipathy to centralization marked the events leading to the Arab Revolt in the Hijaz in 1916. As was the case in Karak, a local elite manipulated tribal resistance to Ottomanism for its own ends. Hijazi localism, rather than Arab nationalism as understood in Damascus or Beirut, was the defining feature of Arabian politics between 1908 and 1916.

THE ORIGINS OF THE ARAB REVOLT:
OTTOMANISM VERSUS LOCALISM IN THE HIJAZ

The late Ottoman Hijaz was an unlikely crucible for Arabism. The province was among the most backward in the Ottoman Empire. Its cities, steeped in ancient privilege and religious superstition, lacked the adversarial press, Arabist notables, and educated middle class that were the hallmarks of early Arab nationalism in Greater Syria or Iraq.[25] The Hashemite rulers of Mecca were at best late converts to Arabism and had as late as 1911 defied the weight of Arabist opinion by aiding the Young Turks' suppression of the Idrisi's rebellion in 'Asir. In launching his revolt in 1916, the sharif of Mecca appealed to educated Hijazi opinion in traditional rather than Arabist terms. Hussein's proclamations, and the articles and editorials of his mouthpiece *Al-Qibla*, accused the "atheistic" CUP of tampering with the Islamic legitimacy of the Ottoman state and called for the preservation of the ancient privileges of the Hijaz.[26]

Formed in a part of the Ottoman Empire "that was not at all nationalistic," Hussein's revolt therefore marked an "ironic beginning" to the Arab Movement. However, if Arabist doctrine had few converts in the Hijaz, the inhabitants of the province, whether townspeople or bedouin, were united in their hostility to the centralizing bent of Ottoman reform. Until 1916, local resistance found tangible expression in tax riots in the towns, as well as in bedouin opposition to the extension of the Hijaz Railway and the threat this posed to the *surrah* they received to protect the pilgrimage. By 1908 the opposition of the tribes had escalated to the point of a general tribal revolt that required six thousand troops for its suppression. Scattered attacks on the railway continued after the Young Turks came to power in 1908, and partial peace was maintained between 1909 and 1914 only by the prompt payment of subsidies to the Bani 'Attiyyah, Harb, and Billi tribes and by the fortification of the railway's main stations and watering points.[27]

The Hashemites shared the bedouins' antipathy to Ottoman centralization. While publicly welcoming the Hijaz Railway, the incumbent clan of the Dhawi 'Awn privately feared that it would provide Istanbul with the means to curtail their power in Mecca. The arrival of the Hijaz Railway in Medina in 1908 had proven to be a means for the consolidation of the Ottomans' grip on the district. Medina and its environs were detached from the Hijaz *vilayet* and made into a separate *mutasarrifiyyah* (Ottoman subgovernate); and although bedouin affairs continued to be administered by a representative of the sharif of Mecca, it was the writ of the Ministry of the Interior and the local branch of the CUP that prevailed within the city walls.

The Young Turk revolution coincided with Hussein ibn 'Ali's accession to power in December 1908, and the confusion following the fall of Abdul Hamid allowed Hussein to consolidate his grip on Mecca. But within a year of his appointment, he had come into conflict with the CUP over the extension of the railway southward from Medina. Tensions with the Young Turks continued to escalate until 1914, when the latter began to promote the claims of a rival clan, the Dhawi Zayd, whose leader 'Ali Haydar professed support for the railway's extension to Mecca.[28] The outbreak of war brought matters to a head. It was the discovery of a Unionist plot to unseat him in January 1915 that seems to have convinced Hussein of the need to seek outside support in order to preserve his family's position as autonomous rulers of the Hijaz.[29]

The realities of wartime Arabia dictated that Hussein turn to Great Britain, whose chief representative in Egypt, Lord Kitchener, had already rebuffed an approach from 'Abdullah in 1914. As occupiers of Egypt, the Hijaz's traditional source of grain and subsidy, the British had considerable influence over the rulers of Mecca. Cairo's leverage was increased once Turkey joined the Central Powers and a naval blockade was imposed on the Red Sea and the trade routes into Kuwait. Moreover, the outbreak of war encouraged the British to conclude treaties with rival Arabian princes who could potentially threaten Hussein's hold on the Hijaz. The latter included the Idrisi ruler of 'Asir, whose followers had invaded Hashemite territory in 1915, and Ibn Sa'ud, who had been in conflict with Hussein over the oasis of Khurma since 1910. British support promised to secure the Hijaz against these regional rivals, as well as provide the means to combat the intrigues of the Young Turks in Mecca.

Conducted by divergent power centers with competing interests, Britain's wartime strategy in Arabia was, however, at best complex and most often confused. Grand strategists in Whitehall, aware of the need to conciliate the competing actors of the "Eastern Question" became more cognizant of the limits of British power and of the rival ambitions of Russia and France. The government of India, which occupied Aden and had responsibility for the Persian Gulf, favored the manipulation of local princes in order to pave the way for direct colonial control over Mesopotamia. Its "men on the spot"—Shakespeare until his untimely death in 1915, and H. St. John Philby—preferred to put their faith in Ibn Sa'ud as the coming power in Arabia. As a result, it was only gradually that the Sharifian inclinations of Lord Kitchener and his protégés in Cairo and Khartoum began to influence imperial policy. In contrast to India, Cairo argued that Arabism could be harnessed to the imperial purpose and (no doubt more fancifully) that an alliance with a direct descendant of the Prophet Muhammad such as the Sharif Hussein could provide an antidote to the Ottoman call to jihad.[30]

In pursuit of these aims, the Arab Bureau in Cairo reinitiated contacts with the Hashemites. In the course of the famous "Hussein-MacMahon" correspondence that ensued, the sharif agreed to take up arms in support of the Allied war effort against the Turks. In return, Britain undertook to support Arab independence within boundaries broadly circumscribed by its secret agreement with France (the Sykes-Picot Agreement). The question of the compatibility of the two sets of undertakings has long exercised historians but need not detain us here. The most balanced assessments conclude that a pledge of Arab independence was given, but that it was not incompatible with Britain's undertakings with the French.[31] Under the pressure of events, both the sharif and Britain chose to defer their differences until the postwar settlement, the contours of which were impossible to predict in 1916.

It seems clear, however, that the local politics of the Hijaz and Hussein's dynastic ambitions, rather than Arabist sentiment, guided his preparations for the revolt. Rather than marking the culmination of the Arab Awakening, "it makes better sense to view the revolt as the death rattle of the traditional Ottoman order, the last gasp of a repetitive cycle of tension and struggle between Istanbul and the provincial elite."[32] Conservative in its aims and traditional in its content, Hussein's uprising marked an unlikely beginning for a new state system in the Arab east.

THE COURSE OF THE ARAB REVOLT (I):
THE WAR IN THE HIJAZ

It was nonetheless Hussein's negotiations with the British in Cairo that brought the Arabist dimension of the revolt to the fore. Once the decision to break with Istanbul was made, the language of Arabism provided a useful tool for conducting a dialogue with a European power imbued with nineteenth-century notions of national self determination. Once the correspondence with MacMahon raised the possibility of Sharifian rule in Syria and Iraq, Arabism also offered a basis for legitimizing a new realm outside the traditional confines of Hashemite influence.[33] In the autumn of 1915 Faisal had already found support among Damascene notables and the secret societies active there, and the uprising in the Hijaz was initially planned in concert with a similar movement in Syria headed by members of the Arabist movement al-Fatat. The latter continued to play a useful role as propagandists and Hashemite emissaries once the revolt was launched.[34]

Arabism was also a means of recruiting the core of a regular army from former Ottoman officers. Members of al 'Ahd, an Arabist secret society that drew its following from Arab officers (in particular Iraqis) in the Ottoman army, were especially prominent in what came to be known as the "National Arab Army." The Ahd's acknowledged leader, 'Aziz 'Ali al-Masri, was briefly (and also unhappily) Hussein's chief of staff, and Iraqi officers led the Arab forces that took part in the battles around Ma'an and Tafila in 1918.[35] However, men like Ja'far al 'Askari and Nuri al-Sai'd were the exceptions rather than the rule among the Arabs serving in the Ottoman cause. Only a fraction of Ottoman deserters and a small minority of prisoners of war joined the Arab forces. On the whole, the nationalist officers kept to training and operational tasks in the Hijaz or in the forward base established in Aqaba after 1917.[36] The bulk of the Hashemite army consisted of bedouin irregulars who functioned as guerrillas on Allenby's "eastern flank" as he advanced into Palestine.

The bedouin irregulars stamped the Arab Movement with a tribal character. This ensured that whatever the motives of its instigators, the form and content of the Arab Revolt reproduced traditional patterns of political change in the rural hinterlands of the Middle East.[37] A protean Arab sentiment, for the most part in the form of ethnic pride in being Arab, was certainly in evidence among the tribespeople.[38] However, the ideas of the Damascene secret societies meant no more to the rank and file of Hussein's following than they did to the tribespeople of al-Karak. In the Hijaz during World War I, the bedouin, in the words of T. E. Lawrence, "were fighting to get rid of an empire, not to win it."[39]

The forces of the revolt failed to take Medina, which held out until January 1919, and instead progressed northward toward Damascus by the creation of a "ladder" of tribal allies along the western edge of the Arabian plateau. Guns, grain, and gold, made available by a British subsidy that ran to £125,000 per month, were the means by which the ladder was fashioned.[40] Where material incentives failed, the threat posed by the Hashemite advance was often enough to elicit a tribe's submission.[41] The two forms of cooperation made for an unstable relationship with the tribes. Some defected once the Hashemite army moved on or once payments ceased. In the areas liberated from the Turks, Hashemite authority was patrimonial. A Council of Ministers was established at Mecca, but actual power was wielded by the staff of the Hashemite princes waging the campaign. Their agents—most often recruited from their own relatives, the eight-hundred-strong network of ashraf—were dispersed among the tribes, where they mediated local disputes and enforced Hussein's writ in cooperation with local notables according to the norms of tribal practice.

Wartime food shortages and the disruption of food supplies through the blockade of the Hijazi coast and the Indian Army's control of trade routes into Kuwait held the key to the Hashemite advance. Contemporaries such as Ranzi, the Austrian consul in Damascus, saw clearly that the revolt "was not only the making of the dismissed Amir [Hussein]," but traced its cause to the "the food crisis of the tribes." The latter was in turn attributed to "woefully insufficient" deliveries of food, particularly grain, from Syria and Palestine. Together with the closure of the sea route, the shortage of grain left the Hijazi tribes "in dire straits and therefore dependent on the good-will of the English."[42]

In the first phase of the revolt, therefore, it was British subsidy as much as Sharifian prestige that enforced Hussein's leadership. Moreover, it was the threat of famine, induced by naval blockade and the disruption of food supplies to the Hijaz, that allowed the sharif to channel local solidarities and rally the bedouin.[43] Otherwise, the Hashemites' patrimonial methods failed to weld their following into a coherent national movement. Beyond the pecuniary ties forged by British gold, the only ideological element that joined the Hashemites to their local supporters was a common antipathy to Ottoman centralization. Hussein manipulated the bedouins' interest in autonomy for dynastic ends, and only adopted the rhetoric of Arabism once the fortunes of war opened new vistas for himself and his sons in the Fertile Crescent. The trajectory of the Arab Revolt meant that in the spring of 1917 it was the tribes of Transjordan that held the key to the glittering prospects promised by MacMahon, and the occupation of Wajh by Faisal in February 1917 opened the way for their induction into the revolt.

THE COURSE OF THE ARAB REVOLT (II): THE WAR IN TRANSJORDAN, JULY 1917–SEPTEMBER 1918

In southern Syria as in the Hijaz, the outbreak of war and the Allied naval blockade inflicted bitter hardship on the population. The memoirs of 'Aw-dah al-Qusus record that the blockade brought shortages of sugar, rice, and kerosene, and that the choking off of imports "raised the price of cloth ten-fold." Matters were exacerbated by Ottoman requisitions. Draconian meas-ures were envisaged that would leave cultivators with a minimal supply of seed and a meagre daily ration of three hundred grams of wheat per per-son. At the same time, grain, camels, and horses were purchased at unfa-vorable prices and with a paper currency that devalued rapidly in the face of wartime inflation.[44] An additional burden was imposed by the general mobilization decreed by the Porte, threatening to conscript all men of mil-itary age.[45]

A cycle of inclement weather and environmental disaster added to the burdens of war. Until the 1917–18 season, the war years were marked by drought and harvest failure. In 1914, al-Karak and southern Syria suffered an infestation of locusts "that destroyed all fruit trees and crops despite the governments best efforts to combat the plague."[46] The decline of cereal production was accelerated by the drain of seed, men, and, above all, draft animals to the war effort. Even in the face of soaring food prices, the result was a steady fall in the surplus marketed through official channels and a contraction of the area of grain cultivation.[47] The greed of speculators and misguided attempts by the authorities to corner the grain market brought famine to the towns and coastal provinces of Syria by the winter of 1915–16.[48]

Hunger and the exactions of the Ottoman war regime were the most likely cause of the deep well of Arabist sentiment revealed by T. E. Lawrence's reconnaissance of the Hawran and Transjordan in May and June 1917.[49] By then, most of the northern bedouin had established links with the Sharifian forces ensconced at Wajh under Faisal, and the Arabist party in Damascus counted such tribal shaykhs as Nuri al-Sha'alan of the Ruwalla; his son Nawwaf, "the most advanced thinker in the desert"; and Talal al-Fayez and his son Mashhur of the Bani Sakhr as adherents.[50] However, of all the Transjordanian bedouin, it was only a dissident section of the Huwaytat—in effect 'Awdah abu Tayeh and his Jazi followers—who openly declared support for the revolt in 1917. 'Awdah, together with individual tribesmen from the Shararat, the Sirhan, and the Ruwalla, was recruited into the Hashemite confederacy between February and July of 1917, and he spearheaded the advance through the Wadi Sirhan, which took Aqaba on the 6th of July 1917.[51]

The occupation of Aqaba provided a base for expansion into southern Syria, and Arab forces under Zayd, the youngest of Hussein's sons, occupied Wadi Musa and Tafila with the support of local villagers in the autumn of 1917.[52] However, Zayd found himself overextended in trying to take al-Shawbak, where the Hishah forest had become a vital source of lumber for the Hijaz Railway, and Ma'an held out in the face of repeated Arab assaults until the end of the war.[53] North of the Wadi al-Hasa, al-Karak, where "Sami Pasha's energetic action in 1910 ha[d] not faded from popular memory," remained firmly in the Ottoman orbit throughout the war.[54]

Two British incursions were mounted across the Jordan with the aim of establishing Faisal in central Transjordan in the spring of 1918. The first "Transjordan raid," launched in late March, briefly occupied al-Salt, but failed to take Amman. Outfought and out-thought by the Turks, the army was forced to retire across the Jordan on April 2. The second Transjordan raid (April 30–May 4, 1918) was compromised by poor intelligence and the failure of promised support from the Bani Sakhr to materialize. The failure of the two raids dealt a severe blow to British prestige—and consequently to the credibility of the Arab Movement. Moreover, Allenby's forces were weakened further by the withdrawal of men and material to meet the Ludendorf offensives on the Western Front.[55] As a result, the forces of the revolt made little progress north of the al-Hasa divide until the defeat of the Central Powers, and until Allenby's victory at Megiddo brought about a general Turkish collapse in the closing stages of the war.

By September 1918, when hostilities in Transjordan ceased, the northern tribes had played a relatively minor role in the revolt. While sections of the Ruwalla were involved in "minor disturbances" in the vicinity of Dera'a as early as October 1916, the tribe as a whole extended only passive support to the Hashemites before May 1918.[56] Both Nawwaf and Nuri continued to receive Turkish subsidies while enriching themselves from the contraband trade.[57] The latter shifted decisively to the Sharifian side only after his camp at Azraq was bombed by the Turks in June 1918.[58] The Bani Sakhr appear to have hedged. The paramount shaykh of the tribe, Fawwaz al-Fayiz, refused to supply camels for the Turkish attack on the Suez Canal in 1915 and signaled his allegiance to Faisal in January 1917.[59] However, his brother Mithqal recruited three hundred men to the Turkish cause, and Fawwaz himself attempted to deliver Lawrence to the Ottoman authorities in Zizya in June 1917.[60]

By agreement with Jamal Pasha, absolute ruler of Syria during the war, the tribes of al-Karak were exempted from conscription in return for supplying auxiliaries to the Ottoman forces operating in their vicinity. Reinforced by Ottoman cavalry and bedouin from the Bani Sakhr, the Matalqa Huwaytat, and the Ruwalla, al-Karak's shaykhs raised five hundred horsemen for an attack on the forces of the revolt in July 1917. While the bedouin held back at the crucial moment, the Karakis engaged the Sharifians in a three-hour battle at Kuwayra, looting five hundred sheep in the process.[61] The Turks found it necessary to exile a number of Christian notables from al-Karak (as well as from the related tribes of Madaba) in the latter half of the war.[62] However, the loyalties of the Majali and prominent shaykhs such as Husayn al-Tarawnah remained Ottoman until the fall of Damascus.[63]

In al-Balqa, the 'Adwan and their tribal followers supported the Turkish cause. The memoirs of Fritz von Papen, then with the Fourth Army, record that the Ottomans "maintained excellent relations with . . . the nearby Arab tribes whose sheikhs often visited Es Salt to make their obeisances." Al-Balqa's Christians, however, were consistent sympathizers of the revolt throughout the war. After the first Transjordan raid occupied al-Salt, the town's Christians (as well as tribal allies and supporters from the faction known as the Harah) chose to evacuate the district alongside the retreating British.[64] By contrast, Transjordan's Circassian minority under Mirza Pasha Wasfi was active in support of the Turks.[65] Circassians in Wadi al-Sir fired upon British forces during the second Transjordan raid, and a "tribal brawl" broke out between their kinsmen in Suwayleh and Salti Christians during the first Allied incursion.[66]

From the perspective of the Hashemite historians, the stalling of the northward progress of the revolt until the last stages of the war is surprising. No doubt there is some truth to their contention that the Turks played on local differences and went out of their way to conciliate local shaykhs and notables. In Karak the Ottomans fanned a feud between the Christian clan of al-Halasa and the Yusuf section of the Majali. The latter's shaykh, Rafay-fan al-Majali, who had succeeded Qadr as the most influential figure in the district, was made an Ottoman *mutasarrif* after the Ottoman garrison withdrew in the fall of 1918.[67] Once the Sykes-Picot Agreement was made public by the victorious revolutionaries in Russia, the Turks also played effectively on fears that Allied victory would bring rule by Christian powers and cast doubt on the motives of the Hashemites.[68] Finally the shaykhs of the Bani Sakhr and the 'Adwan, as well as less significant figures among the Ruwalla, were recipients of Turkish honors and subsidies that kept them from openly siding with the sharif.[69]

Nevertheless, an alternative explanation for the passivity of the tribes is needed, particularly as honor and subsidy were also available from the Sharifian side. The sanction of Ottoman repression must have been of key importance in the first phase of the war in Transjordan. The Turkish hold on Transjordan had been reinforced since 1914 by the presence of the Ottoman Fourth Army, which had its supply center at Jiza some forty kilometers south of Amman. Together with the mobility bestowed by the Hijaz Railway, this allowed the Ottomans to police the Balqa and reinforce their hold on al-Karak and Ma'an at the first sign of trouble. In the summer and autumn of 1917 both Faisal and Lawrence were reluctant to push on into the Balqa and 'Ajlun for fear that Turkish retribution would fall on defenseless villages should an uprising prove premature.

The Bani Sakhr, as the second Transjordan raid illustrated, would have been the logical choice to form the next rung of the Hashemite ladder after the capture of 'Aqaba. However, the concentration of Ottoman forces in the western part of the tribe's *dirah* (tribal territory) placed severe constraints on its room to maneuver. While "unassailable" in the steppe east of the Hijaz Railway, the Sukhur faced "retribution . . . once the summer droughts force[d] them back into the pastures west of the railway." Moreover, their estates at Jiza, Dulaylah, Natl, and elsewhere along the Hijaz Railway added to the tribes' vulnerability, enabling the Turks, in the words of a British intelligence report, "to put a further turn on the screw" by denying them summer provisions and threatening the incomes of their shaykhs.[70]

The plight of the Bani Sakhr illustrates the fact that, in contrast to the Hijaz, the logistics of food supply in the north Arabian desert (Badiyat al-Sham) worked against the revolt. An Arab Bureau report in the winter of 1917 argued that the various components of the great 'Anaza tribal confederation that held the key to the revolt's success in Syria (the Dhana Muslim—Ruwalla, Muhallaf, and Wald 'Ali on the Shami side of Syrian Desert, and the Amarat to the east) would not join the revolt while the Ottomans controlled the settled areas and, therefore, the markets on which they relied for subsistence. Even the most powerful of the northern bedouin, Nuri al-Sha'lan of the Ruwalla, would "not fight openly for the Sharif until his tribe of over 70,000 souls is secure, not only of arms, but of food."[71]

Moreover, the last year of war, when Allenby was well established in Jerusalem and could counterbalance Turkish power, brought ample rain. According to contemporary reports, the bumper harvests that resulted left "the bulk of the rural population in (the) grain producing districts of inland Syria . . . with enough grain in the summer of 1918."[72] With Ottoman resources stretched by the confrontation with Allenby and the need to supply Ma'an, it is likely that cultivators in Transjordan were able to evade requisitioning agents and accumulate the grain surpluses documented by Damascene observers in the Jabal Druze. This was almost certainly true of those bedouin landlords who could harvest their crop and then follow their kinsmen into the steppe east of the Hijaz Railway, where the grain could be exchanged for contraband or Sharifian gold.[73] As the grain flowed south to provision the forces of the revolt in Aqaba, Transjordanians could gain access to the guns and gold the revolt traded in without the risk of actually participating.

Once the minorities are excepted, the pattern of participation in the revolt in Transjordan seems to be of scattered initiatives in support of the Sharifian cause north of the Hasa divide, with collective action in its favor being confined to the Huwaytat and the villagers in the environs of Tafila and Wadi Musa. Variations in the power and reach of the Ottoman state and—as was the case in Hijaz—the incidence of food shortage and hunger best explain overt support for the Arab Movement. In the grain-deficient south, where the hold of the Ottoman state was both recent and unsure, the specter of hunger drove sections of the Huwaytat into the arms of Faisal. From al-Karak northward, the presence of the Fourth Army was a deterrent to opportunistic action in favor of the revolt before 1918. By then a good harvest and slackening Ottoman impositions may have left a surplus of grain in the hands of cultivators. Both *fallah* and bedouin could afford to straddle the fence until Faisal's victory appeared inevitable.[74]

WAR'S AFTERMATH: FAISAL'S RULE
AND THE RESURGENCE OF THE LOCAL ORDER

Faisal's reign in Damascus lasted twenty-two months (October 1918–July 1920) and was initiated by his father annexing Ma'an and Aqaba to the Hijaz.[75] From the beginning, his fledgling government faced almost insuperable problems. Allied forces occupied much of Syria as part of three Occupied Enemy Territory Administrations (OETAs). France's control of OETA North in particular threatened to choke the landlocked interior under Faisal's control. The economy of Syria was in any case devastated by war.

Agricultural production and distribution was severely disrupted, and the towns and coastal areas were close to famine from hoarding, speculation, and graft. The monetary system was in a state of near collapse due to the devaluation of the Turkish lire in the first months of the new regime. The road and railway system had been damaged during the war, and transport was almost at a standstill.[76]

In the midst of the postwar chaos, Anglo-French policy moved fitfully toward implementing the Sykes-Picot Agreement. By 1920 the French interpretation of Sykes-Picot had prevailed, and British forces withdrew from the Syrian interior. Faisal was unable to head off a French occupation of Damascus after the formal division of Syria between the powers at St. Remo in April 1920. Proclaimed king by the Syrian Congress in March 1920, he was forced to abandon his capital four months later as the French army of the Levant under General Gouraud advanced upon it from Beirut. Faisal moved to Haifa and thence to Europe to pursue his cause by diplomatic means. Many of his supporters in the Istiqlal Party fled Damascus for neighboring Arab countries after an engagement with the French at Maysalun. The greater part of these exiles established themselves in Amman, which was rapidly turned into the center of resistance to the French.

Transjordan dissolved into tribal strife as Ottoman rule collapsed. Contemporary accounts speak of the educated and the propertied fleeing the country, while crowds burned the land registries and tax offices in an effort to rid themselves of fiscal obligation or debt.[77] The situation deteriorated further under Faisal. Although local shaykhs and "petty notables" from Ma'an, 'Ajlun, and al-Salt took part in Damascene politics, the unified Faisalite administration established in Amman wielded little effective power. The gendarmerie were underpaid and inadequate, and most of Transjordan's inhabitants refused to pay tax. In al-Salt, the population drove out officials charged with conducting a census and registering the population for conscription.[78] Even before the withdrawal of the British from OETA East in December 1919, bedouin raiding resumed. The Bani Sakhr attacked farms belonging to Salti Christians between Madaba and Amman, and the Balqa tribes began to demand restoration of the land allocated by the Ottomans to the Circassians.[79]

On the eve of the French occupation of Damascus, the instability in Transjordan threatened to spill over into Palestine. The sedentary clans of Bani Kananah—perhaps encouraged by members of the Istiqlal native to the Hawran, including such radical nationalists as Ahmad Muraywid and Ali Khulqi (the latter a native of Irbid)—raided Jewish settlements in Galilee. The raiders engaged British forces at Samakh and suffered a number of casualties as RAF planes strafed them on their way back across the Jordan. Kayed al-Ubaydat, the paramount shaykh of the *nahiyah* (the lowest level of the Ottoman provincial hierarchy) was among the dead.[80] The Samakh raid seemed to confirm Allenby's fears that abandonment of OETA East would leave Palestine's right flank "in the air, threatened by all the Druze and bedouin tribes."[81] Herbert Samuel, who was high commissioner in Jerusalem and cautiously sympathetic to Zionist pleading, now called for the occupation of Transjordan west of the Hijaz Railway.[82]

Samuel's advice was at first resisted by Whitehall, which was fearful of the cost of occupying Transjordan. However, the fall of Faisal brought renewed interest in the country. The area lay astride the lines of communication between Mesopotamia and the British base along the Suez Canal, and France's occupation of Damascus prompted the fear of a further move southward to cut the land corridor with Iraq.[83] Therefore the foreign secretary, Lord Curzon, recommended an "inexpensive solution," whereby requiring a token presence east of the Jordan would be used to keep the area in the British sphere.[84] In August 1920, a day after Faisal's departure for Europe, Samuel convened a meeting of shaykhs and notables from al-Karak and al-Balqa at al-Salt and informed them that Transjordan was to be placed under a British mandate. However, the inhabitants were to form their own administrations in each of the Salt, Karak, and 'Ajlun districts, subject to the advice of British political officers responsible to the high commissioner in Jerusalem.[85]

Regional animosities prevented representatives from 'Ajlun from attending the meeting with Samuel. Therefore the message was relayed to them by a Major Somerset (later Lord Raglan) at a meeting in Um Qais on September 2.[86] Istiqlalists, including Muraywid and Khulqi, attended the Um Qais meeting, and their presence injected a more radical tone into the proceedings. The assembled shaykhs demanded that Somerset accept a series of nationalistic demands, including the incorporation of parts of the Hauran north of the Yarmouk into the government of 'Ajlun's jurisdiction, the unification of the three local governments under a single ruler, a British (as opposed to a French) mandate over Syria, and above all a guarantee that Transjordan would be excluded from Zionist colonization. Somerset was forced to sign a "treaty" incorporating these provisions (the so called Treaty of Um Qais) before proceeding to Irbid.[87]

In any event, the government of 'Ajlun formed at Irbid proved unable even to rule the *qaza* (Ottoman district). Friction with the al-Kura soon became apparent, whose paramount shaykh, Klayb al Shraydah, was not represented on the governing council formed in Irbid. Within a week, a separate government of Kura had been established, with Dir Abu Sa'id as its capital. Following the example of Kura, the dominant clans in four of 'Ajlun's *nahiyyats* (Jabal 'Ajlun, al-Wustiyya, al-Mi'radh, and Jarash) established autonomous administrations.[88] The most notable event in 'Ajlun at the time had a tribal rather than an Arabist coloring. The villagers of Ramtha—then still under titular French control as part of the Hawran—

repelled a bedouin raid on the district, inflicting a severe defeat upon the Bani Sakhr.[89]

Farther south, an elected council was established at al-Salt to rule the district alongside the head of government, Mazhar Raslan (a native of Homs who had served as governor of the same district under Faisal). The 'Adwan were represented on the council, but the Bani Sakhr boycotted its proceedings in favor of a rival government established at Amman by Mithqal al-Fayiz's Damascene brother-in-law, Sa'id Khayr. As a result the Balqa also divided along tribal lines.[90] A council similar to Salt's was established in Karak under Majali leadership. As was the case elsewhere, its procedures remained tribal and it failed to pay its gendarmerie or impose taxation on the district's tribes. Despite the best efforts of Alec Kirkbride, the British advisor, the grandly named "government of Mo'ab," lapsed into internecine tribal conflict and an acrimonious rivalry with Tafilah to its south across the Hasa divide.[91]

The pattern throughout Transjordan at the end of Faisal's rule was of a resurgent local order and a renewal of the tribal particularisms on which it was based. The only effective steps toward stabilizing the country were taken by the British. One of the political officers dispatched by Samuel, Captain Brunton, formed a regular body of cavalry and machine gunners in Amman. The new force had the explicit aim of curbing bedouin raids upon the settled population and was initially recruited from the Circassians settled by the Ottomans for the same purpose.[92] In October 1920 the force successfully collected taxes from Sahab and imposed peace after tribal strife in Madaba.[93] Shortly afterward it was taken over and expanded by Frederick Peake into the new "Reserve Force" which was to be the nucleus of the future Jordanian army.[94] By the time of its formation, however, the arrival of the Amir Abdullah in Ma'an had eclipsed the local governments and set in motion the events that eventually created a separate entity called Transjordan.

CONCLUSION

The years of war and revolt that marked the end of Ottoman rule in southern Syria provide ample support for Charles Tilly's contention that war places unusual demands on rural actors.[95] In Transjordan, however, as elsewhere along the desert marches of the Ottoman Empire, the nature of the local order was such that the results of war making were more in keeping with the ideas of Ibn Khaldun than with the sociology of state making in the West. In Western Europe, war imposed new burdens on a more or less "captured" peasantry, extending the extractive capacity of the state as well as its fiscal resources and, in the long run, promoting centralization and state building. In southern Syria and the Hijaz, the onset of war diverted men and material to the frontiers or deployed them along extended lines of communication. At the same time, external subsidy, in the form of British guns and gold, gave tribal actors the means to wage war on the state and to weaken and eventually undermine the "infrastructural power" of the imperial center.

Viewed through the lens of war and famine rather than the rival histories of Arabism, material incentives, rather than Sharifian prestige, determined the course of Hussein's revolt. The Ottoman entry into the war brought naval blockade and the disruption of food imports in Syria and the Hijaz. The exact impact of these shifts in supply varied with the pattern of development in the late Ottoman period, but in grain-deficient regions like the Hijaz and southern Transjordan, tribes such as the Huwaytat were left more exposed than the more self-sufficient tribespeople north of the Mujib line. The looming threat of hunger provided a lever that the Hashemites and their British allies used to co-opt the southern bedouin and construct the northern rungs of a ladder of tribal allies that took Aqaba in July 1917. However, Transjordanians from al-Karak northward, where grain supplies were more secure and the Ottoman presence more forbidding, preferred to straddle the fence until the last months of the war, and it was Allenby's victory and the Turkish collapse, rather than the forces of the revolt, that carried Faisal into Damascus in 1918.

In Transjordan, as in the Hijaz, guns, gold, and grain, rather than the appeal of Hashemite nationalism, determined the course of the Arab Revolt and its aftermath. Since Transjordanians were largely tribal and for the most part illiterate, their view of the revolt is exceedingly difficult to determine. Nonetheless it may be surmised that the Transjordanians shared the Hijazi bedouins' ethnic pride and, by 1916 at least, their hostility to the rule of the CUP in Istanbul. National sentiment may be discerned in the actions of individual shaykhs like 'Awdah abu Tayeh and in the friendly reception T. E. Lawrence received on his reconnaissance of the Hawran in 1917. During the Faisalite period, a broad Arabist current became apparent in Transjordan, not least in the anti-Zionist form that motivated the raiders of Samakh and the participants in the Um Qais meeting. During the war years, however, Arabism remained latent. Tribesmen for the most part evaded or avoided the state and only took up arms when the Ottoman order weakened and there were good prospects for material gain or pecuniary reward.

In form and content, Hussein's Arab Revolt was essentially a Khaldunian movement. In the words of Albert Hourani, it was "almost the last instance of a recurring process in the history of the region before modern technology transformed the world."[96] The world of Ibn Khaldun had, however, changed by the time World War I broke out, and local actors—whether tribesmen or Hashemite—could no longer challenge the Ottoman order on their own. To rise against the Porte, the sharif of Mecca needed external—and in the wartime Hijaz, inevitably British—support. As a result, the power of the movement he launched "was not its own but borrowed from a more powerful patron which in the end . . . abandoned it."[97] Having entered Damascus, his armies could not hold its citadel. In Transjordan this meant that the years of war and revolt brought a transition to localism rather than to Arabism.

NOTES

1. For examples, see Madi and Musa, *Tarikh sharq al-Urdunn fi al-qarn al-'ishrin*.

2. Musa, "The Rise of Arab Nationalism and the Emergence of Transjordan," p. 250.

3. Ibid.

4. Tibi, *Arab Nationalism: A Critical Inquiry*, p. 89; and al-Sayigh, *Al-hashimiyyun wa al-thawra al-'arabiyya al-kubra*.

5. Kazziha, *The Social History of Southern Syria (Transjordan) in the Nineteenth Century*, pp. 28–29.

6. Their continuing importance was highlighted by Jordan's intemperate reaction (reported in *Al-Hayat*, 3 June 1996) to remarks by Mustapha Tlas, Syrian defense minister and sometime historian of the Arab Revolt, that questioned Jordan's "nationalist" origins; and by the imprisonment of the prominent Islamist Layth Shubaylat on charges of insulting the royal family in a speech that drew heavily on al-Sayigh's opinion of the Hashemites' role in the revolt (*Al-hashimiyyun wa al-thawra al-'arabiyya al-kubra*). See "Fi thikra wa'ad balfur: muhadharat al-muhandis Layth Shubaylat fi mujammma' al-naqabat" (manuscript, 'Irbid, 11 July 1995).

7. Gelvin, "The Social Origins of Popular Nationalism in Syria: Evidence for a New Framework," p. 645.

8. Gelvin, "Demonstrating Communities in Post-Ottoman Syria," p. 23.

9. In other words, strengthening what Michael Mann has called the "infrastructural power" of the state—its geostrategic capacity to penetrate civil society and impose effective rule throughout the realm. Mann, "The Autonomous Power of the State: Its Origins, Mechanisms and Results," pp. 7, 9–11, 29.

10. Zeine, *Arab-Turkish Relations and the Emergence of Arab Nationalism*, p. 16.

11. Eugene Rogan, "Incorporating the Periphery: The Ottoman Extension of Direct Rule over Southeastern Syria (Transjordan), 1867–1914." (Ph.D. diss., Harvard University, 1991), p. 11.

12. See Antoun, *Arab Village: A Social-Structural Study of a Transjordanian Peasant Community*; Andrew Shryock, "History and Historiography among the Balqa Tribes of Jordan" (Ph.D. diss., University of Michigan, 1993); J. M. Hiatt, "Between Desert and Town: A Case Study of Encapsulation and Sedentarisation among Jordanian Beduin" (Ph.D. diss., University of Pennsylvania, 1981); Gubser, *Politics and Change in al-Karak, Jordan: A Study of a Small Arab Town and Its District*.

13. Rogan, "Incorporating the Periphery," pp. 11–13.

14. See Peake, *A History of Jordan and Its Tribes*, pt. 2, passim.

15. Rogan, "Incorporating the Periphery."

16. Issawi, *The Fertile Crescent, 1800–1914: A Documentary Economic History*, p. 270. See also Mustafa Hamarneh, "Social and Economic Transformation of Trans-Jordan, 1921–1946" (Ph.D. diss. Georgetown University, 1986).

17. Issawi, *Fertile Crescent*, p. 313.

18. Rogan, "Bringing the State Back: The Limits of Ottoman Rule in Transjordan, 1840–1910," pp. 32–57.

19. The exact proportions of land held by the two systems is impossible to determine. Auhagen estimated that only 15 percent of agricultural land remained in *fallah* hands by 1907, and there is evidence of land hunger in the tightening of the terms of tenancy in the same decade. However, against this must be set Kurd 'Ali's view that 95 percent of the land was "equitably distributed" in 'Ajlun, Balqa, and Karak, and the fact that the only documented reports of land transfers are from well-watered valleys such as the Ghor and the Yarmouk gorge or areas formerly grazed by bedouin in the Balqa. See Issawi, *Fertile Crescent*, pp. 330–31.

20. Martha Mundy, "Shareholders and the State: Representing the Village in the Late 19th Century Land Registers of the Southern Hauran" (manuscript, Irbid, 1992).

21. Rogan, "Incorporating the Periphery," pp. 153, 188–90.

22. Ochsenwald, *The Hijaz Railway*, p. 119.

23. Ochsenwald, "Opposition to Political Centralisation in South Jordan and the Hijaz," pp. 297–306.

24. Rogan, "Incorporating the Periphery," pp. 178–88.

25. Ochsenwald, "Ironic Origins: Arab Nationalism in the Hijaz, 1882–1914," pp. 189–90.

26. See Dawn, *From Ottomanism to Arabism: Essays on the Origins of Arab Nationalism.*

27. Ochsenwald, "Opposition to Political Centralisation," pp. 302–3.

28. Dawn, *From Ottomanism to Arabism*, p. 51.

29. Ibid.; and Kostiner, "The Hashemite Tribal Confederacy," p. 107.

30. Fromkin, *A Peace to End All Peace: The Fall of the Ottoman Empire and the Creation of the Modern Middle East*, pp. 79–111, 146–50.

31. Dawn, *From Ottomanism*, p. 115; Albert Hourani, "The Arab Awakening Forty Years Later," pp. 209–12. The question of Zionism, and of the morality of Arthur Balfour later undertaking to establish a Jewish national home in Palestine, had not yet arisen. In any case, according to Hourani, "The Hashemites did not oppose it strongly after Britain withdrew its support for [them] in Syria" (211).

32. Mary Wilson, "The Hashemites, the Arab Revolt, and Arab Nationalism," p. 205.

33. Ibid., p. 214.

34. Tauber, *The Arab Movements in World War I*, pp. 62–8, 78–9, 122–34.

35. Tauber, *Arab Movements*, pp. 117–21.

36. Kostiner, "The Hashemite Tribal Confederacy," p. 136.

37. In the words of Albert Hourani, the course of the Arab Revolt "showed how a new dynasty emerged. . . . An urban family, that of the Hashemite sharifs of Mecca, created around itself a combination of forces, partly by the formation of a small regular army but even more so by making alliances with rural leaders, and it was able to do this by providing both a leadership that could be regarded as stand-

ing above the different groups in the alliance, and an aim that could persuade them to rise above their divisions." Hourani, "Arab Awakening," p. 206.

38. St. Antony's College, Private Papers, Arab Bureau, Cairo, *Arab Bulletin* (henceforth *AB*), no. 32. This ethnic sentiment long predated the modern Arab Awakening. According to Albert Hourani, "As far back in history as we can see them, Arabs have always been exceptionally conscious of their language and proud of it, and in pre-Islamic Arabia they possessed a kind of 'racial' feeling, a sense that, beyond the conflicts of tribes and families, there was a unity which joined together all who spoke Arabic and could claim descent from the tribes of Arabia." Hourani, "Arab Awakening," p. 260.

39. Quoted in Kostiner, "Hashemite Tribal Confederacy," p. 136.

40. Ibid., p. 137.

41. Ibid.

42. Quoted in Schatkowski-Schilcher, "The Famine of 1915–1918 in Greater Syria," pp. 229–58.

43. It can be seen that the Hijazi tribes initially faced exchange failures that disrupted previous patterns of food distribution and undermined what had become a form of moral economy guiding exchange relations between Ottoman authorities and local producers. As the British blockade disrupted imports, this wartime shift in entitlements took on political coloring. It followed on a decade of CUP policies that threatened the claim on the Ottoman state embodied in *surrah* payments, while British subsidy allowed for an alternative claim—conditional on participation in the revolt—on the largesse distributed by the sharifs. The net effect was to turn famine and food shortage into a lever that allowed Hussein to mobilize the bedouin to his cause. This use of the term *entitlements* follows Amartya K. Sen, in *Poverty and Famines: An Essay on Entitlement and Deprivation*. Sen argues that the threat of famine stems from shifts in entitlements, or "those means of commanding food that are legitimized by the system in operation in [any] society" (p. 45). Entitlements in Sen's definition include "the use of production possibilities, trade opportunities, entitlements vis a vis the state," but explicitly exclude illegal means, such as looting or brigandage, that Arabian tribes habitually resorted to in war or peace. In order to fit Sen's notion to the anarchic world of the bedouin, it seems necessary to expand the ambit of entitlements by linking them to a wider moral economy. This has been accomplished by Jeremy Swift, "Why Are Rural People Vulnerable to Famine?" pp. 8–15. Swift distinguishes between "exchange failures," the loss of exchange entitlements or those "bundles" of goods that could be obtained through barter, truck, and trade; "production failures" caused by drought or disease; and the loss of "assets," which are disaggregated in turn into "investments," "stores," and "claims" on kin, patrons, or the state.

44. It seems likely, however, that the inaccessibility of its rural hinterland spared Transjordan the full brunt of these wartime impositions. With the diversion of its coercive resources to the Suez campaign and to the protection of the Hijaz Railway, the internal reach of the Ottoman state was impaired. The embattled provincial authorities had to rely on local proxies or a skeletal apparatus of elderly employees to collect grain. Thus in Karak 'Awdah al-Qusus and Husayn al-Tarawnah were brought in as partners of the requisitioning agents supplying Medina with local grain; and in 'Ajlun Saleh al-Tall (a native of Irbid) went about his duties as grain

commissioner *(ma'mour souq al-hubub)* with a meagre escort of four gendarmes. Local sympathies and lack of means of such men must have made sabotage by evasion and concealment an easy matter for local cultivators, and, significantly, al-Qusus's enterprise ended in failure. See al-Qusus, "Mudhakkarat Awda al-Qusus" (Memoirs of Awda al-Qusus) (manuscript, n.p., n.d.). Al-Tall's memoirs record resort to "weapons of the weak" such as occurred in the village of Hatem in the Kafarat district, where grain was concealed in a false wall. Saleh Mustafa al-Tall, "Kul Shay' li al-Taleb Milhim Wahbi al-Tall: Mudhakkarat Saleh Mustafa al-Tall" (Everything for the student Milhim Wahbi al-Tall: Memoirs of Saleh Mustafa al-Tall) (manuscript, Irbid, 1951), p. 40. On weapons of the weak, see Scott, *Weapons of the Weak: Everyday Forms of Peasant Resistance.*

45. Al-Qusus, "Mudhakkarat Awda al-Qusus," p. 104.

46. Ibid.

47. Somerset Papers, St. Antony's Collection, St. Antony's College, Oxford, Boxes 66 and 84.

48. Schatkowski-Schilcher, "The Famine of 1915–1919."

49. Jeremy Wilson, *Lawrence of Arabia: The Authorised Biography of T. E. Lawrence,* pp. 412–15.

50. St. Antony's College, Private Papers, Boxes 45, 46; Bidwell, *Arab Personalities of the Early Twentieth Century,* pp. 106, 114–15.

51. Jeremy Wilson, *Lawrence of Arabia,* pp. 369–75, 416–17.

52. Madi and Musa, *Tarikh sharq al-Urdunn,* pp. 52–3.

53. St. Antony's College, Private Papers, Boxes 64, 73, 75.

54. Bidwell, *Arab Personalities,* p. 154

55. Matthew Hughes, "The Transjordan Raids: Linking Up with the Arabs, March-May 1918" (Ph.D. diss., London, Kings College, 1995), chap. 4.

56. St. Antony's College, Private Papers, Box 71.

57. Bidwell, *Arab Personalities,* p. 100; St. Antony's College, Private Papers, Boxes 92, 97.

58. Jeremy Wilson, *Lawrence of Arabia,* p. 528.

59. Bidwell, *Arab Personalities,* p. 101

60. Kazziha, *The Social History of Southern Syria,* p. 27; and Jeremy Wilson, *Lawrence of Arabia,* p. 415.

61. Al-Qusus, "Mudhakkarat Awda al-Qusus," pp. 109–10.

62. Ibid., pp. 113–14; St. Antony's College, Private Papers, Box 88.

63. Kazziha, *Social History,* p. 27; Musa, "Rise of Arab Nationalism," p. 250.

64. Madi and Musa, *Tarikh sharq al-Urdunn fi al-qarn al-'ishrin,* pp. 55, 76–77.

65. Kazziha, *Social History,* p .28.

66. Matthew Hughes, "The Battle of Meggido and the Fall of Damascus: 19 September to 3 December 1918" (manuscript, Department of War Studies, King's College, London, 1995).

67. Al-Qusus, "Mudhakkarat Awda al-Qusus," pp. 128–29; St. Antony's College, Private Papers, Box 88; Madi and Musa, *Tarikh sharq al-Urdunn fi al-qarn al-'ishrin,* p. 55.

68. Madi and Musa, *Tarikh sharq al-Urdunn fi al-qarn al-'ishrin,* pp. 53–56. Nuri al-Sha'alan was particularly suspicious of the Sykes-Picot Agreement and British duplicity. At a meeting with T. E. Lawrence in Azraq in the spring of 1917, Nuri seems

to have extracted a pledge from Lawrence to submit to retribution and even death if Britain failed the Arabs. Jeremy Wilson, *Lawrence of Arabia*, pp. 414, 1071.

69. Madi and Musa, *Tarikh sharq al-Urdunn fi al-qarn al-'ishrin*, pp. 53–6; al-Qusus, "Mudhakkarat Awda al-Qusus"; St. Antony's College, Private Papers, *AB*, no. 88.

70. Bidwell, *Arab Personalities*, p. 114.

71. St. Antony's College, Private Papers, Box 71. Similarly it was argued that on the other side of the Syrian Desert the Amarat would not join the revolt "until our frontier on both Euprates and Tigris is far enough northwards to control the Amarat markets."

72. Schatkowski-Schilcher, "The Famine of 1915–1919."

73. St. Antony's College, Private Papers, Box 91.

74. In terms of the framework developed above, the northern tribes seem to have retained enough production entitlements to remain above a subsistence threshold, and were therefore not driven to revolt out of desperation or out of outrage at the violation of the norms of their risk-averse moral economy.

75. Kazziha, *Social History*, p. 33.

76. Khoury, *Urban Notables and Arab Nationalism: The Politics of Damascus, 1860–1920*, p. 82; Qasimiyyah, *Hukumah al-'Arabiyyah fi Dimashq*, pp. 218–25, 231–33.

77. F. G. Peake Papers, Imperial War Museum, London, "Biographical Fragments."

78. Kazziha, *Social History*, pp. 34–5; Musa, "Rise of Arab Nationalism," p. 252.

79. Kazziha, *Social History*.

80. Frederick. G. Peake, "Transjordan," 378.

81. Hughes, "The Transjordan Raids," p. 233.

82. Wasserstein, *The British in Palestine: The Mandatory Government and Arab-Jewish Conflict, 1917–1929*, pp. 73–89. The railway itself marked the so-called Meinertzhagen Line that Chaim Weizman wanted as the eastern frontier of Palestine. A. S. Klieman, *Foundations of British Policy in the Arab World: The Laird Conference of 1921*, pp. 205–8.

83. H. Diab, "Ta'sis Imarat Sharq al-Urdunn," *Shu'un Falastiniyya*, no. 50–51 (October-November 1975): 271. Cited in Hani Hourani, *Al-tarkib al-iqtisadi al-ijtima'i li sharq al-Urdunn: muqaddimat al-tatawwur al-mushawwah* (The Socio-Economic Structure of Transjordan: A Prologue to Distorted Development).

84. Mary C. Wilson, "King Abdullah of Jordan: A Political Biography" (Ph.D. diss., Oxford University, 1984), pp. 205–7; Diab, "Ta'sis," p. 271.

85. Eyewitness accounts of the al-Salt meeting report that Samuel tried to tempt the gathering by promising supplies of sugar and rice. Al-Qusus, "Mudhakkarat Awda al-Qusus," p. 134. However, the assembled notables remained unenthusiastic until Samuel agreed to pardon two fugitives from the Palestine government, 'Aref al 'Aref and a youthful Haj Amin al-Hussaini, who had attended under the protection of Rafayfan Majali and Sultan al-'Adwan. Abu Nowar, *The History of the Hashemite Kingdom of Jordan*, p. 25.

86. Madi and Musa, *Tarikh sharq al-Urdunn fi al-qarn al-'ishrin*, pp. 103–4.

87. Ibid., pp. 104–9.

88. Madi and Musa, *Tarikh sharq al-Urdunn fi al-qarn al-'ishrin*, pp. 109–14;

Hamarneh, "Social and Economic Transformation of TransJordan," pp. 109 ff. Jordanian historians hold that these essentially tribal rivalries may have been encouraged by Somerset, who "seemed to excel in the . . . craft of 'divide et impera.'" Abu Nowar, *History of the Hashemite Kingdom,* p. 31. See also Hamarneh, "Social and Economic Transformation," p. 110. Against this must be set Somerset's own papers, which at times show him working to unify 'Ajlun with the other districts to the south. Thus a letter to his father dated January 28, 1921, speaks of a meeting in Jerash "a week ago . . . where we had an unsuccessful meeting to try and combine Salt and 'Ajlun." St. Antony's College, Private Papers, Somerset Papers.

89. Musa, "Rise of Arab Nationalism," p. 253.

90. Madi and Musa, *Tarikh sharq al-Urdunn fi al-qarn al-'ishrin,* p. 115.

91. Hamarneh, "Social and Economic Transformation," pp. 108–9.

92. Dann, *Studies in the History of Transjordan, 1920–49: The Making of a State,* p. 21.

93. Ibid., pp. 21–25.

94. Jarvis, *Arab Command: The Biography of Lieutenant Colonel F. G. Peake Pasha,* pp. 69–70.

95. Tilly, *As Sociology Meets History,* p. 121.

96. Albert Hourani, "The Arab Awakening Forty Years Later," p. 206.

97. Ibid.

3

The Climax and Crisis of the Colonial Welfare State in Syria and Lebanon during World War II

Elizabeth Thompson

The first and most profound effect of World War II on Syria and Lebanon was fear—fear of famine. "In early September 1939 we were preparing for the new school year when the airwaves carried terror to our souls, pounding us all day with news reports of the Second World War," recalled a Lebanese schoolteacher. "In the next few days, I saw acute pain rise in the breasts of the generation that had lived through the catastrophe of the First War. . . . Work stopped, and business dwindled as a wave of profound pessimism engulfed the country."[1] The famine of World War I had killed as many as five hundred thousand Lebanese and Syrians. With blockades and poor harvests, fear of its morbid return reigned for the first three years of World War II, fueling riots, hunger marches, and opposition movements.

Déjà vu struck rulers as well as the ruled. General Georges Catroux, the leader of the Free French forces in the Levant who claimed rule of Syria and Lebanon in 1941, recalled his earlier term of service in these countries after the last war. As in 1918, the French were outnumbered by British troops and competed with them for prestige and power, through the delivery of foodstuffs and aid. In 1941 as in 1920, Catroux faced the task of imposing French rule on a hostile population. And as he did so, he recognized many familiar faces among French sympathizers and the nationalist opposition.

But Syrians and Lebanese confronted war and French rule in a manner radically different from twenty years before. Most salient was the emergence of new mass movements organized by political parties, labor unions, religious groups, and women. These movements aimed most of their demands at the government—for political freedom, decent wages, and full

education and health care. While women in World War I typically had suffered alone, portrayed in numerous photographs as lone mothers dying of
hunger with their children, women entered World War II armed with charitable, educational, and political organizations that would mount incessant
protests claiming not only their right to bread but their political rights and
right to national independence. While men in the last war had been
drafted into the Ottoman army and sent far from home, in this war they
were not mobilized. They too entered the war with highly organized movements that would demand government intervention on behalf of workers,
families, and business.

And the French position had radically changed since the last war. In
1918, the French had sought to aggrandize their empire; in 1941, they
struggled to reconquer it, to take it back from the Vichy government and
fend off encroaching German occupation. In June 1941, Syria and Lebanon were the first major territories outside of Africa that the Free French
reclaimed by force, a year after Charles de Gaulle founded the movement
in London and a scattering of colonies. The Free French were still weak because of their small numbers, and they had had to rely on overwhelming
British support in the Syrian campaign. Moreover, they were still either unknown or suspect in the eyes of most French, and they sought desperately
to justify their claim to represent true France. Syria and Lebanon were thus
to become Free France's "city on a hill." There, Catroux sought to realize
the ideals the Gaullist movement claimed were authentically French (and
absent in the Vichy regime): republicanism, honor, and a fighting spirit.
Free France had little materiel and only "moral capital" with which to re-
capture the prestige of being a Great Power.[2]

The combination of these three wartime phenomena—fear, social solidarity, and French weakness—produced a critical political opening for
change in the relations between the mandatory state and society. This
change has been described mainly in terms of how Syria and Lebanon
achieved independence during wartime. In 1943 the nationalist opposition
won elections, and in 1944 it took over the reins of the states' most essential services. In these accounts, independence was the start of a new era, as
the organization of national governments touched off a boom in spending
and a mobilization of new political interests.[3]

In many of these standard histories, however, a subnarrative exists on the
broader nature of the mass mobilization that occurred in both countries,
beginning in the 1930s, which suggests that the nature of the war's political
opening was more complex than a simple confrontation over independence. While bourgeois nationalists demanding independence were the
most prominent among 1930s opposition movements, they had allied with,
and depended upon, other social groups who were virtually excluded from
the halls of parliament and French negotiating tables: workers, women,

Muslim leaders, and minorities. These groups sought more than independence: they demanded reform of the regime and inclusion in the civic order, the norms and institutions that shape state-society interaction. By the mid-1930s, pressure from these groups brought bargaining over the extension of social rights and state services to the center of politics, establishing the basic outlines of a colonial welfare state.[4] However, by 1939 this bargaining had reached a stalemate, as bourgeois nationalists elected to parliaments balked at guaranteeing the right to welfare, and as the French suspended all politics at the outbreak of war.

The political opening created by wartime conditions did not merely strengthen opposition to the French but also altered the prewar pattern of political bargaining and, consequently, the trajectory of state formation at independence. The changes occurred in two phases. In the early years of the war, welfare not only expanded but its colonial attributes were also challenged. Between 1941 and 1943, social mobilization and French weakness combined to establish welfare as a right, not as a gift of paternalistic colonial rulers. Also the state committed itself to delivering benefits directly to citizens, challenging the colonial privileges of the bourgeoisie. In the second phase, from 1943 to 1946, spending on key social services like education and public health boomed, reaching levels never attained under the French. However, the 1943 election of nationalist elites and achievement of partial independence shifted the terms of bargaining once again. With the French out of their way, ruling nationalists faced less pressure to cede to the demands of the social movements, frustrating aspirations of those who sought revolution along with independence.

The war thus brought the colonial welfare state both to a climax and to a crisis. Wartime conditions had strengthened both the nationalists and the social movements but had also transformed their relationship. While in the 1930s the social movements were weakly organized, dependent allies of the nationalists, they became by war's end powerful rivals who wielded significant influence over the urban masses. The civic order polarized anew around the fate of the colonial welfare state. Nationalists sought to defuse the crisis in divergent ways: Syria adopted a more etatist approach to social policy, Lebanon a more liberal one. Each of these policies was rooted in the hybrid attributes of the colonial welfare state, which had relied heavily on a mix of public and private institutions.[5]

In sum, a focus on mobilization around social rights suggests that the war not only inaugurated a new era of independence but amplified and polarized prewar debates about the state's obligations to its citizens. The welfare model is useful not only in tracing the trajectory of state formation from French rule to independence but also in placing Syria and Lebanon in a comparative historical context. The linkage between war and the rise of the welfare state has been explored mainly in the context of industrialized countries. These studies commonly observe that wars accelerate the expansion of welfare states.[6] The Syrian and Lebanese cases challenge such a unilinear model, in that wartime expansion of their welfare state was halted late in the war. Study of welfarism in a colonial context, both in its similarities to and departures from Western European cases, is a potentially valuable contribution to the revisionist literature on welfare states.

PREWAR ORIGINS OF A COLONIAL WELFARE STATE

In the years 1920 to 1945 the intimate matters of the Syrian and Lebanese household became the target of sustained and intense public scrutiny: how much food families could buy; whether they were giving their babies sterile milk; how clean mothers kept their homes; how much time families allowed for their children's education; whether mothers or children should be permitted to work; and whether fathers should be the sole breadwinners. These and similar issues were debated at political club meetings, labor union rallies, ladies' charity socials, and feminist conferences, and in newspapers, cafes, and government offices.

Such public discussion had arisen before World War I, in the context of Ottoman reform and the need for social progress to safeguard the empire. But after 1918, the arena for debate was widened and utterly transformed by three new factors: prolonged social dislocation after the war, the construction of sovereign nation-states from former Ottoman provinces, and foreign occupation. Newly organized states hurried war relief to citizens to justify their rule: While Faysal's Syrian government heralded health relief and the building of schools as a new era of progress and liberation for the Arab peoples, the French in Lebanon hurried to deliver relief in the name of their civilizing mission. The French used their war relief to win the award of Syria and Lebanon as French mandates by the League of Nations in 1922. Social services would remain a cornerstone of French claims to rule.

By 1939, the mandatory states had committed themselves to a variety of social policies that struck deeper into society than the Ottomans ever had. But the transformation was not merely one of degree: the spirit of that commitment had begun to change. Whereas in the immediate postwar years the state had provided relief in the spirit of exceptional charity by a Great Power toward what it perceived as a backward society, by the 1930s Syrian and Lebanese citizens were demanding state services as a right. Social policy came to be formulated not in French bureaus but in what may be termed the civic order, the arena of interaction between the state and nonstate spheres that shapes public life.[7] The key components of the prewar civic order were, first, the formal, centralized state apparatus built by the French; second, the state's mediating networks of local collaborators and agents; and third, the state's clients and engaged opposition, who mobilized to extract more benefits from, and win greater participation in, government.

The French ruled Syria and Lebanon from their headquarters in an Ottoman palace in Beirut. The two countries were in practice Siamese twins, joined by a common, centralized administration, the French High Commissariat. The commissariat employed roughly one-third of all French officials in the territories and wielded complete control over the hefty Common Interests budget, mostly derived from customs dues. Its 1928 budget amounted to about 10 million £LS (Syrian and Lebanese liras), compared to the budget of 19 million £LS that year for all local governments.[8] In addition to customs duties, the High Commissariat disbursed extrabudgetary sums allocated directly from Paris to pay for administrative and military costs and to subsidize quasi-public French hospitals and schools, averaging an additional 14 million £LS per year before the war.[9]

The High Commissariat built its local administration by recruiting the remnants of Ottoman bureaucracy willing to serve them, and by establishing alliances and clienteles with the most conservative, pliable, and Francophile elements they could find. In Lebanon, the French quickly replanted the hundreds of French missionaries ousted by the Ottomans during the war, and cultivated the Maronite Church, with which the French had long historical ties. They also cultivated the urban bourgeoisie in Beirut with the award of contracts and trade opportunities. In Syria, the French had little previous loyalty and a far more organized opposition to confront. They cultivated a clientele of mostly rural notables—landowners, tribal chiefs, sympathetic religious patriarchs, and minorities. In contrast to their policy in Lebanon, they sought to isolate and disarm the urban bourgeoisie, which mounted stiff nationalist opposition to the mandatory regime. In both countries, French collaborators became agents and mediators between the central state and the populace.

The third component of the civic order, nonstate actors, was a highly varied group. It consisted of both recipients of state services and opponents to the regime. In the 1920s, the state clients who mobilized most vigorously were workers employed by foreign concessionary companies and consumers of the public utilities that these companies ran, who organized strikes and boycotts, respectively, to protest unfair labor practices and utility rates. In addition, opposition newspapers and women's charities mounted campaigns for more stringent public health protections. This fledgling civic order was besieged in these years by those who opposed its very existence. Syrian notables and tribal leaders organized armed resistance against the French, culminating in the massive revolt of 1925–27, which was begun by the Druze and then spread to major cities.

Two factors—one political, the other economic—transformed the civic order from an arena defined in the 1920s by patronage and military repression to an arena animated primarily by demands for political and social rights in the 1930s. Political change resulted both from the Syrian rebels' defeat and from the League of Nations' requirement that a constitution and elected government be installed in the mandates. With force and persuasion, the French imposed constitutions in Lebanon in 1926 and in Syria in 1930, and conducted carefully orchestrated elections of handpicked favorites soon afterward. This process provoked the organization of political opposition among Lebanese Sunnis seeking unity with Syria and among Syrian nationalists opposed to French rule altogether. In Syria, the unification of nationalists into a loose federation called the National Bloc was a watershed, marking a transition from armed, military opposition to political means of opposition. Lebanese Sunnis gradually abandoned their policy of abstention from politics as well. By the mid-1930s, rudimentary political parties would open offices in major cities of Syria and Lebanon and recruit thousands of followers, particularly among students.

The economic factors that transformed the civic order were complex, and can be only summarized here. From the mid-nineteenth century, new classes of urban elites arose around the twin pillars of landownership and ties to the Ottoman bureaucracy. An urban middle class emerged shortly before World War I as a political force through the establishment of political, cultural, and sporting clubs. These were largely professional men, often poorer relations of the elite notable families: doctors, engineers, lawyers, and journalists. Bourgeois women's charities and cultural clubs also emerged as more women attended schools. At the same time government reform and dislocation of the local economy, as the region was drawn into the world economy, transformed the working populations of the cities. By the early 1930s, workers-only labor unions emerged out of former guilds in transport, printing, and public works sectors. With petitions, rallies, and strikes, they confronted both the bourgeoisie and the state as their employers, demanding higher pay and better work conditions.

In sum, the civic order took shape in the 1930s as a triangle of relationships between the French state, collaborating mediators, and their clients and opposition. Virtually excluded from the civic order were the subalterns of mediating elites, such as peasants, children, most women, and the urban poor who were not recruited by active opposition groups. The structure of the civic order influenced the strategies of the three groups as they jostled for power. The supreme power of the High Commissariat made it the dominant player. The division of elites into collaborationist and nationalist camps produced a politics of intense bargaining for political allies and influence. As a result, the French, the mediators, and the nationalist opposition vied with one another for influence over the larger but weaker groups among the urban masses, particularly organized workers, women, and religious groups.

While independence was the most prominent issue to animate the civic order, social policy was also a central terrain of debate, one at first cultivated by the French themselves. Social policy was, from the earliest years of occupation, privileged as a top priority among French officials. The high commissioner played the role as chief relief officer in the days following the Allied occupation in 1918 and retained centralized control of social services in his offices in Beirut, via a partially privatized patronage system. Christian charities (mostly French) administered a large proportion of health services in conjunction with a skeletal public health department. They also ran a large number of schools. As Catroux would later claim during the war, these supposedly private schools, hospitals, and clinics were actually semipublic agencies, as they depended for their very existence on subsidies from the High Commissariat.[10]

Emergency aid and self-justifying beneficence bestowed upon a populace do not, however, create a welfare state. It was only in the 1930s that popular demand for a sustained state role in social affairs was organized by various actors: civil servants, Syrian and Lebanese philanthropists, nationalists seeking a broader political base among lower classes, labor unions, the Communist Party, and women's organizations. Social services were claimed by these groups as a matter of right, in the course of massive strikes and demonstrations between 1934 and 1939; these were fueled first by economic depression and the dismissal of parliaments and boosted in 1936 by sympathies with the Arab revolt in Palestine and by rising expectations, with the reinstatement of national governments and the resumption of treaty negotiations.

Social rights were by no means, in the minds of agitators, the principal goal. Under nationalist leadership, the protests were framed primarily in terms of demands for self-government and independence from French rule. Workers', women's, and parents' grievances were used to support arguments that the French had violated the terms of the mandate: with economic policies that inhibited growth, industrial development, and employment; with chronic shortages of schools; and with low levels of health care. Many of these grievances were sent by petition to the League of Nations in Geneva, as proof that the French had betrayed the terms of the mandate charter awarded by the League, and so ought to withdraw.

In response, French strategy sought to convert challenges based on political claims into bargains over social rights. The willingness of the state to bargain over social rights was enhanced in the mid-1930s by the election of the left-leaning Popular Front government in France. However, idealism was not likely the main impulse to bargain. By introducing social policy initiatives, the French were able to exploit the ambiguity latent in the opposition's demands. For even as the groups rejected the very fact of French rule, they continued to demand more state intervention, not less, in social affairs. Amid criticisms of the emphasis on French language in schools, there were constant calls for more state schools. Amid criticism of industrial policy favoring concessions to French firms, there were calls for state support of a national economy and for state protection of workers. The French responded in piecemeal fashion to these specific grievances and sidestepped fundamental challenges to their rule. To complaints about the lack of schools, they funded more schools. To complaints about poor safety regulations, they stepped up inspections. To complaints about unemployment, they created jobs. In sum, the French responded to the mid-1930s challenges by augmenting their long-standing policy of paternalistic social spending.

In the process, the French were forced to expand their skeletal system of social services well beyond what they had understood to be their commitment when the mandate was assigned. The transformed civic order thus planted the roots of a colonial welfare state. Basic financial and legal commitments won from the state further nurtured the notion of citizens' social rights. Workers', parents', and mothers' claims to those rights were incorporated into nationalist ideology (if not practice) and into the language of government officials themselves. A closer look at the main branches of social policy—public health, education, and labor protection—will illustrate how the process of political bargaining extended state commitments to welfare.

Public Health

Beginning in the 1920s, women's groups and newspaper columnists badgered the French to increase funding for public health and speed responses to epidemics. Pressure was also exerted in the international arena, where doubt was cast on public health statistics reported to the League of Nations. In response, the state built a basic, if rudimentary, system of hospitals and clinics from virtually nothing after the war. By 1939, there were about one hundred hospitals, clinics, orphanages, and asylums, both public and private (the French ones subsidized by the state). Local state public health departments were reorganized and their staff of inspectors enlarged and empowered with stricter regulations on food vendors, restaurants, schools, and other public places. The high commissioner's budget for public hygiene and assistance averaged in the 1930s about 500,000 £LS, rising from 2.0 percent to 2.6 percent of combined global budgets for Syria and Lebanon between 1929 and 1938, a time when most departments' budgets were slashed. In addition, hundreds of thousands more liras were spent through the early 1930s on relief to refugees, particularly Armenians and Assyrians. More important for our purposes was the growing public sentiment that state-subsidized health care was a right, not a gift from the state. Writing in the quasi-official journal *Dimashq* in 1940, Dr. Joseph Aractingi, who had headed the public health administration in Syria since the early 1920s, stated that sound hygiene laws were "the right of the Syrian people."[11]

Education

The number of schools and students in all territories under French mandate—state and private—roughly doubled in the fifteen years prior to the war, totaling 2,554 schools with about 280,000 students in 1938, compared to 1,590 schools with 126,000 students in 1924. As in public health, the delivery of publicly funded benefits was channeled through both public and private institutions. Of the 280,000 students in 1938, only 92,000 were in state schools. Another 55,000 attended the semipublic French schools that were closely regulated and heavily financed by the High Commissariat. And 120,000 students attended local private schools run by Muslim and Christian groups.[12]

And as with public health, pressure to expand state educational services came from the population and, in turn, from the League of Nations. In the mid-1930s, thousands of students each year were being turned away because there was no room in existing state schools. Nationalists demanded universal education as not just a social right but a political right, claiming that an educated citizenry is a precondition of democracy. Parents' groups, particularly among urban Muslims, sent dozens of complaints to the League of Nations' Permanent Mandates Commission. The French defended their policy by claiming that drops in state revenue during the depression prevented the hiring of new teachers, and that localities had failed to contribute their required portions of funds for the construction of schools, required by existing law dating from the Ottoman era.[13]

The pressure apparently had some effect. In 1938, the French used extrabudgetary funding to open twenty-eight new government schools in Lebanon, the first new schools in years.[14] Moreover, as with public health spending, education spending rose throughout the 1930s, when the depression was forcing deep cuts in administrative and public works budgets. Education spending in all of the Levant states rose from 4.6 percent of global budgets (1.4 million £LS) in 1929 to 8.6 percent (2.4 million £LS) in 1938.[15] The figure rises to 9.2 percent if subsidies to French missionary schools are included.[16]

Labor

State involvement in labor issues took three main forms: job creation, labor regulations and protections, and cost-of-living allowances. Labor unions' strikes and demonstrations against unemployment pressured the state to adopt a major job-creation program in 1933. High Commissioner Damien de Martel inaugurated a public works program to combat unemployment, with a budget of 10 million £LS, and ordered a further study to develop import substitution industries. Funding for workers' technical education was also increased, and, after the franc was devalued in 1936–37, De Martel introduced cost-of-living wage increases for civil servants, including teachers.

The unions also called for safer workplaces and for social security. Under pressure as well from the International Labor Organization, the High Commissariat decreed laws on industrial hygiene and the protection of working women and children in 1935 and 1936. Unions heralded the laws as a first step toward comprehensive labor laws protecting workers against long hours and accidents. Between 1936 and 1939, the unions united into (illegal) federations to pressure the reinstated parliaments into adopting such labor codes, which would include unemployment and work accident pensions, minimum wage standards, and the legalization of their federations. Syrian and Lebanese unions, as well as leaders of the women's movement, explicitly invoked as a model contemporary events in France, where in 1935–36 democratic socialists and Communists joined labor unions to agitate for substantial new state intervention in economy and society, and to bring the Popular Front to power.[17] By 1937 workers won virtual state recognition of their right to organize against their employers.[18] The proposed labor codes, however, foundered in parliaments dominated by the bourgeois owners of businesses that employed the union members.[19]

With the establishment of rudimentary social rights to health, education, and job security, in the form of both legal protection and fiscal commitments from the state, the cornerstone of a colonial welfare state had been laid. The growing acceptance of the notion of social rights in Syria and Lebanon mirrored contemporary developments in 1930s France and Britain. The term "welfare state" itself had become current in Britain by the late 1930s, while in France the foundations of "l'état providence" were laid with universal unemployment insurance laws in 1928 and 1930. The etatism of the era spread internationally the idea that citizens should claim from the state a commitment to improving their welfare.

However, the nature of state commitments by 1939 was limited. Only under external pressure did the state formulate benefits in terms of legal right, in the exceptional case of the 1934–35 protective labor laws. Even as the French government increased education spending, it continued to claim that it was not the state's obligation to do so. Although the language of rights was increasingly employed, it was more a political ploy than a description of institutionalized reality. Second, there was a profound reluctance on the part of nationalist elites to make good on demands for social rights. The parliaments they controlled after 1936 refused to adopt labor codes and made no significant allocations of funds for education or health. The level of state commitment may be compared those made by the British and French states to their own citizens prior to World War I, when the first legislative guarantees and financial entitlements were established.

Moreover, the way in which services were delivered and funded was distinctly colonial. In stark contrast to the situation in metropolitan France, social welfare in Syria and Lebanon was not primarily funded through taxes on the middle and upper classes. Syrian and Lebanese elites resisted taxation, especially by a foreign ruler, and constituted such a thin layer of the population in their unindustrialized societies that potential revenues were limited anyway. Social spending in the mandates was financed, as a result, primarily through the High Commissariat, via Common Interests' customs revenues and subsidies from Paris. The colonial welfare state was, at its origin, a stopgap measure designed to forestall demands for independence, not the product of an evolutionary social contract binding state and society through a commitment to higher taxes.

Another distinctively colonial feature of Syrian and Lebanese welfare was the mediated delivery of what were largely state-funded services. In diverting political grievances into social claims, the French turned to their post–World War I legacy of paternalistic social spending, which was funneled preeminently through the loyal constituencies they had cultivated: rural landlords and tribal chiefs, missionaries, indigenous religious leaders. These elites were the civilian pillars of French rule. They were cultivated with the award of power over other citizens and with financial support. As the French were pressured into expanding social policy, these elites became important vehicles not only of political control but also for the delivery of social services. The French in a sense could kill two birds with one stone: the need both to award power to mediators and to appease demands for social rights. In addition, mediators were often bargains. Nuns in French schools, for example, did not require full salaries.

The corollary of mediated state services was a hierarchical bias in benefits, which tended to favor the urban bourgeoisie, landowners, Christians (particularly in Lebanon), and males more than peasants, workers, Muslims, and women. European welfare states were closely tied to states' needs for healthy, literate military recruits, and needs to pacify growing numbers of industrialized urban workers. These conditions did not hold in Syria and Lebanon, where the indigenously recruited Troupes spéciales were not used for foreign wars, and where the urban workforce remained a small percentage of the population. On the other hand, as we have seen, the state did need to appease urban middle classes and elites who could potentially lead an armed rebellion, as Syrians had done in 1925–27. Elites were not only taxed lightly but enjoyed disproportionate use of public services. They were the main clients of state-funded hospitals and French institutions of higher education. Even oppositional nationalists sent their children to state-subsidized schools like the Maristes' lycée in Damascus and the Jesuit

St. Joseph's University in Beirut. Conversely, school shortages afflicted rural and Muslim areas most, while state labor policy continued to discourage unionization of workers against their employers and landlords. And existing law not only permitted lower pay for women workers but sanctioned their exclusion or marginalization in higher education, teaching, the civil service, and industry. Mediation and hierarchy of benefits contrasted with European welfarism, which aimed to level differences through the direct delivery of universal benefits to citizens. Welfare remained in Syria and Lebanon a privilege, not a right.

By late 1938, the bargaining process that had produced the colonial welfare state reached a critical juncture. Workers and women sought a far more radical transformation of state duties and citizens' rights than had so far been attained in the emergent colonial welfare state. In late 1938, frustrated Syrian unions sent an ultimatum to parliament, threatening a general strike unless it passed the proposed labor code. Women's unions, too, showed impatience with their alliance with nationalists, as the nationalist governments continued to ignore their calls for women's suffrage, increased employment of women in the civil service, and reforms in personal status law.

But in 1938 workers and women lacked the power to pressure the governments into adopting a more egalitarian, rights-based social policy. Ruling nationalists refused such reforms, in part due to their self-interest—as employers, fathers, and husbands of workers and women—and in part because of the greater pressure they felt from conservative religious interests that had a stake in mediated government. Syrian Islamic groups contributed in the winter of 1938–39 to the unrest that brought down the National Bloc government, with protests against reforms in the personal status code that would have virtually permitted civil marriages for the first time and appeared to undermine the historical priority of Islam among religions. Meanwhile Christian groups in Lebanon, including French Jesuits, staunchly defended their position as mediators in the colonial welfare system, standing in opposition to parents who sought the reallocation of funds from private to public schools and preaching against personal status reforms that would undermine patriarchal families. And the French, who in the Popular Front years were sympathetic to social demands and popular participation in government, withdrew their support as conservative governments took power in Paris. In late 1938 they replaced De Martel with a conservative high commissioner, Gabriel Puaux, who established close ties with religious patriarchs and voiced his preference for installing a monarchy in Syria.

The juncture turned to crisis when the independence treaties approved by the Syrian and Lebanese parliaments were flatly rejected by the French parliament. Labor strikes and mass street demonstrations brought down the iron hand of Puaux, who suspended the parliaments and constitutions of both governments in the months before the outbreak of World War II in September 1939. The struggle over the colonial welfare state was frozen in place for the next two years.

REALIZATION OF A COLONIAL WELFARE STATE, 1941–43

High Commissioner Gabriel Puaux boasted that it was "easy to govern" in the first year of the war, as his hundred thousand French troops "inspired everyone to respect France's wishes."[20] Puaux wielded, in addition to this big stick, a carrot of 50 million francs sent from Paris to ensure imports of necessary goods and to stanch unemployment by reviving De Martel's public works program. However, Puaux did not revive De Martel's bargaining policies. Labor leaders who mounted strikes to protest low wages and layoffs were arrested, as was most of the Communist leadership, by January 1940. The civic order of the 1930s was stilled as it had been in the early 1920s, under martial law and military repression.

The war's second year would not be so calm. The June 1940 occupation of France and inauguration of Vichy rule in Syria and Lebanon aggravated conditions beyond endurance. Funds from France were cut, as was vital trade. The British instituted a shipping blockade, shut off the oil flow from Iraq to Tripoli's refinery, and closed borders to important markets in Iraq and Palestine. To cope with these stresses, Puaux laid the foundations of a state-led wartime economy, while using Vichy rhetoric to discipline an anxious population. In a speech on August 30, 1940, he called on youth to "calm down" and to espouse their duties of "discipline and work," just as the state would do. He directed the High Commissariat to plan planting of sugar beets and rice and to impose a state monopoly on the transport of necessities to ensure supplies to Mount Lebanon and the rural poor. The Tripoli oil refinery was refitted to process remaining oil stockpiles. Yet shortages and inflation continued, igniting sporadic protests. In November, Puaux decreed harsh penalties for hoarding and black marketeering. The pillar of French claims to rule, its guarantee of welfare, was crumbling, and Puaux lamented, "The inhabitants [of the Levant] had been accustomed by us, perhaps too quickly, to consider the Republic as a wet nurse with an inexhaustible breast."[21]

The bottom fell out of Puaux's tenuous social order upon the arrival of his successor, the pro-Vichy General Henri Dentz, in December 1940. More than fifty thousand workers were unemployed in Damascus alone, and breadlines grew long. The cost of living had doubled since the war's start, without comparable pay raises. The first hunger marches took place in January 1941, in Damascus and Aleppo. In February, the Syrian nationalist leader Shukri Quwwatli seized leadership of protests against unemployment, high prices, and shortages, and organized a shopkeepers' strike that spread to all of Syria's major cities. In the face of French tanks and mass arrests, the strikes spread to Lebanon's cities in March, some of them organized by the few labor leaders not yet jailed. Nationalist leaders used the threat of continued strikes to oust Vichy's puppet governments and lower bread prices. In April 1941, Dentz dismissed the Puaux-era Councils of Directors. Khalid al-Azm, the new Syrian head of state, promised immediate public works jobs, welfare for youth, an ambitious public health program, and increased supplies of food. In May, bakers were forced to reduce the price of bread. Social pressure and Vichy's lack of funds had forced the state back to the bargaining table.

Two months later the Vichy government fell to Free French and British invaders. The Free French were even weaker in resources than Vichy had been. Not only did they not enjoy subsidies from the metropole, but their rule coincided with the deepest economic slump of the war, plunging state tax revenues to new lows. They were thus forced not only to bargain but also to adopt a positively liberal policy in order to establish their rule. Under Georges Catroux, from July 1941 to June 1943, the Free French reinstated much of the civic order of late 1930s, with its three-way structure, bargaining strategies, and familiar players.

This proved to be no simple return to the past, however. As political prisoners were released and opposition groups permitted to reform, they attracted more followers than ever among those suffering from wartime hardships. Fearing rebellion during wartime, the French were forced to cater to social demands as never before. They compensated for their lack of funds by taking significant steps toward the direct delivery of state welfare benefits, bypassing colonial mediators, and toward the institutionalization of social rights through legislation. In early 1943, bargaining would reach a new pitch, as the French and their nationalist opponents sought to sway the loyalties of the urban masses in anticipation of the long-delayed parliamentary elections. As a result, the period of Free French rule brought the colonial welfare state to a new climax.

Catroux had no choice but to promise a return to the democratic liberties and colonial beneficence that had been cast aside by Vichy. The Free French were making a barely legal and desperately absurd claim to rule in the Levant, as they still occupied only a few minor colonies and commanded only a few thousand troops. Their claim to the mandate was doubly jeopardized by Vichy's abandonment of neutrality for collaboration with the Germans, perceived by many as a renunciation of their membership in the League of Nations. Finally, they did not enjoy the confidence of their British and American allies. The Free French had therefore to base their claim to represent true France on antifascist, democratic principles. To rally the population, the government also had to promise war relief. And so on

June 8, Catroux dropped flyers from airplanes proclaiming promises to abolish the mandate, establish independence, and reopen trade within the British-occupied regions of the Middle East: "it is not to repress your freedom but to assure it, to chase Hitler's forces from Syria and make your rights, and those of France, respected."[22] The Vichy rhetoric of "duty" was replaced by claims to social and political rights.

In reorganizing the state and civic order, Catroux made explicit reference to policies of the leftist Popular Front between 1936 and 1938, now constructed in Free French ideology as a golden age before disaster. The independence treaties negotiated then would be revived, and as soon as wartime conditions permitted, elections for parliament would be held. Catroux even considered reinstating the governments dismissed by Vichy-collaborator Puaux in 1939. Under pressure from de Gaulle, however, Catroux postponed such a return as too risky to French interests: democratic symbols would be subordinated to the preservation of empire.[23]

The Free French were too weak in 1941 to control a return to the combative parliamentary politics of the 1930s. They lacked critical funds and staff. Fully one-third of top French bureaucrats and all but 2,500 troops had opted to return with Dentz to Vichy France. The Free French would not fully replenish their civil and military ranks in Syria and Lebanon until 1943. And their tentacles of support among nonstate mediating bodies were attenuated, as most French missionaries were pro-Vichy: Catroux exiled the Jesuit rector of St. Joseph University, Père Chanteur, to Cairo for continuing to lead his students in prayers for Marshal Pétain. In addition, Free France enjoyed no subsidies from Paris with which to rebuild such support. Neither could the High Commissariat rely on customs duties to finance itself, as wartime trade was to remain severely restricted under the guidance of the Middle East Supply Centre (MESC), run by the British and Americans. Indeed, the period of Free French rule was the most impoverished of the war, as total state spending sank, in real terms adjusted for inflation, to roughly half of 1939 levels.

So Catroux reneged on his promise of independence and instead announced a transition period of conditional independence in autumn 1941, wherein he granted more autonomy to local governments and appointed longtime conservative collaborators to head the states: Shaykh Taj al-Din in Syria, and Alfred Naccache in Lebanon. Catroux also maintained the tight control of the High Commissariat (renamed the Délégation générale) over the military, police, and vital Common Interests administration, which included not only the sizable customs revenues but the foreign concessions that owned and managed much of the Levant's public utilities and transport, the tobacco monopoly, and the Tripoli oil refinery.

However, revived opposition movements mushroomed as soon as Catroux announced conditional independence in autumn 1941. In Lebanon, the prewar rivalry between Bishara al-Khuri and Emile Eddé would solidify into opposing parties. In Syria, the bourgeois National Bloc/rural landowner cleavage reemerged, as the Bloc attacked the latter associated with Shaykh Taj's government. Labor federations and the Communist Party in both countries would gain unprecedented strength by late 1943, with revived campaigns for the long-sought labor code and for pay raises. Syrian and Lebanese feminists, too, reignited their prewar women's unions in a more independent spirit, distancing themselves slightly from their nationalist allies by demonstrating behind their own banners. Syrian Islamic groups, before the war scattered in various cities under individual personalities, would unite by 1945 into a branch of the Muslim Brotherhood.

Inflation and food shortages immediately engaged the reconstituted civic order. The years 1941–42 were the darkest days of wartime hardship. The summer harvest of 1941 was poor, and both public panic and government alarm rose: "Fearing a famine like that of 1917–1918, all of Mount Lebanon speaks of protests and demonstrations," French police reported on September 9.[24] Ten days later, similar reports came from Aleppo and Damascus. Food prices soared far beyond wage raises (the cost of food rose 450 percent and the general cost of living rose about 300 percent between January 1939 and January 1943).[25] Infant mortality, a primary indicator of public health, peaked throughout the Middle East in 1942.[26]

The threat of popular revolt was taken extremely seriously by the weakened French. Urban populations, those with the greatest capacity to unsettle the fragile Free French regime, were hit hardest. The 1942 crop would also be poor, and despite MESC food shipments, fear of famine would not subside until the bountiful harvest in June 1943.[27] Hunger marches began as early as September 1941 and peaked in the summer of 1942 and again in the spring of 1943, in all major cities. Communists, labor unions, and nationalists took credit for organizing them, but the prominence of women in French police reports about the marches is also striking: Women appear to have led at least ten demonstrations in Beirut and Aleppo during the summer of 1942 alone. Aleppo was shut down in early June 1942, and hundreds of women marched to the governorate building, shouting "We want bread!" and "Death to Governor Nabih Martini!" In Beirut, a Muslim woman started a demonstration in May 1943 after officials at city hall dismissed her complaint about poor distribution of flour. She returned to her quarter and led a crowd toward the city center, forcing shops to close and demanding lower prices and larger rations.[28]

Thousands of workers also staged increasingly disruptive strikes. French police recorded major strikes in nearly every month of 1942 and 1943, especially among textile and public sector workers seeking wage raises to match inflation. While Vichy-era unemployment diminished in 1942, as British military demand fueled the creation of thirty thousand jobs, wages remained extremely low. Wages would rise by 1943 at only half the rate of inflation. Workers also protested import-export bans of cotton and silk, which curtailed production.[29] With each month, the size and number of labor unions grew, and labor federations began to coordinate united actions not just against employers but targeting the state as well.

Thus two issues dominated politics between 1941 and 1943: bread supplies and workers' wages. The French, their appointed heads of state, and nationalist opposition leaders each in turn sought to exploit mass unrest over food shortages and rising prices. These inter-elite rivalries would shape government policy, producing a variety of legal and financial commitments that amounted to the awarding of new rights to a broader array of social groups.

Catroux took the initiative in the late summer of 1941, when he established a new department in his cabinet called the "Section sociale." By September, the Section began producing numerous social studies and legislative proposals to ameliorate the condition of workers and to offset the hardships of inflation. Their intent, as in French strategy of the 1930s, was to diffuse calls by opposition nationalists for immediate independence and to sway the loyalties of urban masses toward French allies in government. The section's proposals would result in important legislation granting workers and families unprecedented rights to security and benefits.[30]

Catroux similarly sought to exploit the bread issue. In April 1942 he established a Wheat Office (Office du blé) under the auspices of the Common Interests administration to impose a state monopoly on grain supplies and assure the delivery of surplus Syrian grain to Lebanon, which depended on Syria for half of its needs. His intent was to make the (French) state the primary and direct provider of this most essential foodstuff. But he was thwarted in this effort by Sir Edward Spears, the British minister to the Levant, who sought to assure MESC (that is, British) control, and by Shaykh Taj, who asserted Syrian control. The parties negotiated to create a new, joint commission to oversee grain collections and distribution, which was eventually named the Office des céréales panifiables (Cereals Office).[31]

The bread-supply issue was most prominent in Syrian politics because Syria was the main producer of grain. In the summer of 1942 the Cereals Office attempted its first collections of grain, but landowners and peasants balked at state-set grain prices and hid the grain from Cereals Office collectors. Catroux saw an opportunity to recoup French prestige by using French troops to extract the grain by force, thereby bypassing landowning intermediaries. However, Spears checked Catroux's plan. In August 1942, Spears approached the prime minister, Husni al-Barazi, a large landowner from Hama, and arranged to hold landlords responsible for the collection of grains on their lands, under threat of deportation if they did not produce the grain. At least thirteen landlords were deported and collections increased. However, landowners in both Syria and Lebanon were greatly compensated for their compliance, and emerged from the war tremendously enriched by MESC schemes to increase local production. Peasants, on the other hand, would not reap similar rewards, and lived at subsistence levels.[32]

The establishment of direct state benefits did, however, proceed on the other end of the bread chain: distribution to urban consumers. The Syrian head of state, Shaykh Taj al-Din, known for his fiery populism in speeches, carved his own wedge of prestige by introducing a system of subsidies to the urban masses. He sold grain for less than the Cereals Office paid for it, at a cost of 8–10 million £LS per year. The deficit was covered by instituting a two-tiered pricing system, wherein the middle class paid more for grain and sugar to offset the discount offered to lower classes. Shaykh Taj also built a coalition of merchants, among whom he tolerated war profiteers and the rural Alawi and Druze minorities. In so doing, however, he plunged the state into debt and opened it to charges of corruption.[33]

The nationalist opposition mounted an offensive against Shaykh Taj's conservative coalition beginning in late 1942, upon the return of the National Bloc's leader, Shukri Quwwatli, from exile. The Bloc took over leadership of hunger marches from unions, women, and others and coordinated a sustained campaign against the alleged corruption of Prime Minister Barazi, ousting him in December 1942. The next month, Shaykh Taj died, and his funeral, significantly, drew sympathetic crowds into the streets. Following Taj's lead, his successor Jamal al-Ulshi raised the price of bread paid by the urban middle class from 8 to 8.5 piasters per kilo and proposed a new income tax, claiming the need to finance bread subsidies to the poor.[34] In early February, the Bloc organized students and merchants in a five-day strike to protest the increase, accusing Ulshi of pocketing the new revenues. The Bloc continued to provoke protests through March, expanding its complaints to include opposition to sending grain to Lebanon. Catroux, fearing Spears's growing ties with the Bloc, dismissed Ulshi on the pretext of disobedience.[35] Quwwatli and the nationalists had successfully exploited the bread issue to discredit their main opposition in the upcoming elections, but at the cost of more firmly allying their cause with middleclass interests against those of the poor.

Syrian bread politics had repercussions in Lebanon, where Catroux also failed to turn bread into political gold. Lebanese hunger marchers, alarmed by the National Bloc's calls to stop grain exports, demanded bread subsidies like those instituted by Shaykh Taj in Syria. Through his control of the Cereals Office and Common Interests, Catroux sought to position himself as defender of Lebanese interests. But he gained little ground, for Bishara al-Khuri and his Constitutional Bloc pounded Catroux's head of state, Alfred Naccache, for ineffectual government.

Catroux exploited the wage issue to better profit, especially in Lebanon. He used it first as a means of securing the loyalty of the underpaid bureaucracy, still laden with pro-Vichy sentiment, and then in an attempt to sway the urban masses toward supporting his conservative allies as the summer 1943 elections approached. Labor unions acted quickly to steal Catroux's initiative and pushed state wage policies far beyond their original intent. The result was to position the state for the first time as the legal protector of all workers. In contrast to the stalemate of the late 1930s, when nationalist parliaments in both countries refused to enact labor laws, the state now aligned itself with workers against the bourgeoisie.

Legislation began with Catroux's decrees in October and November 1941 to increase cost-of-living allowances for civil servants and establish a minimum wage for all workers in public sector enterprises in both Syria and Lebanon. Lebanese unions immediately threatened a general strike unless pay raises were extended to the private sector. The Lebanese government issued such a law in December but suspended implementation when employers objected. Unions mounted a series of strikes, which crested in a general upheaval in March 1942. Seven unions combined in a joint committee to advance their cause. An August 1942 law finally granted private sector workers a smaller pay increase, one that fell well below real inflation rates. Also in 1942, the Délégation générale enacted rent control laws and established a Labor and Artisanate Office subsidized by de Gaulle to promote local wool spinning and other industries.[36] In October 1942 the Lebanese government decreed family allowances for married civil servants; and the unions again demanded their extension to all workers.[37]

In May 1943, three months before elections, the Délégation générale and Lebanese government promulgated an omnibus wage law, which guaranteed all workers in commerce and industry increases in minimum wages, family allowances, and cost-of-living allowances.[38] The law also decreed equal pay and benefits for men and women who performed similar work.[39] The Free French had vowed to reverse Vichy policy and advance a liberal position in defense of women's work. At the time the omnibus wage law was decreed, they publicized a showcase munitions complex called De Gaulle Park in the press, featuring one hundred Lebanese women in white laboratory coats manufacturing truck parts.[40] But while women who worked in factories and for the civil service stood to gain from the labor legislation, the laws did not affect the many more women homeworkers who sewed clothing to substitute for wartime cuts in clothing imports.

Also in May 1943, the Lebanese state promulgated a second landmark law, modeled on an 1898 French law, that guaranteed work-accident insurance in the public sector and a variety of heavy industries deemed essential to the public interest.[41] It required employers in mining, construction, transport, electric, and other industries to pay injured workers a daily pension during recovery, or permanently in cases where they could not return to work. In the case of death, the worker's family would receive an indemnity. The law also required first-aid care facilities in the workplace. A third and final 1943 labor law established the Service des affaires sociales in Lebanon to help conciliate labor disputes.[42] It was based on a 1909 Ottoman law on strikes that had never been implemented, but which had required government mediation. And like the Délégation générale's Section sociale, the Service was to study labor issues and prepare legislative proposals. In addition, it was to undertake assistance to workers for the protection of children, prisoners, and families.

These new labor laws unleashed strikes throughout Lebanon during May and June and for months to come, as employers resisted workers' demands to implement their provisions. Workers fought tooth and nail, factory by factory, to claim their rights from employers. Workers also sought government intervention to enforce their new rights. In June 1943, the government intervened on behalf of striking tailors, who then obtained a 30 percent raise. Workers at a stocking factory, wool factory, and tobacco plant also sent representatives to the government seeking protection, but obtained only partial compliance in October 1943.[43] The government's apparent laxity in enforcing the new labor laws may have been due at first to a time lag in setting up the regulatory apparatus. However, it also reflected the politics behind the laws' promulgation. The work-accident and omnibus wage laws were decreed in Lebanon in the fervor of the 1943 election campaign by Eyub Tabet, the conservative interim president and stiff opponent of the nationalist opposition, the Constitutional Bloc. As the Constitutional Bloc represented a large portion of the commercial-industrial bourgeoisie, the intent of these decrees was clearly to sway workers' support away from the nationalists. Workers would find that after the August elections, the new Constitutional Bloc government was reluctant to enforce the labor laws.

The wage issue in Syria was not exploited as vigorously by the ruling elite faction, in part because the National Bloc had already destroyed its conservative opposition by May 1943. In November 1942, Shaykh Taj al-Din issued two decrees guaranteeing severance pay and setting minimum wage standards, the latter in compliance with Catroux's 1941 decree. Cost-of-living laws were also issued, although they covered only civil servants. The decrees may be read, like Shaykh Taj's two-tiered bread policy, as part of his effort to woo the urban workers away from the National Bloc. Moreover, the laws were primarily designed to appeal to workers in large industries, many of which were owned by members of the National Bloc. They significantly exempted constituencies loyal to Shaykh Taj: landlords with agricultural workers, employers of domestic servants, and artisanal and family businesses did not have to comply with the new wage and severance standards.[44]

Like their Lebanese counterparts, Syrian workers staged numerous strikes in Aleppo, Homs, and Damascus to extend the labor laws, but to less effect. This was likely because the outcome of the elections had been virtually decided with Ulshi's dismissal in March. Ata al-Ayyubi, the elderly interim chief of state, was on good terms with many National Bloc leaders.[45]

On the eve of the summer 1943 elections, the colonial welfare state ruled by the Free French had not only been rebuilt from the "scorched earth" Catroux said he found after Vichy's departure, but significantly transformed. The state had assumed new financial commitments to the population at large, in the form of bread subsidies, and new guarantees of legal protection for workers, in the form of minimum wages, family allowances, equal pay for men and women, cost-of-living increases, and severance pay. Despite their limitations and often self-serving origins, the new labor laws armed workers with unprecedented rights. These laws positioned the state as the primary guarantor of families' economic welfare in a way undreamed of in the 1930s. The change was made possible only by the peculiar circumstances of the war that had transformed the civic order and the roles that the French and the urban masses played in it. The masses were far more organized, and the French needed their support, and feared revolt, more than before. The laws and subsidies represented, finally, a clean break from France's former colonial paternalism and a true commitment of the state to social welfare.

The nationalists, meanwhile, had been pushed to show their allegiance to their own bourgeois interests, which drove a wedge in the cross-class nationalist coalitions of the 1930s. The Communist Party and Islamic groups both positioned themselves as the true defenders of the poor; their memberships soared in this period. Because of this split, and growing food supplies, the Free French no longer feared revolt by the spring of 1943. Also by that time, they had secured a government base in reconquered Algiers. Catroux felt confident enough to call elections for the following summer, although his boss, Charles de Gaulle, was uncomfortable with the extent of bargaining required: "I came to think his desire to charm and his leaning toward conciliation did not always answer to the kind of sword play which was imposed upon him."[46]

It is well-known that the nationalists won the 1943 elections; it was, however, neither a resounding victory nor a referendum against state welfarism. Nationalist candidates won through their manipulation of a two-stage electoral system designed in the 1920s to favor rural and urban elites over unknown and poorer candidates. The list system promoted patronage politics of personal clienteles, and it disadvantaged formal political parties.[47] Voter turnout tells the story. Most of the urban masses did not vote in the summer 1943 elections (turnout was as low as 33 percent in major Syrian cities and 25 percent in Beirut). Nationalists won their biggest majorities in the countryside, where peasants were corralled to vote for local notables—except, significantly around Hama, where Akram Hawrani won a seat in parliament on promises of land reform. The nationalist Constitutional Bloc actually lost in Beirut to its Francophile opposition. And a significant number of urbanites voted for Communist candidates. The Communist Party, through its organizing of hunger marches and labor unions, had won the reputation of defender of the poor. The joint Syrian-Lebanese party fielded six candidates on a platform of workers' rights, democracy, and independence, while several more sympathizers ran independently. Procommunist candidates earned forty thousand votes in all of Syria and Lebanon, and nearly 12 percent of all votes cast in Lebanon alone, a show of promising strength, although they failed to win a parliamentary seat.[48]

The nationalist victory would nonetheless transform the civic order for a second time during the war. The new governments' disinterest in social bargaining was made immediately clear. In Lebanon, President Bishara al-Khuri, a Maronite Christian, and Prime Minister Riad al-Sulh, a Sunni Muslim, cemented their victories with a pact that would unite a significant portion of the Muslim and Christian landowning bourgeoisie. In October 1943, workers petitioned the Lebanese government to enforce the neglected May 1943 labor laws and to increase subsidies, schooling, and protections for workers and their families. In response, Sulh merely called on workers to cooperate with their bosses in the national interest.[49] Similarly, Khuri dismissed petitions from women for the right to vote. In Syria, President Shukri Quwwatli, a landowner and industrialist himself, would bring the National Bloc's urban, Sunni, and bourgeois constituency closer to their erstwhile rivals, rural elites, in face of growing challenges from Communists and Islamists. As in Lebanon, Quwwatli's government urged the population to withhold their demands until the war was done and full independence achieved.

The year 1943 was, then, another turning point in the evolution of the colonial welfare state. Would workers, women, and others succeed in expanding their social and political rights and the scope of direct state benefits? Or would they confront the same resistance from national governments as in 1938–39?

NATIONAL GOVERNMENTS AND THE LEGACY OF COLONIAL WELFARE, 1944–46

Catroux left the Levant to take up a position with the Free French government newly established in Algiers in June 1943. With him departed the brief and final effort to reignite French prestige through bargaining over social policy. His successor, Jean Helleu, showed little interest in such a project and instead engaged in brute efforts to promote French cronies and to withhold power from the recently elected Syrian and Lebanese governments. Upon these governments' reasonable and expected demand to revise their constitutions, Helleu stonewalled. To their demands to acquire control of the police, military, and Common Interests, he turned a deaf ear. Helleu's intractability only raised the ante. When in November the Lebanese parliament proceeded unilaterally to amend the country's constitution, expunging references to the mandate, Helleu staged a coup; arrested President Bishara al-Khuri, Prime Minister Riad al-Sulh, and other cabinet officials; and precipitated the biggest political crisis of the war. Thirteen days of protest began on November 10 with crowds tearing down pictures of Charles de Gaulle from public walls.

Allied pressure forced the French not only to reinstate the Lebanese government but also to relinquish their civilian powers in both countries. On January 1, 1944, the French transferred to the national governments the main pillar of their rule: the Common Interests administration. By the end of 1944, the only important institutions still left in French hands were their own army, the Troupes spéciales (the locally recruited military), and the Serail building, French headquarters since World War I. Journalists, women's leaders, labor organizers, and politicians alike heralded the dawn of a new era, wherein imperialist obstacles to social and economic progress were finally cleared.

There was no instant revolution, however. In the years 1944–46, the civic order was decolonized with ambiguous implications for the colonial welfare state. On the one hand, major players in the civic order continued to follow strategies set in the 1930s. Labor unions, Communists, and feminists continued to make demands in the belief that the key to equality and social well-being lay in extending state regulation and benefits. Islamists and the Maronite Church intensified their critique of direct state intervention in society. Nationalists in both countries continued to appeal for cross-class unity with calls for full independence, in 1945 mounting campaigns to claim control of the Troupes spéciales and to oust French troops.

On the other hand, decolonization transformed the triangulated structure of the civic order that had produced the colonial welfare state. First, nationalists now filled the shoes of the French, occupying the state apparatus and controlling the ranks of state mediators. Withdrawal of the French removed the rationale for a split between nationalist and collaborationist elites that had fueled their rivalry for mass loyalty and social bargaining. Second, nationalist rulers were insulated from social pressure in a way the French had not been: the British had strongly backed them against the French, and as long as their troops remained on Syrian and Lebanese soil, pressure from highly mobilized labor unions, Communists, Islamists, and feminists could not seriously threaten the new regimes. Third, the states were administratively weakened in 1944, as less experienced Syrians and

Lebanese replaced the ubiquitous French advisors throughout the bureaucracy. Links between the state and many of its quasi-public mediating agencies were broken: French schools, hospitals, and concessionary companies that had delivered a large portion of state-subsidized services were now clearly private agents of a foreign country. Both states focused less on promoting social change, and more on internal administrative, fiscal, and judicial reform, particularly on abolishing inefficient dual French and Arabic procedures. Fourth, as result of the above, the state's opposition, once a cross-class coalition, now distinctly represented those groups marginalized or excluded from power—workers, women, and Islamists—and they were more frustrated and disgruntled than ever.

The polarization of class interests altered political bargaining strategies. The former strategy of French rulers, who employed social policy to divert calls for independence, had no place in this civic order. Indeed, at times the nationalist rulers would reverse the French tactic, using the need for full independence as a reason to postpone fulfillment of social demands. The opposition, no longer bound to elites by the cause of independence, now amplified their own demands. In Syria, the opposition was now split between two powerful movements: secularist Communists who looked to the state to guarantee social rights, and Islamic groups that defined social rights in terms of limitations on the state. In Lebanon, a powerful federation of labor unions coordinated protests across the country. While bread was now plentiful, inflation still depressed most families' standard of living. In both countries, women's unions launched all-out suffrage drives, uninhibited by their former deference to nationalists' insistence on independence first. Fearful especially of the Communists, Syrian and Lebanese nationalist elites responded by forming closer alliances with the very conservatives they once opposed, especially religious interests.

In the years 1944–46, ruling nationalists' efforts to reduce tensions in the civic order would modify the colonial welfare state but not alter its basic attributes. First, the states responded to demands to expand welfare with two major social policy initiatives: expansion of public education and adoption of comprehensive labor codes. Initial efforts were made, too, to finance social services through taxation, now that extrabudgetary subsidies from Paris had disappeared. Social spending, particularly on education, expanded rapidly. However, as will be shown below, no substantial new initiatives in welfare spending were undertaken, and the proportion of state budgets devoted to health and education would remain at levels characteristic of the colonial welfare state. Second, in keeping with past practice, mediation of services and rights continued. But it took new forms, marking a divergence in the state formation of the two countries. While Syria adopted etatist and corporatist policies, Lebanon adopted liberal ones. In sum, while the states were no longer colonial, they retained the low funding of social services, mediated structure, and obstacles to direct access to rights and privileges associated with the colonial welfare state. This limited response produced a precarious balance of forces that would inform the politics of both countries in postwar years.

The states' major new legal commitment to enhanced social rights was the passage of comprehensive labor codes. In January 1944, Lebanese labor unions united in a general federation and demanded credit for mobilizing many of the thousands of protesters in November 1943. They petitioned the government to recompense them for their national service by reducing inflation and reviving the 1930s labor code proposals. Unions in both countries brought far greater strength to bear on the issue than they had five years before: Wartime industries had swelled their ranks and Communist party membership ballooned on the heels of Red Army victories. Membership in unions is estimated at fifty thousand, and in the Communist party ten thousand, by war's end.[50] In 1944–45, the unions and Communists staged continuous strikes, demonstrations, and conferences with parliamentary representatives, and finally achieved the passage of labor codes in both countries in 1946. The labor codes formally legalized workers-only unions and the right to strike (except in the public sector). They also instituted demands made since the 1930s, including eight-hour workdays; overtime, sickness, and severance pay; retirement pensions; vacations; and the reinforcement of rights already won, like the minimum wage and work-accident protection.[51]

Women, too, campaigned for new rights on the basis of their contributions to the independence struggle. By 1944, the Syrian and Lebanese women's unions had achieved a much higher profile than in 1939. The Lebanese women's union capitalized on the mass mobilization of women over bread supplies to organize prominent demonstrations by hundreds of women in November 1943. The union used that momentum to stage a successful boycott of Beirut markets in 1944, forcing merchants to reduce food prices. Both the Syrian and Lebanese women's unions positioned women as defenders of the family, supporting campaigns to win family allowances, to fight corruption in rationing programs, and to increase vigilance against epidemics. Women workers also mobilized in labor unions and the growing women's wing of the Communist Party, which explicitly linked women's work to claims for rights as full-fledged citizens. Imilie Faris Ibrahim, a prominent Lebanese Communist and feminist, argued in an article published in December 1943 that women deserved the vote because they worked hard for the good of the country at factory jobs and in the fields.[52] At the end of 1944, the two women's unions sent delegates to the highly publicized Arab Women's Conference in Cairo, which called on Arab governments to grant women the vote, hire women for government posts, and expand girls' education and welfare for poor women and children. They also demanded that states adopt newer interpretations of Islamic law on personal status that granted women more rights in marriage, divorce, and child custody.[53]

Because of their ties to the powerful labor movement, women did win new rights in the labor codes, to equal pay, paid maternity leave, and severance pay if they quit their jobs to marry. They also won state commitment to girls' education because it fit with nationalists' ideas about the need to educate mothers for social progress.

However, women's grassroots support was much weaker than that of labor, and they would fail to gain the political and civil rights that were so necessary to furthering their welfare. Even though leaders of the women's movement were relatives of powerful nationalists, they could not compete with an opponent that posed a greater potential threat to nationalist rule: religious groups mobilized vigorously against the women's movement. In Lebanon, Catholics and Maronites held conferences calling on women to respect their traditional domestic roles and give up their jobs. The Lebanese parliament killed proposals in 1943 and 1946 to grant limited suffrage to educated women. In Syria, Islamist groups protested Muslim women's increasing presence in public and against reforms of personal status laws. Islamists had allied with Shukri al-Quwwatli in the 1943 elections, and expected a payback. When Quwwatli did not block social mixing of men and women, protests led to violent clashes. Islamist pressure, however, made the government reluctant to move on women's reforms. When delegates returned from the Cairo women's conference, they met ridicule in the press and condescension from government officials. In sum, women's nationalist allies in both countries let them down after independence.[54] Women would not fully attain the vote until the 1950s and would never achieve the personal status reforms they sought.

Education was a less inflammatory issue and so became the second major initiative taken in social policy, although not without intense bargaining. Universal education had, as we have seen, long been claimed by nationalists as both a political and social right of citizens in a democracy. Between 1944 and 1946, the Lebanese state opened nearly 150 new schools, raising enrollment from 30,000 to 41,000. In 1943–1945, Syria opened 30 new state schools, also adding about 10,000 students to state rolls.[55] The Syrian state went beyond expansion of the mandate system: the education advisor Sati al-Husri, who had designed the Iraqi school system, revamped the national school curriculum to standardize and Arabize it. In a nod to the demands of women and labor, al-Husri's guidelines also called for equal educational opportunity for boys and girls and for more technical schools, although these were long-term goals not fulfilled during the war. Education would become the strongest pillar of postwar social policy in Syria. The number of state schools and students enrolled in them would quadruple in the fifteen years following the war, twice the rate of expansion under the French between 1924 and 1938.

The Lebanese did not expand or reform state education to the same extent. They did little to alter the state system's French-style curriculum or the balance between public and private schools, limiting reform to a 1946 law stiffening the state's regulation of foreign and private schools. In 1945, only 21 percent of Lebanese students attended state schools, compared to 58 percent of Syrian students, and the gap would grow after the war. One reason for the differing policy was the legacy of a century of educational policy. Ottoman reforms had supplanted Islamic schools while permitting foreign and Christian schools to flourish. The French had, as we have seen, encouraged Christian institutions and relatively neglected state schools with their Muslim majorities. So while Syrian Islamists had long ago lost a firm foothold in education, weakening their quest to assert greater control over education, their Christian counterparts in Lebanon were in a much stronger position to protect their mediating role in educational affairs.

New financial commitments to citizens' welfare resembled patterns in legal commitments: they tended to amplify rather than modify colonial welfare policy. While their scope was initially restricted by the wartime economy, beginning in 1946 state spending in all areas boomed. The most significant factor was the availability of new sources of revenue: customs duties that had once flowed to the French, and income taxes, both of which would grow rapidly once wartime restrictions on trade were lifted. Syria had adopted an income tax in 1942; Lebanon adopted a war profits tax in 1942 and an income tax in 1944. The income taxes replaced Ottoman *temettu* taxes, which had been levied only on certain professions, with general levies. Direct tax revenues jumped by nearly 40 percent in Syria and 50 percent in Lebanon from 1945 to 1946, signaling the transition from wartime trade restrictions. These revenues would more than quadruple in Lebanon and more than double in Syria, in real terms, between 1944 and 1951.[56] A third potential source of revenue was loans: between 1947 and 1951 the Syrian state would run deficits, a fiscal tool shunned by the French, who in the prewar years remained committed to balanced budgets.

Both the Syrian and Lebanese governments heralded expanded budgets, particularly in public works and education. Figures 1 and 2 show that by 1945 state budgets had nearly recovered from devastating wartime cuts: spending rebounded to 1939 levels, totaling about 30 million £LS for both states and the Common Interests budget, when adjusted for inflation. The trough in wartime spending during World War II, shown in figure 1, reflected mainly the precipitous drop in customs revenues to the Common Interests budget controlled by the Délégation générale. From 1944, the steep rise in state budgets reflected the reprise of trade and the transfer of Common Interests revenues to the states. The Common Interests, once the

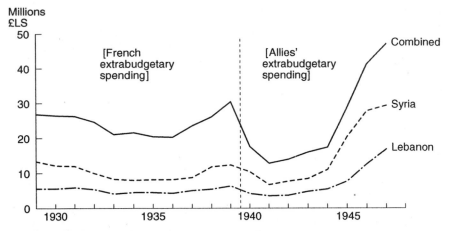

Figure 1. State expenditures, 1929–1947, adjusted for wartime and postwar infla-
tion to 1939 Syrian and Lebanese liras.
Combined: Budgets of Syrian and Lebanese states and the Common Interests.
Syria: Includes budgets of Lattakia and Druze territories; excludes Alexandretta.
French extrabudgetary spending: Averaged 14 million £LS per year for military and
social-cultural subsidies, to 1940.
Allies' extrabudgetary spending: Totaled 242 million £LS (adjusted) between 1940
and 1944.
SOURCES FOR ALL GRAPHS: Ministère des affaires étrangères (France), *Rapport à la Société des Nations sur la situation de la Syrie et du Liban (Années 1930–1939)*; Conseil
supérieur des intérêts communs, *Receuil de statistiques de la Syrie et du Liban, 1944,*
pp. 176–83, and *Receuil de statistiques de la Syrie et du Liban, 1945–47,* pp. 170–75;
Office Arabe de presse et documentation (Syria), *Receuil des statistiques syriennes
comparées (1928–1968)*, pp. 114–23; United Nations, *Statistical Yearbook, 1948,* p.
374; Lloyd, *Food and Inflation in the Middle East, 1940–45,* pp. 189, 363; Himadeh,
The Fiscal System of Lebanon, pp. 12–13, 97; and Hudson, *The Precarious Republic,* p.
309.

mainstay of the common administration binding the two countries, would
be formally abolished in 1950, when Syria and Lebanon dissolved their
customs union.

The years 1944–1945 were also a honeymoon period, allowing for
higher rates of social investment. Inflation increases leveled off after rising
steeply each year since 1939, and the cost of living would actually begin to
fall in 1946. Nominal increases in budget allocations, therefore, from this
point onward did more than merely compensate for inflation (see fig. 2).
Second, the states did not yet face prohibitive military costs, which they
would after the French withdrawal in 1946. As a result, spending on health
and education reached unprecedented highs before the war's end. In

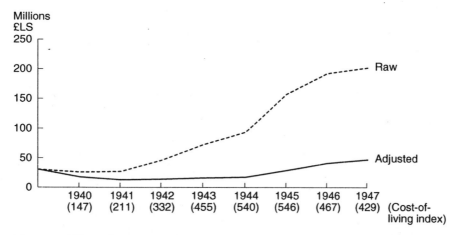

Figure 2. Effect of wartime and postwar inflation on state spending: comparison of raw and adjusted levels, 1939–1947.
Each line represents the combined total spending per year by the Syrian and Lebanese states and Common Interests.
Raw: Reflects actual amounts reported in annual budgets.
Adjusted: Reflects the real value of the raw total, adjusted to 1939 £LS according to annual cost-of-living indexes. The indexes were calculated by the Common Interests to reflect increased prices of housing, food, and other necessities in Beirut.

1945, Syria's spending on health and education totaled 2.8 million £LS (adjusted for inflation to 1939 levels), higher than the previous peak of 2.3 million in 1939. Likewise, Lebanon's budgets for health and education, totaling 934,000 £LS (adjusted to 1939 prices), surpassed its 1939 peak of 781,000 (figure 3). Public works spending showed the same patterns.

Postwar spending skyrocketed: By 1951, global spending by both Syria and Lebanon dwarfed the highest levels of spending attained in the mandate period, at about 106 million £LS, adjusted for inflation.[57] By 1951, health and education spending had increased, in real terms, eight times over 1943 levels in Syria; six times in Lebanon. The major portion of new government spending, however, covered new military and administrative costs. By 1950–51, 44.4 percent of Syria's budget was allocated to the Ministry of Defense, up from .10 percent in 1944 and 16.5 percent in 1945.[58] Lebanon's defense spending rose from virtually nothing to 20 percent of the ordinary budget in the same period.[59] As figure 1 suggests, the postwar spending boom substantively incorporated into state budgets for the first time the extrabudgetary military spending of the French through 1940, and of the Allies during World War II.

Did postwar economic expansion fuel the long-sought expansion of the

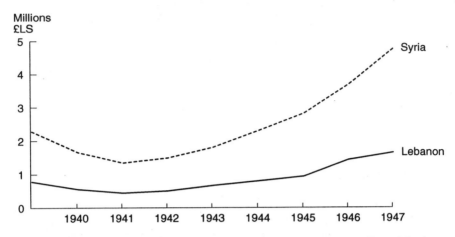

Figure 3. Health and education spending by states, 1939–1947, adjusted for in-flation to 1939 price levels.
Each line represents the combined total budgets for the ministries of public health and education in each country, adjusted for inflation (see fig. 2).

colonial welfare state? Increases in postwar social spending were real, but they remained within ranges familiar in the colonial welfare state. Between 1944 and 1951, Lebanon's education budget grew from 2.6 million £LS to 9.8 million £LS (when adjusted for inflation, from 484,000 to 2.5 million in 1939 £LS); but as a percentage of overall spending in the ordinary budget, it grew only from 8.9 to 10.8 percent. Syria's education budget in the same period grew from 9.8 to 46.8 million £LS (1.8 million to 12.2 million in 1939 £LS), an increase from 16.4 to 17.6 percent of state spending. Figure 4 shows that the percentage of combined state spending on education and public health in the two states peaked in 1943 and 1944 and then leveled off in the 1950s, at just under 20 percent in Syria and 13–15 percent in Lebanon in 1951. These levels were slightly above those of the 1930s, but not dramatically so. Similarly, public works spending in Syria ballooned from 9.6 percent of the state budget to 25 percent between 1943 and 1947, but then fell back to 7.3 percent in 1950–51, slightly lower than the prewar average.[60]

More important, while there was a quantitative expansion in social spending, there was no qualitative expansion. Public health and education remained the sole major areas of social spending into the 1950s. In Syria the supply budget, which encompassed subsidies for food rations, dwindled after the war. The Social Affairs budget disappeared in 1944. A new budget line for the Ministry of Labor was established in 1948, following the adoption of the labor code, to finance mediation and subsidize union services.

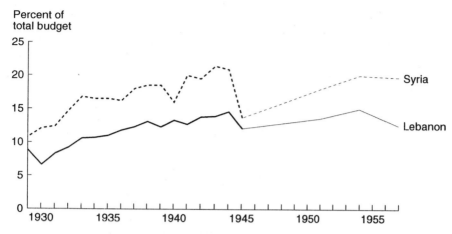

Figure 4. Health and education as a percentage of overall state spending,
1929–1957: postwar trends compared to the period of French rule.
Each line represents the combined budgets for the ministries of public health and
education, as a percentage of the total budget, for each year in each country.

But the ministry's expenditures remained quite low: 279,000 £S in 1949,
rising to 836,000 £S in 1957, less than 1 percent of the state's budget. In
Lebanon, cost-of-living subsidies disappeared. And while a Ministry of Social Affairs was established in 1952, its budget barely reached 3 million £L,
just over 1 percent of total spending, in the 1950s. A Ministry of Finance official noted in 1961 that Lebanon's only real social services remained health
and education: "Not only is the relative expenditure on social services low
in Lebanon but also the standard of service is very poor." He lamented that
Lebanon had not followed the example of Sweden, where in 1957 spending on social services had represented 41 percent of state expenditures,
compared to Lebanon's 17 percent and Syria's 21 percent. The difference
was due not to levels of spending on health and education but to the lack of
social security and cost-of-living allowances. The official blamed the tax system set up at the end of the war for taxing the wealthy only lightly, thus providing only 11 percent of state revenues by 1957.[61]

In sum, aside from Syria's massive investment in education, there was no
permanent reapportionment of state funding to welfare, either in the later
years of the war or afterward. As before, legal and financial benefits to
workers remained limited, women remained excluded, and elites continued to enjoy a disproportionate share of state largesse. Substantial public
works investments and allocations to ministries of economy and agriculture
may have promised long-term benefits to all, but they profited bourgeois
merchants and industrialists first. Income taxes were levied mostly on

poorer wage earners. Unions and the two Communist parties vigorously opposed the new income taxes as regressive violations of the rights of lower classes.[62] And financial commitments that might have reinforced new legal rights of workers were neglected. The labor codes provided for old age, sickness, and accident pensions, but neither state allocated funds for them. Moreover, the codes excluded other social security benefits demanded by workers, such as low-cost health care. Feminists' calls for a comprehensive welfare system for poor women and children went unheeded along with their other demands.

The Syrian state did formalize support for women and workers by establishing official umbrella organizations. The Syrian General Union of Workers' Syndicates was created in 1948 to oversee implementation of the labor code. The Syrian Women's Union combined the dozens of women's organizations active in the country, and by 1946 published an official women's magazine. The official unions were modestly funded, and appear to have served more as regulatory and policing bodies than as vehicles of social support. They each usurped the powers of the grassroots-organized national labor federation and Syrian women's union. Their intent appears to have been corporatist, binding these groups to state patrons and so blunting their opposition.[63]

The Lebanese state also repressed the labor movement, but its methods were less etatist. While the Service des affaires sociales, established by the French in 1943 to mediate labor disputes, languished, the 1946 labor code was viewed by critics as primarily a policing instrument. Membership and activities of labor unions were highly controlled. Passage of the code coincided with a government anti-Communist campaign, and in 1948 the Communist Party would be outlawed. Although it would continue to operate illegally, the Lebanese party would not play the political role that it had in the 1943 elections or that the Syrian party would in the postwar period. No official women's union was established in Lebanon, but the preindependence women's union remained firmly in the grasp of women from prominent nationalist families and devoted largely to charity works.

From 1944 onward, Syrians and Lebanese both struggled over the extent of state intervention in social and economic affairs. Differences of opinion and interest were deeply rooted in the hybrid legacy of the colonial welfare state, which, as we have seen, combined direct state intervention with mediated and privatized agencies. While the war had vastly increased state controls to the benefit of many, powerful private interests also resisted a permanent extension of the public sector and state welfare. While it is beyond the scope of this essay to examine fully the postwar conflicts over the issue, a general observation on the linkage of variant outcomes in Syria and Lebanon may be advanced.[64] It comes as no surprise that Lebanon would follow a nonstatist, liberal approach to social policy, given the much higher degree of privatization in education and health care in the period of French rule. Syria, on the other hand, had not had nearly the same density of missionary activity and had built much stronger state education and health systems before the war. As a consequence, antistatist interests were much weaker in colonial Syria. Moreover, Syrian nationalists, to a greater degree than their Lebanese counterparts, had centered their ideology on the need to capture the state in order to advance social progress. This ideology reflected the Syrian bourgeoisie's bases of wealth in agriculture and industry, which required state subsidies. The strongest wing of the Lebanese bourgeoisie was commercial, and it saw greater profit in laissez-faire policies.

While Syria pursued a stronger commitment to state welfarism, both countries retained essential features of the mandate-era civic order and colonial welfare state until well after the war's end. The principal players remained, and bargaining over social policy continued to inform political conflicts. Mediated delivery of social services also continued, whether through corporatist state bodies or privatized organization, as did basic patterns of spending on health education and public workers that were biased toward elites and against women, workers, and peasants.

While World War II was heralded in Europe as the springboard of full-fledged welfarism, the war appears to have had a more somber effect in Syria and Lebanon.[65] Most evidently the reason lay in the precarious economic basis of the colonial welfare state, where social spending had been covered disproportionately through French subsidies rather than through taxes on the middle class and elites. Industrialized Europe, aided by the Marshall Plan, was simply in a stronger position to raise vast revenues and redistribute national income. Nationalists in government reasonably argued that Syria and Lebanon had first to broaden investment in production in order to generate levels of wealth that might fund expanded welfare. Groups mobilized after the war to demand welfare were also stronger. European veterans could demand a payback for the sacrifices their governments required of them in wartime. In Syria and Lebanon, males had not only not been recruited to military service, but the French rulers who had demanded wartime sacrifices of the civilian population had departed. Social demands had their biggest impact in Syria and Lebanon during the war, not afterward, as a disgruntled, unconscripted male population organized national, grassroots movements. Civilian social mobilization in protest of wartime policies must be distinguished from military mobilization in wartime when we examine the impact of wartime mobilization on state expansion.

We must also account for the effect of wartime decolonization, in contrast to European experience. The linkage between war and state expansion was decoupled in the colonial context. While the war effort bloated states in Europe and North America, state expansion in Syria and Lebanon was primarily within administrative, military, and economic organs controlled by the French and British, organs that they would take with them when they departed. The withdrawal of the MESC and Allied military forces left an institutional vacuum in 1945–46, one that was not fully reconstituted until the 1950s.[66] The departure of the French High Commissariat, which had been the primary agent of social policy under the French, left a more enduring vacuum with profound consequences for welfare.

The legacy of wartime expansion was thus selectively nurtured, and so cannot be explained solely via the particular structural constraints of less industrialized, colonized countries. Indeed, the choices made in expanding the postwar states owed much to the politics of social spending during the previous decade. As we have seen, varying strengths of statist and privatist interests determined that Lebanon would choose to fill the social policy vacuum only minimally, whereas Syria devoted much larger resources to rebuilding the welfare state. Also, the fact that the states did not allocate increased revenues to the poor cannot simply be explained away as the result of lack of means. While we have seen that the states' capacity to fund social investment rose sharply at the war's end, we must also take account of how funds were actually spent: investment in postwar development mirrored prewar and wartime policies that had funneled crucial subsidies and economic privileges to elites and left workers greatly impoverished by inflation. And we must also view spending patterns in the context of contemporaneous legal commitments to social rights, where state policies explicitly sought to limit their extension to workers, women, and peasants in a context of class polarization induced by the war and independence.

In sum, while the war undoubtedly fueled the general postwar expansion of the states, it also generated a transformation in the nature of the states. By 1939, social groups and state policy had converged around a politics of social rights poised to produce a colonial welfare state. In 1946, the now-independent states began to steer politics away from rights-based welfarism toward liberalism and corporatism. The war may be said to have triggered, in its first phase, the realization of a colonial welfare state, and in its late years, a crisis of that state, as newly empowered and polarized forces conflicted over social policy and the expansion of rights and state services. While the colonial welfare state's initial expansion mirrored trends in Europe, the subsequent leveling off of social spending (as a percentage of total spending) stood in contrast. This contradictory effect of the war on the welfare state resulted from the conditions specific to colonial rule and decolonization.

Contrary to top-down arguments about the effect of war on welfare states, grassroots social mobilization was, as we have seen, the primary motor of institutionalizing the colonial welfare state during World War II. Both nationalist elites and the French reacted to, and then sought to exploit, the mobilization of workers and women in strikes, demonstrations, and hunger marches. The preeminent goal of the MESC and rationing programs in Syria and Lebanon was to stanch incipient revolt. Catroux immediately founded the Section sociale to study and propose ways of alleviating social stress, with the goal of securing Free French rule and preserving empire. Nationalist politicians assumed leadership of protests well after they had begun, and forged alliances with women's and labor leaders in the independence struggle, with the goal of capturing control of the state.

Furthermore, the shape of the colonial welfare state was determined more by the relative strengths of the various grassroots interests than by the design of state social engineers. Hence, highly mobilized, urban, industrial workers obtained minimum wage guarantees, family allowances, and cost-of-living increases, while nonunionized peasants, domestic servants, and women homeworkers did not. The smaller and mainly bourgeois women's unions were unable to bring the same pressure on governments to grant women the vote. And finally, powerful mediating bodies like religious groups, landowners, and industrialists were able to maintain subsidies and privileges granted by the colonial welfare state and to block direct access to rights and state benefits by their subalterns.

Future scholarship may profitably explore further the place of Syria and Lebanon, and possibly other colonies, within the broad spectrum of welfare regime types developed in recent scholarship. This revisionist literature has undermined unilinear models of the welfare state as the unique product of industrialization and as a wholesale shift from liberal, laissez-faire public policy that assigned individuals responsibility for risk to state assumption of collective social insurance involving the expansion of the state apparatus and disbursement of vast sums of entitlement spending.[67] A historical variety of processes is now understood to have produced diverse outcomes in differing countries: "There never was one view of how social justice was to be achieved any more than there was one route by which to achieve effective democratic governance."[68] In France and Germany, for example, top-down reforms and statist policies prevailed, while in Britain and the United States grassroots mobilization and nonstate initiatives informed early welfare developments. Among the latter, not only did industrialized workers and veterans mobilize for welfare protections, but women played important roles both in applying pressure on states and in designing programs.[69] Some states relied heavily on private agencies and market regulations and incentives to address the needs of the poor, while others built overarching public administrations to deliver services directly.[70] Working definitions of the welfare state have as a result been scaled back and become more flexible. As two early revisionists defined it, the welfare state is simply "the predictable delivery of publicly funded benefits to people without imposing systemic degradations and restrictions upon them."[71] Broadly speaking, welfarism is a system that supersedes the boundary of the state, that may include both public and private agencies, and that takes shape through negotiations between rulers and ruled over social rights.[72]

While virtually all of this recent scholarship has concerned industrialized countries, we have seen that colonies like Syria and Lebanon shared some of these characteristics in process and outcome. Syrians and Lebanese mobilized first in the 1930s, an etatist era in which the belief in the state's unique responsibility and capability to advance social progress was nearly universal. Their programs imitated liberal models emphasizing social rights and democratic equalities. The mix of private and public agencies delivering social services that resulted from the bargaining process was not in itself atypical within the spectrum of emergent welfare regimes, although the origin of that mix in colonial practices of rule was distinctive.

Finally, among the more compelling aspects of the evolution of welfare state, apparent in the Syrian and Lebanese cases, is their malleability. We have seen how World War II stretched and reshaped the Syrian and Lebanese states, altering the direction of social policy and institutions. The American case demonstrated a similar ability to shift direction. As Theda Skocpol has argued, two distinct welfare regimes followed one upon the other, roughly divided by World War I. A maternalist welfare state emerged out of the system of veterans' pensions established after the Civil War, only to give way to a new configuration focused on the welfare of male industrial workers in the 1930s.[73] Similar to the American case, the phases of Syrian and Lebanese welfare policy were conditioned by the politics inherent in a variable civic order, one first transformed with the end of armed rebellion in the late 1920s, and then again during World War II, with the accelerated polarization of classes and the accession of the elite nationalist opposition to power. Wars do not simply, or always, accelerate previous trends in (welfare) state formation, but may instead alter their trajectory.

NOTES

1. Qurtas, *Dhikrayat, 1917–1977*, p. 139.

2. Catroux, *Dans la bataille de Méditerranée*, pp. 137–38, 200–201.

3. See, for example, Longrigg, *Syria and Lebanon under French Mandate*, pp. 293, 339–40; Khoury, *Syria and the French Mandate: The Politics of Arab Nationalism, 1920–1945*, pp. 583, 604–12, 626–30; Khoury, "Syrian Political Culture: A Historical Perspective," pp. 13–27; Yahya M. Sadowski, "Political Power and Economic Organization in Syria: The Course of State Intervention, 1946–1958" (Ph.D. diss., UCLA, 1984), pp. 115–202; Tibawi, *A Modern History of Syria, including Lebanon and Palestine*, pp. 364–78; Hassan, *Jil al-shaja'a hatta 'amm 1945*, pp. 174–97; Salibi, *The Modern History of Lebanon*, pp. 186–95; al-Hakim, *Suriya wa al-intidab al-Faransi*, pp. 314–50; Boustany, *Introduction à l'histoire politique du Liban moderne*, pp. 159–78;

Gates, "The Formation of the Political Economy of Modern Lebanon: The State and the Economy from Colonialism to Independence, 1939–1952," pp. 97–109, 189–95, 324–36.

4. Although Syria and Lebanon were technically mandates, a term coined by the League of Nations to distinguish their supposedly temporary and limited nature from that of colonies, the French tended to ignore the distinction. I use the term *colonial* here to emphasize the fact that the essential attributes of the mandatory states were shared with colonies.

5. This article is drawn from research presented more fully in my book, *Colonial Citizens: Republican Rights, Paternal Privilege, and Gender in French Syria and Lebanon*.

6. See, for example, Porter, *War and the Rise of the State*, pp. 149–93.

7. I have borrowed the concept of civic order from Isser Woloch, who used it in his analysis of the reorganization of the French state's institutional links with society in the Napoleonic era. As Woloch defines civic order: "It is meant to encompass the values, policies and institutions at the juncture of state and civil society—the framework, in other words, for the collective public life of the French people. . . . I visualized the civic order in an almost physical sense, as embodied by buildings in the urban landscape, whose influence extended, unevenly and ever more faintly, into the countryside . . . the departmental administration; the town hall or *mairie;* the local schools; several new courts or tribunals; the institutions of poor relief." See Woloch, *The New Regime: Transformations of the French Civic Order, 1789–1820s*, pp. 14–15.

8. Ministère des affaires étrangères (France), *Rapport à la Société des Nations sur la situation de la Syrie et du Liban (Année 1928)*, pp. 148, 155. Hereafter abbreviated to: MAE, *Rapport . . . (date)*.

9. Longrigg, *Syria and Lebanon*, p. 266.

10. Catroux, *Dans la bataille*, p. 202.

11. Joseph Aractingi, "Al-Mudiriya al-'amma lil-sihha wal is'af al-'amm fi Suriya" *Dimashq* (1 September 1940): p. 3.

12. MAE, *Rapport . . . (Année 1924)*, p. 95, and *Rapport . . . (Année 1938)*, p. 215.

13. MAE, *Rapport . . . (Année 1933)*, p. 79. The argument is repeated in other 1930s reports. The French, for their own purposes here, hid behind the requirement by the League of Nations that mandatory powers respect local laws.

14. MAE, *Rapport . . . (Année 1938)*, pp. 139–41.

15. MAE, *Rapport . . . (Année 1930)*, p. 158, and *Rapport . . . (Année 1938)*, p. 180.

16. In 1935, for example, approximately 2.5 million francs in Service des oeuvres subsidies and 850,000 francs in public education department subsidies went to private schools, compared to an overall budget of 26 million francs for public education. The French and private schools also received undocumented amounts of additional French aid through other government channels and from private sources in the metropole.

17. Abdullah Hanna, *Al-Haraka al-'ummaliya fi Suriya wa Lubnan 1900–1945*, pp. 422–23. On women's organizations' use of French and American models, see articles on conferences with French feminists in the Damascus newspaper *Les Echos*, 9 and 12 February 1935, and the regular references to American women's movements in the Beirut women's journal *Al-Mar'a al-jadida* (The New Woman), published in Beirut by Julia Dimashqiyya in the 1920s.

18. A 1934 Lebanese law (DL 294) and a 1935 Syrian law (DL 152) revising the

1912 Ottoman corporation law required unions to include both employers and workers in each industry, subjected them to tight state supervision, and banned federations among workers of different industries. In 1937 Syrian unions threatened a general strike when the government imprisoned labor leaders for defying the law. Both state governments eventually backed down and from then on tolerated the new workers-only union movement. See Sanadiki, "Le Mouvement syndical en Syrie," pp. 55–70; Couland, *Mouvement syndical au Liban 1919–1946*, pp. 221–33.

19. Hanna, *Al-Haraka al-'ummaliya*, pp. 442–70; and Couland, *Mouvement syndical*, pp. 237–50.

20. Puaux, *Deux années au Levant*, p. 118.

21. Ibid., 159–60.

22. Catroux, *Dans la bataille*, pp. 137–38.

23. Ibid., pp. 217–18; and de Gaulle, *The Complete Memoirs of Charles de Gaulle*, pp. 201–5.

24. Ministère des affaires étrangères, Archives diplomatiques, Nantes. Série Beyrouth—Sûreté générale, carton 20, "La crise du blé a pris des proportions considérables," 9 September 1941. (Hereafter abbreviated to MAE-Nantes, carton x.)

25. Conseil supérieur des intérêts communs, *Receuil de statistiques de la Syrie et du Liban, 1944*, p. 158.

26. Lloyd, *Food and Inflation in the Middle East, 1940–45*, p. 328. Data for Syria and Lebanon are not available, although a crude calculation of births against deaths of infants under one year of age in 1944, the only year numbers are available, suggests that infant mortality was still high despite regional improvements after 1942. The crude 1944 Syrian infant mortality rate, of 77 per thousand, was nearly as high as that of the Netherlands during its 1945 famine.

27. While Syria and Lebanon joined the Middle East Supply Centre in 1941, benefits from the new center were slow to accrue. Not until late 1942 was the MESC able to mount full-scale operations to assure food supplies and shipping. And while the MESC had managed in the winter of 1941–42 to import more than one hundred thousand tons of Australian wheat to the Levant, public confidence in the MESC scheme remained low, shaken by the Pearl Harbor attack and German advances on the MESC's headquarters at Cairo between May and October 1942. Confidence grew only after the American landing in North Africa in November 1942 and the German defeat at Stalingrad in January 1943. See Lloyd, *Food and Inflation*, pp. 87–89; and Wilmington, *The Middle East Supply Centre*, p. 47.

28. MAE-Nantes, cartons 20 and 70.

29. MAE-Nantes, cartons 76, 1074, and 1107.

30. Reports and drafts of laws for nearly all of the initiatives taken, dating months before the laws were passed, suggest the Section sociale's central and proactive role in granting workers' rights in this period. MAE-Nantes, cartons 2921 and 2922. See also Godard, *L'Oeuvre politique, économique, et sociale de la France Combattante en Syrie et au Liban*, pp. 183–84.

31. Arrêté 229/FL, 21 avril 1942, portant création d'un Office du blé pour la Syrie et le Liban, printed in *Bulletin officiel des actes administratifs de la délégation* 8 (30 April 1942), p. 229. The Office des céréales panifiables (OCP) apparently superseded Catroux's Wheat Office, although officials customarily continued to refer to the OCP as the Wheat Office. See Godard, *L'Oeuvre politique*, pp. 125–26, 130; Go-

dard, "Etude statistique de la situation économique en Syrie et au Liban," p. 393; and E. L. Spears, "Memorandum on the First Year of the Wheat Office (O.C.P.), Syria and the Lebanon, June 20, 1943," private papers, Middle East Library, St. Antony's College, Oxford. I am grateful to Steven Heydemann for providing me a copy of the latter document.

32. The story is told from differing points of view in Spears, *Fulfilment of a Mission: Syria and Lebanon, 1941–1944*, pp. 173–202; Catroux, *Dans la bataille*, pp. 268–82; and Lloyd, *Food and Inflation*, pp. 115–16, 144–56.

33. Godard, *L'Oeuvre politique*, p. 133; and Catroux, *Dans la bataille*, p. 256–57.

34. Syrian government notice, printed in *Le jour*, 11 February 1943, and reprinted in Godard, *L'Oeuvre politique*, p. 134.

35. Al-Hakim, *Suriya fi al-intidab al-Faransi*, pp. 324–28; and Khoury, *Syria and the French Mandate*, pp. 596–99; MAE-Nantes, carton 70, Sûreté générale reports dated 20 and 23 March 1943.

36. MAE-Nantes, carton 2922, Délégation générale decree of 30 October 1941, 18 November 1941 (arrêté 405/FL), and Lebanese government decrees of 15 December 1941 (DL 125/NI) and 27 August 1942 (DL 204/NI); Couland, *Mouvement syndical*, pp. 288–89; and Godard, *L'Oeuvre politique*, pp. 184–85.

37. Decree DL 231/NI of 19 October 1942, *Journal officiel de la République libanaise* (1942); Couland, *Mouvement syndical*, p. 290.

38. DL 29/ET of 12 May 1943. Typescript copy in MAE-Nantes, carton 2922.

39. Article 4 of DL 29/ET guaranteed women pay and benefits equal to those of men. The law also limited family allowances to the first wife, in cases of polygamy.

40. *Le Jour*, 22 May 1943. In 1942, the Free French had set up women's committees in London to prepare social legislation to improve the status of women, children, and families as part of their effort to help France "catch up" to other welfare states. De Gaulle's decree granting French women the vote in 1944 was taken in the same spirit.

41. DL 25/ET of 4 May 1943, *Journal officiel* (1943): 6805–10.

42. DL 2031/NI of 26 January 1943, summarized in Couland, *Mouvement syndical*, p. 290.

43. Couland, *Mouvement syndical*, p. 292–95.

44. Hanna, *Al-Haraka al-'ummaliya*, pp. 479–82.

45. Khoury, *Syria and the French Mandate*, p. 600.

46. De Gaulle, *Complete War Memoirs*, p. 202.

47. Khalaf, *Lebanon's Predicament*, pp. 121–45; Hudson, *The Precarious Republic*, pp. 211–61.

48. MAE-Nantes, carton 20, "Communistes informations, 1941–43"; al-Malla, *Safhat min tarikh al-hizb al-shiyu'i al-suri (1924–1954)*, pp. 137–43; Couland, *Mouvement syndical*, pp. 272–73; Khoury, *Syria and the French Mandate*, p. 601.

49. Couland, *Mouvement syndical*, pp. 294–95.

50. Ibid., p. 276; Laqueur, *Communism and Nationalism in the Middle East*, pp. 149, 151; al-Malla, *Safhat min tarikh*, pp. 155–59.

51. Syrian DL 279 of 11 June 1946, published in *Al-Jarida al-rasmiya*, no. 25 (13 June 1946) and Lebanese law of 23 September 1946, published in *Al-Jarida al-rasmiya al-lubnaniya*, no. 40 (2 October 1946); Hanna, *Al-Haraka al-'ummaliya*, pp. 486–506; and Couland, *Mouvement syndical*, pp. 333–78.

52. Imilie Faris Ibrahim, "Sawt al-mar'a: haquq jadida" (Women's voice: New rights), *Al-Tariq* 2, no. 20 (29 December 1943): pp. 15–17.

53. Badran, *Feminists, Islam, and Nation: Gender and the Making of Modern Egypt,* pp. 238–46.

54. See, for example, *L'Orient* (Beirut), 13 February 1945. On the importance of political-coalition building to feminist goals and achievements, see Cohen and Hanagan, "The Politics of Gender and the Making of the Welfare State, 1900–1940: A Comparative Perspective," pp. 469–84.

55. Matthews and Akrawi, *Education in Arab Countries of the Near East,* pp. 351, 422.

56. Direct tax revenues in Lebanon increased from 5.5 million £LS in 1944 to 17 million in 1951 (from about 1 million to 4.4 million in 1939 £LS); those in Syria increased more modestly from 16 to 27 million £LS (about 3 million to 7 million in 1939 £LS).

57. The actual total, before adjustment to 1939 levels, was 370 million £LS: 104 million £LS in Lebanon (counting both the ordinary budget and the Development Works budget) and 266 million £LS in Syria. For data on these and all other figures presented here, see Himadeh, *The Fiscal System of Lebanon,* pp. 12–13 and 97 passim; Office Arabe de presse et documentation (Syria), *Receuil de statistiques syriennes comparées (1928–1968),* pp. 115–18; Conseil supérieur des intérêts communs, *Receuil de statistiques de la Syrie et du Liban, 1944,* 2:176–83, *Receuil de statistiques de la Syrie et du Liban, 1945–1947,* 3:170–75; and MAE, *Rapport . . . (Années 1930–38).* Inflation is calculated according to the cost-of-living index in Lloyd, *Food and Inflation,* p. 363.

58. Office Arabe de presse et documentation (Syria), *Receuil des statistiques syriennes,* pp. 116–18. Syria's defense spending jumped tenfold in one year as the French transferred control of the military, from a mere 16,679 £LS in 1944 to 16.5 million £LS in 1945. It then doubled in 1947 to 32 million £LS and reached 102.5 million £S in 1950–51, when Syrian state expenditures totaled 230.7 million £S. (Figures are not corrected for inflation.)

59. Himadeh, *Fiscal System of Lebanon,* pp. 12–13.

60. Office Arabe de presse et documentation (Syria), *Receuil des statistiques syriennes,* pp. 117–18. Prewar averages of public works spending were calculated on the basis of figures reported in annual reports to the League of Nations for public works spending by the state of Syria, 1930–38. The average was 944,000 £LS per year, or 11 percent of the state's budget. These figures exclude additional funds spent on public works by the Common Interests administration.

61. Himadeh, *Fiscal Policy of Lebanon,* pp. 35, 89–91, 106–7.

62. MAE-Nantes, carton 76, "Ouvriers"; George Hakim, "The New Income Tax: Unfair to Right of Workers and Employees" (in Arabic), *Al-Tariq* (5 February 1945): 9–11; Himadeh, *Fiscal Policy of Lebanon,* p. 107.

63. Sanadiki, "Le Mouvement syndical en Syrie," pp. 142–45, 183–85.

64. See Sadowski, "Political Power and Economic Organization in Syria"; and Gates, "The Formation of the Political Economy of Modern Lebanon."

65. Bruce Porter equivocates on this point by arguing both that the world wars accelerated preexisting trends toward welfare and that the intensive collectivism of total war was in fact the origin of welfare states. See his *War and the Rise of the State,* pp. 180–81 and 192–93. Eric Hobsbawm argues that World War II was particularly

defined by state ideologies promising a better society: "Social and economic reforms were introduced, not (as after the First World War) in response to mass pressure and fear of revolution, but by governments committed to them on principle. . . . the logic of the anti-fascist war led towards the Left." Hobsbawm, *The Age of Extremes*, p. 163. Charles Tilly draws less direct and longer term linkages between increasing requirements of warfare and European states' expanding commitments to the citizens who fulfilled them. In his view, welfare was the flip side of intensified policing and coercion. See his *Coercion, Capital, and European States, AD 990–1990*, pp. 67–126.

66. Lebanese and Syrian bureaucrats complained well into the 1960s that the French had so monopolized decision making in the various branches of state that their departure crippled the bureaucracy. Poorly trained lower-level cadres were encased in an overly centralized apparatus. See, for example, Iskandar, *Bureaucracy in Lebanon*, pp. 11–15.

67. Three useful overviews are Baldwin, "The Welfare State for Historians," pp. 695–707; Skocpol, *Protecting Soldiers and Mothers: The Political Origins of Social Policy in the United States*, pp. 12–30; and Gordon, "The New Feminist Scholarship on the Welfare State," pp. 9–35. A pivotal volume that both represented prevailing orthodoxy in the early 1980s and signaled a shift from monolithic models is Flora and Heidenheimer, *The Development of Welfare States in Europe and America*.

68. Ashford, *The Emergence of the Welfare States*, p. 2.

69. Koven and Michel, "Womanly Duties: Maternalist Policies and the Origins of Welfare States in France, Germany, Great Britain, and the United States, 1880–1920," pp. 1076–1108; and Skocpol, *Protecting Soldiers and Mothers*, chaps. 6–9.

70. Castles, "Social Protection by Other Means: Australia's Strategy of Coping with External Vulnerability," pp. 16–55.

71. Skocpol and Ikenberry, "The Political Formation of the American Welfare State in Historical and Comparative Perspective," pp. 87–148.

72. See works cited above by Linda Gordon and Charles Tilly.

73. Skocpol, *Protecting Soldiers and Mothers*, pp. 525–31.

4

War, Keynesianism, and Colonialism
Explaining State-Market Relations
in the Postwar Middle East

Robert Vitalis and Steven Heydemann

For much of this century, but especially in the past two decades, sociologists, economists, historians, and political scientists have found productive and stimulating common ground in exploring the effects of war on processes of state formation and economy building in Europe. Their efforts have helped clarify the connections between war making and the processes through which large-scale political and economic institutions are constructed. Yet these findings have been largely ignored by scholars interested in explaining similar processes in the postcolonial states of the developing world.[1] The reasons for this lack of interest are not hard to discern. As Charles Tilly rightly stresses, there is little reason to think that the processes underlying the emergence of modern states in Europe will "provide an adequate explanation of the formation, survival, or growth" of late-developing states in the Third World.[2] The emergence of such states into a fully consolidated state system and a highly structured global economy presents daunting challenges to those who would draw on early modern Europe to explain postcolonial processes of state making or the construction of economic institutions.

Among the most powerful distinctions between early and late processes of state and market formation is the extent to which state forms and regulatory practices in much of the Third World have been shaped by the experience of colonialism. Indeed, for the first half of the twentieth century Middle Eastern peoples experienced full-scale war not as a national-state-defining enterprise of the sort Tilly so famously describes but as a manifestation of imperialism directed by outsiders. For local power holders in the Middle East, the experiences of World Wars I and II were heavily mediated by the dynamics of colonial domination and nationalist resistance. And theorists of late development have concluded that this reality weakens or even severs the causal link between war making and state formation in a decisive way. Because war making was not undertaken by local actors, shifts in state capacity, the emergence of new state institutional configurations, and the reorganization of state-society relations are seen as later processes—consequences of the transition from colonialism to "postcolonialism" rather than the experience of the World Wars.

As a result, the macrohistorical effects of war on processes of state and economy building in Europe seem to offer an unpromising starting point for theorizing about the relationship among war, states, and markets in the developing world.[3] The profound gaps separating western Europe from the peripheral states of the mid-twentieth century would appear to require such conceptual stretching that the results would hardly justify the effort.[4] Tilly's caution against adopting a grand teleology of state building has been widely noted in subsequent research, as have Gershenkron's efforts to delineate the distinctive trajectories of late developers. Reactions against the "conceptual hegemony" of Europe have led scholars of the developing world to focus, appropriately, on disentangling local processes from their embeddedness in Europe, whether as prototype or as archetype.

Yet in the absence of theoretical frameworks that illuminate the effects of World Wars I and II on processes of state and economy building in the developing world, our understanding of these processes cannot be considered complete. Theories of state and market formation in the developing world that overlook the effects of these conflicts, especially World War II, seriously underestimate the weight of external variables in explaining the global shift among late developers from market-based to statist developmental strategies in the postwar period. Such theories neglect the causal weight of wartime interventions in constructing the frameworks for postwar import substitution industrialization (ISI), even while ISI is often viewed as a consequence of postcolonial economic nationalism and, later, decolonization in Africa and Asia. They overlook the importance of wartime regulatory norms in facilitating the shift from non- or even antidemocratic forms of market liberalism to statist, often authoritarian forms of populism in much of the Third World.[5]

This chapter examines the experience of World War II and its effects on state-market relations in one part of the developing world, the Middle East, with a focus on Egypt and Syria. Careful attention to the wartime political economy and the new forms of foreign intervention that were its hallmark move us toward an "adequate explanation" of how institutional arrangements for governing the economy first arose in places like Egypt and Syria. In the process, we are able to think critically about various forms of postdependency theorizing and interpretation in historical-comparative political economy. Our work challenges in particular a pronounced domestic bias in existing accounts of state institutional formation in the Middle East, evident in the tendency now to downplay the causal effects of external factors in the making of markets and states on the periphery and to assume that institutions emerge in relative isolation from the international system. But we also take issue with a second and more interesting sociological approach to the question of how to explain the global diffusion of particular models of state formation and repertoires of state intervention. By and large, scholars such as Meyer and McNeely, who emphasize the convergence of political units within the postwar international system around a limited number of state forms, have neglected two critical concerns. They have not provided adequate explanations of mechanisms and agency through which models of state management are installed, adapted, and consolidated.[6] And in emphasizing states as isomorphic at a high level of organizational abstraction, they overlook the profound variation that exists within particular state forms—such as import-substituting models of development—and thus cannot account for the diversity of outcomes that even similar models generate. Our chapter addresses both of these issues.

EXPLAINING STATE-MARKET RELATIONS IN THE MIDDLE EAST

European responses to the economic and administrative demands of World War II had profound implications for domestic processes of state formation and for the organization of state-market relations in the Middle East. Specifically, during World War II distinctive norms concerning appropriate strategies of state intervention were exported throughout much of the Middle East as a result of regulatory regimes established by Allied agencies. These norms were grounded in the Keynesian views of economic intervention and management held by leading British and to a lesser extent American officials of wartime regulatory agencies in the Middle East.[7] They reflected, as well, the lessons learned by British officials through their roles in the design of economic regulatory agencies in England during World War I.[8] With vast authority to organize economic activity, Allied regulators forcefully imposed their administrative and managerial norms throughout the region. The institutional consequences that followed the diffusion of these norms reached across the Middle East but were especially important in Egypt and the Levant (Syria, Palestine, Iraq, and Transjordan).[9] They became elements in the regulatory repertoires of local governments and thus influenced in significant ways the postwar, postcolonial trajectories of state building, state intervention, and state-market relations that later came to define the political economies of these states.[10]

We focus on the prewar, wartime, and immediate postwar experiences of economic regulation and economic institution building in two cases: Egypt and Syria.[11] We first offer a general argument for wartime economic regulations as a critical juncture in the organization of state-market relations in the Middle East. We then review how Allied forces organized wartime regulatory regimes in the region. In the third section of the chapter we examine in detail the role of the single most important Allied regulatory institution, the Middle East Supply Centre (MESC), which we view as the central mechanism behind the diffusion of Keynesian notions of economic planning into the Middle East. We then turn to a more detailed account of the impact of MESC regulatory regimes in four key areas—agricultural production, trade regulation, taxation, and labor—emphasizing how certain kinds of MESC intervention became the object of bargaining between local and Allied officials, while others did not. Finally, we demonstrate the effects of wartime regulation on the emergence of postwar political economies in Egypt and Syria, tracking the legacies of wartime experiences in shaping postwar patterns of state-market relations in the two countries.

Why Syria and Egypt as cases? In part, this choice reflects the biases of our previous research.[12] Yet the choice is not entirely path-dependent. Egypt and Syria represent broadly different instances of wartime regulatory experience. Egypt was the focal point of Britain's Middle East interests during the war, the headquarters of Allied regulatory institutions, and a prominent site for both the emerging presence of the United States in the Middle East and the negotiation of Britain's gradual, reluctant postwar disengagement from the region. Syria, governed by France under a League of Nations mandate, was much less central to the Allies' strategic interests. British policy in Syria and Lebanon was driven principally by a concern to ensure that France honor its commitment to grant these states their independence, and to minimize economic disruptions that might encourage the spread of Axis influence among populations whose commitment to the Allies was, at best, contingent.[13] In Egypt, wartime regulatory regimes were administered directly by the Middle East Supply Centre; in Syria and Lebanon, however, MESC operated under the auspices of the Spears Mission, an organization established by Britain to oversee the whole of its wartime relationship with Lebanon and Syria—military and political, as well as economic. The Mission was headquartered in Beirut rather than Damascus, and the force of its presence in Syria was thus circumscribed both by the role of French mandatory authorities and by its distance from the center of Syrian political life.[14]

Despite these differences, however, the institutional and political-economic consequences of wartime economic regulations in these two cases were broadly similar. In both cases, Allied interventions exhibited a distinctive pattern in the extent to which they influenced domestic practices of economic management. These interventions largely succeeded in restructuring the organization of agricultural production and food supply; had more limited but still considerable success in shaping the management of foreign trade and promoting the development of import-substituting local industries; and attempted, with little success, to persuade the Syrian and

Egyptian governments to shift from indirect to direct forms of taxation as a response to the dramatic increases in money supply (and inflation) that followed the war-driven influx of Allied resources.

Labor management, on the other hand, permits a different take on the role of MESC, shedding light on the *indirect* consequences of wartime economic regulation, and in this instance the experiences of Syria and Egypt were quite varied. In Egypt, the war created significant new demand for labor and promoted new forms of labor mobilization. Yet the regulation of labor was not a high priority for MESC, whose officials were more concerned with limiting unemployment caused by wartime fluctuations in demand. With the end of the war, the threat of large-scale unemployment in Egypt helped drive the postwar expansion of large public works projects and the formation of a substantial public sector. In Syria, on the other hand, wartime demand for labor was more limited and new forms of labor mobilization (the press gang) ended shortly thereafter, with few clearly discernible effects on state policy toward Syrian workers.[15] In both Egypt and Syria, postwar governments would dramatically expand the scope of state intervention over the affairs of labor, imposing corporatist forms of interest representation on workers in both countries during the 1950s and 1960s. In this area, too, Middle East practices reflect the diffusion of global norms of interest organization, but outcomes cannot be explained by the styles of intervention introduced during World War II.

In both Egypt and Syria, therefore, World War II stands out as the crucial missing piece in the historical puzzle of the emerging statist alternative to the colonial-watchman economies that had been constructed over the previous half century. The uneven pattern of Allied intervention noted above represents a critical juncture in the postwar development of domestic political economies in both countries. Despite the broad differences in their starting points, the converging vectors of Syrian and Egyptian transitions from more liberal to more statist and populist developmental projects in the postwar period can be traced back to their wartime regulatory experiences.

The significance of the war—as a shock that punctured the more liberal regulatory equilibrium of the prewar era—was not that it helped usher the region from lower to higher levels of state intervention. After all, the rise of statism characterizes the reorganization of political economies throughout the developing world between 1945 and 1960, and it is entirely reasonable to suppose that, even without the war, statist development strategies would have taken hold in the Middle East. The more important question, for which the experience of the war holds the answer, is why this transition took the form it did in our two cases. Why was it, for example, that in Egypt and Syria the public sector dominated the rise of import substitution industrialization (ISI), while in Latin American cases the private sector took the lead in the consolidation of ISI?[16] Why did state elites in postwar Syria and Egypt perceive of state regulation and state management of the economy as appropriate solutions to some of the urgent problems associated with the construction of postcolonial economies but not others? Why did certain kinds of regulatory practices and institutional capacities become prominent in these states, such as a high propensity to regulate agricultural production and foreign trade, but a low propensity to impose direct taxes on citizens?

What shaped these patterns of intervention? The answer is quite straightforward: Allied preferences and the balance of Allied versus local command of critical resources. The two core interests of the Western powers were to ensure the supply of Western armies and to minimize the impact on import-dependent Middle Eastern populations of the disruptions in global trade that resulted from the requisitioning of global shipping capacity by the military. These two imperatives threw up nearly overwhelming administrative challenges but placed an urgent premium on resolving two problems: feeding local populations and making sure that local economies did not impose demands on global shipping capacity. Driven by these concerns, Allied administrators were prepared to permit the lowest levels of local discretion in the areas of food supply and trade management. And because the Allies controlled ships and thus held the fate of local populations in their hands, they had the power to impose their preferences in these areas.

At the same time, Allied regulators recognized the potential for social instability associated with war-driven shifts in local economies, notably the inflation caused by military spending in countries with limited access to goods. As a result, MESC officials concerned themselves with broader questions of macroeconomic management, but their efforts in this regard were less unilateral. Implementation of economic policies was contingent on local administrative capacities and local political circumstances. As a result, local governments exercised more discretion in the strategies they adopted to manage the money supply. Almost invariably, these took the form of indirect taxation rather than the politically more demanding forms of direct taxation urged by Allied officials.

In short, in these areas as in many others, wartime regulatory changes did not just promote the transition from market liberalism to statism. They shifted Middle East political economies onto a distinctive path, constructing a singular, if flexible, template for how statism would become organized. The Allied regulators, who directed the day-to-day work of wartime economic coordination, built new regulatory agencies, supervised the management of local economies, and negotiated economic policies with local officials, were acting as the microchannels through which a powerful set of Keynesian ideas about the efficacy of state economic management were filtered into the region. If state elites in Egypt and Syria were not themselves steeped in the techniques of demand management, they were nonetheless heavily influenced by the "Keynesian-esque" regulatory environment that Allied bureaucrats created, one in which state intervention easily acquired legitimacy as a solution to problems of economic development.[17]

Allied regulators not only made intervention more accessible as a strategy, they also offered up specific institutional mechanisms (such as price control boards, state purchasing agencies, agricultural production committees, and import oversight commissions) that Syrian and Egyptian officials could appropriate, make use of in devising economic policies, and then absorb into the bureaucratic apparatus of their postwar states.[18] In adopting Allied regulatory practices, local officials lowered the costs of constructing institutions for the management of postcolonial economies. But they also privileged the formation of state capacities in those areas most heavily subject to MESC regulatory intervention while neglecting others, notably the capacity to impose direct taxes on citizens. Just as important, local officials helped fix a pattern of state-market relations in which interventionist norms became deeply and pervasively embedded as the organizing principles of postcolonial economic policy in these two states.

As we suggest above, however, the processes through which interventionist norms were transmitted, received, adapted, and transformed belie any simplistic notion of passive local governments acquiescing to the dictates of colonial or postcolonial powers. Instead, Allied bureaucrats and local officials engaged in explicit processes of bargaining over the design of regulatory regimes. And despite the presumption of stringent Allied control, local officials often carried the day. The practices of economic management that resulted from this bargaining were just as firmly embedded in local political and economic dynamics—and in the politics of nationalism and anticolonialism—as they were in Allied strategic and administrative concerns. The result was a set of policies and institutional outcomes that bore the clear imprint of their origins in Allied regulatory agencies, and in the administrative norms that prevailed among British wartime economic planners, but that also reflected the contours of local political struggles and the organization of domestic social conflicts. During the war, but even more so in subsequent years, regulatory regimes were adapted, exploited, and transformed in the context of domestic struggles over the role of the state and the scope of legitimate state intervention in the economy.

In short, what World War II helps us explain is not the move from market-liberal to interventionist political economies *in general,* but the *specific institutional and regulatory form* this movement took.[19] The outcome of wartime regulatory innovation was to articulate a pattern of state-market relations that was far removed from the economic liberalism of the prewar era. Moreover, this pattern reflected norms of economic management that helped legitimate and make possible the populist, redistributive, and aggressively state-managed economies of Syria and Egypt in subsequent decades after the war.[20] There is little question that this pattern had certain features in common with the later developmental strategies of postcolonial states elsewhere. Yet the wide variation among late developers in terms of their postwar economic trajectories—including huge discrepancies in performance, inward versus outward orientation, and even in their responsiveness or resistance to the current wave of economic liberalization—suggests that differences within this broad pattern are critical to understanding how it is that what often appears to us as a coherent developmental model can produce such widely differing political and economic outcomes.

STATE AND MARKET BEFORE THE WAR

It is broadly true to say that before the Colonial Welfare and Development Act of 1940, Colonial Governments acknowledged little responsibility for economic affairs. Nor was there any great tradition of state interference in industry or commerce in the non-colonial countries, India, Egypt, Iraq, Syria, where much the same attitude persisted.

A. R. PREST

To understand and assess our claims about the effects of wartime regulatory regimes, it is important we resist the almost inevitable tendency to exaggerate the coherence of colonial governance or to impose contemporary intellectual images of "the state" on the past. For example, analysts generally credit the British occupation with a successful administrative revolution inside Egypt's ministries. Elizabeth Thompson details in her chapter in this volume the extent to which popular mobilization prompted French colonial officials to expand state administration within Syria during the interwar period. Yet until the 1930s British colonial administrators in Egypt received no formal or specialized training, and the ideal of the generalist who improvised solutions to whatever problems arose in the field was well entrenched among those who ran the empire.[21] Nor were the policies of French administrators in Syria driven by a vision of how to transform the Syrian state into a mirror image of the French bureaucracy. Although the colonial presence altered the regulatory environment in both countries, Egypt and Syria nonetheless arrived at the moment of World War II with economies subject to low levels of state intervention and to forms of intervention that were largely market enhancing.

In Egypt, the British colonial project was essentially Africa's first experience with structural adjustment. The debts incurred by Muhammad 'Ali and his descendants had led by the 1870s to the takeover of the Egyptian treasury, the imposition of an austerity regime, rebellion by those made to pay, and ultimately British armed intervention and occupation. As today, structural adjustment went hand in hand with a quite literal "privatization" campaign that turned over ownership and control of vast royal lands and industries to private investors.[22]

In the realms of production and distribution, British imperialists oversaw the reconstruction and extension of the system of Nile control works under the authority of the public works ministry, one of the earliest organizations serving to create the (shaky) effect of a modern administrative state. But this effort was the limit of intervention for authorities who were charged with facilitating debt repatriation under prevailing Victorian norms. In the three decades preceding the occupation, Egypt's hastening pace of incorporation on the then "frontier" of the world economy followed a kind of "Klondike-on-the-Nile" model. Unlike what occurred in other parts of Africa, investors had found power and transport ventures attractive, and British officials continued to support a model of privately dominated and privately initiated economic development. There was little government oversight or regulation of these domains, as we have come to understand such notions. Alexandria was a virtual enclave, and the cotton trade that fueled the city's rapid (and of course unregulated) growth was run, like the city itself, by its leading families and firms. Building was also essentially unregulated, and the "old" city of Cairo was rapidly ringed by enclaves of its own: Zamalak, Bulaq al-Dakrur, Heliopolis, and Ma'adi. Public services were contracted out to concessionaires, at a price, generally paid by consumers. Oligopoly emerged as the market-controlling institution of choice by the narrow stratum that occupied the commanding heights. And twenty-five years after the British occupation in 1882, there was still no ministry charged with governing agriculture, the country's leading sector.

By World War I, both Egyptian nationalist factions and the leaders of the expatriate business community were demanding that government do more to support local enterprise. When Egyptian investors in particular in the 1920s successfully obtained subsidies and other guarantees for their investments, they were not cautiously laying the groundwork of etatism but instead desperately trying to catch up with the networks of British colonial officials, foreign financiers, and local interlocutors that had monopolized rent circuits over the previous three decades of industry- and economy-building. They shared with these competitors a broad understanding of the proper roles of government as an investment subsidizer and guarantor (distributor) of first resort but a regulator only of last resort. Any hint of a redistributive role, however, particularly one that challenged the existing balance of claims or rights with respect to property, was portrayed as foreign contamination of deep-rooted cultural norms.

These points are usefully summarized in John Waterbury's reminder: "We should not forget that it was a very limited state. No Keynes or FDR [or, we might add, Stalin or Attaturk] burst upon the Egyptian scene in the

1930s to deal with the economic crisis."[23] World War II in fact appears to have arrested a new, mid-to-late-1930s "liberalizing" wave in the tariff regime. And if there even existed a significant cadre of officials, Egyptian or non-Egyptian, in the decade or two before 1939 intent on transforming the regulatory powers of the state, the task would have been formidable. Land-lords and capitalists both had to be dragged from a Victorian past to an etatist future.[24]

If the war thus propelled Egypt into the new Keynesian world order, for-eigners engineered the shift. Egypt served as the central command post for the entire Middle Eastern theater, and the harbor at Alexandria became the main base for the British Mediterranean fleet. Allied authorities, backed by swelling ranks of foreign soldiers and civilians and the creation of a virtual shadow government in Cairo, seized control of the economy's commanding heights for the duration of hostilities. Most local producers and consumers could exercise little direct influence over basic institutions of the wartime state's economic apparatus. Martin W. Wilmington, the semiofficial historian of the Middle East Supply Centre—effectively the country's, if not the region's, first "superministry" of the economy—argues that its top officials purposely tried to design strategies for maintaining the facade of government sovereignty given "nationalist sensibilities." They hoped to "preclude the impression that the British government was usurp-ing governmental powers in the capital of a foreign country where its troops were quartered as allies, not occupiers."[25]

Syria's trajectory marked a different path to a similar end. First, of course, when France was formalizing direct control over Damascus and en-virons in the 1920s, under the terms of the League of Nations mandate, the British were just beginning the transfer of power to an independent Egypt-ian government. More crucially for our argument, however, is that in the 1920s the French state was initiating a particular type of "development" *(la mise en valeur)* project throughout the empire in support of neomercantil-ism at home.[26] French mandatory officials pursued policies that were thus typically "late" colonial in character. France assumed control of Syria's monetary system; linked Syria's currency to the French franc; exported to the metropole responsibility for macroeconomic policy; held local govern-ments responsible for the costs of maintaining French forces in the coun-try; controlled all major sources of public revenue; and, despite League of Nations prohibitions to the contrary, systematically privileged French in-vestment and economic activity in the country.[27]

Institutionally, French authorities greatly enlarged the bureaucratic and regulatory machinery of the post-Ottoman Syrian state, notably in those ar-eas related to the collection of revenues and the maintenance of (French) security. Yet French-dominated institutions functioned, by and large, as a system of exclusion. They operated as a "dual structure" in which the

French High Commission and its staff in the field "exercised an almost unlimited influence over the local administration and political life."[28] The growth of French intervention in the Syrian economy and the establishment or expansion of foreign-owned monopolies in such areas as communications and rail transport thus reflected the intent of mandate officials to maximize their capacity for extraction rather than any kind of statist development project on the part of a Syrian national or business elite. Writing in the 1950s, Syrian economist Edmund Asfour stressed that "the French mandatory government did not try . . . to hurry the pace or affect the pattern of economic development in the long-run interest of the country. There was no place in the central state budget for significant expenditure on development projects. . . . Trade and banking policy was designed to encourage trade with France and further strictly the ends of the French commercial empire, often to the detriment of valid Syrian interests. Industries were not given assistance or protection and in fact grew very little, while agriculture, the mainstay of the economy, was generally neglected."[29]

France's policy of repeatedly reorganizing Syria's borders and creating autonomous substates based on ethnic or religious identity further fragmented administration and the formation of a national economy. In March 1942, therefore, when Major General Sir Edward Spears arrived in Beirut as England's Envoy Extraordinary and Minister Plenipotentiary for the Levant States the organization of Syria's political economy had been profoundly influenced by two decades of French rule and the impact of economic policies intended to subordinate Syria's economy to French economic priorities. Indeed, expressions of Syrian economic nationalism that various political factions deployed against the French clearly associated "statism" with the mandate—in the form of intrusive and unjust state regulation that harmed the economic interests of the elites who dominated the nationalist movements.[30] Like their Egyptian counterparts, however, Syrian business elites were disturbed less by the emerging liberal (as opposed to democratic) economic order than they were by their exclusion from it.[31] Resistance to French rule during the war often led Syrian political elites to embrace interventionist policies put forward by British officials from the Spears Mission, partly to ensure Syrian representation in questions of economic governance that French officials were less inclined to grant.[32] In this way, nationalist politics led quite directly to the integration of Allied regulatory norms into Syrian administrative practices.

In both Egypt and Syria, therefore, colonial management of local economies in the prewar period had produced limited and highly selective state regulatory capacity. In both cases, colonial officials operated with a liberal economic framework but used state intervention to secure their own economic advantage. Neither colonial nor local elites viewed the state as an instrument of development, seeing it rather as an instrument for generating and directing the flow of resources within economies in which the private sector remained the dominant actors. Both sought the consolidation of liberal rather than democratic or redistributive patterns of state-market relations. Under these conditions, capitalists and landed elites in Syria and Egypt struggled not to overturn the existing regulatory order, but to expand its boundaries in ways that would permit them to enjoy its full benefits. In both cases, it was World War II that decisively altered the scope and intensity of state regulation of the economy, replacing the liberal prewar organization of state-market relations with more interventionist regimes. Initially, this shift greatly expanded the economic opportunities available to local elites, who dominated the institutions that managed access to rents in the postwar period. Later, however, these institutions were used to undermine economic liberalism, and became the tools through which a new generation of populist political leaders would accomplish the marginalization of the nationalist elites of the prewar and wartime period.

DEBATING REGULATION:
THE GENESIS OF WARTIME INTERVENTION

For capitalists and landowners in Egypt and Syria, World War II marked a critical turning point. Wartime exigencies led to the creation of regulatory bureaucracies and normative frameworks that would become increasingly central to the dynamics of postcolonial state building. Interventionist practices defined a set of norms that legitimated state control of the private sector and linked the fortunes of capitalists and landlords, both political and economic, to the actions and policies of the state. In so doing, wartime regulatory regimes contributed in substantive ways to the creation of a distinctive sense of how states function and how they relate to business.[33] They boosted local industry and gave rise to market-protecting import substitution policies that altered the relationship of local economies to global markets. Not least important, they also helped to develop the institutional and bureaucratic capacities that made it possible for new cadres of state officials to carry out their designated functions. In various domains—the creation of official statistical bureaus, the training of bureaucrats, the introduction of domestic price controls, the creation of credit facilities, the deepening of import-substituting patterns of industrialization, and the establishment of government monopsonies over agricultural produce—the contours of postwar, postcolonial state forms and practices were shaped by the regulatory regimes introduced during World War II.

One recent explanation for the shift from market-oriented to statist political economies focuses on the difficulties associated with the formation of market-supporting institutions.[34] In this view, state elites adopt interventionist strategies of economic management only after they have been undermined in their efforts to build the institutional frameworks needed to support a national market. The rise of intervention is thus explained as a fallback strategy on the part of state elites frustrated by the demands of market building.

As the historical record makes clear, however, the new patterns of state intervention and the postcolonial development strategies that resulted from wartime economic transformations cannot be interpreted as an embrace of statist approaches on the part of local politicians and Allied bureaucrats frustrated by the unwillingness of local capitalists to play a developmental role, or by the difficulties of creating national markets. Rather, state intervention was organized around an explicit and durable division of labor between states and markets, with open debates surrounding each decision to permit the encroachment of the former on the latter. Neither the Allied officials directing the regulatory regimes introduced during the war, nor the local officials who were mostly responsible for implementing them, viewed state intervention as an uncontested good. Their principal concerns were not the difficulties of creating and sustaining national markets, which had become more consolidated in Egypt during the interwar period than in Syria. Rather, administrators struggled with the demands of managing a system of state controls, the problems of reengineering economies to meet social needs, and the political difficulties that seemed certain to follow the introduction of sweeping economic regulations.

Getting the prices right, ensuring adequate supplies of trained administrators, enhancing bureaucratic capacity, and negotiating the political implications of regulation and intervention: these were the issues that shaped the design of regulatory regimes in the Middle East during World War II. Allied officials were not driven by apprehensions about the capacity of states to create and sustain market mechanisms but by their determination to respond to the immediate social and military needs arising from the exigencies of war. And they tended to view intervention as a temporary response to emergency conditions. Indeed, they expressed their concerns about the possibly corrosive effects of expanded state intervention on the functioning of capitalism in the Middle East that echoed debates then under way in Europe and the United States.[35]

Such concerns emerged quite clearly at, for example, a regional conference convened in August 1943 by the Middle East Supply Centre to discuss issues of food rationing and distribution. E. M. H. Lloyd, then-economic advisor to the British minister of state in Cairo and chair of the conference, opened the meeting with comments that evoked the mix of caution, regret, and hesitation that accompanied the expansion of state intervention throughout the Middle East as a result of the war:

There is no easy solution to the problem we are to discuss at the Conference. Government control is always unpopular. It requires a sufficient and reasonably competent staff; and above all it needs to win general acceptance and a fair measure of support from traders who have to be controlled. In no country is it wholly satisfactory. In Britain I can only claim that it is a good deal more satisfactory than in the last war. Indeed, conditions in the United Kingdom in 1916 and 1917 resembled in some ways those now prevailing in the Middle East—widespread profiteering and natural hesitation on the part of Government to launch out on the uncharted and perilous waters of State interference.

These considerations make it all the more remarkable that Middle East governments should have attempted to do as much as they have done. We all know that rationing and control of distribution can never be 100 percent perfect; but if the need is sufficiently great, there is some force in the view that even an imperfect attempt at rationing and control is better than doing nothing.[36]

Reluctance to risk the perils of state interference captures quite accurately the initial response of local governments to the policy recommendations of Allied officials. Aware that their governments lacked the bureaucratic capacity or institutional strength to adopt a wide-ranging regulatory role, Middle Eastern leaders exhibited something of the hesitation identified by Weir and Skocpol on the part of politicians asked to consider policy options to which their state structures were incapable of responding.[37]

Yet administrative concerns tell only a small part of the story. By and large, domestic political considerations were as powerful a predictor of local responses to wartime regulation as state institutional configurations and capacities. Such considerations heavily influenced the character of the negotiations among Allied and local officials over the scope and implementation of regulatory policies, and thus had a significant influence on the nature of regulatory regimes, the kinds of solutions that were adopted to resolve particular problems, and the kinds of administrative instruments created to implement them.[38] As we indicated above, Allied officials were more heavy-handed in imposing controls in some areas (agricultural supply and pricing) than in others (taxation), but in every case shifts in regulation provided the impetus for domestic political conflicts.

In responding to price inflation resulting from wartime expenditures, for example, Allied officials worked to persuade regional governments to apply "remedial" policies "on orthodox lines," that is, "higher taxation, loan issues, savings campaigns, control of prices and distribution, and rationing."[39] Yet in reviewing various ways to soak up excess purchasing power, local officials exhibited deep reluctance to introduce taxation schemes, for both administrative and political reasons. Allied pleas to do so "fell on deaf ears." Instead, local governments exhibited a "greater readiness [to] control prices and distribution and to enforce rationing," as well as to rely on indirect taxes.[40] Doubting their capacity to tax and lacking the political will to ensure compliance, local governments negotiated a form of state intervention that was more consistent with their particular capacities and political circumstances—with lasting effects on the political economies of these states. Throughout the region, mechanisms to control prices and distribution were much more fully developed in the postwar period than those associated with taxation, and were consistently relied upon as a central feature of postwar economic development strategies.

In general, therefore, the scope of wartime regulations, their manner of implementation, and their effectiveness were influenced by a range of domestic factors, both political and economic. These included local institutional capacity; local economic conditions; whether a particular state or territory was independent, a colony or former colony, or ruled by a European power under the auspices of a U.N. mandate; whether Britain or France was the mandatory power in a given territory; and the pattern of nationalist politics in a particular state. Regulatory regimes also differed depending on whether the object of regulation was a commodity deemed critical for the sustenance of citizens, such as wheat, which was tightly controlled across the region and governed by a rather consistent set of policies, or a product regarded as less essential to the maintenance of daily life.

Just as important, regulatory policies emerged through a rather consistent pattern of trial and error in which reliance on markets was replaced by state intervention in specific and delimited instances when private traders and merchants sought to maximize their own profits (whether by hoarding or otherwise) rather than respond to local needs. Whether such instances constituted broad-based evidence of market failure or provided justification for more elaborate regulatory regimes was a hotly debated topic at the time. Yet these debates indicate that the control and regulation of markets were viewed as much more daunting tasks than their creation or maintenance. Thus, even as regulatory regimes expanded throughout the course of the war, and even as local governments overcame their earlier objections to such regimes and began to appropriate them to serve local political and economic aims, Syrian and Egyptian political and business elites continued to see the private sector as pivotal to the economic development of Middle Eastern states.

As this summary suggests, the making of wartime regulatory regimes in Syria and Egypt was a highly interactive and dynamic process, engaging local and Allied officials in ongoing negotiations about fundamental issues of state policy, state structure, and state-market relations. In turn, these negotiations were influenced by a broad range of factors, from the Keynesian preferences of Allied regulators and the political ambitions of nationalist governments in the region to the lobbying efforts of American exporters in Washington. They also had far-ranging consequences for the postwar structure of the political economies of the region.

As the war progressed, regulations became consolidated. Syrian and Egyptian leaders came to view regulatory policies as highly effective mechanisms for extracting resources from society. Similarly, they learned that the institutions created to implement these policies offered important bases of political power and patronage.[41] As the end of the war approached and pressure began to grow for the removal of wartime regulatory agencies—pressures originating not only among private sectors within the region but also and importantly among exporters based in the United States and Europe who had long complained about wartime restrictions on their business activities in the Middle East—Allied regulators in the region began negotiations with governments within the region about how, or whether, to dismantle the regulatory institutions put in place just years or months earlier.[42] In Syria and Egypt, the withdrawal of Allied involvement did not provide a justification for state shrinking; just the opposite. Local governments independently decided to sustain the regulatory regimes initiated at the urging of the Allies, and to incorporate regulatory institutions into their expanding state structures. As one observer of the time noted with regard to import-licensing regimes, to take just one case, "It was left to Middle Eastern Governments to retain what portions of their import-licensing system they desired—most in fact retained completely powers which they found most valuable as a means of financial control."[43]

The appropriation by Middle Eastern governments of wartime regulatory agencies and practices occurred on a fairly broad basis, underscoring the linkages between these regulatory regimes and the postwar economic structures of the region. It is important to emphasize, however, that the integration of wartime regimes into postwar state structures cannot be seen as a comprehensive, seamless process that explains fully the formation of contemporary economic structures across the Middle East. We have noted that business and political elites in postwar Lebanon colluded to roll back wartime regulations. And we have emphasized that the transmission of regulatory norms was highly selective. A number of policy outcomes considered crucial by Allied officials were essentially ignored by local governments, and little trace of them remains. Most important among these was the sense among Allied bureaucrats of the compelling value of regional economic integration, and the powerful benefits of building comparative advantage on a regional rather than a state level.[44] The sense of disappointment on their part that integration was an early casualty of the postwar peace was tangible.[45] Tracing this process of selective transmission, its wartime trajectory, and its legacy for the postwar political economies of the region requires a more focused review of policy making in specific cases.

We take up this task in the following sections of the chapter, focusing on how wartime regulatory regimes altered the existing arrangement of state-market relations that had characterized the Egyptian and Syrian political economies during the interwar period.

THE RISE OF THE MIDDLE EAST SUPPLY CENTRE

Many factors influenced the patterns and trajectories of wartime economic regulation, but the circumstances that led Allied authorities to intervene can be traced directly to a particular event: a shortage of shipping. With the onset of war and the extension of fighting into North Africa, Britain's transport requirements confronted the need to enlarge and then supply its forces in the Middle East. This difficult task became even more complicated after 1940 with the fall of France, Italy's entry into the war, and the resulting loss to British forces of Europe's Mediterranean coastline. As Wilmington notes, "Overnight the link between the Desert Army and the arsenals of Britain and the United States had been lengthened from 5,000 miles to 12,000 miles and more."[46] German submarine attacks, competition for scarce shipping space between civilian and military cargoes, and disorganization at overburdened ports all compounded the difficulty of ensuring the provision of essential military supplies to Allied forces in the Middle East.

Stricter management of shipping and massive reductions of nonmilitary trade seemed the only solutions to the shipping crisis of 1940. Yet civilian shipping requirements could not easily be subordinated to military needs. Middle East states imported considerable quantities of essential foodstuffs and manufactured goods. These items represented an estimated 6 million tons of imports during peacetime, a level of trade requiring almost 100 percent of peacetime shipping capacity in the region.[47] Dramatic reductions in civilian imports without corresponding efforts to increase local production and improve local systems of distribution would have threatened food supplies and endangered the health, if not the survival, of local populations. In Syria and Lebanon, memories of the widespread starvation resulting from the Allied blockades of World War I had provoked considerable hoarding, along with "one of the most spirited import sprees the region had known" as soon as war seemed imminent.[48] The shipping crisis also threatened export-dependent sectors of Middle Eastern economies, as access to peacetime export markets was disrupted.[49] Moreover, nationalist and colonial politics interacted with strategic and economic concerns. British leaders were determined to avoid political instability that might follow economic adversity and thereby create openings for Axis advances in the region and bolster the more radical of the nationalist forces they confronted.

These considerations reinforced a growing British recognition—developed through a protracted process of intrabureaucratic wrangling among numerous ministries and other government agencies in England—that a wartime shipping regime could succeed only if accompanied by a region-wide plan to reduce its potentially disruptive effects. Some agency would have to coordinate agricultural production and distribution, substitute local manufactured goods for imported products, and supervise civilian trade to ensure that only essential imports were permitted to occupy scarce shipping space. Long-term strategic factors worked alongside the shipping crisis to produce a distinctive strategy for wartime economic mobilization in the Middle East, a strategy designed to insulate the populations of the region from the economic consequences of the war by expanding and coordinating local production as well as local capacities for economic management. Though intended to resolve the immediate issue of the shipping crisis in ways that would not undermine the position of Allied powers in the region, this strategy had far-ranging consequences for the Middle Eastern states whose economies were to be reorganized to accommodate the loss of imports.

British authorities did not underestimate the magnitude of the task they faced. Wilmington emphasizes that neither Middle Eastern governments nor the colonial powers had prepared for the challenges of coordinating the economies of the region:

> Nowhere was there a master plan of war economics, nowhere a central agency endowed with power and plenipotentiaries to set the pace for a regional alignment of consumption and production. There was no general scheme of rationing . . . [, no] remotely adequate scheme of commodity allocation to industry anywhere. Few price controls and no schemes for the allocation of labor were in effect. No drastic measures for the stretching of supplies . . . had been enacted. Few steps had been taken to convert land to food production. No important campaigns against inflation had been launched. Only feeble warnings and deterrents had been addressed to the hoarder and the profiteer, and no drastically effective regimes of import control had appeared.[50]

As impressive as Wilmington's record of Allied unpreparedness might be, it is nonetheless incomplete. It overlooks the fact that there was little coordination among colonial powers as to how to respond to the administrative gaps he identifies. It also neglects to point out that competition among France, Britain, and the United States over the terms of wartime economic management—an extension of their larger economic competition in the region—ensured that inter-Allied bargaining and conflict would define how the Allies responded to the demands of managing the economies of a region larger than the United States.[51]

As a major step toward creating the infrastructure needed to manage a wartime shipping regime, British authorities established the Middle East Supply Centre in April 1941. The Centre was created as a civilian office based in Cairo, operating under the auspices of the British Ministry of Shipping. Initially, the mandate of MESC was rather narrowly framed, focusing on collection of data needed to assign priorities to various civilian imports and thus determine the allocation of cargo space for civilian goods. MESC was created as an advisory body without executive power to enforce its recommendations.[52] Yet even this apparently modest assignment implied an extraordinary range of tasks, and the executive power of MESC soon grew to match. As defined by W. W. Elliott, an administrator attached to the Spears Mission, the functions of MESC were:

> To develop local production of essential food and materials in the Middle East through the co-operation of individual Middle Eastern governments. . . .
>
> To ensure that the demand for imports of civilian goods and equipment to the Middle Eastern countries was restricted to essentials; and to ensure that these essential needs were, in fact met. . . .
>
> To assist Middle Eastern governments in the administration of services and in the control of distribution so that the imports which did arrive were used to the best purpose. . . .
>
> To provide a Centre for the exchange of information on problems of agriculture and industrial production, transport, distribution, and economics generally; and to make available technical experts to advise on these problems.[53]

It would be hard to exaggerate the degree of intervention needed to achieve these goals. Simply to determine whether a particular food item was essential, for example, meant knowing how much of it was produced within the region and where; what local consumption levels were (implying a need for accurate demographic data in a region where rates of census avoidance were high); what kinds of replacements or substitutes could be found; how much it would cost to deliver them; what the effects would be of diverting crop production from one part of the region to another; and, not least, making sure that sufficient funds and credit were available to ensure that local alternatives could be purchased at one point for resale at another. For manufactured goods, allocation of shipping space required calculations of a similar complexity. As MESC expanded beyond its advisory role to become more active in the implementation of import-reduction schemes, its tasks became even more intricate; its reach extended into virtually every aspect of Middle Eastern economic life.

To carry out the range of tasks expected of the Supply Centre would have proven daunting under virtually any circumstances, and MESC experienced any number of growing pains. Its operations were hampered at the outset not only by the enormity of its role but by interagency rivalries; a lack of cooperation from military services concerned with preserving their autonomy in the allocation of shipping space; and the absence of coordination with U.S. authorities, the other major supplier of shipping to the region and not yet a participant in MESC. From its inception, Free French officials, including Charles de Gaulle himself, strenuously lobbied the British for inclusion in MESC, arguing that France's role in Syria and Lebanon demanded that it be given an equal voice in MESC. Already chafing at what they took to be de Gaulle's presumptions about the scope of his authority, this was a prerogative the British were determined not to extend.[54]

Despite this inauspicious beginning, by its second year of work and until it was dissolved in 1945 MESC exercised an extraordinary role in the management of regional economies. In summer 1942 MESC became a joint Anglo-American operation, and the United States was increasingly willing to rely on MESC recommendations to guide the civilian component of its lend-lease program in the region. The Supply Centre had established its reputation within Allied governments and agencies as an accurate provider of information needed to make decisions concerning the priority of shipments of goods throughout the Middle East. Within the span of a few years, MESC operations reduced the flow of imports shipped into the region from 6 million tons to about 1 1/2 million tons. Its staff had put in place region-wide import-control programs that largely determined what kinds and what amounts of foreign-made goods were available on local markets. It had become a leading direct importer of essential commodities such as pharmaceuticals, tires, grain, meat, and cooking oils. It regulated regional distribution networks, directed census-taking efforts, encouraged the development of local production in ways that influenced postwar industrialization patterns, and managed programs to eradicate locusts and other threats to agricultural production and public health.

As might be expected of an operation on this scale, MESC activities were highly controversial, generating strong reactions, both positive and negative, from a variety of directions. American and British exporters criticized the intervention of MESC in their trading relationships with Middle East customers. Local businesspeople lodged similar complaints. Both groups pursued vigorous lobbying efforts to undermine MESC's authority and deregulate shipping. Governments and businesspeople in the region disparaged MESC's authority to review and prioritize their import requests. They also resented MESC's intervention into local markets as field officers worked to coordinate regional supplies with local demands. These were not by any means trivial concerns.

Perhaps more significant, MESC's regulatory role cut deeply into prewar economic and political arrangements, redirecting the trajectory of local economies and thus reshaping relations among various political and economic groups at the domestic level. This process proceeded differently in Egypt and Syria, though it moved the political economies of these states in similar directions. Crucially, MESC activities were guided by a notion of the state as the agent of social equity, a clear and critical departure from the elitist market liberalism, if not laissez faire attitude, that shaped processes of state building before the war. Social justice as a responsibility of the state was a central principle underlying the work of the Supply Centre. Through its efforts this perspective became integrated into local perceptions concerning the appropriate purposes of the state in ways that profoundly altered the trajectories of postwar state formation. The Supply Centre took over agricultural production and distribution to ensure not only that food would be available in adequate measure but that it would be available at the same price and quality to every Syrian or Lebanese. It introduced rationing schemes to ensure that access to critical goods would be guided by some notion of equity in distribution.[55] It undertook censuses of local populations in part to ensure fairness in the allocation of scarce resources. It bought grain directly from peasants at above fair market rates, producing substantial improvements in their standard of living.[56] And officials of the Centre explicitly contrasted their efficient and rational approach to governance with what they characterized as the corruption and inefficiency of local politicians—sentiments that were typically phrased in the best traditions of colonial paternalism, if not outright racism.[57] Through these explicit commitments to the state as the agent of social equity, the Centre highlighted and deepened tensions in the core of the state project in the Middle East, making explicit the contradictions between the antipopulist market liberalism that formed the elites' vision of the state and an emerging vision of the state as the agent of redistribution and social equity that was articulated by reformist intellectuals and politicians as well as by labor unions. The Centre thus helped to frame deep social conflicts that would be resolved only with the demise of nationalist elites and their replacement by populist systems of rule in the decades after the war.

In the following sections of this chapter we review the dynamics through which the political economy of wartime regulation took shape in Egypt and Syria in three distinct arenas: agricultural production and supply, foreign trade, and taxation. We end with a brief assessment of labor regulation, a domain that was shaped to a far lesser extent by wartime intervention, even while new war-driven patterns of labor mobilization fed the larger move toward more statist developmental strategies, especially in Egypt.

Regulating Agricultural Production and Supply

From the outset of the war, Allied officials feared the consequences of wartime shipping disruptions on Middle East food supplies among local populations and struggled to balance the equally urgent need to provide for both civilian and military consumption. Allied assessments of regional food production identified inefficiencies in the distribution of food across the region: surpluses in one country were not available to redress shortages in a neighboring state, typically due to a simple lack of adequate transport. These studies found a reliance on imports in countries that showed the potential to be self-sufficient, and underscored the widespread use of practices deemed threatening to the stability of large urban areas: the hoarding of crops by villagers and of basic commodities by urban dwellers, price gouging by urban merchants, and smuggling of crops to areas outside the control of Allied forces (especially from Syria to Turkey). When combined with the volatility of harvests due to natural fluctuations in rainfall, and restrictions on the export of scarce goods from the United Kingdom to the Middle East, the conditions encountered by MESC officials when they set up shop in the region in mid-1941 were nothing short of dire.

In Syria and Lebanon, in particular, mass famine was a real possibility, and this threat led MESC officials operating within the Spears Mission to adopt a particularly heavy-handed approach to the management of agricultural production and supply. During its first season of operation, hoarding and speculating had led to severe grain shortages. The initial response of MESC staff was to flood the markets with low-priced wheat. More than one hundred thousand tons of wheat originally destined for Europe was diverted to the Levant "to induce speculators and hoarders to unload their stocks."[58] But as Spears admitted, "The absorptive capacity of the hoarders was underestimated." Imported wheat was bought up as soon as it hit local markets, and prices immediately returned to their speculative levels.[59]

In the face of this failure, MESC staff in the Levant abandoned market-based methods of price management and moved to impose a thorough control regime that governed the entire grain economy of Syria and Lebanon, bringing with it a raft of regulatory and interventionist practices that rapidly became consolidated within local state structures. To oversee this effort, the Spears Mission created an agency known as the Wheat and Cereals Office (also called the Office des céréales panifiables, or OCP), which included representatives from Syria, Lebanon, France, and England.[60] The inclusion of local representatives had implications that reached well beyond a challenge to French authority. This step made Syrian and Lebanese bureaucrats responsible for the regulation of their own agricultural economies, socialized them into the administrative culture of the Spears Mission, and provided training in the management of large-scale regulatory enterprises—expertise that technocrats such as 'Izzat Tarabulsi, one of several Syrians appointed to MESC agencies, later placed at the disposal of the postwar Syrian state.

Under OCP auspices, a centralized system of grain collection, transport, processing, and distribution was created, prefiguring the apparatus of food control that developed in independent Syria. Its tasks included everything from acquiring the foreign exchange needed to purchase grains, to equipping the OCP with trucks, sacks, and weighing equipment. The OCP became the monopsony purchaser of Syrian wheat, with prices fixed by MESC economists. To ensure compliance with directives that restricted the sale of wheat to the OCP, it created a dense network of village and district level committees to determine local grain requirements and develop estimates of grain production. Even the transport of wheat required a license in an effort to curtail smuggling.

As might be expected, the politics of managing Syria's food supply were hugely contentious. Damascus was a site of particular unrest.[61] Riots and protests were commonplace as MESC officials struggled to determine how much wheat Damascus really needed. Rumors abounded that MESC was skimming Syrian grain for British troops. Mobs collected outside bakeries whose owners sold bread made from adulterated flour. Absentee landowners and grain dealers, whose profits were threatened by OCP's practice of direct cash purchases of wheat from peasants, encouraged noncompliance with OCP collection efforts.

To cope with these circumstances the OCP gradually expanded its reach, essentially nationalizing a number of bakeries and nine flour mills. Spears induced Syria's prime minister Husni al-Barazi to become a local advocate of grain collection. Barazi traveled throughout Syria with an OCP delegation, urging landowners and peasants to sell their wheat. Implicit in his pleas was the threat of coercive collection by French forces if they did not comply. Soon, "knowledge of the risk involved in flouting the authority of the O.C.P. . . . percolated to the remotest corners of Syria," and it was able to buy wheat at the rate of three thousand tons per day.[62]

Alongside this enormous administrative apparatus, MESC constructed an entirely new bureaucracy for the collection of demographic and agricultural data. From the outset, MESC officials recognized that the work of the OCP would founder without adequate census information, of which only the most rudimentary was then available. They believed, accurately, that existing population counts dramatically overstated urban populations, to the detriment of the countryside. Local committees were unwilling or unable to direct new population counts. Early efforts to manage grain distribution in Lebanon through a system of ration cards had proven ineffective (Spears claimed that the prime minister of Lebanon held seventy-three ration cards). In response, OCP staff created a statistical agency (Bureau de statistiques et de liaison), with the mandate to undertake nationwide census counts and detailed crop estimates in Syria and Lebanon.

These were to be the first "modern" censuses in the history of the Levant, and they proved no less contentious than any other aspect of this enterprise. In spring 1942, separate censuses were conducted throughout Syria and Lebanon, with urban areas placed under curfew to ensure an accurate count. As Spears recalled, "The O.C.P. census of the Syrian towns produced some astonishing results. Damascus and Aleppo, taken together, revealed an overestimate of 96,000 souls, and Deir ez Zor proved to have a population of only 28,000 instead of 65,000. When it was learnt in Homs that a census was soon to be made by British and French officers under curfew conditions, panic-stricken householders immediately registered 5,000 new deaths at the municipal office; even excluding this sudden decrease, the new figures were 18 per cent. lower than those of the previous census."[63] Counting was accompanied by the formal registration of households to permit the implementation of a food-rationing scheme—information that was later used in Syria to revise lists of eligible voters.

With new population figures in hand, wheat provisions to Damascus were cut. Rioting broke out to pressure the Syrian government to increase the city's allocation. An OCP decision to reduce the "ration of the wealthier .classes [in Damascus] . . . to the level prevailing elsewhere" also prompted riots in March 1942. As with other aspects of the food supply program, popular mobilization against intervention led MESC not to cut back, but to broaden its role. With the Syrian government unwilling to assume responsibility for an unpopular rationing system, the role of the Bureau de statistiques et de liaison "evolved first from liaison into supervision and [then became] one of direct control" of the entire wheat distribution scheme.[64]

By the time Spears wrote his memorandum to the Foreign Office in June 1943, he was able to claim that the OCP's efforts had been a resounding success. He took credit for averting famine and for giving Syria and Lebanon "a taste of honest and efficient administration which were conditions totally unknown there." He expressed his hope that local governments would eventually develop an "attachment to the scheme."[65] In Syria, the government certainly did.

"Wars pass," wrote Guy Hunter, a historian of MESC, "but economic problems do not."[66] Syrian politicians were no less concerned than officials of the Spears Mission about the imperative necessity to ensure food security, especially for highly mobilized urban populations. Following the war, the OCP was absorbed into the Syrian bureaucracy, as were several other agencies created by MESC to manage food production and supply. For a short period, a small number of British technical experts stayed on, but over time the functions of OCP agencies were absorbed into a range of ministries, from the Ministry of Economy to the Ministries of Agriculture and Supply, and managed entirely by Syrians. Throughout the 1940s and 1950s, and quite apart from their flawed and halfhearted attempts at agrarian reform, the Syrian governments of this period steadily broadened the role of the state in the agricultural economy, retaining many of the regulatory regimes first introduced by the OCP. These included price controls, marketing controls, and oversight of food distribution.[67] The statistical and data collection capacities created by the Bureau de statistiques et de liaison supported the production of Syria's *Al-majmu'a al-ih'saiya* (annual statistical abstract), published first by the Ministry of Economy and later by the Ministry of Planning. In general, and without exaggerating the extent to which later practices grew directly out of Syria's wartime experience, it is clear that Syria's postwar capacity to manage the agrarian sector has critical links to the role of MESC in the construction of a pervasive program of agrarian regulation during the war.

In Egypt, entrenched patterns of agricultural production posed two distinct and related problems for economic administrators: how to meet the increased need for food production and how to minimize the adverse effects of a drastic decline in fertilizer imports. The Egyptian economy was built around estate production of cotton for export on the world market. Unlike during World War I, however, when producers and merchants reaped the windfalls from rising wartime demand for their goods, world cotton market prices began a precipitous decline early in 1940 that indeed rocked the foundations of the political economy.[68] Following protracted negotiations through the late spring and summer, which were bound up with the British Embassy's intervention to remove one government presumed insufficiently loyal and secure the cooperation of a successor, British authorities agreed in August 1940 to purchase the entire domestic cotton crop.[69] Producers planted their fields in anticipation of even greater windfalls, but in 1941 British authorities drove a harder bargain, linking its support to a system of invasive regulation of cotton production and marketing.[70]

In this case, the wartime administration invented many of the arrangements that have since come to stand for etatism in Egyptian agriculture, including a strict currency exchange control regime, the closing of the first cotton futures market in the world, and the conversion of the state to monopsonist.[71] According to Richards, these unprecedented policy changes contributed to undermining the one-hundred-year-old 'izba system of estate production. From the time of the war, large landowners turned increasingly to renting out their estates for cash.[72] The cornerstone of this new and transforming regulatory regime was a series of laws controlling cotton production by forcing growers to alter their regular pattern of crop rotation and fixing upper limits on the percentage of lands that could be planted with the traditional cash crop. Wartime officials combined these restrictions with cash incentives to farmers who shifted additional acreage to food production.

These regulations succeeded in shrinking the cultivated acreage to 50 percent of the prewar level, and, for the duration of the war, cotton trickled to rather than flooded the market.[73] Officials continued this regime after the war, relaxing controls very briefly in 1950 before reinstating them one year later. The result was a shift in agricultural output over time, in-

cluding increases in rice, sugarcane, fruits and vegetables, and the introduction of wholly new crops such as flax, jute, and sugar beet cultivation
under the guidance of MESC.[74] But, as is widely noted about the intervention, the massive shift out of cotton and into staple grains—wheat, barley,
millet, and maize—was able only to offset the steep fall in yields caused by
the virtual cutoff of fertilizer shipments.[75] And the increased rate of exploitation to make up for food imports exhausted soil resources.[76] In Egypt
as in Syria, therefore, agricultural inputs and outputs were subjected to an
increasing degree of control, until governments had taken over purchase
and distribution of most key commodities, including fertilizers, wheat and
other grains, sugar, tea, coffee, and cooking oil.[77] And as in Syria, the
spillover effects of these regulatory innovations into postwar Egyptian food
policies are clearly visible.

The Regulation of Foreign Trade: Centralization, Coordination, and State-Led ISI

The scale of MESC's role in the regulation of trade was similar to the extent
of its role in the management of agriculture. Controlling the flow of goods
into and out of the Middle East was the raison d'être of the Middle East
Supply Centre, making the regulation of domestic trade its principal task.
Moreover, its control over access to shipping was complete, giving MESC officials extraordinary leverage in their negotiations over trade with Syrian
and Egyptian representatives, whose economies were heavily import-dependent. As in the case of agriculture, the implications of regulating trade
encompassed an enormous range of economic activities, leading MESC officials to become deeply engaged in the restructuring of a wide array of domestic economic arrangements and in the development of significant new
forms of state capacity.

Three specific factors helped determine how economic arrangements
were restructured and what specific forms of state capacity were produced
through the intervention of the Supply Centre. First, MESC was above all
an agency of economic coordination, evaluating and prioritizing the import requirements of some fifteen states and territories, reconciling these
needs against available shipping space, communicating with government
agencies in Washington and London and with private vendors to supply essential goods—but only essential goods. To make these determinations in
any reasonable fashion required the construction of a centralized, region-
wide trade management apparatus, including local agencies that mediated
between MESC and domestic business interests. The specific mechanism
MESC adopted to regulate trade flows was a system of import licensing. To
allocate licenses, governments provided MESC with data detailing import
requirements for a six-month period (later annually), for everything from

"heavy machinery to razor blades."[78] This represented a level of data collection that vastly exceeded the prewar capacity of local governments and demanded considerable expansion in their collection of basic economic information. And because MESC worked with local representatives and governments to attach priorities to specific requests, the import licensing scheme made private enterprise highly dependent on government mediation, shifting the balance of public-private power in matters of economic decision making. In Syria, these issues were especially acute because by 1941, "the volume of imports [had sunk] to a lower proportion of the prewar level than it [had] in any other Middle East country."[79]

Second, MESC's role in regulating foreign trade became a channel for imposing direct state control over domestic economies on the part of local governments, but here too this happened in ways that favored the development of quite distinctive state capacities. Once again, the participation of local bureaucrats in trade regulation—though poorly trained and in short supply—helped transfer administrative norms from MESC to local bureaucracies. And once again, MESC policies were heavily influenced by a view of the state as the mechanism for ensuring that economic outcomes would be socially just (and therefore politically justifiable in the West). As Hunter writes:

> Undoubtedly the most effective controls were in the rationing and price control of essentials, and here the partly effective control of M.E.S.C. over the distribution of imported goods and the governmental control of grain through the Wheat Collection Schemes were of outstanding importance. M.E.S.C. was able to make it a condition of supply that scarce essentials should be fairly distributed at controlled prices. In taking this attitude it was fair to insist that the British and American publics were not prepared to go short of supplies and to risk their sailors and ships in order to put enormous profits into the hands of Middle East black-marketeers. In the distribution of tires, cotton textiles, and some medical supplies, M.E.S.C. *rigidly insisted* that the receiving Government should establish a satisfactory scheme for distribution according to need and essential use before supplies were released.[80]

In Syria and Lebanon, the regulation of essential goods gave rise to no less than eight separate advisory boards. These included a Joint Supply Council, on which Syrians and Lebanese were the only representatives and which was responsible for approving import and export forwarded by the other boards.[81] The authority of these boards was considerable, and their work quickly expanded beyond mediating between MESC and local business to encompass the control of domestic production in critical areas. The extent to which this new role cast the state as supervisor rather than ally of the private sector, and the resistance of private capitalists to this shift, was amply demonstrated by the intense opposition of mill owners and textile merchants in Aleppo and Damascus to a proposal by the Textile Advisory Board to impose government control over the entire textile sector.[82] Nor was this economic oversight role, once taken on, quick to disappear at the end of the war—even though Spears and his American counterparts were anxious to see the resumption of free trade in the region and determined to secure the competitive position of their countries' commercial interests. Despite state controls, local prices for many imported goods were considerably higher than global prices, and governments reaped windfall profits from their monopoly over trade in various commodities. Given politicians' reluctance to tax, they were not inclined to give up this source of revenue. Nor were local manufacturers inclined to see protectionism disappear. Syrian industrialists lobbied for the continuation of protectionist legislation after the war, hoping to expand their operations before more competitive Western producers could reenter local markets.[83]

In the Egyptian case, the system of import licenses, quotas, and excluded goods that was installed beginning in the fall of 1941 was based on a division of labor. For a combination of political and administrative reasons, once the schedule had been formulated the Egyptian government was responsible for distributing of licenses. The result was a political entrepreneur's dream come true. We know this conceptually from the recent accounts of rent-seeking and governance in Egypt and elsewhere in postcolonial Africa, as well as anecdotally from the lurid tales of the Wafd party in office between 1942 and 1944 and Durrell's unforgettable portrait of those in Cairo and Alexandria "in a money daydream . . . who have skimmed the grease off the war effort in contracts and profiteering."[84] Nonetheless, as elsewhere in the region, all decisions on licenses were forwarded for review by MESC, which held effective veto power through its influence on shipping and supply commissions in London and Washington.[85]

Though few details are available as yet, this particular regulatory regime emerged as the result of "long drawn-out and difficult negotiations" with the Allied authorities.[86] For instance, MESC exploited Egypt's dependence on fertilizers at different points to obtain wheat, barley, rice, and millet for export. A British organization—the United Kingdom Commercial Corporation—received all fertilizers shipped to Egypt and released them to the Egyptian government only with the authorization of the regulators. And the government organization that determined fertilizer allocation for different crops included British authorities as members.[87] While such authorities saw no need to gracelessly trample the myth of Egyptian sovereignty—Lampson never called for armor to surround the finance ministry—Allied control over the supply of strategic goods gave them significant leverage over arenas deemed of vital importance.

Third, and perhaps most important, trade restrictions gave MESC a stake in the development of local production capacity for items that could no longer be imported. In other words, MESC became an agent in the construction of import substitution industrialization in the Middle East, and its intervention gave a particular cast to the form of ISI. For MESC officials, the move toward ISI raised much deeper issues than those posed by rationing or price controls, interventions that were perceived as flexible and potentially short-term. Tinkering with the organization of industry was a different matter. MESC economists had an intuitive sense that the path on which they set local industrialization would determine future prospects for economic development. To mention again Hunter's account, he emphasizes the importance MESC officials attached to the long-term effects of their actions:

> The struggle for imported supplies was a war problem, and one likely to cease after the war when normal trade could be resumed. But its corollary, the effort to increase local production, at once entered the field of possibly permanent economic improvement; and it was in this field that the work of M.E.S.C. had its chief interest in the future
>
> Although there was an urgent need for some products which could have been made in the Middle East, a good deal of care had to be taken not to create uneconomic industries which would wither away altogether when lower priced and better quality goods from the industrial West were again freely available. The war and consequent shortages acted almost as a high tariff wall behind which it would have been possible to create a number of enterprises; but the temptation was resisted.[88]

Despite the reticence Hunter attributes to MESC, it helped launch a number of industrial enterprises in both Syria and Egypt, especially in the fields of mining, chemicals production, and construction supplies. In addition, Syrian manufacturers seized on the sudden absence of foreign competition to ramp up their own production and capture the profits held out to them by closed wartime markets. Their efforts led to a tremendous industrial boom. Indeed, increases in local output made it possible to meet military requirements for many items without imposing hardship on civilians.[89] Private investment in industry soared. According to Wilmington, "For years afterwards the business community of the region mused about the war years as something akin to a golden age of bustle and confidence."[90]

The golden age was not to last. Crucially, and somewhat ironically given industrialists' enthusiasm for protection, MESC officials helped construct a version of ISI that transformed industrialization into a state project. If private capital drove the wartime expansion of import-substituting sectors—with public investment largely limited to heavy industry and food processing—wartime controls represented the first critical moves toward state appropriation of industrialization in both Egypt and Syria. With MESC support, states established a range of heavy industries and thus helped construct industrial public sectors. Control regimes institutionalized the role of government as the direct manager of industry and created significant financial incentives for them to expand their role in the years after the war. MESC also provided local governments with a discourse that linked economic management to norms of fairness and social justice and gave intervention a powerful element of legitimacy. It is not surprising therefore that the end of the war did not bring about the removal of tariff barriers as Hunter expected. In fact, the sheltering of local economies gave rise to protectionist coalitions of state managers and industrialists who worked together to embed state-managed ISI within the political economies of postwar Egypt and Syria. The lower-priced and better-quality goods (presumably British goods) that Hunter expected to flow into the region after the war did not materialize. Instead, the pattern of industrialization that MESC officials feared was precisely the one they helped to construct: state-dominated forms of import substitution embedded first within nationalist-liberal, and later within populist, strategies of economic development.

Tax Policy and the Limits of MESC Authority

Among the many changes associated with wartime shifts in the economy of the Middle East was rampant inflation. Spending by Allied armies and expenditures by MESC itself combined with restrictions on trade to produce vast increases in money supply and corresponding increases in local prices. Despite extensive use of price controls and more limited reliance on rationing of scarce goods, the money supply in Syria (in pounds sterling) grew by more than 1,000 percent between August 1939 and June 1945, while local commodity prices jumped by 860 percent in the same period.[91] For allied authorities, the concern that inflation might generate social instability led them to explore a range of strategies for absorbing excess purchasing power, including tax reform. In this area as in others, MESC officials expressed confidence that reforms would bring lasting benefits to the region, but managing fiscal policies was a lower priority and their efforts lacked the urgency and intensity of their intervention in trade and agriculture. As a result, Middle East authorities exerted less pressures to overcome entrenched local interests in the area of taxation, providing considerably more latitude for local politicians to shape policy outcomes. MESC economists encouraged local politicians to impose considerably higher direct taxes on their populations, but in the face of local resistance they abandoned this tack and shifted to other ways of absorbing purchasing power, such as the sale of gold, a policy that was developed by a MESC economist, R. F. Kahn, who was a colleague of Keynes at Cambridge, and reviewed by Keynes himself in his capacity as a director of the Bank of England.[92]

For Syrian politicians, the idea of shifting from indirect to direct forms of taxation posed a considerable political dilemma. State revenues were derived almost entirely from indirect taxes, principally customs duties. Syria had no income tax at all until 1942 and then assessed taxes of only 3–4 percent on fixed-wage earners. Agricultural income was largely exempt from taxation. The move to direct taxation would thus alienate virtually every electoral constituency, as well as cut into the prerogatives of the land owners and capitalists who sat in Syria's cabinet and national assembly. This is not to say that Syrian politicians made no effort to respond to the urgings of MESC economists. In 1944, avoiding policies that targeted the commercial elite, the government attempted to impose direct withholding on the wages of textile workers. Yet even singling out workers proved ineffective. News of the change prompted a strike among mill workers in Aleppo, and the government relented.[93] By the end of the war, and in the absence of strong Allied pressure, little remained of MESC's efforts to shift the organization of tax policy in Syria.

In Egypt, the situation was similar. Taxes in Egypt increased more during the war than in neighboring Arab states, but in an oft-cited 1945 address the president of the National Bank of Egypt admitted that "Egypt still remains one of the least taxed countries in the world."[94] And the increase in indirect taxes such as customs duties more likely exacerbated rather than checked rising prices. Egyptian officials apparently preferred price-fixing and rationing schemes. As a result, former prime minister Isma'il Sidqi's projection, on the eve of the war, of the state's need for new sources of development revenues went unheeded.[95] Colonial arrangements (the debt administration and the system of commercial treaties known as the Capitulations) tightly constrained the state's fiscal powers. Egypt had no income tax until these controls were dismantled in 1937–38. The government imposed four new taxes in January 1939—on movable property, on commercial and industrial profits, on professional earnings, and on salaries and wages. During the war these schedules were adjusted mildly upward and were supplemented by an excess profits tax passed in 1941. Significantly, this emergency levy was never applied to agricultural land rents, though these had soared together with property values.[96] Nonetheless, the government made up for the loss in revenue from the import decline, and by 1944 direct taxes netted £E 14 million or approximately 30 percent of all taxes and customs duties.[97]

As in Syria, these wartime arrangements did not outlast the fighting. Firms proved more resourceful than the overtaxed employees of the finance ministry, where reforms designed to close up loopholes in the tax regime and raise rates were enacted after protracted negotiations, in 1949.[98] In the intervening years, the state reverted to its pattern of relying on import duties, which increased both absolutely and relative to other taxes in the postwar period. Thus, by 1948, direct taxes totaled £E 11.8 million, down from 1944, while customs and excise duties climbed to £E 51 million or 71 percent of all revenues. The share was identical to that of 1939.

Labor and the Indirect Consequences of MESC Intervention

Despite the close association between Keynesian economics and problems of employment, MESC regulators were virtually silent on the issue of labor policy in the Middle East. In part, this reflected an appreciation of the difference between agrarian and industrialized economies, and in part the perception of Allied regulators that wartime demand would itself provide sufficient employment to avoid serious labor shortages in the region. What stands out about the war period, however, especially for Egypt, were the indirect effects of MESC's intervention in other areas on how the state managed the regulation of labor. Even without direct forms of intervention, the war caused significant shifts in the relationship between the state and local labor markets.

Labor power represented Egypt's primary contribution to the war effort. In contrast to the small numbers of citizens absorbed by the Egyptian army, the number of workers employed by the Allied armies in the Cairo, Alexandria, and Canal Zone bases peaked at 210,000 in 1943, and these massive new flows into military construction and service sectors represented the overwhelming share of the growth in the ranks of the wartime urban labor force.[99] Syrians were similarly recruited for defense works, though the 30,000 mostly unskilled workers employed in the peak year of 1943 did not represent the same order of magnitude as in Egypt, where shortages of skilled and semiskilled labor of all classes were acute.[100]

For the duration of the war, officials did little more than let the market, that is, wages, govern the allocation of labor resources. At most, and under pressure from newly legalized labor unions and their core constituencies, the state directed firms to pay (nominal) cost-of-living allowances and began to subsidize some basic commodities as hedges against the inflationary spiral of prices and rents.[101] The real problem for politicians would come once the war ended. With the steep decline in demand for labor, the recent flood of migrants to Cairo and other urban centers would be transformed into a reservoir of unemployed and impoverished city dwellers.[102] In 1943 the Egyptian government unveiled the country's first five-year plan, outlining future public outlays for infrastructure and social and industrial construction. A new hydropower station and fertilizer-manufacturing complex anchored the plan, which needed and received the endorsement of the allied economic authorities, not least because both the Roosevelt and Churchill governments recognized the centrality of these industrial schemes to postwar Middle East policy.[103] The Egyptian government, no less clearly, viewed these and related policies as designs for coping with the postwar unemployment problem.[104]

The obvious example is the steep rise in tariff levels imposed on top of the protection already provided to the cottonseed oil producers, the distilleries, the giant spinning mills, the canning industry, the sugar monopoly, and other privileged economic actors by the wartime diversion of shipping space and the import control regime put in place by MESC. Despite these war-driven forms of protectionism, the tariff on manufactures rose 50 percent in 1941 and ratcheted up twice more in 1942 and 1943. True, firms and their agents may well have been motivated to shore up their (un)competitive positions in the postwar market, but for politicians these rents were the price for maintaining uncompetitively high employment levels. In archival data from the late 1940s, firms are explicit about the existence of this bargain.[105] And, by the time of the 1952 revolution, at least some large investors were looking for alternatives.[106]

LEGACIES OF ALLIED REGULATION

By the end of the 1940s, citizens of Egypt and Syria were subject to political economies that had been profoundly restructured as a result of MESC intervention. Allied regulators had shifted the prewar, liberal trajectory of state-market relations in these countries, and in the Middle East more broadly, onto a new trajectory. Their impact certainly varied, leaving only faint traces in some areas while having tremendous weight and longevity in others. Where the Allies perceived regulation to be critical for success of the war effort, and where local political and economic actors perceived regulation to be in their immediate (but not always long-term) interests, interventionist norms became deeply embedded within domestic political economies. Where the Allies attached a lower priority to economic outcomes, and where local politicians associated regulation with high political costs, wartime innovations were more fleeting in their effects. Yet the overall shift in state-market relations was unmistakable and reached even into areas, such as labor, that were not part of its formal mandate. Above all, in both Egypt and Syria the regulation of markets would come to be seen as a normal and appropriate response to questions of development. For a decade after the war, certain groups of capitalists would struggle to overcome the accelerating move toward statist development strategies. But the normative and institutional legacies of the war had become too deeply consolidated in these states to be forced aside. Within only fifteen years, little was left in either Egypt or Syria of the economic liberalism of the prewar period that capitalists would recall with increasing nostalgia.

Though mediated by the vastly different colonial contexts of Egypt and

Syria in the 1940s, wartime economic policies created new institutional arenas within which capitalists, landowners, colonial representatives, and local
politicians struggled to secure their interests. These transformations were
not in any sense *necessarily* antagonistic toward capitalists—the merchants,
entrepreneurs, industrialists, traders, and others whose activities dominated the economies of both countries before and during the war. Indeed,
the rise of wartime regulatory regimes designed to substitute local production for foreign imports and administer the purchase and distribution of
essential commodities had widely differing effects on capitalists, strengthening and enriching them in some instances, eroding their power and well-
being in others. Capitalists and state institutions alike often benefited considerably, however, from wartime rents: the windfall profits resulting from
the supply and maintenance of foreign troops, foreign aid, wartime contracts, and, notably in Syria and Lebanon, levels of inflation that greatly enriched those who controlled the supply of necessary goods.

Capitalists thus fared reasonably well during the years of the war, and in
both Syria and Egypt the immediate postwar period was a time of rapid private sector growth. Yet in both countries wartime economic practices
helped consolidate notions of the economy as a legitimate object of regulation, and of the state as the necessary agent of economic coordination and
management. They valorized the belief that a "national" economy could be
directed to achieve distributive justice. They extended "rational" administrative practices into the management of agricultural production and supply—at least in Syria—in ways that disrupted long-standing patterns of
agrarian production based on sharecropping relations between landlords
and peasants. Moreover, and perhaps most important, these notions and
practices, and the institutions through which they were effected did not disappear with the end of the war or the departure of colonial powers. In both
Egypt and Syria, wartime regulatory institutions and practices were appropriated by nationalist movements. They were carried over and incorporated
into postwar, postindependence processes of state formation and economy
building.

CONCLUSION: CRITICAL PERSPECTIVES
ON THE MIDDLE EAST SUPPLY CENTRE

This chapter brings together ideas, institutions, and actors to trace the specific routes through which a particular set of developmental norms were
transmitted into and institutionalized within a specific set of political
economies. This argument, which locates one important force behind Middle East state and market formation at the intersection of externally imposed wartime economic regulations and the domestic political contexts of

the region, has implications for a range of contemporary debates concerning the relationship between state and market in late-developing states, and the relationship between domestic and international influences shaping patterns of state and market formation. In particular, the chapter challenges revisionist explanations of the political economy of state formation in the Middle East, arguing that postcolonial conflicts between statist and market-oriented visions of economic development—conflicts that resulted in the marginalization of private sectors in our two cases, Egypt and Syria—cannot adequately be understood without reference to war-related transformations that reshaped the institutional arena within which struggles between private capitalists and state actors were played out. The state-led and import-substituting economic development strategies that became dominant in Syria and Egypt after World War II, as in much of the developing world, did not reflect simply the inability or unwillingness of local capitalists to shoulder the burdens of development.[107] Nor do they indicate a lack of state capacity to create and manage markets.[108] Rather, they can be seen as a product, at least in part, of three interrelated aspects of the experience of World War II in the Middle East: (1) wartime efforts of Allied powers to manage and organize the local economies of Egypt and Syria in keeping with their sense of military priorities—and in keeping with a set of administrative preferences influenced by the increasing acceptance of Keynesian interventionist strategies; (2) the negotiations between Allied officials and local leaders over how to implement these efforts; and (3) the transformation in the balance of power between state actors and local capitalists produced by the policies that resulted from this process of bargaining.

Inevitably, however, there are gaps in detailing the causal links that illuminate the relationships at the core of this study. Despite access to diplomatic archives and to the small secondary literature about the work of MESC, we are aware that much remains hidden from view. A more fine-tuned judgment about MESC and its role is difficult, given how little we actually know about the history of specific economic institutions in the Middle East and of specific policy making arenas, episodes, and outcomes. British officials at the time understandably celebrated rather than looked critically at their wartime statist experiment, and found it convenient to explain most economic problems as the result of local administrative deficiencies, tradition-bound peasants, and local political corruption. Nonetheless, Vitalis has previously documented incidents of collusion between British officials and Egyptian capitalists in subverting export controls and rationing rules.[109] Clearly, paeans to the efficiency of Anglo-Egyptian planning need systematic review, as do the earnest testimonies in the British Parliament that the massive allied operation imposed no particular burden on the Egyptian populace. As Milward proposes, the massive influx of soldiers and civilians strained the resources of Middle Eastern countries "to the utmost," and if Egypt was "relatively well off" in the war, it was despite the Allied administration, which he says contributed to famine in India in 1943.[110]

We know that London viewed MESC as vital to the refashioning of neocolonial arrangements in Egypt and the Levant, which led the U.S. government in turn to oppose plans to reconfigure MESC as a joint Anglo-American regional development agency.[111] Assistant Secretary of State Acheson and other top officials, such as Roosevelt's confidant Patrick Hurley and the senior U.S. representative to MESC James M. Landis, prevailed in the policy debate, backed by the findings of the business leaders and government officials who comprised the special Culbertson economic mission to the Middle East.[112] This opposition was framed in terms of continuing statist economic structures at the behest of Great Powers. The irony is, of course, that the statist currents grew stronger in the first postwar decade, aided by the U.S. Embassy, which was pressing in the late 1940s for more comprehensive forms of planning; U.S. technicians, who were designing land reform schemes in Egypt in 1951–52; U.S. funding ($40 million by 1954); and the U.S. consulting firms who were paid to design the Nagib-Nasser regime's import substitution industrialization program.[113]

In reality, U.S. officials were among the most fervent early disciples of import substitution industrialization, and were the conduits to Egypt and the rest of the Middle East region for ideas, routines, and rationales that were widely adapted in the decade following the war's end. As we have seen, specific policies constructed in an ad hoc fashion to cope with the exigencies of conflict came to serve as organizational templates. Postwar administrators, suddenly more easily able to see why and how it was possible, for instance, to substitute for the Alexandria Cotton Futures Market or to distribute agricultural inputs, "reinstalled" these wartime programs. In related fashion, to the extent that there were cadres who were already inspired by Turkish, Soviet, or U.S. alternatives to the "liberal" state that had become naturalized over the previous half century, the war opened up a significant political space for these new statist currents.

In part, our arguments challenging the purely domestic and "nationalist" origins of statism in the Middle East derive from a problematic historiography in which statism is seen to emerge "first" in places such as Latin America and Turkey, and only much later, in the 1960s and beyond, in Egypt, Africa, and Asia. This narrative, a product of post-1968 intellectual trends, is intent on constructing ISI as an act of resistance within the global order and, significantly, in defiance of alleged U.S. preferences for unregulated markets. But this reading is called into question by, for instance, archival accounts of postwar U.S. initiatives in the Philippines and elsewhere, as well as a new wave of economic histories of the Southern Cone that trace the multifaceted and contingent origins of the statist programs and currents of the 1940s to the 1960s.[114] Far from emerging against U.S. interests, scores of countries adapted ISI projects under the guidance of the U.S. state. In India, where "socialist" currents allegedly had envisioned and pressed for such reforms before the war, nonetheless, following the allied intervention, these policies took on a distinctly new cast. In Turkey, where the Soviet project was particularly influential, and which in turn influenced particular Indian intellectuals, Americans had a remarkable influence in reconfiguring these policies, as is now widely recognized.

The allied experiment in the Middle East during World War II may thus be a critical link in a much broader account of global shifts in economic arrangements. As Wilmington reminds us, MESC influenced the European experiment in World War II while other of its cadres went on to administer UN development projects and the regional commissions such as Economic Commission for Latin America (1949) that proved so critical to ISI in Latin America. The unfortunate irony is that this legacy has somehow been lost, and the countries of the Middle East are now more likely to be portrayed as places where the vestiges of colonialism first had to be obliterated before authorities there could experiment with public planning, industrial development, and economic regulation.

NOTES

This essay is in every sense a joint venture, and the order of the names is the result of a coin toss. Heydemann thanks Joel Migdal, Michael Barnett, and David Waldner for critical readings of earlier drafts of this article, as well as Columbia University for a grant that funded travel to archives in the United Kingdom. Vitalis thanks Philip Khoury for originally supporting the research he presents in this essay and Ellis Goldberg for countless conversations that shaped these ideas. Both of us are grateful to our coparticipants at the November 1994 SSRC workshop, "War as a Source of State and Social Transformation in the Near and Middle East," and to the Ford Foundation for funding it.

1. For a valuable exception to this, see Rock, *Latin America in the 1940s: War and Postwar Transitions*. On the Middle East see Barnett, *Confronting the Costs of War: Military Power, State, and Society in Egypt and Israel;* Gongora, "War Making and State Power in the Contemporary Middle East," pp. 323–40; and Lustick, "The Absence of Middle Eastern Great Powers," pp. 653–84.

2. Tilly, *The Formation of National States in Western Europe*, p. 46.

3. A major work on the international diffusion of Keynesianism, for example, includes no non-Western cases other than Japan. Hall, *The Political Power of Economic Ideas: Keynesianism across Nations*. In contrast, Drake, *The Money Doctor in the Andes: The Kemmerer Missions, 1923–1933*, establishes the significant extent to which pre-Keynesian economic models were absorbed into the interwar economies of Latin America through the self-conscious efforts of a leading U.S. economist, Edwin Walter Kemmerer.

4. When Europe-centered approaches have been applied to the developing world, the results often have been disappointing. Such work often appropriates uncritically the concepts and categories developed by scholars of Europe and imposes them on Third World settings, exporting definitions of war and of the state that seem wholly unsuited to Third World contexts. According to one scholar of Africa, for example, the lack of European-style war making in Africa has led to the emergence of "permanently weak states" plagued by inefficiencies that war making would have required them to overcome if they wished to survive. Herbst, "War and the State in Africa," pp. 117–39. On conceptual stretching see Collier and Mahon, "Conceptual 'Stretching' Revisited: Adapting Categories in Comparative Analysis," pp. 845–55.

5. Similar importance has been attached to wartime interventions in the construction of the postwar regulation of interstate relations, as well. See Burley, "Regulating the World: Multilateralism, International Law, and the Projection of the New Deal Regulatory State," pp. 125–56.

6. See Meyer, "The World Polity and the Authority of the Nation-State," pp. 41–70; and McNeely, *Constructing the Nation-State: International Organization and Prescriptive Action.* See also Powell and DiMaggio, *The New Institutionalism in Organizational Analysis;* Steinmo, Thelen, and Longstreth, *Structuring Politics: Historical Institutionalism in Comparative Perspective;* and Strang, "British and French Political Institutions and the Patterning of Decolonization," pp. 278–95.

7. For example, the economic advisor to the British minister of state in Cairo was a Cambridge economist and pupil of Keynes, R. F. Khan, who also had previous government experience in overseeing wartime economic planning on the British Board of Trade. For several months in 1942 Kahn served in Cairo as deputy director of the Middle East Supply Centre. Lloyd, *Food and Inflation in the Middle East, 1940–1945,* pp. 84, 86.

8. This refers in particular to Lloyd, who was also an economic advisor to the British minister of state in Cairo, during 1943 and 1944. During World War I, Lloyd served as assistant secretary in the British Ministry of Food.

9. The effects of this intervention on Iran's economy are detailed in Millspaugh, *Americans in Persia.* Millspaugh led two U.S. missions to Persia, one during the interwar period and a second during World War II, to develop its institutional capacity in the area of economic management and to oversee its macroeconomic policies. In both instances, he left Persia at the request of the government due to concerns over the extent of his mission's intervention in economic policy making.

10. The experience of the Middle East was not in any way exceptional. Indeed, Alan Milward argues that World War II represents a critical turning point in the organization of agricultural production on a global scale. Our purpose, rather, is to understand how global shifts in regulatory norms produced distinctive outcomes in one region as a result of their interaction with a particular political and social environment. See Milward, "The Second World War and Long-Term Change in World Agriculture," pp. 5–15.

11. Syria as used here refers to the territory that would eventually become the state of Syria, not to the area known as Greater Syria, which encompasses Lebanon as well.

12. Heydemann, *Authoritarianism in Syria: Institutions and Social Conflict,*

1946–1970; and Vitalis, *When Capitalists Collide: Business Conflict and the End of Empire in Egypt.*

13. Disruptions in food supply caused in part by a British blockade of Ottoman Syria during World War I led to massive starvation, an experience British authorities hoped not to repeat. See Schatkowski-Schilcher, "The Famine of 1915–1918 in Greater Syria," pp. 229–58.

14. The Mission was named after its director, General Sir Edward Spears. See his autobiography of this period, *Fulfilment of a Mission: The Spears Mission to Syria and Lebanon, 1941–1944.*

15. The Syrian government did pass a major piece of labor legislation in 1946, shortly after the final withdrawal of French forces: the 1946 Labor Code. However, its passage had relatively little to do with the impact of wartime regulation on Syrian labor. See al-'Azm, *Mudhakkirat Khalid al-'Azm* (Memoirs of Khalid al-'Azm), 2:5–116.

16. For a summary discussion of ISI in the Middle East see Richards and Waterbury, *A Political Economy of the Middle East: State, Class and Economic Development,* pp. 25–39. They refer to state versus private sector participation in ISI in the Middle East and Latin America on p. 36. On the institutional and political consequences associated with different forms of ISI, see Kaufman, "How Societies Change Developmental Models or Keep Them: Reflections on the Latin American Experience in the 1930s and the Postwar World," pp. 110–38; and Ranis, "The Role of Governments and Markets," pp. 85–100.

17. It should be clear from this discussion that our reference to Keynesianism is not intended to imply that Middle East governments applied policies conforming in any strict sense to Keynes's economic theories. It refers instead to a general appreciation for the potential of interventionist approaches among the economists and planners who were posted to Allied regulatory agencies in the Middle East.

18. Although MESC was active throughout the Middle East, state officials differed in the extent to which they found the institutional and regulatory legacies of MESC useful in the project of postwar economic development. In Lebanon during the 1950s, for example, a powerful business class that relied on Lebanon's status as an entrepôt economy forced the dismantling of many of the regulatory regimes established by MESC during the war. See Gates, *The Merchant Republic of Lebanon: Rise of an Open Economy,* pp. 109–34.

19. Implicit in this is a second claim, that the specific organization of state-market relations in the postwar Middle East has had long-term consequences that are critical for understanding the dynamics of the contemporary political economies of the region. To fully develop this claim, however, is beyond the scope of this chapter.

20. The subsequent consolidation of interventionist norms was no doubt facilitated by their easy compatibility with more radical, anticapitalist notions of development that were becoming prominent in Syria and Egypt during the late 1940s and 1950s. Indeed, it is one of the major ironies of this period that Western international financial agencies like the International Monetary Fund concurred with Soviet economists on the value of state intervention, agrarian reform, centralized planning, and the positive role of the public sector.

21. Lee, *Colonial Development and Good Government: A Study of the Ideas Expressed by*

the British Official Classes in Planning Decolonization, 1939–1964, pp. 37–39; William B. R. Cohen, "The French Colonial Service in French West Africa," pp. 491–514.

22. Vitalis, *When Capitalists Collide,* pp. 34–9.

23. Waterbury, *The Egypt of Nasser and Sadat: The Political Economy of Two Regimes,* p. 233.

24. Vitalis, "The End of Third Worldism," pp. 13–33.

25. Wilmington, *Middle East Supply Centre,* pp. 35, 43. Few Egyptians were fooled, however, particularly when in other venues the essential nature of the country's position and contribution to the war effort were being portrayed without inhibition. As a South African writer, C. Z. Kloetzel, described in an article originally for the *Palestine Post,* by providing the "Egyptian fleshpots" coveted by the military nomads from the desert, "Cairo is accomplishing an important task[,] . . . strengthen[ing] the striking force of the Army as a whole." *Egyptian Gazette,* 8 January 1943.

26. On the post–World War I shift in French economic policy see David K. Fieldhouse, "The Economic Exploitation of Africa."

27. A more critical assessment of French economic policies in Syria and Lebanon is presented in Khoury, *Syria and the French Mandate: The Politics of Arab Nationalism, 1920–1945,* pp. 85–94, 277–84. For a less critical view see Longrigg, *Syria and Lebanon under French Mandate,* pp. 133–35; 265–83.

28. Albert Hourani, *Syria and Lebanon: A Political Essay* (Oxford: Oxford University Press, 1946), p. 170, quoted in Ralph E. Crow, "The Civil Service of Independent Syria, 1945–1958" (Ph.D. diss., University of Michigan, 1964), p. 55. Crow elaborates on the notion of the dual administrative structure erected by the French.

29. Asfour, *Syria: Development and Monetary Policy,* p. 5.

30. Khoury, *Syria and the French Mandate,* pp. 205–18, 277–84.

31. On the consensus among a cross-section of Syrian elites about the need for market-supporting forms of state intervention as the basis for Syria's postindependence economic growth, see Yahya Sadowski, "Political Power and Economic Organization in Syria: The Course of State Intervention, 1946–1958," pp. 152–66.

32. For example, Syrian leaders expressed their opposition to French plans for the management of Syria's wheat crop during the war by encouraging the Spears Mission to devise an alternative program and construct a MESC-run administrative agency, the Wheat Office, to manage it. British officials were persuaded that Syrians preferred this course of action due to their deep distrust of the French High Commission. See Sir E. Spears to Mr. Eden, "Memorandum on the First Year of the Wheat Office (O.C.P.), Syria and the Lebanon," June 20, 1943, Oxford University St. Antony's College, Middle East Library, Private Papers, Spears IV/1. However, in assessing his perspective on events in Syria and Lebanon it is important to keep in mind Spears's antipathy toward his French counterparts.

33. Brian Waddell makes a similar argument concerning the effect of World War II on state-business relations in the United States, "Economic Mobilization for World War II and the Transformation of the U.S. State," pp. 165–94.

34. This is the argument advanced in Chaudhry, "Myths of the Market and the Common History of Late Developers," pp. 245–74. Our findings show that Chaudhry's argument does not hold.

35. In 1940, the American Historical Association organized its annual meeting

around the theme of "War and Society," with the explicit purpose of encouraging attention to the ideological and social transformations America experienced in the interwar period and to the likely effects of the "second major war within the space of a single generation." According to one of the papers published after the conference:

> The great wars of the twentieth century have had a more revolutionary influence upon economy [*sic*] than those of the nineteenth century to the extent that they have made necessary a high degree of state intervention for the coordination of private capitalism. . . . Until after 1914 . . . the state continued to serve the interests of business, or, in general, to stand aside permitting private enterprise a free course. This relationship was reversed for the first time since the decline of mercantilism when the material demands of the World War surpassed the limits of private capitalism, *uncoordinated in a national sense* [emphasis added], and the state was increasingly forced to take over the economic, in addition to the military, prosecution of the conflict. . . .
>
> In these and other ways, "statism" has intruded itself with varying degrees into formerly free economies. Capitalism within the nation has been made to subserve a supercompetition between states and blocs of states and thereby has been deprived of so many vital functions that it has been seriously weakened. . . . The discretionary powers of investment, the role of free initiative in production, the "automatic" mechanisms of the free market and other essentials of private capitalism have given way to planning and regulation by the state.
>
> Rothwell, "War and Economic Institutions," pp. 205–6.

36. Lloyd, *Food and Inflation*, p. 219.

37. Weir and Skocpol, "State Structures and the Possibilities for 'Keynesian' Responses to the Great Depression in Sweden, Britain, and the United States," p. 118.

38. See Hall, introduction to *The Political Power of Economic Ideas*, p. 12–13.

39. Lloyd, *Food and Inflation*, p. 195. Lloyd notes that Allied governments later pushed for the sale of gold as an additional measure to absorb excess funds in the region, a policy, he tells us, that had Lord Keynes's personal endorsement.

40. Ibid.

41. In one illustrative incident, a full-scale political crisis erupted in Syria in the winter of 1946–47 in response to allegations of corruption in the management of a former British agency, "the British military organisation 'MIRA' for the purchase of cereals." This agency was transferred to Syrian control on June 1, 1946, under the Ministry of National Economy headed by Khalid al-'Azm. "Immediately a number of far reaching changes were made . . . in the personnel of the organisation, in which were placed a number of [al-'Azm's] political supporters." Al-'Azm's adversaries in the Syrian assembly subsequently accused him in parliamentary debate of corruption and embezzlement of MIRA funds, though the veracity of the charges was questionable. British diplomats sent news of these events to the foreign minister, Ernest Bevin. His terse handwritten response: "This sort of thing usually happens in the state monopolies belonging to new countries." British Legation, "Damascus to Ernest Bevin, Foreign Office, February 24, 1947," FO371/62128, Public Records Office.

42. For example, as early as the fall of 1944, Spears pushed the Foreign Office to relax trade restrictions that he felt handicapped British commercial interests in their trade competition with Americans. See "E. L. Spears to Anthony Eden, Foreign Office, November 18, 1944," FO371/40336, Public Records Office.

43. Hunter, "Economic Problems: The Middle East Supply Centre," p. 189.

44. The rise and decline of Britain's desire to reorganize the Middle East as a regional trading zone is described in Kingston, *Britain and the Politics of Modernization in the Middle East, 1945–1958*.

45. As Wilmington wrote in the 1960s, "More than a quarter of a century has passed since the Middle East Supply Centre was disbanded and the countries so intimately involved in its work decided to go their separate ways in the Middle East. The intervening years of dissension, war, and hatred have denied the promise of M.E.S.C., and the hopes of those who created it, and whose labors made it, for a few short years at least, a working model of Middle East cooperation." *The Middle East Supply Centre*, p. 7.

46. Ibid., p. 15.

47. B. A. Keen, *The Agricultural Development of the Middle East: A Report to the Director General, Middle East Supply Centre, May, 1945*. Wilmington notes a figure of 5 million tons.

48. Wilmington, *Middle East Supply Centre*, p. 17.

49. Prest, *War Economics of Primary Producing Countries*, pp. 8–9. Prest mentions the potential collapse of citrus production in Palestine and declines in cotton exports from Egypt. In both instances British military purchase of crops was arranged to prevent economic hardship.

50. Wilmington, *Middle East Supply Centre*, pp. 29–30.

51. The Allies eventually came to oversee, through the Middle East Supply Centre, the economies of Aden, Cyprus, Libya (divided into Cyrenaica and Tripolitania), Egypt, Eritrea, Ethiopia, Iraq, Lebanon, Palestine, Iran, Saudi Arabia, Somalia (then divided between French and British Somaliland), Sudan, Syria, and Transjordan.

52. In the United Kingdom, actual decisions about the allocation of shipping space and the priority to assign to various goods were made by the Middle East Supplies Committee, and in the United States by the Combined Agency for Middle East Supplies. Lloyd notes (*Food and Inflation*, p. 95) that "since the British were always in the majority in MESC and had set it up under a British Director-General before the Americans arrived, both sides tended to regard it as primarily a British body with the British bearing the main burden of responsibility and their American colleagues watching and criticizing. Moreover, both British and American officials were accountable for their actions to departments in London and Washington with special interests which could not always be reconciled. These divergent interests were most marked in the field of exports to the Middle East." American exporters viewed the war as an opportunity to replace British firms as suppliers to the region and were opposed to the efforts of MESC to restrict imports into the region, viewing it as a British effort to retain their commercial advantage in the region. Ibid., pp. 96–7. See also, Rosen, *The Combined Boards of the Second World War: An Experiment in International Administration*, pp. 71–130.

53. W. W. Elliott, "Civil Transport Problems in the Middle East in Wartime" (paper presented to the Institute of Transport by W. W. Elliott, 1945). Oxford University St. Antony's College, Middle East Library, Private Papers, Middle East Supply Centre I/I.

54. British bureaucrats justified the exclusion of France from MESC on the

grounds that MESC was concerned simply with the rationing of shipping space, and as France controlled no ships it had no valid claim to representation. However, it is readily apparent that British officials were concerned to do nothing that might enhance France's authority in Syria and Lebanon, delay French withdrawal from these territories, or promote postwar French ties in the Levant. The most detailed review of the French and British positions on this matter are contained in "Mr. Holman, Algiers, to Foreign Office, 'Question of French Participation on Middle East Supply Centre,' June 5, 1944," FO371/40336, Public Records Office. For the MESC position see "Office of Minister Resident, Cairo, to Foreign Office, 'Question of French Participation on Middle East Supply Centre,' July 24, 1944," FO371/40336, Public Records Office.

55. Alan A. Milward made the normative dimension of rationing explicit: "In a general sense black markets are socially unjust in the most flagrant way; rationing, by contrast, is often a device for reducing inequalities. The ethics of rationing tend towards the idea of a just reward." *War, Economy, and Society, 1939–1945,* p. 283.

56. "The most important point to consider is how far the incomes of [Syrian] cultivators rose. It is not possible to produce any comprehensive and cast-iron evidence on the subject, but there is little doubt that, generally speaking, the rises in income were large enough to leave them substantially better off in real terms than they were before the war." Prest, *War Economics,* p. 230. In 1942, imported wheat cost £24 per ton. The OCP fixed the local price in Syria at £39 per ton.

57. Spears's memoirs are laden with a casual but repellent racism. In one typical phrase, he refers to the wife of an African general as a "mammy, but as quick as a troop of monkeys." *Fulfilment of a Mission,* p. 43.

58. Lloyd, *Food and Inflation,* p. 145. Lloyd based his account of MESC's work in agriculture in Syria and Lebanon almost entirely on the then-classified memorandum written by Spears as cited in n. 32, above.

59. Spears, "Memorandum on the First Year," p. 1.

60. The French and British, however, held veto power over OCP decisions. The French high commissioner in Lebanon and Syria at the time, General Georges Catroux, had tried to preempt the Spears Mission by creating a French-dominated Wheat Office (Office du blé) to oversee food collection and supply. Spears's proposal for local participation won out when Syrian and Lebanese politicians refused to accept Catroux's fait accompli—and when British officials told Catroux that without a plan acceptable to local officials, the British Army would step in to do the job. Faced with these threats, Catroux folded.

61. Food riots in Damascus and elsewhere in Syria and Lebanon before the arrival of MESC are described in Kirk, *The Middle East in the War,* pp. 89–90. Spears, "Memorandum on the First Year," p. 10, compared disturbances in Damascus to a the whining of a spoiled child and suggested that he was prepared to play the part of the stern disciplinarian. "Damascus," he wrote, had "always been a spoilt city, used to intimidating its rulers, both French and Syrians, by threatening strikes and riots."

62. Spears, "Memorandum on the First Year," p. 9.

63. Ibid., p. 12.

64. Ibid.

65. Ibid., pp. 13–14.

66. Hunter, "Economic Problems: The Middle East Supply Centre," p. 179.

67. On the postindependence expansion of state regulation of agriculture, see Heydemann, *Authoritarianism in Syria*, chaps. 2–3.

68. Fears that the war would prevent Egypt from disposing of the 1940 cotton harvest had, by May 1940, produced a slump that the Alexandrian correspondent for the *Economist* said "assumed the proportions of a regular depression" ("Egypt Faces Facts," *Economist*, 1 June 1940), and later judged "one of the worst crises in [Egypt's] history." ("The Anglo-Egyptian Cotton Deal," *Economist*, 5 October 1940). El-Mallakh argues that interwar policies of stockpiling and the expansion of artificial-fiber technologies reinforced the effects of shipping and the loss of key markets such as France. Ragaei W. El-Mallakh, "The Effects of the Second World War on the Economic Development of Egypt" (Ph.D. diss., Rutgers University, 1955), pp. 58–60.

69. The purchase cost £2.5 million, for a quantity approximately twice Britain's average need, of which 60 percent remained stockpiled in the Delta. Kirk, *Middle East in the War*, pp. 193–203.

70. British authorities forced the Egyptian government to share in the financing of the purchase and refused to raise the prices above the 1940 level. Egyptian authorities paid a surcharge. In later years, the Egyptian government covered the entire outlay for the markedly reduced crop on its own. Ibid., p. 203; El-Mallakh, "Effects of the Second World War," pp. 61–63.

71. *Economist*, 25 May 1940; El-Mallakh, "Effects of the Second World War," pp. 60, 142, 203–4. The Alexandrian Futures market was reopened in September 1948 and operated until the Nasir regime closed it permanently in November 1952.

72. Richards, *Egypt's Agricultural Development*, pp. 172–74; Anhoury, "Les repercussions de la guerre sure l'agriculture Egyptienne."

73. Prest, *War Economics*, pp. 130–31; El-Mallakh, "Effects of the Second World War," p. 63.

74. El-Mallakh, "Effects of the Second World War," pp. 95–6.

75. With increasing demand for food and the need to counter the adverse effects on productivity caused by the interruption of normal crop rotation, the rate of application of fertilizers would have had to rise faster than the already high annual increase based on normal use. Instead, fertilizer imports dropped drastically below prewar levels. See Issawi, *Egypt: An Economic and Social Analysis*, p. 62; Richards, *Egypt's Agricultural Development*, pp. 168–69.

76. El-Mallakh, "Effects of the Second World War," p. 95.

77. Lloyd, *Food and Inflation*, pp. 123, 132; Kirk, *Middle East in the War*, p. 175.

78. Hunter, "Economic Problems," p. 174. According to Hunter, "At the height of its work MESC was handling about 80,000 licences each year" under six directorates: food, materials, medical, transport, programs, and administration.

79. Prest, *War Economics*, p. 225

80. Hunter, "Economic Problems," p. 187. Emphasis added.

81. The other seven boards were the Transport Advisory Board, Joint Paper Advisory Board, Joint Medical Advisory Board, Miscellaneous Supplies Advisory Board, Agricultural Advisory Board, Textile Advisory Board, and Iron and Steel Advisory Board. See "Mr. Mackereth, Beirut, to Mr. Hankey, Foreign Office, 'Supply Council and Advisory Boards in Levant States,' August 2, 1944," FO371/40336, Public Records Office.

82. "The plans prepared by the Textile Advisory Board for the control of textiles have been approved by the two Governments and some legislation has already been issued in the case of Syria. . . . Pressure brought to bear by influential spinners and merchants is causing some hesitation by the Ministers in applying this control but that they sincerely wish to see the introduction of a control scheme as outlined by the Advisory Board, is substantiated by their agreement to the costing of the production of all spinning mills, which was carried out by the firm of Russell & Company" (ibid.).

83. In both Syria and Lebanon, traders and industrialists struggled to shape economic policies, with the former lobbying hard for the overturn of protectionist legislation. In Syria, industrialists carried the day; in Lebanon, traders won out and protectionism declined after the war. See Gates, "The Historical Role of Political Economy in the Development of Modern Lebanon," pp. 29–30.

84. "Lawrence Durrell to Henry Miller, Alexandria, February 8, 1944," in *Lawrence Durrell, Henry Miller,* ed. George Wickes (New York: Dutton, 1963), p. 181; 'Ubayd, *Al-kitab al-aswad* (The Black Book).

85. Lloyd, *Food and Inflation,* pp. 105–16. As Lloyd notes, Washington's compliance was not always guaranteed. Private U.S. trading interests with influence over the determination of cargo space were a critical factor in making it possible for Egypt-based merchants to profit from the war. The terms of lend-lease also opened up new opportunities for U.S. exports to Egypt, which U.S. officials sought to exploit, much to the consternation of the British Foreign Office (96–97).

86. Ibid., p. 102.

87. Ibid., p. 137.

88. Hunter, "Economic Problems," pp. 182, 186.

89. Prest, *War Economics,* p. 225

90. Wilmington, *Middle East Supply Centre,* p. 107.

91. Prest, *War Economics,* pp. 227, 229.

92. Details of the program to sell gold in the Middle East, including the minor but nonetheless interesting role of Lord Keynes, are in Lloyd, *Food and Inflation,* pp. 208–17. Keynes apparently felt that the United States should provide gold for sale in the Middle East, arguing that this might be the last meaningful use the Americans would have for their gold reserves.

93. "Weekly Political Summary No. 125, Syria and the Lebanon, September 5, 1944," FO660/205, Public Records Office.

94. Cited in Prest, *War Economics,* p. 27; and El-Mallakh, "Effects of the Second World War," p. 235.

95. See "A Healthy Financial Situation, but New Sources of Revenue Required," *Manchester Guardian Commercial, Egypt, 1938* (n.d.): 30.

96. Taxes on land were actually lowered, while the rates on rent were increased in 1939.

97. Details are found in El-Mallakh, "Effects of the Second World War," pp. 37, 240; and Issawi, *Egypt,* p. 140.

98. *Egyptian Gazette,* 4 November 1949.

99. See for example al-Disuqi, *Misr fi al-harb al-'alamiyya al-thaniyya, 1939–1945* (Egypt in World War Two), pp. 223–24.

100. Prest, *War Economics,* pp. 126–28, 221; El-Mallakh, "The Effects of the Second World War on the Economic Development of Egypt," pp. 178–82.

101. Beinin and Lockman, *Workers on the Nile: Nationalism, Communism, Islam, and the Egyptian Working Class, 1882–1954,* pp. 288–94; Prest, *War Economics,* pp. 142, 152; El-Mallakh, "Effects of the Second World War," pp. 220–25.

102. Abu Lughod, *Cairo: 1001 Years of the City Victorious,* p. 129; Beinin and Lockman, *Workers on the Nile,* pp. 259–63.

103. For details see Vitalis, "The New Deal in Egypt: The Rise of Anglo-American Commercial Rivalry in World War II and the Fall of Neocolonialism," pp. 211–40.

104. El-Mallakh, "Effects of the Second World War," pp. 187. Beinin and Lockman's argument that "no concrete measures were adopted by either the British or Egyptian authorities to deal with the high level of unemployment" (*Workers on the Nile,* p. 260) is in fact wrong.

105. Tignor, *Egyptian Textiles and British Capital, 1930–1956.*

106. Vitalis, *When Capitalists Collide,* pp. 205–6.

107. This reflects a long-standing and widely held explanation of the rise of state capitalism in the Middle East, articulated by international lending agencies and academics alike.

108. See Chaudhry, "The Myths of the Market and the Common History of Late Developers."

109. Vitalis, *When Capitalists Collide.*

110. Milward, *War, Economy and Society,* pp. 278–81.

111. Tignor, "The Suez Crisis of 1956 and Egypt's Foreign Private Sector," pp. 274–97; Vitalis, "'New Deal' in Egypt."

112. DeNovo, "The Culbertson Economic Mission and Anglo-American Tensions in the Middle East, 1944–1945," pp. 913–33: 922–23; Philip J. Baram, *The Department of State in the Middle East, 1919–1945,* p. 165.

113. Vitalis, *When Capitalists Collide.*

114. See Waisman, *Reversal of Development in Argentina: Postwar Counterrevolutionary Policies and Their Structural Consequences;* Sikkink, *Ideas and Institutions: Developmentalism in Brazil and Argentina;* and Rock, *Latin America in the 1940s.*

PART TWO

War, State, and Society
in the Contemporary Middle East

5

Si Vis Stabilitatem, Para Bellum
State Building, National Security, and War Preparation in Syria

Volker Perthes

Since Hafiz al-Asad's assumption of power in 1970, Syria has been transformed into a fairly strong security state. Political and social control have been firmly established. The extractive capacities of the state and the participation of the populace in regime-led institutions have been enhanced. Regime stability has been maintained even after the collapse of the country's main international ally, the Soviet Union. Moreover, Syrian policy making has been marked by the virtual absence of external interference, that is, by a high measure of national autonomy.[1] Perhaps most important, the state has become a security state in the sense that its prime function, if not its raison d'être for those who control it, has been to serve both national and regime security more than anything else. Economic rationalities, for instance, have regularly been subordinated to the rationality of regime maintenance and control.

The emergence in Syria of such a strong state and stable regime is of particular note in light of both the notorious weakness of postindependence Syria, which was very much an object of regional and international power politics and which even sacrificed its sovereignty to establish a union with Egypt, and the fragility of the Ba'thist military-party regime that, after the failure of the union and a short interregnum of the ancien régime, ruled the country from 1963 to 1970. In hindsight, these first years of Ba'thist rule appear to be a transition period in which the substructure of the postindependence regime was destroyed, while new structures did not provide for political stability. The parties of the ancien régime were banned, its leading representatives driven out of the country, its landed and industrial bourgeoisie seriously weakened, and its bureaucracy flooded with ambitious and often politically committed migrants from the countryside. The new regime, though, was internally fragmented, split between different networks and groups, and weakened by the struggle for power of various military and party leaders. It was not in control of the military, whose involvement in politics it had furthered and legitimized. Nor was the regime able to defend the country. The June war of 1967 revealed that the regime and its armed forces were anything but prepared for the battle that the Ba'th's radical nationalists had promised would come and that would lead to the liberation of Palestine. Furthermore, the regime proved unable to build viable legal institutions, and it was not able to create a legitimizing, nationally integrative myth. Even as late as 1970, important segments of the active population did not fully accept the Syrian state as the legitimate arena for national politics. Some of the country's political elite were openly prepared to consider a capital other than Damascus—notably Cairo, where Nasser's legacy still exerted a powerful appeal, or Baghdad where the exiled Ba'thist old guard wielded influence—as their political reference point.

Only after Asad's takeover was a new, coherent structure of power and control set up and national integration pushed forward. The state apparatus and the armed forces were vastly expanded, decision-making structures were centralized, and popular or professional organizations, such as the trade unions, Peasant's Union, Women's Union, and others, were reorganized into hierarchical, corporatist bodies that could, at the same time, represent, mobilize, and contain all important segments of the population. All these measures helped to establish regime control over the largest part of active society and also helped to make sure that such local or sectoral strongmen as still existed or were to emerge would rise only through regime-controlled organizations, exercise their influence through regime channels, and thereby invest their own power resources in the system. Although it relied on substantial rent income, the regime was by no means independent from domestic resources. It managed, however, not to become dependent on the support of one particular societal stratum alone. And while not regulating all spheres of life—the regime is authoritarian not totalitarian—it has deeply penetrated society, effectively monopolized the means of organized violence, and largely succeeded in making the Syrian nation-state the accepted frame of politics.[2]

I will argue here that the achievement of a remarkably high measure of stateness, as well as the consolidation of the regime, maintenance of its stability, and the capacity to generate substantial external rents are largely the result of the pervasive militarization of state and society, an enormous buildup of the security forces, and an almost constant preparation for war. State building and the strengthening of the means of national security cannot be separated in the Syrian case. As I will explain, however, Syria's experience of war preparation is distinctive in several ways. In contrast to the experience of war preparation and state building in other cases, Syria's reliance on external resources to underwrite its perpetual state of militarization meant that specific shifts in state-society relations that we usually associate with intensive preparation for war—new patterns of bargaining between regimes and social groups, including the emergence of new constraints on the exercise of political authority—did not occur. In fact, Syria's status as a belligerent generated high levels of strategic rent and thus reduced the regime's dependence on domestic resources to fund its programs of militarization and its building of a security state. In this sense, the domestic outlays needed to maintain pervasive militarization can be considered an investment that paid off in the form of even higher levels of strategic rents. In addition, Syria's experience since the early 1970s suggests ·the need to understand and explain war preparation and militarization as an end in itself and not as a prelude to actual war making. After the 1973 war, Syria's continued militarization did not imply that the regime intended to lead a war, or that engaging in actual warfare or even preparedness for all-out war, had been the essential element of Asad's political project.[3] Rather, it is the domestic social and political benefits of protracted militarization, subsidized by external resources, that explain the regime's determination to preserve Syria's status as a security state.

MILITARIZATION AND WAR PREPARATION

War preparation and militarization necessarily involve the mobilization of resources for military efforts and the buildup of military capabilities.[4] This military dimension, however, forms only part of the picture. In the case of Syria under Asad, militarization and war preparation have been an almost all-encompassing feature of the country's political-cultural development and political economy. These processes determine how the regime governs, and strategies of social incorporation help legitimate the regime and the Syrian nation-state and form an important element of resource generation. In the discourse of the regime, the preparation for "the battle" has been given absolute political primacy. All other goals figure as secondary.[5]

In the following sections, I will first give an overview of the expansion of the security apparatus under Asad and the regional context of war preparation and buildup. I will then explain how these efforts served to legitimize the regime and build a fairly strong and consolidated state. It is important to note here that the use of the regional situation to legitimate militarization and the establishment of strong mechanisms of domestic control is not some kind of trick the government played on its people. External threats were (and are) real. However, the policies the Syrian leadership uses to confront these threats have at the same time had a domestic function—namely, the maintenance of stability and control.

The Buildup of Force and Control

Under Asad's rule, the buildup of the security forces has indeed been enormous. The manpower of the regular armed forces, including the gendarmerie and the Syrian contingent of the Palestine Liberation Army, increased from some 80,000 in 1970 to 430,000 by the early 1990s. Even compared to the rapid growth of Syria's population, the expansion of the armed forces is remarkable. In 1970, there were some 13 members of the armed forces for every 1,000 Syrians, growing to more than 35 per 1,000 by the second half of the 1980s. Since then, the total number of persons employed in the Syrian armed forces has remained more or less stagnant, producing a decline in the military/civilian ratio to around 20 military persons for every 1,000 Syrians. Notably, the main buildup took place only from 1974, that is, after the October War of 1973. Also, from 1975 Syria's military expenditures, including estimated expenditure on arms procurement, soared, from only about 10 percent of the GDP in the 1970–74 period— except for the war year 1973, when expenditures were considerably higher—to around 15 percent, with peaks of over 20 percent, in the years till 1986; only thereafter did it decrease, dropping to around 10 percent of the GDP by the early 1990s, and below 7 percent of the GDP by 1995.[6]

Even though the buildup of the 1970s and 1980s was not solely linked to the confrontation with Israel, it has to be seen in the context of this confrontation—which was also how it was generally understood both domestically and abroad. Given that the 1973 war and the ensuing disengagement on the Syrian-Israeli front had not ended Israel's occupation of Syrian territory, and that a negotiated return of the Golan to Syria and a comprehensive Arab-Israeli peace seemed unlikely at that time, Syria had to prepare for a possible renewal of fighting. In addition, the Syrian army had been heavily engaged in Lebanon since 1976. While Syria's Lebanon involvement certainly enhanced the regime's capacity to project its power regionally, it was primarily regarded as part of the confrontation with Israel, inasmuch as one of the major Syrian fears had been that Israel could take advantage of Lebanon's fragmentation. Under the premises of the confrontation with Israel, Syria further increased its armament efforts in the wake of the Egyptian-Israeli peace treaty of 1979, which left Syria as the only credible confrontation state. The widely publicized rationale behind the armament policies of Damascus was now that Syria alone would have to achieve what was called "strategic parity with the enemy"; that is, a military capability that would allow it not only to defend itself against Israeli aggression but eventually also force Israel to make concessions.

At the same time, growing internal unrest provided further incentive to strengthen the regime's security apparatus. From 1979, a close-to-civil-war situation evolved in parts of the country. Only by the employment of warlike means was the regime able to gain the upper hand over its Islamist-led challengers and finally crush their rebellion in the spring of 1982. In the summer of that year, during Israel's Lebanon invasion, Syrian forces were dragged into open war by their Israeli adversaries. This engagement caused catastrophic blows to the Syrian forces, bringing home to the regime and to Syrians in general that the country was far from achieving anything like military parity with Israel, that Syria would not be able to choose the time and place of "the battle," and that war preparation therefore would have to be intensified. Armament efforts were indeed increased considerably in the following years.

In the course of this preparation for the eventual battle with Israel, as it was constantly referred to in official discourse, the armed forces were also professionalized and depoliticized. While political indoctrination still played a role in the armed forces, the general theme of this indoctrination was the army's role in defending the homeland as well as the "revolution," that is, the regime: the army was no longer the breeding ground for an ideology or political project of its own that set the armed forces apart from the state and its leadership. It was transformed from a power center whose leading members pursued their own political ambitions and what they considered their sociopolitical mission into an institution that, though harboring and defending its own corporate interests, would obey orders and preserve the stability of state and regime rather than constantly threaten it. With political primacy given to the needs of national security and war preparation, the army was, for the first time since independence, effectively subordinated to the political leadership. The army and the rest of the security forces now formed the strongest instrument of the state, allowing the latter to monopolize the means of organized violence, including control over the Ba'th Party militia and those Palestinian forces that until 1970 had enjoyed some independence from the Syrian state. Notably, this monopolization of the means of violence in the hands of the political leadership was referred to as a "unification of command"—that is, unification of state, party, and military as demanded in the light of the prospective battle.[7]

There is no doubt that the military regards the Asad regime as "theirs." While Syria under Asad does not represent a full-fledged military dictatorship, it is certainly a dictatorship in which the military wields strong influence. The president himself is a military person, and military and security officers occupy important government positions. Neither the prime minister, nor the minister of finance, let alone parliament, has a say over the military budget or matters of state security. And the highest echelons of the security apparatus, rather than the government or the leadership body of the ruling Ba'th Party, are likely to have a decisive voice once the question of succession to President Asad becomes acute.

Militarization and Social Incorporation

Militarization, of course, does not only denote a particular condition of the relationship between the government and the military, but also denotes a condition of the state-society relationship that includes practices of governance and the political incorporation of society. For more than thirty years, emergency laws have been in force in Syria. Its various security services, or *mukhabarat,* have virtually unchecked powers and a long record of arbitrary encroachments on the freedom and property of citizens. According to the security logic of the regime, the continued application of emergency laws is vindicated or even dictated by the ongoing state of war in which the country finds itself.[8] War and the necessities of the battle, however, are used not only to justify authoritarianism and the lack of personal freedom but also as the rationale behind the development of political institutions. The establishment of the Progressive National Front (PNF), for instance—the coalition body that joins the ruling Ba'th Party with a couple of tolerated smaller parties—has frequently been presented as needed to mobilize "all progressive and popular energies" and put them at the service of "the battle."[9]

Since 1970, parts of the regime structure itself have been reorganized along quasi-military, hierarchical lines. This applies in particular to the Ba'th Party. The principle of collective leadership that had applied within the party until Asad's putsch of 1970 was replaced by a highly personalized style of leadership. Internal party elections were increasingly replaced by the use of appointments. Important policy directions were no longer decided upon by party congresses but commanded and transmitted through the party from the top down; and any discussion of the general party line, as defined by the president, has become off-limits even to the party congress. Moreover, the dividing lines between the party as a political organization and the security apparatus have become blurred, as much of the party's energy is spent on the political control and so-called security evaluations of Syrian citizens.

Beyond the Ba'th Party, much of Syrian society itself has been militarized, and a generally militaristic political culture has evolved. This is largely due to the direct incorporation into state structures of an important part of active society via the security apparatus, and to the militaristic socialization of the country's younger generations in particular. The military and security apparatus are leading agents of socialization, and militaristic values form an important part of the curriculum, as it were, that young Syrians complete from prep school to university. Both incorporation and military socialization have helped to politically contain the population, which over the last three decades has undergone substantial processes of social change and mobilization, including rapid urbanization, increasing literacy, and the formation of more distinct class structures.[10]

By the early 1990s, the security apparatus—including the regular armed forces, an estimated 100,000 police and *mukhabarat,* and some 60,000 civilians employed in companies run by the Ministry of Defense—gave work to almost half of all people employed by the state, or directly employed some 15 percent of the total workforce. Within that number were some 60,000 conscripts drafted into the army or police each year for their two-and-a-half-years of military service. For many a young villager the army still represents a chance to leave the rural environment behind and acquire a career. Many conscripts receive their only professional training during their military service. And many families, not only those from rural areas, consider it an opportunity to place one of their sons in the security apparatus. Given the large number of persons directly connected to the security apparatus, the military is anything but an isolated caste. Rather, it has widely penetrated society. Moreover, given that military persons and others working with the ubiquitous security apparatus are visibly privileged and can usually deliver *wasta* (mediation), and that dealing with the security services has become part of people's daily lives and strategies of survival, few Syrians would not find it advantageous to establish good relations with some military or *mukhabarat* officer.

The military also organizes and commands volunteer militias attached to the Ba'th Party, the Peasant Union, the trade unions, and other mass organizations and runs mandatory military training programs in high schools and universities.[11] Indeed, education in Syrian schools is thoroughly militaristic. Intermediate-level and high school students wear military-style school uniforms; students who participate in parachute or special combat courses organized by the official and quasi-mandatory Revolutionary Youth Organization obtain special privileges such as preferential university acceptance; and members of the youth organization have occasionally been used as police reserves. A Syrian survey among primary school pupils analyzing the contribution of the pedagogic and political programs of the Pioneers of the Ba'th—the mandatory organization for children of primary school age—to the development of children's values and norms left no doubts about both educational goals and achievements at the primary school level. While pointing critically to shortcomings regarding the children's geographic and historical knowledge, the study noted positively the deeply embedded values of sacrifice and martyrdom for the defense of the homeland against its enemies and for the liberation of its occupied territories.[12]

While the young generation is the main recipient of such militaristic socialization, other social segments too are constantly reminded that Syria is at war and that one's personal and the country's collective war preparation efforts are what really counts. Public spectacles are a case in point. Consider the display of combat exercises at the opening ceremony of the Mediter-

ranean Games in Latakia, or the transformation, in public speech and official posters of the president's second son, Bashar al-Asad, from a civilian, almost intellectual eye-doctor to a military officer once he stepped in to replace his late brother as a young representative of the regime and potential
successor to his father.[13] There is a comparatively large output of books
dealing with general—as opposed to specifically Syrian—military issues
and of works of art praising struggle and martyrdom. Employees of the public sector and the bureaucracy are regularly mobilized for "voluntary" unpaid days of labor for the "twin battle of development and liberation," and
even the private sector is forced to participate through what is called, literally, the "war effort" *(al-majhud al-harbi),* a special tax for defense purposes
that is levied on business profits. Amounting to only a fraction of normal
business taxes, this additional war tax is not so much a meaningful source
of government revenues as a reminder to the business class of the state of
war and of their national duty to contribute to the nation's defense efforts.

Legitimation of Regime and State

Not surprisingly, militarization and the pervasive reminders of the state of
war and the country's frontline status have had an important legitimating
function for the Syrian regime. As noted, the demands of the battle have
done more than serve to justify heavy-handed rule and limitations of personal freedom. Since the external threat to Syria and the greater Arab
homeland—as well as Syria's role in confronting these threats—has generally been credible, the militarization of public life has rarely been questioned. And Syria's stance in the Arab-Israeli confrontation has been one
element that has retained for the regime a modicum of domestic legitimacy
during periods of serious public discontent. Consider how Israel's Lebanon
invasion of 1982, as well as the attacks by U.S. forces on Syrian positions in
Lebanon the following year, helped to distract public attention from the
destruction of Hama at the hands of the Syrian army just a couple of
months before Israel's siege of Beirut, and to silence domestic opposition.[14]
Or consider how the constant criticism by, among others, trade unions and
Syria's official Communist Party regarding the regime's handling of social
and economic policies and even its toleration of corruption and the lack of
democracy have always been mitigated by references to the "national
stance" of country and regime.

Asad is probably right when suggesting, if only to a Western public, that
he might lose domestic support if he gave up his tough stance in the Arab-
Israeli context and settled with Israel for less than a domestically justifiable
peace.[15] It is also notable that the army itself and defense expenditures
have hardly ever been the object of criticism. As a matter of fact, regime
representatives themselves have occasionally pointed to the country's de-

fense burden to justify administrative shortcomings or budgetary constraints, but have not, to date, felt any pressure to defend or explain this burden, that is, the military buildup and its presumed economic and social costs. This is so not only because the regime is not practically accountable to the public but also because under the premises of external confrontation and war preparation this burden is an undisputed and largely noncontroversial issue.[16]

We can further assume that both militarization and the incorporation of a large part of society via the security apparatus, as well as the credibility of the external threat and of war mobilization, contributed to the territorialization of political and social life in Syria and, thereby, to the legitimacy and stability of the Syrian nation-state. Militarization, in other words, has helped to further a spirit of Syrianness—an identity related to the territory of Syria within its postindependence borders—and lessen the importance of both regional (subnational) and transnational links and loyalties. Despite official Arab nationalist rhetoric, the actual Syria-first orientation of the government has never been hidden, and it seems to be generally accepted. Distinctions are made, for instance, between "our Syrian people in the Golan" and the "Palestinian brothers" who must eventually assume responsibility for their own future—notwithstanding Syria's aspirations to a dominant position in its immediate geopolitical environment. Lebanon too, despite Syrian domination over much of Lebanese policy, is neither represented in the public discourse, nor—as far as can be judged from largely impressionistic evidence—commonly perceived as part of the Syrian nation-state, but as an independent country in which Syria may have certain tasks and policy objectives. There is the occasional reference to the "one people," but it is, clearly, *sha'b wahid fi baladayn*—one people in two countries.[17]

While other factors also play a role, Syria's frontline position in the Arab-Israeli conflict has certainly helped a great deal to crystallize this distinctive Syrianness. There is considerable agreement among Syrians that their state is the strongest defender of Arab rights and the principal adversary of Israel, that it is the military power and national stance of Syria that Israel primarily seeks to weaken, and that Syria—the nation-state—is accordingly entitled to exert some influence over its weaker Arab neighbors and their regional policies. Israeli attacks on Lebanon, in contrast, do not cause many Syrians sleepless nights. While Syrians may display solidarity with their Lebanese neighbors, there is no indication that they consider such attacks as directed against their own country or people. The territorial boundary between Syria and Lebanon, it seems, is as much established in the hearts and minds of ordinary Syrians as it is recognized and respected by Israel's fighter pilots.

And while other Arab leaders, notably King Hussein of Jordan and Saddam Hussein of Iraq, have enjoyed at times some popularity among Syrians, Damascus is clearly the *qibla* of politics, even for a dissident Ba'thi nationalist from eastern Syria, or a traditional Druze from the Jabal al-'Arab. The legitimacy of the Syrian nation-state and its institutions, including, prominently, the army, is not today in doubt, and the legitimacy of the state certainly exceeds that of the regime and its individual representatives. Regime legitimacy has known its ups and downs, but what the regime doubtless has managed to gain and maintain is a de facto legitimacy built on the fact that there is no one other than Asad who can claim to represent the country and its people. Whether Syrians adore Asad or strongly dislike him, both perspectives are defined in relation to him and his government's policies rather than anyone else's. And national, or nation-state, pride is generally boosted when Asad, regardless of whether or not he is really popular, insists on meeting U.S. presidents not in Washington, as other Arab and Third World leaders do, but in Damascus or Geneva, thereby demonstrating Syria's regional power and importance.

Resource Generation: The War Dividend

Syria is one of few countries that has been able to combine substantial allocations for defense purposes with a comparatively high level of civilian public expenditure. Rather than being overburdened by its spending on defense, since the October War of 1973 Syria has successfully managed to exploit its strategic, regional location as a means of external resource generation.[18] Syria paid for only a fraction of its armament bill, for example; most of its arms imports were paid for by its Arab allies or financed by Soviet soft loans, the largest part of which post–Soviet Russia probably will have to write off. Only Syria's current military spending, as reflected in official defense budgets, must be covered from domestic sources. Although these expenditures are high—ranging from 30–35 percent of the budget—they cannot be considered simply a wasteful burden. Rather, they represent an investment that permits the regime to maximize returns on the country's location and its strategic posture. Military expenditures, in other words, are an investment in military credibility that earn a strategic rent or war dividend in the form of financial transfers. Syria's regional sponsors only put such resources at the disposal of the regime because of Syria's strategic position and its military credibility, that is, its constant preparation for war. On the basis of a comparison of flows of regional aid to Syria with similar flows to structurally similar Arab states that were not at the same time confrontation states, Syria's total war dividend for the 1970s and 1980s can be estimated at about \$12–13 billion, or some 5–6 percent of the country's GDP.[19]

The buildup of a large security machine and the constant preparation for war has no doubt engendered socioeconomic and political costs—consider the absorption of qualified personnel by military rather than civilian sectors of the economy, or the militarization of public life and political culture. Also Syria has not been spared the distorting effects of rent on economic structures and culture—such as a strong import orientation, the relative neglect of agriculture, the disproportionate growth of distributive sectors and of the bureaucracy, and the spread of a rent-seeking mentality among Syrians.

In making these claims about the regime's use of militarization to maximize strategic rent, I am not suggesting that rent-seeking policies represent a rational long-term strategy informed by cost-benefit calculations on the part of political elites. Nor is it my argument that war preparation was intentionally designed from the outset to serve as a strategy for the generation of strategic rents. Indeed, the Syrian regime viewed the buildup of force and the militarization of society as a political and security need. Yet it rapidly learned that it was able to draw economic benefits from its strategic position and hard-line posture. To the extent that the Syrian leadership was aware of the social costs and economic-opportunity losses militarization and war preparation involved, it may have considered these costs as bearable given their political value. Considering that Syria's strategic rent was not dependent on domestic bargaining, and that it could be used freely for infrastructural development as well as for the expansion of state services and the bureaucracy, it served to increase both the autonomy of the state from its citizenry and its penetration of and hold on society.

PREPARED FOR WAR?

In sum, war preparation in Syria has served as a useful means of regime consolidation, social mobilization, social control, and even economic development. Throughout history, of course, there have been many cases where war preparation or even the creation of international tension have been used to increase the infrastructural power of states, particularly to provide governments with enhanced extractive capabilities and to force or convince domestic oppositions to accept a truce with incumbent regimes. The Syrian case therefore is not particularly extraordinary. Its significance, rather, can be found in how its experience challenges our understanding of the relationship between war preparation and state institutional consolidation. First, while domestic resource extraction certainly has increased over the last two or three decades, there is no clear and direct link between this increase and war preparation, setting aside symbolic acts such as voluntary days of labor.[20] Instead, as I have stressed, resources for war preparation largely were generated regionally and internationally. War preparation provided a substantial rent income that not only spared the government the need to bargain with citizens but enabled it to bind strategic groups to the regime by means of domestic rent distribution.

Second, in contrast to many alternative cases of militaristic popular mobilization and pervasive war preparation, Syria has not actually fought a major war for twenty-five years, during which the nation's extensive militarization has continued at a rate largely impervious to changes in the political arena. My assumption is that, since the end of the 1973 Arab-Israeli war and the Syrian-Israeli disengagement agreement of 1974, Syria sustained its constant war preparation efforts but was not actually prepared in a meaningful sense for the "battle."[21] Preparedness to conduct, let alone begin, a war with Israel was not even the central objective of war preparation. Instead, regime stability and control seem to have been much more pivotal. Evidence for this assumption can be found in the patterns that characterize Syria's buildup and use of its military force, in its economic policy orientation, and in the Syrian leadership's handling of the peace process.

Force Buildup

It is notable, first of all, that the main effort to expand the Syrian armed forces took place after the 1973 war, and that their enormous expansion has not paralleled any increase of violence between Syria and Israel. On the contrary, the Golan Heights have been among the quietest Arab-Israeli front since the disengagement of 1974. Syria has not allowed any infiltration into Israel over this front since 1974. And in Lebanon too, where Syrian troops have been stationed since 1976, Syria has eagerly sought to avoid direct military confrontations with Israel, occasionally even at the risk of losing face.[22] Syria was dragged into the 1982 war in Lebanon against its will and at catastrophic costs for its forces. The war revealed openly what the Syrian leadership probably had been aware of: namely, that Syria was in fact not prepared for a war with Israel and was far from achieving "strategic parity" with its adversary. New arms purchases were definitely needed to make up for the losses, particularly given that, as Israeli analyst Yair Evron put it, Damascus had lost confidence that it could avoid war by adhering to the limits or "red lines" that Israel had itself defined.[23]

From 1974 onward, the Syrian leadership has obviously sought to build military capabilities that would enable it to defend the country and which could be used as an instrument of control and power projection. But it has neither sought war nor actually built a force for sustained warfare. In order to avoid or, if need be, fend off a potential Israeli attack, the Syrian leadership has sought to obtain a credible retaliatory deterrent potential—notably in the form of chemical weapons and medium-range missiles, and also by means of the Soviet-Syrian friendship treaty of 1980 that threatened Soviet involvement should Syria proper come under attack. The positioning of Syrian armed forces also reflects defensive rather than offensive options. Strong fortifications have been built on the Golan front. Tanks have been dug in rather than positioned for attack. And while the army and air force have a reputation of poor maintenance levels—with tanks cannibalized and jets grounded for lack of spare parts—the only well-maintained branch of Syria's armed forces, according to Western military observers, has been its air defense.[24] The dialectics inherent in Syria's desire to avoid the "battle" for which it constantly has been preparing is probably best captured in the doctrine of "strategic parity." While this doctrine demands that Arab confrontation states build up a military capability that balances that of Israel, quantitatively as well as qualitatively, it also entails that war must be avoided as long as parity has not been achieved.

As a rule, active troop engagements undertaken by the Syrian leadership of their own free will have always had the character of internal security operations or regional operation that were intended to serve Syria's regional power projection. Syria's enduring involvement in Lebanon, its limited deployment of troops to Saudi Arabia during the Kuwait crisis and war of 1990–91, and its tank concentration on the Jordanian border in 1980 all fall in this latter category. The conflict with Jordan, moreover, was directly linked to that country's support for opposition to the Syrian regime.

The domestic security function of the Syrian military has never been hidden. Ultimately, of course, regime security cannot be traded off against external security, both being deeply interwoven and interdependent.[25] To the extent that a ranking between the two objectives is nonetheless possible, the Syrian regime certainly places a higher priority on its own security than it does on the security of the country's borders. Accordingly, the armed forces have a strong praetorian element, with the best-equipped troops still concentrated in and around Damascus rather than on the front line.[26]

Economic Orientations

While significant efforts have been made to build up an impressive security machine during the almost three decades that Asad has been in power, Syria has not developed a war economy that would have supported sustained warfare. Its productive structure is not geared toward an economy of war, nor are public or private consumption actually made subject to the preparation of war. Militarization, to use Brzoska's terms, has remained "traditional," restricted to a quantitative expansion of the military sector and to militaristic value orientation and behavior. It has not become "technological" or "industrial," which, among other things, would involve the creation of a military-industrial complex.[27]

The experience of Europe during World War II suggests that the buildup of a war economy, and particularly of an economy that is to support sustained warfare, demands "the earliest and most far-reaching militarization of the economy, i.e., maximum expansion and the largest possible mobilization, beginning in times of peace, of war-economy potential at the expense of peace production."[28]

Two of Syria's neighbors clearly fit this description. Israel and Iraq have both spent considerable efforts on building a war economy, directing the economic structure of their countries toward war production. Both have attempted to achieve a substantial measure of self-sufficiency in arms development and production, to allow them to bear a reduction or temporary halt of foreign military supply without being forced to cease operations. In the Syrian case, however, the picture is different. Some ammunition and light weapons are produced domestically, but on the whole—and this is quite astonishing, given the size of the Syrian forces and its defense budget—Syria's arms industries are negligible, less advanced even than those of Jordan.[29] Syria appears, as Yezid Sayigh puts it, "to have opted for reliance on its one secure source of armament"—that is, the former Soviet Union—"rather than embarking on a costly course of local industrialization."[30] Only since the disintegration of the U.S.S.R. has Syria begun to expand its arms production. Even so, this remains limited to the local assembly of imported parts, such as the reported construction of facilities for the assembly of North Korean and Chinese missiles.[31] Since one can reasonably assume that the Syrian government would have been able to raise Gulf Arab funding for a local defense industry had it actually been willing to establish one (consider the fact that Saudi Arabia and the other Gulf monarchies have extended substantial financial support for the buildup of defense industries in both Egypt and Iraq, two countries that, from a Gulf Arab viewpoint, follow much more ambitious and disquieting regional policies than Syria), one is bound to conclude that the absence of such an industry in Syria is intentional and not due to a lack of resources.[32]

Also, the production profile of both public and private industry is far from that of a war economy. Certainly, some basic public industries such as cement, oil refining, petrochemicals, and iron and steel would be of vital importance in a situation of war. Obviously, however, the main purpose of these industries has been to support the gigantic construction and development program that Syria launched in the mid-1970s. Similar to those of many other Third World and Arab countries that have followed a strategy of import substitution industrialization, Syria's industry is heavily dependent on imported inputs and largely oriented toward the production of consumption goods. Strikingly, no machine tools industry worth mentioning— a centerpiece of any defense-related industrialization—has yet come into existence.[33]

Not only has Syria's productive structure remained largely civilian, but the Syrian government has not actually imposed any belt-tightening on the population for defense purposes. Given that arms purchases, as outlined, were for the greatest part covered by foreign aid, the population has been widely insulated from the costs of military buildup. And the defense budget, representing those military costs that have to be borne domestically, has in fact developed in a procyclical manner; that is, it has been reduced in real terms in times of financial constraints and expanded when budgetary conditions improved. The economic crisis of the 1980s thus caused real cuts to the defense budget; defense expenditures were not a cause of the economic crisis.

Syria and Regional Peace Efforts

Since demonstrating in the October War of 1973 its capability to launch an attack, to fight, and to gain at least a political and psychological victory, the Syrian leadership has been prepared to give international and particularly U.S.-sponsored peace initiatives a chance, and has considered a negotiated solution of the Arab-Israeli conflict a possibility.[34] Syria accepted UN resolutions 242 and 338. It also responded positively to Kissinger's mediations that led to the troop disengagement accord with Israel in 1974, and to the early Middle East initiatives of the Carter administration. The Camp David process, on the other hand, left Syria more vulnerable by neutralizing Egypt. And the position of the first Reagan administration, which the Syrians perceived as extremely hostile toward the Arabs and Syria in particular, led Damascus to adopt a more hard-line posture. Nevertheless, Syria supported the 1982 Fez Declaration, which, by demanding a peaceful solution that would guarantee the security of all regional states, made clear the readiness of the Arab states to come to terms with Israel. Syria's reestablishment of diplomatic ties with Egypt in 1989 indicated Damascus's eventual acceptance of the Egyptian-Israeli peace. And while the Syrian leadership remained highly suspicious of Israeli intentions when the Bush administration ventured to bring about a Middle East peace conference in Madrid in 1991, it nonetheless embraced the American initiative. Damascus realized that one alternative to a peaceful settlement of the conflict—renewed war—would be disastrous, particularly since the collapse of the U.S.S.R. deprived Syria of Soviet diplomatic and military support. Moreover, a second alternative—the perpetuation of the no-war-no-peace situation that had marked Israeli-Syrian relations since 1974—was seen as increasingly difficult to sell in a post–cold war environment.

However, and despite Syria's entering into direct negotiations with Israel, the preferred regional constellation for many among the regime elite remains this no-war-no-peace situation.[35] Such a constellation, as noted, allowed, if not compelled, the regime to prepare for war but at the same time avoided actual warfare and produced a wide range of political and economic benefits. It furthered the regime's nationalist credentials and legitimacy both domestically and in the wider Arab environment. It enhanced Syria's international weight. It secured the inflow of a substantial strategic rent. It did not place at risk the country's infrastructure and other developmental achievements. Nor did it put Syria's armed forces themselves at risk. Given that parity was not achieved and was virtually unattainable, any fullscale war with Israel would almost certainly have resulted in defeat. And in all likelihood, such a defeat would have endangered the regime itself, much as was the case, if with some time lag, after the military catastrophe of 1967.

During the period of serious negotiations between Israel and Syria—that is, from the takeover of the Rabin government in 1992 to the fall of Peres in 1996—Damascus was politically prepared to conclude a peace treaty if its basic condition was met, namely, the full withdrawal of Israel from the Golan. Even after the 1996 change of government in Israel, the Syrian leadership reiterated its preparedness to resume negotiations, on the condition, however, that they would resume from where they had left off earlier that year. Syria's interest in the negotiations, however, was not so much a peace treaty or a quick resolution of the conflict with Israel, as the avoidance of war. Indeed, Syria was not in a hurry to establish what has been dubbed "full peace" in an attempt to express more than a simple termination of belligerency. It needed time to prepare for such a peace and for the economic, technological, intellectual, and political challenges it would entail.[36] Domestically, therefore, even at a time when the Oslo Accords had come into force and Jordan made peace with Israel, the official discourse remained restricted to warnings against normalization with Israel, and the issues that Syria would have to face after a peace treaty were not even up for discussion. The peaceful intentions of Syria were frequently stressed, but those of Israel were doubted and the rhetoric of war preparation was maintained.[37]

Only during the negotiations of 1995 did the Syrian leadership become convinced that the Labor government was indeed prepared to give up all of the occupied Syrian territory under certain conditions. As a result, the Maryland talks from December to March 1996 were much more serious and detailed than all previous negotiations. At that point, it seems, the Syrians decided that peace could and should be ventured upon. "We will be able to negotiate a treaty within one or two months of serious committee work, including security arrangements, the water issue, and borders," commented a high-ranking Syrian military officer in the spring of 1996. "The era of military confrontation is over. Israel is there to stay. And as Israel is making progress in its relations with the Gulf states, with Jordan, and with the Maghreb, should we remain on our own?"[38]

What probably helped the Syrian leadership decide that they should proceed to an agreement with the Israelis—once the territorial condition was fulfilled—were the prospects for Syria as a result of the new Mediterranean policy of the European Union. Syrian-European talks about a so-called partnership agreement similar to those the European Union (EU) had already concluded with Morocco, Tunisia, and Israel, and was about to conclude with Jordan, Egypt, Lebanon, and the Palestinian Authority, began in March 1996. Obviously, Damascus had a strong interest in the funds and the technical assistance offered by the EU to make Syria fit for the establishment of a free-trade relationship with Europe by 2010. More important than the potential rent flows involved, European assistance in reforming the Syrian economy and preparing it for competition in a Euro-Mediterranean free trade zone would also make it easier for Syria to face the challenges of a new regional division of labor, once Israel had been fully integrated into a more open Middle Eastern economic and social space.

The Syrians did expect Shimon Peres to win the elections of May 1996 and to restart negotiations after that.[39] The results, however, were different, and with the election of Benyamin Netanyahu the ball shifted to Israel's court. One might argue that by not doing much to speed up negotiations with the Rabin and Peres governments, Damascus missed a chance. Many Syrians, however, would not agree, stressing instead that it was Peres who had called early elections and broken off negotiations.[40] The change in Israel had the immediate effect on Syria of strengthening the hard-liners. For them, Netanyahu's victory, his rhetoric, and his unpreparedness to continue negotiations where they left off in January 1996 all vindicated their skepticism toward Israel and toward the peace process in general.

At the time of this writing, the Syrian leadership sees no point in renegotiating with the Barak government what they already negotiated with its predecessors. The preponderant attitude in Damascus, therefore, is that Syria should wait. Syrian regime representatives are honest when they confirm that Syria, while prepared to negotiate with Barak, is not in any hurry. As noted earlier, peace with Israel is not considered an urgent need, and there is no reason to expect that Syria will settle for less from Barak than it could expect to achieve with Labor. Unless Netanyahu moves, therefore, we may well anticipate a continuation of the Syrian-Israeli no-war-no-peace situation, even if negotiations of sorts are held.

THE CRITICAL DIMENSIONS OF PEACE

Given that only the perpetuation of that state of no-war-no-peace can guarantee that Syria's political economy of war preparation might be maintained indefinitely, peace is a risky affair in the first place, from the regime's perspective. Regional pacification and normalization will most likely reduce both Syria's strategic rent and its international influence. At the same time, peace with Israel held out few prospects for economic gain.[41] Not only does peace thus threaten to push Syria from its frontline status to a much less comfortable backyard position, it is also likely to destabilize Syria's domestic political-economic arrangements.

In not a few historical cases, war and war preparation, while enhancing the infrastructural capacities and increasing a government's access to resources, have at the same time reduced the despotic powers of a regime; that is, they have forced the regime to bargain with societal actors and thereby cede or share some discretion over policy making.[42] The Syrian case appears to offer a contrasting picture. With the end of the Arab-Israeli conflict in sight, and with no other significant conflict likely to replace it, the Syrian regime may have to rely more heavily on domestic resources than on diminishing streams of strategic rents. It may therefore be subject to more extensive domestic political bargaining during the transition to peace than it ever was during times of war preparation and militarization. And as this suggests, such a transition may well call into question the legitimacy of militarization and authoritarian rule. One possible result, therefore, of a decline in both the political and the economic resources that have resulted from militarization could be the reappearance of open political conflicts in which the regime, if not the state itself, could lose capacity and perhaps become seriously destabilized.

In the course of a cautious economic reform and liberalization program, implemented gradually since about 1985, the regime has in fact already relaxed its hold over the economy. Foreign trade, in particular, as well as agriculture and industry have become less subject to government intervention, and the private sector has grown remarkably. Recognizing their increased economic role, the regime has even co-opted some representatives of the business class into the formal decision-making structures of the state. Liberalization measures have, so far, remained controlled, subject to the regime's own rather than the business class' agenda, and below the threshold of anything that could be called democratization. However, given that the contribution of the private sector to tax income, foreign exchange, employment, private income, and goods for local consumption will continue to increase, while other public and foreign sources of revenue are likely to stagnate or decline, one can reasonably expect that those structures that today allow a limited participation of private sector interests in economic policy decisions will be expanded and may even permit societal actors some discretion over the reform and policy agendas. As long as Asad remains at the helm, such piecemeal political reforms are unlikely to threaten regime control. Even so, they may gradually create space for a clearer articulation of contending economic and sociopolitical interests within the political-institutional frame of the system, and they may also prefigure the institutional edifice of a post-Asad Syria.

Regional peace could thereby serve as a critical catalyst, stimulating a gradual transition to a less authoritarian form of government. With regional peace in the air, it is noticeable that Syrians, privately at least, have started to question the future of the security state. Many expect political rather than economic opportunities from a settlement of the Arab-Israeli conflict in the short-term, hoping that peace will bring about a reduction of the political power of the security apparatus, a restoration of respect for the law, an increase in government accountability, and a broadening of public space not subject to tight government scrutiny.[43] Such expectations of declining military and security influence over government and society may still exceed reality, but they reflect the delegitimation threatening the Middle Eastern security state, which Syria so thoroughly represents, once a credible threat and the credibility of war preparation are gone.

There are ample reasons to expect that the state in Syria in the post-Asad period will be weaker than it has become under Asad's rule. Both his skillful leadership and the external threat that he has been able to employ in his state- and regime-building project will most probably be lacking. And the state, as I have indicated, will have to lean more heavily on private-sector resources. Such a weakening of state power will almost certainly open up space for society. Political and social conflicts could then more openly be tabled and negotiated; the political leadership would lose its prerogative of defining the public good and the interests of society; and new parties and pressure groups could come into being.

Such a weakening of state power vis-à-vis society need not, as is sometimes claimed, lead to an implosion of state structures or a disintegration of the state.[44] Regional peace will come in doses and over time, thereby allowing domestic actors to adapt. Picard points out that in a militarized regime like the Syrian, peacemaking will demand some sort of symbolic or economic compensation for the military.[45] This is indeed so. The military itself is likely to play an active role in the technical negotiations preceding a final agreement and, therefore, to consider such an agreement their own achievement. The chief of staff and two of his aides have already been involved in talks with the Israelis, and it is unlikely that security arrangements can be agreed upon without the military's blessing.

The military is also likely to remain the strongest corporate actor on the scene for some time to come, and one should not expect that a largely militaristic political culture will simply dissolve. Both Syria's historical experience and the present structure of authority suggest that a Turkish-style military democracy is much more likely to emerge in the post-Asad period than a full-fledged liberal democracy. While the military elite may well leave day-to-day politics to a civilian government, it would probably step in if such a government tried to undermine its entrenched interests or if government policies threatened to provoke unmanageable social unrest. In contrast to the 1950s and 1960s, however, there is no longer a highly politicized officer corps with a sociopolitical mission that would want to topple existing socioeconomic structures. Today, Syria's military can be expected to guard these structures that, on the whole, are also much to the liking of the local bourgeoisie.

No future Syrian government, on the other hand, would likely have an interest in severely reducing the size of the armed forces or the military budget. Even after an eventual peace treaty with Israel, the former main contenders of the Arab-Israeli conflict will remain on their guard. Other conflicts in the region may erupt or reerupt, and the Gulf Arab states may have a strong interest in Syria's maintaining a military force that could, if need be, help to balance Iraq. The maintenance of a credible force could therefore still be deemed necessary and could also generate some strategic rent—if less than the country has become used to during the last decades of the Arab-Israeli conflict.

There is, above all, a common interest on the part of all existing or emerging domestic power centers—the security apparatus, the state bureaucracy and the public sector bureaucracy, the bourgeoisie, the religious establishment—to maintain both Syria's internal stability and, as far as possible, its regional position. Hardly anyone would like to relive the near-civil-war situation of the late 1970s and early 1980s or suffer through the external vulnerability that Syria experienced during the 1940s and 1950s. Also, while there is much Islamic conservatism today, there seems to be no infrastructure for another violent Islamist uprising.[46] Given that the state has monopolized the means of organized violence and would hardly hesitate to use them again against any movement or group challenging its authority, a serious breakdown of domestic stability would probably have to begin with a split within the security apparatus. One cannot, in fact, rule out the possibility that two or more factions within the army of *mukhabarat* may face each other in a contest for power once the succession question arises. The scenario of a disintegration of the security apparatus is, however, not very likely. Syria may have a history of military coups and coup attempts, but it doesn't have a tradition of civil war or of different parts of the army fighting each other. The corporate spirit within the army is probably too strong for the latter.

In the last couple of years, therefore, leaders from various sociopolitical groups—representatives of the security apparatus and representatives of the Sunni bourgeoisie in particular—have been in contact in order to prepare what they call a "soft landing." The aim is to prevent the occasion of the president's death from sparking individual acts of revenge or sectarian violence against the Alawites, the Shi'ite sect to which Asad and most top-level military and security officers belong. In addition, it is understood that the private wealth of leading military officers will not be touched. In return, high Alawi officers have indicated that they will not necessarily insist that Asad's successor be an Alawi.

Thus, while the legitimacy of the present security state seems likely to disappear, and while the rationalities of regime security and political control that have so far largely determined government politics may gradually be replaced by economic rationalities, it is unlikely that any of Syria's domestic political forces would want to do away with the degree of stateness and national integration that the years of war preparation have helped to achieve. With a broader social base, these achievements could well be maintained even without the threat of, and preparation for, war.

NOTES

1. On the concept and operationalization of state strength see Migdal, *Strong Societies and Weak States: State-Society Relations and State Capabilities in the Third World;* I. William Zartman, "State-Building and the Military in Arab Africa," pp. 239–57.

2. On the corporatization of society see Perthes, *The Political Economy of Syria under Asad,* pp. 170–80.

3. The traditional reading of Syria's state-building process generally omits the regional situation and preparation for war, focusing instead on the attempts of the Ba'thist leadership to modernize political and class structures. See in particular Hinnebusch, "State Formation in a Fragmented Society," pp. 177–97; and Hinnebusch, *Authoritarian Power and State Formation in Ba'thist Syria: Army, Party and Peasant.* Other authors who deal with Syria's war preparation efforts tend to explain them in the context of a regional power struggle and Israel's occupation of Syrian lands. See Seale, *Asad of Syria: The Struggle for the Middle East.* While these views cannot be ignored, I want to emphasize the functionality of an atmosphere of war and war preparation for the particular form of state building Syria experienced under Asad. From a neorealist perspective, the functionality of war preparation for state building is explained in terms of regional power politics and, to cite one insightful example, in terms of a strategic dialogue between the main contenders in the region. Evron, *War and Intervention in Lebanon. The Israeli-Syrian Deterrence Dialogue.* See also Ma'oz, *Syria and Israel: From War to Peacemaking.* Less persuasive is the attempt to depict Syria's efforts to build up military strength as an element of an expansionist tendency driven by a Greater-Syria ideology. See Pipes, *Greater Syria: The History of an Ambition.* The more realist accounts of Syrian defense and war policies (Evron, Ma'oz) have shown that, unlike in Iraq, for instance, any ideological or revisionist ambitions Syrian leaders might have harbored have not driven them into military adventurism.

4. Barnett, *Confronting the Costs of War: Military Power, State, and Society in Egypt and Israel,* defines war preparation, in this sense, as "the government's mobilization of men, money, and material resources for external security" (p. ix). Militarization, according to Michael Brzoska, in "Militarisierung als analytisches Konzept," refers to a

quantitative expansion of the military and security apparatus and the transfer of specifically military values and forms of behavior to basically all sectors of society

5. A prominent example is the preamble of the Charter of the Progressive National Front: "The liberation of the Arab territories occupied after 5 June 1967 is the goal of this stage of the struggle of our nation. It stands in front of all other goals of this stage. In the light of this lofty goal, we have to develop our economic, social, cultural, political, and military plans such as to mobilize all human and material forces and potentials, to organize the national unity of the popular masses, and to strengthen and steadfasten the domestic front." The charter was published in *Al-Thawra,* 8 March 1972.

6. Sources differ on these figures, partly due to varying calculations of foreign exchange rates. My figures, therefore, are approximations. Data on military personnel as a percentage of Syria's population are drawn from U.S. Arms Control and Disarmament Agency, *World Military Expenditures and Arms Transfers* (Washington, D.C., various years). Figures on defense expenditures are taken from Syrian Arab Republic, Central Bureau of Statistics, *Statistical Abstract* (Damascus, various years), and International Institute for Strategic Studies, *The Military Balance* (London: Brassey's, various years).

7. Cf., e.g., Arab Socialist Ba'th Party (hereafter ASBP), National Command, *Nidal Hizb al-Ba'th al-'arabi al- ishtiraki* (The struggle of the Arab Socialist Ba'th Party) (Damascus: ASBP, 1978), p. 114.

8. Cf., e.g., President Asad's speech to the Revolutionary Youth Organization, 8 March 1990, *Tishrin,* 9 March 1990.

9. Cf., e.g., Hafiz al-Asad's policy declaration of 16 November 1970, the day he accomplished his takeover, documented in ASBP, *Nidal Hizb al-Ba'th,* p. 119; Yusuf Murish, *Al-Jabha al-wataniyya al-taqadummiyya wa-l-ta'addudiyya fi al-Qutr al-'arabi al-suri* (The Progressive National Front and political pluralism in the Syrian Arab region) (Damascus: Dar al-Na'ama, 1993), pp. 122 ff.

10. On the social fabric of Syria, cf. Perthes, *The Political Economy of Syria under Asad,* pp. 80–132.

11. These militias and the permanent army reserve add up to about the same number as the standing military force.

12. Cf. Amal Muhammad Mu'ati, "Al-Tarbiyya wa-l-Taghayyurat al-ijtima'iyya fi al-Qutr al-'arabi al-suri" (Education and social change in the Syrian Arab region), *Al-Iqtisad,* no. 319 (August 1990): 19–28.

13. On spectacles and the regime's personality cult see Lisa Wedeen, *Ambiguities of Domination: Politics, Rhetoric, and Symbols in Contemporary Syria.*

14. Cf. Picard, "State and Society in the Arab World: Towards a New Role for the Security Services?" p. 261.

15. See Asad's interview on U.S. television, 1 October 1993, British Broadcasting Corporation, *Summary of World Broadcasts* (SWB), ME/1811, 6 October 1993.

16. See, for instance, Hafiz al-Asad's speech to trade unionists, 16 November 1986, *Al-Ba'th,* 17 November 1986.

17. See Volker Perthes, "Scénarios syriens: Processes de paix, changements internes et relations avec le Liban," pp. 37–56.

18. The following sections draws largely on my "From War Dividend to Peace Dividend? Syrian Options in a New Regional Environment," pp. 277–92.

19. See Perthes, "From War Dividend to Peace Dividend?" and "Kriegsdividende und Friedensrisiken: Überlegungen zu Rente und Politik in Syrien," pp. 413–24.

20. According to Syrian and World Bank data—which, however, cannot in this context be expected to offer more than general indicators—budgeted government expenditures as a percentage of GDP increased from some 23 percent in 1963 to 40–50 percent or more in the 1970s and early 1980s. Due to careful but consequential liberalization efforts since 1985, they decreased again to some 25 percent by the early 1990s. In the same period, the ratio of direct to indirect taxes (i.e., taxes on capital and wages in contrast to levies on consumption, service charges, and customs duties) has changed in favor of direct taxes, which indicates a more intrusive and efficient form of domestic resource extraction. For example, direct taxes accounted for only 28 percent of the 1971 budget but 65 percent of the 1995 budget. See Syrian Arab Republic, Central Bureau of Statistics, *Statistical Abstract, 1971* (Damascus: Syrian Arab Republic, Central Bureau of Statistics, 1972), pp. 294–95; and *Statistical Abstract 1995* (Damascus: Syrian Arab Republic, Central Bureau of Statistics, 1996), pp. 440–41. For budgets as a percentage of GDP, see World Bank, *World Development Report* (Washington: World Bank, various years).

21. Unlike its Egyptian counterpart, the Syrian leadership has never openly stated that the 1973 war had limited objectives, namely to bring movement into the Arab-Israeli stalemate and thereby prepare a political solution, and to boost the domestic and Arab legitimacy of the respective new regime. We can assume however, that Sadat's and Asad's motives in leading the war were quite similar—more so than the latter liked to acknowledge.

22. Consider, for instance, that during "Operation Accountability" of July 1993, Israeli forces attacked Syrian positions in the Beqaa, wounding and killing several Syrian soldiers, without provoking more than a verbal condemnation from Damascus. Syrian restraint, while positively acknowledged internationally, was harmful to its standing in Lebanon, where it provided grist for the mills of those who had always claimed that Syrian troops were certainly not in the country to defend it.

23. Evron, *War and Intervention in Lebanon*, p. 192.

24. This is not to suggest that Syria is ruled by a pacific regime, or that Syria could not, in a desperate situation, seek to launch a surprise attack against Israeli positions. In fact, it is impossible to know what strategic options the Syrian leadership discussed for worst-case scenarios, such as strong international pressure and/or internal unrest. Any provocative or aggressive posture likely to start a war, however, would be inconsistent with the practice the Syrian government has been following for the past twenty-five years, and with the strategic doctrine that this practice as well as the Syrian force structure reveal—namely, an orientation toward deterrence and defense. See Evron, *War and Intervention in Lebanon;* Michael J. Eisenstadt, "Syria's Strategic Weapons," *Jane's Intelligence Review* 5 (April 1993): pp. 168–73.

25. See Migdal, *Strong Societies and Weak States*, p. 24.

26. According to observers, it is notable, for instance, that the few modern T-80 tanks the Syrian army possess are all in the service of units charged with the protection of the regime, such as the presidential Republican Guard.

27. See Brzoska, "Militarisierung als analytisches Konzept."

28. Eichholtz, *Geschichte der deutschen Kriegswirtschaft 1939–1945*, p. 1:19.

29. See Yezid Sayigh, *Arab Military Industry: Capability, Performance, and Impact*, pp. 144 ff.

30. Ibid., p. 145.

31. See Eisenstadt, "Syria's Strategic Weapons."

32. Syria's Ministry of Defense actually owns two of the country's largest companies: the Military Construction Establishment and the Military Housing Establishment. The two companies, both founded under Asad's rule, in 1972 and 1975, respectively, employ almost 10 percent of all civilian government employees. The majority of their construction and engineering work, however, is civilian in nature or even carried out on behalf of civilian clients.

33. The centrality of a machine tools sector for the buildup of a military-industrial basis has become clearly evident in the Iraqi case. See Timmerman, *The Death Lobby: How the West Armed Iraq*. The failure to establish a strong machine tool industry is a major point of criticism in critical accounts by Syrian academics of their country's path of industrialization. See in particular Hilan, *Al-Thaqafa wa-l-Tanmiya al-iqtisadiyya fi Suriya wa-l-Buldan al-mukhallafa*(Culture and economic developments in Syria and the countries left behind).

34. See Ma'oz, *Syria and Israel: From War to Peacemaking?*

35. Some, even among the regime elite, have a different understanding of things and have accepted that Syria, eventually, needs peace. See Perthes, "Scenarios syriens," pp. 37–56.

36. See Perthes, *Scenarios for Syria: Socio-Economic and Political Choices*.

37. See for instance the statements of Hafiz al-Asad and the Syrian chief of staff, Hikmat al-Shihabi, on the occasion of "Army day," 1 August 1994, in BBC SWB ME/2063, 2 August 1994.

38. Personal communication, Damascus, 1996.

39. This assessment was shared by Israel's chief negotiator at the Maryland talks. See Savir, *The Process: 1,100 Days that Changed the Middle East*, pp. 282 ff.

40. See the interview with Syria's ambassador to Washington, Moualem, "Fresh Light on the Syrian-Israeli Peace Negotiations," pp. 81–94.

41. International agencies expect a peace dividend for the region mainly through three channels: by means of intraregional trade and cooperation in a new Middle East that would integrate Israel; by means of investments from regional and international sources; and through reduced military expenditure and the release of revenues for development purposes. While it is generally doubtful that any substantial reduction of defense expenditure will occur either in Syria or Israel in the short run, the opportunities to attract foreign investment and to benefit from intraregional trade are markedly more limited for Syria than for its neighbors. See Perthes, "From War Dividend to Peace Dividend?"

42. The "despotic power" of a regime denotes the "range of action" that it "is empowered to undertake without . . . negotiations with civil society." Mann, "The Autonomous Power of the State: Its Origins, Mechanisms, and Results," p. 113. World War I is the classic European case. Consider, for instance, the British government's granting of universal suffrage parallel to the introduction of conscription, or the incorporation by the German government of trade union representatives into the statist system of raw material and production controls.

43. See, for instance, Hilan, "The Effects on Economic Development in Syria of a Just and Long-Lasting Peace," pp. 74 ff.

44. The disintegration thesis is expressed most prominently by Pipes, "Syrie: L'après-Assad," pp. 97–110.

45. Picard, "La Syrie et le processus de paix," pp. 56–69.

46. For a detailed account the best documented work on the Syrian opposition thus far is Lobmeyer, *Opposition und Widerstand im ba'thistischen Syrien.*

6

Changing Boundaries and Social Crisis
Israel and the 1967 War

Joel S. Migdal

FROM DOOM TO BOOM

The sudden end of the June 1967 war brought not only unrestrained rejoicing in Israel but, just as palpably, a collective sigh of relief. What Israelis had called the "waiting period," between Egypt's blockade of the Straits of Tiran on May 22 and the beginning of the war on June 5, had been a time of unbearable tension in the country. Israelis saw the closing of the straits as a tripwire for war and waited those fourteen days with a sense of impending doom.[1] This was a moment, as Itzhak Galnoor recounted, of "public confusion, lack of confidence in the political leadership and some threats of military insubordination."[2]

The dark warnings of Arab leaders about what would happen to Israel if their forces were to triumph had been all too explicit. Only a week before the outbreak of fighting, Egypt's president, Gamal Abdel Nasser, had threatened that "this will be a total war. Our basic aim is the destruction of Israel." And the head of the Palestine Liberation Organization, Ahmed Shukairy, had added to the sense of looming tragedy, "Those native-born Israelis who survive can remain in Palestine. But I estimate that none of them will survive."[3]

I recall receiving a letter from Israel in May of that year describing a sense of resignation and foreboding on the part of the writer and her fellow kibbutz members. She wrote of people going about their daily chores with their heads hanging; a sense of fatalism gripped Israel's Jews. But the sudden and complete military victory in June stood Israelis' emotions on their head. The war itself was a fleeting, almost surreal, interlude. Bill Stevenson, a veteran British war correspondent, recounted how "the clocks stopped in Israel on Monday, June 5, 1967, and they started again a week later."[4]

The drastic mood swing began in the last couple of days of the war. On June 9, the fifth day, one Israeli woman wrote of "the two weeks of dreadful tension when all of us faced what we thought might, quite literally, be extermination, and the death of the young State, and our own total abandonment by the world. And then, the four breathless, incredible days and heights of victory."[5] Indeed, that sense of being collectively plucked from the precipice at the last possible moment—a feeling of miraculous, redemptive deliverance shared by religious and secular Jews alike—inaugurated a period in which Israelis seemed all but oblivious to the postwar currents sweeping them up. Like a death-row convict celebrating wildly after having been granted a pardon minutes before execution, Israelis followed the Six-Day War with a six-year spree that veiled many of the domestic difficulties caused or exacerbated by the war.

These six years, which ended with the October 1973 war, or what Israelis call the Yom Kippur War, both followed and preceded sharp economic downturns in the country. But that interwar period wiped out thoughts of recession and unemployment. Per capita income grew at among the highest rates in the world, at 8.5 percent a year, and personal consumption reflected the spreelike atmosphere, ballooning ominously at a rate of about 12 percent annually. Collectively, Israelis were recklessly living beyond their means.

Profound social and political difficulties simmered beneath the surface of this economic explosion, involving an increasingly beleaguered state organization and its relations with the Israeli population. Indeed, the central dynamics of state-society relations came under severe strain in the generation following the 1967 war.[6] I will underscore three of the central problems: First, at a time of continuing tension in the Middle East—so high that it prompted a nuclear standoff between the superpowers in 1973—the Israeli state found itself with diminishing capabilities to govern its own society effectively. Second, deep and abiding divisions about what the character of Israeli society should be rent both political and social life. And, finally, the society's model of social integration came to be seen as a failure, resulting in more intense and open social conflict.

Why did such fundamental problems afflict the state, society, and state-society relations in the wake of Israel's greatest military triumph? In this chapter, I will argue that the boundary changes that the war effected unglued important social and political relationships. Three core ideas related to boundary changes will be developed:

1. *Upsetting understandings of institutional reach.* The stability that social and political institutions bring to everyday life depends upon the

population's understanding of their reach. Boundary changes bring into question the reach of those institutions and, in so doing, lead to crises in society's central dynamics.

2. *Challenging the principle of universalist exclusion.* Reconstituted boundaries of the territory governed by the state open to question the established principles about the character of the state and its relationship to its population. In Israel, the civic principles of the pre-1967 period had the paradoxical effect of using the principle of universal citizenship as a method of exclusion, especially for Jews of Middle East background. The boundary changes opened the way for a contending ethnonational set of principles, which these Jews found much more inclusive.

3. *Undoing labor segmentation and social fragmentation.* Territorial boundary changes can have a deep impact on social boundaries. In Israel, the new borders changed the character of the labor market, opening the door to new types of social and physical mobility and undoing the old social boundaries that had been marked by social fragmentation and segmentation. For society, the change in social boundaries led to heightened tensions; for the state, the change resulted in new, increased demands on it without a corresponding growth in capacity to deal with those demands.

From a comparative perspective, the timing of this volume, the beginning of a new century, is opportune for revisiting the issue of the effect of the 1967 war through its transformation of boundaries. After World War II, the cold war had imposed an extraordinary stability on states' boundaries. Significant border changes came only with the dismantling of the colonial empires, and, even there, many new states' boundaries remained the same as when the territory had been ruled by Europeans. One would be hard-pressed to name more than a handful of cases in which state boundaries changed or states disappeared entirely during the more than forty years of the cold war.

But its end brought a host of boundary changes in a short period, including the disintegration of the Soviet Union itself, Yugoslavia, Czechoslovakia, and Ethiopia. As one of the few cases of state boundary changes in the decades leading up to the 1990s, Israel and the 1967 war offer some important insights into the process of how border changes affect labor markets, state-society relations, and ethnic relations.

In the following section, I will look first at the social dynamics that undergirded Israel's state and society in the two decades leading up to the Six-Day War. I will then analyze how the crisis transformed those dynamics. Finally, I will tie the crises in state, society, and state-society relations to the 1967 war's transformation of state boundaries.

STATE AND SOCIETY BEFORE THE WAR

Three key features had marked pre-1967 Israeli society: the important and growing role of the state in people's daily lives; increasing consensus among Israel's Jews about the extent and character of the state; and a focus on societal integration, at least among the more than 90 percent of the citizenry who were Jews. But, in the wake of the war that had so united this population, each of these cornerstones began to show worrisome fissures. Before analyzing how border changes that resulted from the war affected these three elements, I will survey the three.

Israel's first prime minister, who dominated political life for nearly half a century, worked single-mindedly from the moment of the state's founding in 1948 to make the state the dominant and central institution in people's lives. Through an orientation that he called *mamlahtiyut* (which can be translated loosely as *statism*), David Ben-Gurion was determined to bring about a revolution in Jewish society.[7] His first target was the abiding wariness of nationalism that had marked Jewish writings and thought since the Enlightenment.[8] And, what was even more important, he battled the very institutions that he and others had built in the generation before independence. His own political party, Mapai, and the powerful labor federation that he had headed, the Histadrut, along with numerous other organizations had played key roles in creating a viable Jewish presence in Palestine during the thirty years of British rule. While Ben-Gurion certainly saw an important role for them in the period of statehood, he feared their divisive, even sectarian, tendencies. His aim was to shift the ability to allocate key resources in the society from the political parties, the Histadrut, and the once-powerful Jewish Agency (another organization he had headed) to the bureaucracy of the new state and thereby build a political center that would gain the loyalty and obedience of the population.

In its first two decades, the success of the new state in centralizing the allocation of key resources and in overcoming the long-standing distrust of nationalism among Jews was truly impressive. It quickly became the central focus of people's lives, engendering not only endless complaining about its oversized and often unresponsive bureaucracy but also fierce loyalty that had a religious-like fervor.[9] Tension continued to fester between the institutions that had predated the state and Ben-Gurion, and by no means did their leaders lose every battle with him. Health insurance, for example, remained outside the state's direct control. But the swelling state bureaucracy assumed responsibility for education, welfare, labor exchanges, and more. Centralization brought increased state capabilities—from the battlefield to the control of the economy to the regulation of everyday social relations. An import-substitution economic strategy also heightened the activity of the state in the economy. All in all, the state organization grew to alarming proportions and insinuated itself into the daily lives of everyone living within the crazy-quilt boundaries Israel ended up with after the 1948 war.

Beyond the growing role of the state organization, a second feature of pre-1967 Israeli life was a developing consensus about the nature of that state. Prior to 1948, the Zionist political institutions were understood by Jews and non-Jews alike to have two highly sectarian qualities to them. First, those organizations represented and advocated for the Jews, against the claims of Palestine's Arabs and, sometimes, against those of the colonial British rulers. Second, sectarianism also marked the relations among the Jewish political institutions. There was a unified framework incorporating the Jewish groups, but inclusion in it was voluntary. At various moments, key groups simply dropped out. And, of those that remained inside, representing most of the Jews, each had significant autonomy to pursue its own ends.[10] S. N. Eisenstadt, Israel's leading sociologist, labeled the weak framework consociational, one in which the framework served largely as a mediating forum among groups rather than one that set the tone for all political debate.

Once an independent state existed, important changes occurred in people's thinking about political institutions. The old mediating framework's "place was taken by an ideology of national social ethos articulated within a constitutional democratic-pluralistic State, based on universalistic premisses, universalistic citizenship and the access of all citizens to the major frameworks of the State."[11] This quotation from Eisenstadt points to a fundamental element in the character of the state, as well as an underlying tension. The change was critical, altering the political framework from a sectarian one claiming to speak for a people or nation—the Jews of Palestine, but not others in the country—to one asserting the right to represent all peoples within its boundaries. Both Jews and Arabs fell under the new state's "universalistic premisses [and] universalistic citizenship." Eisenstadt's reference to "the access of all citizens to the major frameworks of the State" meant that the new political entity, at least in theory, provided equal rights to non-Jews and equal entrée to the administrative services of the state. Its "universalistic principles," in the words of Erik Cohen, "would govern relations between all citizens."[12]

To put the matter a bit differently, the state (unlike the prestate political institutions) was constituted so as to interact with a civil society—a population united by its civic ties in which all held the key role of citizen—not simply the Jews in society.[13] The declaration of independence, the Basic Laws that were to be the backbone of an as-yet-unwritten constitution, the judiciary, and many other key state institutions were created on the basis of an imagined society made up of equal citizens. While the construction of the state was geared to such a civil society, no such society bound through civic ties yet existed. Further complicating the picture was the fact that political leaders also defined the state as Jewish (what Eisenstadt obliquely referred to as a national social ethos), which put some of civil society—the Arabs—at a disadvantage. I will come back to this tension because it is so central to the internal dynamics of Israel, especially after the 1967 war. It is worth noting here that Arabs faced a kind of Alice-in-Wonderland existence: a set of laws and institutions designed to give them, like everybody else, equality and day-to-day practices that discriminated against them at every turn.

Before the war, however, this inconsistency tended to be somewhat muted. A combination of the terrible dislocation of Palestine's Arab community during the 1947–48 war and the effects of the state's military rule of the Arab population until 1966 dampened Arab demand for equal access to the state's services and agencies.[14] The promotion of a fragmented labor market in which the state prohibited Arab movement beyond their own localities reinforced the low profile of Arab citizens. In short, state policies and the trauma of 1948 veiled the dissonance that Arabs faced every day.

In what can only be understood as a supreme paradox, these conditions, which created the invisible Arab as a clearly less privileged citizen, allowed state leaders to proceed in building the civic orientation of the state, one whose institutions were geared to be universal rather than in the service of a particular group. In practical terms that meant the establishment of the rule of law, with its implied universality for all groups; the development of strong legal institutions, most notably the Supreme Court; and the emergence of other key agencies designed to protect the citizenry, including the offices of the attorney general, state comptroller, and ombudsman. The character of the state, even with the encouragement of a markedly Jewish ethos or civil religion and even with the repression and strong control of the Arab population, was being forged in the years before the 1967 war with strong universal components, premised on the development of a society forged by civic ties. Indeed, evidence mounted that even many of the country's Arab citizens related positively to the civic dimensions put forth by the state.[15] No more important sign for the development of a universalistic state was evident than the granting in 1950 "of Israeli citizenship to the country's Arab residents [which] constituted a renunciation of the ethnonational principle."[16]

Consensus developed not only about the character of the state but on the extent of its reach. From 1937, when the British tabled a plan to partition Palestine between the Arabs and the Jews, Zionists had engaged in a loud debate about whether or not to compromise by taking only a portion of the promised Palestine in exchange for political independence in that truncated territory.[17] Once independence was achieved, however, this debate quickly faded. Shlomo Avineri, the renowned political philosopher and onetime director-general of Israel's Foreign Ministry, noted a new implicit understanding about what the character of the state should be:

> One issue which was central to the political debate within the Jewish Yishuv (community) in the late 1930s and the 1940s—the debate about partition—was over. The armistice lines of 1949 were considered by practically all Israelis as the realistic definite borders of Israel. If, prior to 5 June 1967, the Arab countries had been ready to sign a peace agreement with Israel on the basis of the existing frontiers, there would have been an overwhelming Israeli consensus in favour of accepting this, perceiving this Arab readiness as a major concession and a tremendous achievement for Israel. With very few exceptions on the lunatic fringe of Israeli politics, there was no irredentist call in Israel during the period of 1949–1967, advocating an Israeli initiative to recapture Judea and Samaria, or even the Old City of Jerusalem. This post-1948 consensus was visible across the spectrum of Israeli politics.[18]

Avineri's point is a very important one. The haphazard and irrational borders with which Israel was left after 1948 took on a kind of sanctity of their own. They imparted a stability to state and society. The state molded its reach to them and people simply assumed that those arbitrary lines would permanently define the extent of Israeli society. Borders, then, affect both institutional development (by defining the limits of an institution's reach) and public culture (by providing the frame for a sense of we-ness, or common identity—what it meant to be an Israeli).

Finally, besides the growing role of the state and the developing consensus on its nature and territorial reach, a third mark of the pre-1967 period was an emphasis on social integration among Jews. The huge influx of Jews immediately after the 1948 war posed serious challenges for both state and society. Not only did the country's Jewish population triple in the three years after Israel's founding, but the majority of the new Jews were from the Middle East, culturally distinct from the dominant groups that had migrated earlier from eastern Europe. The state's response was an attempt to assimilate the new Jews into the dominant eastern European culture through an ideology of *mizug galuyot,* or what we might call the melting pot.

While this model had worked relatively well in absorbing early waves of immigrants during the prestate period, it ran into serious bumps in the 1950s. The proportion of immigrants was now extremely high, and the Middle Eastern Jews came much less prepared or willing to take on many of the values and symbols of the dominant groups.[19] Critics have emphasized the shunting of Middle Eastern Jews into low-paying, low status jobs—often in remote parts of the country with very little infrastructure. The immigrants quickly became the blue-collar class in a labor market that gave them limited opportunities for physical or social mobility. Here, the boundaries did not simply divide "us" from "them"; they provided the bases for the distribution of people in society, including their centrality or peripherality. New immigrants were relegated to the outer reaches of the frame. Just as the borders provided the space within which imagined civic equality would develop, the border also framed the scaffolding for real social and economic inequality that emerged.

In terms of income per person, by 1967 families originating from Africa and Asia (mostly the Middle East and Arab North Africa) had a bit less than 50 percent of the income of their counterparts of European origins.[20] Even after taking into account factors such as length of residence in the country, education, and age, an "ethnic gap" in income of 5–15 percent persisted.[21] Erik Cohen added a cultural dimension to the problem of economic inequality: "Oriental culture, in which at least some of the Oriental communities [African and Asian, mostly Middle Eastern] had been deeply steeped, has made no perceptible imprint on Israel's cultural life. Oriental civilization was generally considered 'backward' or 'Levantine,' and Oriental immigrants were asked to shed their way of life as quickly as possible."[22]

These criticisms and gaps notwithstanding, the period before the 1967 war "was marked by the relative success in the absorption of immigrants. . . . A society made up of numerous, highly varied cultures underwent a rapid and sometimes painful process of consolidation."[23] This point is not made in order to minimize the problems. Rather, the period before 1967 is remarkable for the emphasis on integration in public, academic, and government discourse, even as real, serious problems abounded. Indications existed of seething anger and deep resentment on the part of many immigrants—against Ashkenazim, old-timers, the Histadrut, and the Mapai (the Labor Party). But the cauldron, while bubbling, rarely boiled over. Practically all Jewish groups were absorbed into almost all state and civic institutions (as followers and receivers of services rather than leaders), including schools and the military. Immigrants and old-timers alike participated in and promoted the new civil religion—only Arab citizens were largely excluded from that.

Israeli institutions and civic culture held out the promise of upward mobility for new immigrants. Indeed, as one sociological study gathering data on mobility and opportunity put it, "Israel has developed into an extraordinarily meritocratic society. . . . It is a country that both beckons to potential immigrants and integrates them into the mainstream of social life."[24] After 1967, as we shall see, serious protests arose against this formulation. Critics claimed that the meritocracy demanded accepting the dominant European Jews' rules of the game, especially the primacy of education, while Middle Eastern Jews had inferior educational opportunities and less access to education. But before the war, the emphasis was much more on integration into the Israeli institutions and civic culture than on a critique of them.

WAR AND THE CRISIS IN SOCIAL DYNAMICS

The years following the Six-Day War brought unrestrained euphoria to Israel. But in a period of heady economic growth and consumption, and of a self-image as a regional powerhouse, Israeli state and society demonstrated clear signs of stress. The three processes that we have discussed—the state's increasing centrality, the emerging social agreement about its character and reach, and the emphasis on social integration of Jews into the new Israeli society and culture—all developed in the context of new, fixed boundaries. When the 1967 war suddenly changed those boundaries, these three processes changed dramatically. Military, economic, and political shocks that came a bit later—the 1973 war and the long period of economic stagnation in its wake, as well as the 1977 defeat of the Labor Party (formerly Mapai), which in one form or another had dominated politics for half a century—exposed and exacerbated social dynamics stemming from the 1967 war.

The State's Diminishing Centrality

The Israeli state, so domineering in the first two decades after Independence, suffered surprising blows after the 1967 war, both to its centrality in society and its capacity to govern. It is difficult to disentangle the issue of state centrality and capacity from Ben-Gurion's resignation in 1963 and from the once-dominant Labor Party's painful demise. The state's legitimacy rested in no small measure on continuing allocative roles still played by the party and Ben-Gurion's own towering stature in coping with threat and crisis.[25] Nonetheless, one must not underestimate the amount of state institution building that had gone on in the first twenty years of the state to facilitate policy making and the bridging of differences among key groups. After the war these institutions' capabilities eroded; "it became more difficult to overcome crisis and potential breakdowns with the old tools of accommodation and compromise."[26]

Several key signs of the changing status of the state were the mushrooming public protests and labor strikes directed against it, especially by newly independent groups "outside the rigid structure of Israeli politics; growing debt and faltering ability to finance public expenditures; reduced dependence of the population on state capital; and difficulties in mediating among competing demands by groups in the population, leading to high inflation, among other economic and social plagues."[27]

Israelis have always been political animals; political decisions have been too important to their daily life for them to remain aloof.[28] Anyone who has sat on an Israeli bus as the hourly news is broadcast knows that. But in the prewar period high attentiveness was not matched by organized activity to influence government or by social initiative, especially by organized protest groups.[29] By the 1970s, this diffidence vanished. This process must have been spurred by the international political mobilization of 1968 and the following years. But it had a decidedly local flavor in a country with such a quiescent society and domineering state. Where once the relationship between state and society had been analogous to a marriage in which the husband had taken all the public roles and the wife had faded into the background, now it resembled one in which the wife was newly assertive, making all sorts of new demands for changes in the relationship.

Leading the way at the beginning of 1971 was a group of mostly young Jews of Moroccan origin who called themselves the Black Panthers, after the notorious Black militant organization in the United States (again, the connection to international factors, especially the rise of a new identity politics, is evident). While the Black Panthers' demands were comparatively rather mild—they asked the government to clear slums, provide housing, and stop discrimination—their effect was electrifying. "Although the number who actually joined the Black Panthers was not very large," wrote Cohen, "the spontaneous movement quickly gained popularity and triggered off the expression of widely-felt resentment and dissatisfaction among Oriental Jews."[30] Other protest groups formed later, especially following the 1973 war. Social movements, including Gush Emunim and Peace Now, began to see organized demonstrations as a legitimate tool, and both organized a series of massive protests over the next two decades.

As time went on, much protest centered on the boundary question, the future of the occupied territories. The war had dramatically changed Israel's borders, creating a sense of uncertainty about the appropriate reach of the state and its character. Violence against the state came from both sides. Jewish settlers from Gush Emunim (less than 10 percent of those surveyed) battled soldiers and police when they felt state leaders were contemplating giving up parts of the newly conquered lands, what came to be called territorial compromise.[31] On a far more massive scale, Palestinians in the West Bank and the Gaza Strip rallied, violently and nonviolently, against the state. Their protests culminated in the Intifada, an unarmed but violent continuous struggle, which began in 1987 and petered out by 1993. Palestinian citizens of Israel, too, joined the stream of demonstrations. Starting in 1976 with rallies that ended in a confrontation with the army and the shooting of several Arabs, Israel's Arab citizens have marked Land Day as a means of expressing their frustrations with the state. All in all, a state that had escaped having more than occasional outbursts of unorganized political protest in the pre-1967 period found itself increasingly preoccupied and wearied by all sorts of planned public protest after the war.

Labor unrest was a second avenue of protest. As in the case of the Black Panthers, much of the impetus for the wildcat strikes that blanketed the country after 1967 came from dissatisfaction among Jews of Middle Eastern origins. Strikes were not unheard of before 1967, to be sure. A wave of labor stoppages crippled many enterprises in the mid-1960s. Even then, the strikes concentrated in the public, not private, sector.[32] That wave, however, had subsided in the prewar recession and a reinstitution by the state and the Histadrut of strict labor discipline. Within two years after the war, however, the strike craze was fully under way, again concentrated in the public sector. In 1970, strikes resulted in 390,000 lost workdays, three-quarters of them in the public sector.[33] In one startling statistic, the number of persons involved in labor stoppages and lockouts for every thousand workers, rose from 23 in the years 1948–59 to 218 in 1975–88.[34]

As the state become a target of surging unrest after 1967, its centrality to people's lives diminished, as did its capabilities. As one professor of business put it, "The constant rise in the standard of living and the receipt of personal reparations money from Germany materially reduced the dependence of citizens on the political apparatus or the government system."[35] Not only did the economic dependence of the population on the state decrease, the state showed signs that it could not control social demands put upon it. Even as productivity lagged, the state continued to promote increases in public and private consumption. The only way to do that was to find outside money to continue catering to growing consumption. It is not surprising, therefore, that one clear sign of the state's increased weakness was ballooning foreign and domestic debt.[36] The state could not take the steps necessary to make Israel live within its means.

The state's inability to balance available domestic resources against demands for growing consumption led to a host of serious problems. Investment dropped, balance of payments worsened, and the state's liquidity diminished.[37] But the two clearest signs of state weakness were debt and inflation. By the early 1980s, the state spent nearly a third of the country's GNP on transfer payments and debt service, and, in 1985 the debt burden reached 127 percent of GNP.[38] Spiraling inflation was another sign of the state's inability to mediate demands even as it made substantial cuts in domestic financing of defense. The fifteen years after 1970 wreaked economic havoc on Israel, as first the Labor government and then the Likud government lost control of the economy. At the beginning of the 1970s, clear signs of accelerating inflation already existed; by 1979, rates reached a level of over 100 percent per year and soared to nearly 500 percent in 1984.

Growing Disagreements about the State's Character and Reach

At the same time that the state's centrality and capabilities diminished, bitter debates broke out about what the character of the state should be. No single powerful figure, as Ben-Gurion had been in the prewar period, could dominate the controversy. What had seemed to be settled before the war—the civic, universal model of the state in the territory under its control—became a source of bitter dispute, both inside and outside the halls of government.

The territorial controversies are well-known and need little comment here. Avineri captured the deeper importance of the new political battles:

> What appeared to have been closed in 1948–9 by the dual impact of the acceptance on the part of Israel of the UN partition resolution and the outcome of the War of Independence, became once more an open question. The national consensus that Israel had to be defended, and defended at all cost, from within its 1949 borders, was broken and for the first time since Independence the question of the Israeli boundaries was reopened. While there was virtually no dissenting voice regarding the unification of Jerusalem, the future disposition of the West Bank and Gaza became the focus for the most acrimonious and divisive debate in Israel since its inception. For the debate is not only about policies, it is about the boundaries of the polity itself.[39]

Deep social and political conflicts about the nature of the state followed closely on those over Israel's eventual permanent international boundaries. At issue was whether the state held, for the Jews, a kind of stewardship over the historical Land of Israel or instead served as the representation of the population—largely but not exclusively Jewish—in a given territory, even if that territory was somewhat arbitrarily defined by twentieth-century circumstances. The tension between its ethnonational foundation as the *Jewish* state and its universal, civic nature—first and foremost found in its rule of law—now burst to the top of the public agenda.[40] The Jewishness of the Israeli state and society has remained a central topic of public and academic discourse to this day.[41] Certainly, the rise of the Likud after 1967 and its control of government for nearly fifteen years were not unrelated to deeper questions about the character of the state.

In the renewed ethnonational conception, the state was downgraded from the centrality of *mamlahtiyut* to the role of guardian of Jewish society. That society was defined independently of the state, as a product of the *true* territorial legacy of the Jews. Jewish nationhood was defined through its relation to the ancient homeland, and the state was simply an expression of the nation. As Alan Dowty summarized this view, the Jews, like any other people have "a distinct character that is inextricably linked to [their] statehood. The essence of nationhood was particularism, not a vague set of liberal principles that few states observed in practice anyway (especially when their survival was at stake)."[42]

The Arabs would have only a limited role in such a state, much more as subjects than equal citizens. In the ethnonational image, then, society was not a civic construction in which the state played a pivotal role in forging the society by developing universal institutions, as had been widely accepted before 1967. Society's very existence, the dissenters contended, stemmed from Jewish national rights, largely territorial rights.[43] Arabs did not share in those rights; and this implied that they were not full members of society and that the state was not theirs in the same way that it was the Jews'. While I will concentrate below on group relations among Jews, it is worth noting that the problematic status of Arabs after the war led to "a reality of growing hostility, estrangement, and hatred" that governed relations of Jews with Arab citizens.[44]

Faltering Images of Social Integration

In addition to the eroding position of the state and the divisive debates about its ultimate reach and character, a third social dynamic coming out of the boundary changes of the 1967 war was the faltering of Israel's model of social integration among Jews, which led to deteriorating group relations. The slide down the slope of ethnic enmity took many observers by surprise. If anything, the 1967 war's initial impact was to strengthen social integration, especially feelings of solidarity among Israel's Jewish population. One anthropologist captured its effect: "The virtually traumatic experience of the Six-Day War in 1967 . . . was highly concentrated in time, packed with action, and dramatic in its outcome. The hypertension of this drama, whose result was seen by many as a miracle, streamed down to all levels of the nation. All strata of the highly variegated and motley society experienced themselves united by the bonds of common peril and salvation, an experience that overrode all the other particular exigencies of various social strata and individuals."[45]

It became a truism in Israel that the participation of Jews of Middle Eastern origin in the deliverance of the country from its moment of peril in 1967 cemented their place in society. The heroism of many of their children in the war itself established the credentials of the Middle Eastern immigrants as central members of the society. Additionally, by the mid-1970s, evidence appeared indicating that the ethnic wage gap was beginning to shrink.[46] Indeed, the widening income differential between Jews of European and Middle Eastern backgrounds in the prewar period stabilized in the late 1960s and then shrank to its lowest point since 1951—at precisely the time that the Black Panthers burst on the social scene.[47] While noting that domination by Jews of European background remained at the highest levels of society, one observer pointed out that "the economic expansion after the Six-Day War brought with it increased entrance of Orientals into white-collar occupations. They became bank tellers, secretaries, sales people, and moved into service jobs such as television and radio repair, became bus and taxi drivers, food-stand and boutique owners; they also entered the ranks of the expanded regular army, especially in N.C.O. positions."[48]

But the solidarity born in the experience of the war and the narrowing economic differential afterward did not prevent a serious deterioration in ethnic relations among the Jews. Perhaps, as Virginia Dominguez has argued, the problem of ethnicity comes only after a collectivity such as Israeli society develops a sense of collective self.[49] Whether the 1967 war had such an effect or not, both the sensitivity and open dissatisfaction of Jews of Middle East background increased rapidly within a few years of the war. Smooha, for example, found that leaders of Jews with Middle Eastern origins were much more likely than leaders of, say, Romanian Jews to cite invidious comparisons and other forms of discrimination.[50]

Public and academic discourse came to be focused on issues of discrimination, prejudice, unequal access, and segregation. Jews of Middle Eastern background became more conscious of, and outspoken about, their inferior status. No event had more impact in crystallizing dissatisfaction than the actions of the Black Panthers. Their demonstrations were followed by a host of new studies confirming the ethnic gap and active discrimination. Ethnic parties sprouted up, and ethnic anger was taken out on the ruling Labor Party, as Jews of Middle East origin flocked to the opposition Likud.

If the dominant discourse before 1967 had been one of social integration, in the aftermath of the war the talk was of "immigration without integration."[51] Anger welled up; one Yemeni intellectual challenged some of the sacred cows of Israeli society by stating that the children of Middle East Jews had died in the war "in order that the Abromoviches and similar people . . . might be appointed as civil servants."[52] The Black Panthers displayed the same sort of animus: "Their whole attitude," wrote Cohen, "was permeated by the conviction that the Orientals had been oppressed and cheated by the Ashkenazi-dominated establishment or even used for its ulterior purposes."[53]

It is important to add that the sense of dissatisfaction did not lead many of the non-European Jews down the path of separatism. Even the few ethnic parties did not trumpet a separatist ideology. From the violent protests of the Black Panthers to the treatises of academics and writers, the call most often was for inclusion and equality, not a breaking off from the dominant groups.[54] The prosperity of the immediate postwar period made the prospect of integration continue to seem attainable. At the same time, it heightened the frustration of second-class status, resulting in an increasingly vitriolic reaction against the methods and outcomes of the existing model for integration.

The three postwar crises that I have singled out—the diminishing centrality of the state, deep divisions in society about the nature of the state and its final borders, and growing ethnic tensions—intersected with one another. Israel faced growing social polarization, intractable divisions between Jews and a growing Arab minority, as well as ethnic venom expressed by one segment of Jewish society against another; and, on the future status of the occupied territories and the character of the state as universal or ethnonational, Israelis also faced off against each other. And, throughout the fray, no referee was in sight. The diminished Israeli state seemed paralyzed by the social divisions and unable to make hard choices. Its declining capacity to guide the society left Israel by the early 1980s with an economy spiraling out of control and an inability to come to terms with the question of where the society was headed. The war that had been heralded as redemptive, as the antithesis of the Holocaust, seemed within several years of its conclusion to have had satanic effects on Israeli state and society. What was it about the 1967 war that so unsettled state-society relations?

SHIFTING BOUNDARIES

Fixed boundaries lend stability to political and social life. People's behavior becomes predictable, social values become ensconced, and the established social roles of institutions—from the family to businesses to the state—become the defining elements for the character of interactions in a society.[55] Institutions of everyday life depend upon the population's clear sense of their reach—*who* is inside an institution and *who* is outside, *which* sorts of interactions they govern and *which* are external to their realm, *what* is private space and *what* is public space. These whos, whichs, and whats may institutionalize exploitative and brutal relations, or egalitarian and caring ones; ones based on individual autonomy, or those promoting group sensibilities first. Whatever the specific character of the institutions, their structure of benefits and sanctions carve out stable social roles and modes of interaction.

Institutions depend upon the permanence of boundaries. Shifting boundaries lend all sorts of uncertainty to the underpinnings of institutions. Boundary flux changes the calculus of incentives; it undoes the understanding of the institution's reach and, with it, the whos, whichs, and whats that provide the parameters for behavior in the society. Ideas and practices embedded in institutions have meaning and influence in a certain space, both social space (say, that of a family) and physical space (as in the jurisdiction of a municipal agency). Sudden shifts in the boundaries of that space can subvert the rules and practices that characterize a single institution. Changes affecting multiple or central institutions in a society can lead to crisis in society's central dynamics, both by opening routine rules and practices to question and by lending uncertainty to the relevance and efficacy of society's central institutions, such as the church or state. The effect of boundary changes is particularly salient when the new borders are hotly contested.

Ian Lustick is one of only a handful of scholars who analyze the relationship of boundary changes to broader questions of state-society relations. His brilliant book *Unsettled States, Disputed Lands* analyzes how and when boundary changes may occur outside the context of war.[56] He asks which circumstances move a polity from a point where lopping off some of the territory that the state controls (Ireland for Great Britain, Algeria for France, and the West Bank and Gaza Strip for Israel) is unthinkable to a point where such an act is an actively debated policy choice.

Raising the question of border changes, as Lustick does, is important in a broader theoretical sense, as well. When the concept of the state reentered academic discourse in the 1980s, all too frequently it was treated as a given; as an independent variable it seemed inviolable and unchanging.[57] Rosenau remarked that scholarly discourse seems to assume that "the state is to politics what the hidden hand is (à la Adam Smith) to economics."[58] Along with several other scholars, Lustick shifted the focus of comparative politics, asking how the state may change from a seemingly impenetrable rock to something that is shaped and transformed by the currents in society or in the larger international system.[59] His insight that states are not permanent fixtures but may contract or expand in size (or disappear altogether) furthered the entire enterprise of state studies.[60]

It is the possibility of border changes that concerns Lustick. In technical terms, the shifts in boundaries are his dependent variable, and he looks to changes in state-society relations for his answers (the independent variable). The question I am exploring stands Lustick's formulation on its head. What is the effect of boundary changes and continuing contestation over those changes, which now comprise the independent variable, on state and society, which here comprise the dependent variable?

It would be incorrect to say that by themselves the boundary changes stemming from the 1967 war caused the crises in Israel's social dynamics. We can follow Galnoor, however, in stating that the war created a "broken path."[61] By undoing Israel's boundaries, the Six-Day War chipped away at the hold of key institutions and unraveled the understanding of the character of state and society, opening a new period of intense debate about the future. Conquering and then holding territories that had been ruled by Jordan, Syria, and Egypt undermined existing institutional patterns in Israel and precipitated crises in Israel's central social dynamics. Reopening the question of Israel's borders in 1967, after a twenty-year hiatus in which the state's territory seemed to achieve some permanent status in the minds of many in the international community and among Israelis themselves, led to divisive debates in the country about the fundamental nature of society. These debates spilled over into the political realm and had profound effects on state-society relations and relations among groups in the society.

Boundary Changes Open New Questions about the Construction of Society

In addition to the territory marked by the 1949 armistice lines, at the 1967 war's end Israel ruled the Golan Heights, the Sinai Desert, the West Bank, and the Gaza Strip. The latter two, with their dense Palestinian populations and their relation to Jews' construction of a "territorial legacy," had a particularly profound effect on social dynamics in Israel. At the simplest level, the occupied territories presented Israelis with choices on issues that the vast majority had previously assumed were closed. In the immediate aftermath of the war, Israeli leaders seemed not to have assimilated these choices, giving indications that they assumed the territories would be returned in exchange for peace and recognition by Israel's enemies. But quickly the issue of choice pushed itself onto the public agenda, leading to debates about what had previously been undebatable—incorporating new territories permanently into the state.

But the change in political boundaries had several other key effects that went beyond the question of the territorial reach of the state. First, the conception of an expanded Israeli state was accompanied by a rationale for its enlargement; that is, the new reach demanded a set of principles different from those that had supported the zigzag boundaries that had existed from 1949 to 1967. What emerged was a debate that went far beyond the question of where to draw the lines for Israel's permanent borders. The controversy was an intense, still ongoing division between those supporting the old principles (with their heavy emphasis on universalism and citizenship) and the new rationale based on the ethnonational rights of Jews over the state's other citizens.

The bitter dispute over the meaning of the state not only divided those in Israel along ideological grounds but also deeply affected group relations. Most obviously, the debate affected Israel's Arab citizens and their relationship to the dominant Jews. But it also injected itself into group relations among Jews. The ethnonational principle offered the hope of quicker and more complete integration to frustrated Jews of Middle East origin. The established model of a universalistic state implied, as I noted earlier, a civilly constructed society. Such a society placed demands on citizens to conform to modes of interaction through *civil* behavior. Exactly what civil behavior entailed, however, turned out to be defined by the dominant European-Jewish groups. Much of the discrimination against those from North Africa and Asia, as Jews from a Middle East background knew all too well, was based on the claim or assumption that they did not possess civil attributes. Their acceptance into full membership in society, then, was attenuated and subject to unspoken tests, which in the eyes of those controlling major institutions they repeatedly failed. "They were thought," noted Arnold Lewis, "to exhibit instability, emotionalism, laziness, boastfulness, inclination to violence, uncontrolled temper, superstitiousness, childishness, and lack of cleanliness."[62]

An ethnonational definition of society would subject Jews of Middle East background to no such tests. Ethnonationalism would mean automatic acceptance for such Jews, as is.[63] In part, their gradual switch to the Likud reflected a desire to hook into that party's model of society. Israel's universal institutions, by their very exclusion of those who did not fit the criteria of "civil," had created their own in-group qualities. Run, as they were, almost exclusively by Jews of European roots, they created what Danet called an institutional culture marked by *mishpahtiyut,* or familism.[64] "It is almost a commonplace," wrote Cohen, "that all the major institutional spheres of Israeli society—the government and the Knesset (Parliament), the political parties, the Histadrut (The General Federation of Labour), the major economic enterprises and corporations, the universities, state schools, and the cultural activities—are dominated, on the national and often also on the local level, by people of Ashkenazi [European] origin and by expressly Western values."[65]

The effect, oddly, was that institutions based on universalism used universalism as a method of exclusion, creating their own ethnic in-group.[66] The change in Israel's boundaries opened the question of what sort of society would be most consonant with rule over an extended territory and well over a million Palestinians in the newly conquered territory. Those Jews who had been excluded from the central institutions before the war took advantage of the reopened question about the nature of society to push for a redefined ethnic in-group. The new group would be ethnonational, not civic in character, leading to their automatic inclusion, as well. Outliers would then be the Palestinians, both citizens and those in the occupied territories.

Boundary changes thus account for a new contending model of what society should be. This model opened the door to inclusion in central institutions for Jews of Middle Eastern background and, at the same time, to new negativism toward, and exclusion of, Arab citizens (and certainly noncitizens in the territories).[67] It is not surprising that Danet found almost no drop in the institutional culture of familism, between the war and 1980, in what were constructed as universal institutions.[68] What may have changed is that after 1967 a multifaced battle developed over the lines of who was in, and who was outside, the family.

Boundaries Change the Labor Market

The effects of the wartime change in boundaries did not end with struggles over where the final borders should be drawn or with ideological divisions about the sort of society that went along with different boundary configurations. Another key impact of the war's final demarcation lines was on the country's labor market. The war created a new reservoir of low-wage workers in the conquered territories who had access to work opportunities in Israel across formerly impenetrable lines. This new worker pool affected the entire labor market, most markedly those who had occupied the lowest rungs of the labor ladder before the war. The high-level mobilization of the Israeli economy before, during, and after the war lifted the country out of recession. Palestinians from the territories filled much of the new labor demand by taking low-paying jobs. The mobilization and the existence of the new Palestinian labor pool from the West Bank and Gaza Strip enabled Israeli Arab citizens and Jews from Middle Eastern countries to take advantage of all sorts of positions at the next level up—they became subcontractors, foremen, supervisors, and the like.[69]

Their occupational mobility often demanded new physical mobility as well. The result was that the Israeli economy, and its labor market in particular, shed much of the fragmentation and segmentation that government policies, wittingly or unwittingly, had engendered during the first two decades of statehood.[70] Those barriers to physical and social mobility, the internal boundaries, had been most obvious in the case of the Arab population of the country but had existed for new Jewish immigrants from other parts of the Middle East too, as we shall see below. Because Israel seemed so militarily secure now, and because demand was so high for all sorts of labor, state leaders may have seen the breakdown of the old segmentation and the social relations that went along with it as largely cost-free. In fact, the costs turned out to be staggering: reorganization of society, with its new Gazan and West Bank underclass, prompted the erosion of the state's privileged position, leading to important and profound changes in state-society relations.

In the years of high immigration right after the creation of the state, governmental policies had attracted new immigrants, especially those of Middle Eastern origin, to so-called development towns. Subsidized housing and low-interest loans were the biggest inducements drawing immigrants to these isolated new communities, "outside the main stream of Israeli society geographically as well as socially."[71] More than any other settlements in Israel, these towns were ethnically constituted, with as many as two-thirds of residents from a Middle Eastern background.[72]

The state also gave incentives to certain kinds of industries to locate in the development towns, especially ones using labor-intensive technologies and low-skill labor.[73] In effect, an ethnic division of labor developed in Israel that was geographically based. Isolation meant that new immigrants from Middle Eastern countries were concentrated in jobs and locations that impeded their physical and social mobility. Concentrated at the lower end of the occupational ladder and shunted to the geographical margins of the country, Jews with Middle Eastern roots formed a labor force within a labor force. Spatially, Israel was divided by what Oren Yiftachel has called "internal frontiers."[74]

Segmentation and fragmentation, then, were the hallmarks of the pre-1967 economy. The deep recession immediately before the war, fell hardest on precisely those in the isolated, low-skill industries.[75] "To sum up," wrote Swirski, "residential segregation, the predominance of intragroup marriages, the segregated and unequal school system, and the ideological apparatus that portrays the Orientals as culturally deprived or backward— all work to reproduce the ethnic division of labour that emerged in Israel during the fifties and sixties."[76]

Arab labor in Israel was even more disadvantaged. Even before the creation of Israel, many Arabs (especially those living in the coastal portions of Palestine that became Israel) had begun to commute from their villages to low-skill jobs in the cities. With the imposition of military administration of the Arabs after Israeli independence, that pattern continued. Now, however, severe restrictions were placed on how far and under what conditions Arab workers could commute to outside jobs, making them available for the lowest-skill labor but only in their local regions. They, too, formed a niche within a fragmented and segmented labor force.

Even before the 1967 war, signs emerged that the social boundaries associated with the segmented labor market, with its clear ethnic division of labor, were beginning to fray. The end of military administration ended the forced confinement of Arab labor. Since the geographic isolation of Jews from Middle Eastern origins was maintained through incentives, rather than force, it is not surprising that many began to move from the development towns. One study in the early 1960s found that interurban movement from these communities was four times the national average.[77]

But it was the boom after the war, coupled with the reconfiguration of the labor market through the addition of Palestinians from the conquered territories, that opened wide the gates to new physical and social mobility, undoing the old social fragmentation and segmentation.[78] Economic boom created a high demand for labor at all levels of the Israeli economy; in fact, unemployment rates until the late 1980s averaged just 3.6 percent. Amir described the result: "The 1967 war changed the composition of the labor force in Israel; there now existed accessible reserve labor which was cheap, unskilled, and nonorganized [Palestinians from the occupied territories]."[79] For both Arab citizens of Israel and Jews from Middle Eastern background, the demands higher up on the occupational scale, coupled with the availability of low-skill labor to replace them at the low end, resulted in new social and physical mobility.[80] The changing of the internal social boundaries and the external physical boundaries became coupled processes.

The mobilization of new social groups increased demands upon the state—many of them, as we saw, expressed in terms of ethnic and labor protest.[81] Indeed, the end of the old residential isolation and labor market segmentation broke down the state's ability to dampen demands put upon it. As new political and social demands strained the capacities of the state's relatively young institutions, it became less and less able to regulate inter-group relations and to put brakes on Israeli consumption. And, with the reemergence of the ethnonational model of society expressed by the Likud, many Jews with Middle Eastern origins found a ready way to express their dissatisfaction.

It might also be noted, in conclusion, that some of the elements leading to the crisis in Israel's social dynamics also put limits on that crisis. The unrestrained economy, with its soaring levels of personal consumption and low unemployment, allowed for high mobility and thus very focused bread-and-butter demands by Jews from Middle Eastern backgrounds. Their aims were not separation but inclusion and participation. They did not build exclusive institutions but integrated into established ones, such as the Likud itself. At least for some of the problems we have discussed, that meant an avenue for the creation of new institutional stability in the future.

CONCLUSION

When the 1967 war broke out, the Israeli state was only twenty years old. Its institutions had not hardened over many decades or centuries. Still, in a short period, those institutions had created remarkable stability in the relations between the state and those it governed. State organizations from the Knesset on down had become naturalized, that is, many in society, especially among the Jewish population, accepted the reach of those institutions and the rightness of their establishing codes for social behavior. To be sure, there was no shortage of grumbling about particular rules, but little questioning arose about the appropriateness of those organizations to make the rules.

Immediately after the harrowing days of May and early June 1967, very few Jewish citizens saw the outcome of the war as anything but an unmixed blessing. What they and Israeli political officials could not foresee was how unsettling to state institutions and the relations between the state and society the change in boundaries brought about by the war would be. If the prewar boundaries had taken on a kind of sanctity in those two decades, all sorts of doubts came to the surface about what the new proper boundaries and reach of political institutions should be. In a setting where the state had been elevated to a very special status comparatively, the postwar border changes, mixed with a number of other domestic and international factors, weakened the state and transformed its relation to society.

As I write these words, early in the new century, in the midst of intense negotiations with the Palestinians and Syrians, the questions of Israel's permanent boundaries, including who constitutes the nation, the nature of citizenship, and the proper role of state institutions are as contested now as they were thirty years ago. If a glimmer of hope can be seen on the horizon that some of the most wrenching disputes will recede, it is that today's debates are much more focused now on the signed agreements with the Palestinians and what they require of Israel. The absence of a viable alternative to the Oslo Process, as well as a growing sense of inevitability about the return of the Golan Heights to Syria, has channeled many of the divisions into questions of how to implement the agreements and how far concessions should go. Those are not inconsequential questions. But, if they can be resolved and final agreements between Israel and the Palestine Authority, and between Israel and Syria, can be ratified, the effect could be similar to Israel's withdrawal from the Sinai Desert and its settlements there, such as Yamit, in the late 1970s. In that case, emotions ran very high at the moment; then, as now, musings about the possibility of civil war could be heard in the street. But the permanent settlement with Egypt came to be nearly unquestioned within a few short years after the withdrawal occurred. If the Israeli people and state are fortunate, the same will occur in the context of a final peace with the Palestinians and the Syrians.

NOTES

1. Hammel, *Six Days in June: How Israel Won the 1967 Arab-Israeli War,* p. 33.
2. Galnoor, "Israeli Society and Politics," p. 179.
3. Chesnoff, Klein, and Littell, *If Israel Lost the War,* front matter.
4. Stevenson, *Strike Zion!* p. 1.
5. Quoted in Stevenson, *Strike Zion!* in front matter.
6. Among the new works looking at the effects of the 1967 war on Israeli society are Barzilai, *Wars, Internal Conflicts, and Political Order: A Jewish Democracy in the Middle East;* Levy, *Trial and Error: Israel's Route from War to De-escalation;* and Pedatzur, *The Triumph of Embarrassment: Israel and the Territories after the Six-Day War.*
7. Liebman and Don-Yehiya write, "Statism affirms the centrality of state interests and the centralization of power at the expense of nongovernmental groups and institutions. In terms of symbols and style, statism reflects the effort to transform the state and its institutions into the central foci of loyalty and identification. Statism

gives rise to values and symbols that point to the state, legitimate it, and mobilize the population to serve its goals." Liebman and Don-Yehiya, *Civil Religion in Israel: Traditional Judaism and Political Culture in the Jewish State,* p. 84.

8. See the discussion in Keren, *The Pen and the Sword: Israeli Intellectuals and the Making of the Nation-State,* pp. 1–5.

9. Indeed, academics have written of the development of Israel's own civil religion, in which the state stands at the center. See Liebman and Don-Yehiya, *Civil Religion in Israel,* p. 84, where they write, "In its more extreme formulation statism cultivates an attitude of sanctity toward the state, affirming it as an ultimate value." They go on to note that "the establishment of an independent Jewish state only a few years after the Holocaust evoked an outburst of enthusiasm from Jews both in the Diaspora and the Land of Israel. . . . The joy and enthusiasm evoked by the creation of Israel had the character of Messianic sentiments. In this context many believed the state to be the fulfillment of the traditional Jewish vision of redemption" (pp. 85–86).

10. "During the prestate period it was possible to cultivate the civil religion of one subgroup without hampering the basic unity of the Jewish population. The political leadership of the various camps interrelated through a complex network, compromising on some disputed issues and principles and ignoring many others. Avoiding issues was possible in the absence of statehood and political sovereignty. Available resources, money, and jobs were distributed by the political leadership according to a key; according to a negotiated formula, each group received an allocation based roughly on its voting strength." Ibid., p. 81.

11. Eisenstadt, *The Transformation of Israeli Society: An Essay in Interpretation,* p. 186.

12. Cohen, "Ethnicity and Legitimation in Contemporary Israel," p. 113.

13. Dowty, *The Jewish State: A Century Later,* pp. 61–73.

14. Lustick, *Arabs in the Jewish State: Israel's Control of a National Minority.*

15. See for example Peres, "Modernization and Nationalism in the Identity of the Israeli Arab," pp. 479–92.

16. Peled, "Ethnic Democracy and the Legal Construction of Citizenship: Arab Citizens of the Jewish State," p. 435.

17. Galnoor, *The Partition of Palestine: Decision Crossroads in the Zionist Movement.*

18. Avineri, "Political Ideologies: From Consensus to Confrontation," p. 198. A powerful argument about Israel's pre-1967 war boundaries is made by Adriana Kemp, "'Talking Boundaries': The Making of a Political Territory in Israel, 1949–1957" (Ph.D. diss., Tel-Aviv University, 1997) (in Hebrew).

19. "Newcomers are expected to change cultural traditions and ways of life that are considered unsuitable or irrelevant to life in Israel. This social definition puts pressure on people who come from Asian or African countries to adopt Western codes of behavior." Herzog, "Political Ethnicity as a Socially Constructed Reality: The Case of Jews in Israel" p. 140.

20. Liron, *Deprivation and Socio-Economic Gap in Israel,* p. 12. The figures are for 1968–69.

21. A large number of studies were surveyed by Raphael Roter and Nira Shamai. See "Social Policy and the Israeli Economy, 1948–1980," p. 162.

22. Cohen, "The Black Panthers and Israeli Society," p. 149.

23. Gorny, *The State of Israel in Jewish Public Thought: The Quest for Collective Identity*, p. 39.

24. Kraus and Hodge, *Promises in the Promised Land: Mobility and Inequality in Israel*, p. 59.

25. See Divine, "Political Legitimacy in Israel: How Important Is the State?" pp. 205–24.

26. Galnoor, "Israeli Society and Politics," p. 178.

27. Ibid., p. 181.

28. Wolfsfeld, *The Politics of Provocation: Participation and Protest in Israel*, p. 15.

29. See Migdal, "Civil Society in Israel," p. 125. On the manipulation of consensus in Israeli society by political elites, see Barzilai, *Wars, Internal Conflicts, and Political Order*.

30. Cohen, "The Black Panthers and Israeli Society," p. 147.

31. Weisburd, *Jewish Settler Violence: Deviance as Social Reaction*, p. 111.

32. Plessner, *The Political Economy of Israel: From Ideology to Stagnation*, p. 139, states that "in 1965 almost 63 percent of all workdays lost in strikes were in the public sector. Even more impressive, over 71 percent of all strikers were in the public sector, although its share in employment was only less than 23 percent."

33. Ibid., p. 139.

34. Shalev, *Labour and the Political Economy in Israel*, p. 257.

35. Aharoni, *The Israeli Economy: Dreams and Realities*, p. 195.

36. Plessner, *The Political Economy of Israel*, p. 177.

37. Aharoni, *The Israeli Economy*, pp. 85–86; and Rivlin, *The Israeli Economy*, p. 3.

38. Plessner, *The Political Economy of Israel*, p. 178.

39. Avineri, "Political Ideologies," p. 199.

40. On the concept of ethnonationalism, see Connor, *Ethnonationalism: The Quest for Understanding*. While universalism implies rationalism in Weberian terms, ethnonationalism (a loyalty to one's own kind), Connor maintains, rests on passions and nonrational factors. On the growing debate between the civic and ethnonational models after the 1967 war, see Dowty, *The Jewish State*, chap. 10.

41. See two recent volumes, for example: Liebman and Katz, *The Jewishness of Israelis: Responses to the Guttman Report;* and Dowty, *The Jewish State*.

42. Dowty, *The Jewish State*, p. 13.

43. See Kimmerling, "Between the Primordial and the Civil Definitions of the Collective Identity: Eretz Israel or the State of Israel?" pp. 262–83.

44. Peleg, "The Arab-Israeli Conflict and the Victory of Otherness," p. 228. Also, see Cohen, "Ethnicity and Legitimation in Contemporary Israel," p. 114.

45. Deshen, "Political Ethnicity and Cultural Ethnicity in Israel During the 1960s," p. 142.

46. Roter and Shamai, "Social Policy and the Israeli Economy, 1948–1980," p. 163.

47. Remba, "Income Inequality in Israel: Ethnic Aspects," p. 203.

48. Swirski, *Israel: The Oriental Majority*, p. 28.

49. Dominguez, *People as Subject, People as Object: Selfhood and Peoplehood in Contemporary Israel*. Commenting on Dominguez, James Armstrong writes, "Ethnic divisions within Israeli society are only problematic insofar as there is some idealized, subject-constructed sense of peoplehood which is compatible with those divisions."

"The Search for Israeliness: Toward an Anthropology of the Contemporary Mainstream," p. 123.

50. Smooha, *Israel: Pluralism and Conflict,* p. 193.

51. See Shama and Iris, *Immigration without Integration.*

52. Y. Nini, quoted in Cohen, "The Black Panthers and Israeli Society," p. 154.

53. Cohen, "The Black Panthers and Israeli Society," p. 154.

54. See Herzog, "Political Ethnicity as a Socially Constructed Reality: The Case of Jews in Israel," pp. 140–51. On the question of inclusion versus segregation, see the important work by Aronoff, *Israeli Visions and Divisions: Cultural Change and Political Conflict.*

55. "By institutions I mean established organizations and the rules and practices that govern how these organizations function internally and relate to one another and to society." Sikkink, *Ideas and Institutions: Developmentalism in Brazil and Argentina,* p. 23.

56. Lustick, *Unsettled States, Disputed Lands: Britain and Ireland, France and Algeria, Israel and the West Bank-Gaza.*

57. Evans, Reuschemeyer, and Skocpol, *Bringing the State Back In.*

58. Rosenau, "State in an Era of Cascading Politics: Wavering Concept, Widening Competence, Withering Colossus, or Weathering Change?" p. 14.

59. Other examples of those looking at the state as a dependent variable are Jackson, *Quasi-States: Sovereignty, International Relations, and the Third World,* (New York: Cambridge University Press, 1990); Jackson and Rosberg, "Why Africa's Weak States Persist: The Empirical and the Juridical in Statehood," pp. 1–24; and Migdal, Kohli, and Shue, *State Power and Social Forces.* In the context of Israel, one book rejecting the notion of the state as a black box is Levy, *Trial and Error.*

60. On that enterprise, see Migdal, "Studying the State."

61. Galnoor, "Israeli Society and Politics," pp. 193–94.

62. Arnold Lewis, "Ethnic Politics and the Foreign Policy Debate in Israel," p. 28.

63. Cohen, in "Ethnicity and Legitimation in Contemporary Israel," wrote, "It is claimed that Oriental Jews are entitled to gain such access—by sheer virtue of being Jews, and not because of some particular process of absorption and resocialization" (p. 120). I am indebted to Ovadia Shapira for reminding me that Erik Cohen made this important point over fifteen years ago. Also, see Lewis, "Ethnic Politics and the Foreign Policy Debate in Israel," p. 33.

64. Danet, *Pulling Strings: Biculturalism in Israeli Bureaucracy,* p. 95.

65. Cohen, "The Black Panthers and Israeli Society," p. 149.

66. Cohen, "Ethnicity and Legitimation in Contemporary Israel," p. 116.

67. On the growing negativism toward Arabs, see Sprinzak, *The Ascendance of Israel's Radical Right.* For a different explanation of the enmity that Middle Eastern Jews demonstrated toward Arabs, see Peled, "Mizrahi Jews and Palestinian Arabs: Exclusionist Attitudes in Development Towns," pp. 87–111.

68. Danet, *Pulling Strings,* p. 243.

69. See Haidar, *On the Margins: The Arab Population in the Israeli Economy,* pp. 97 ff.

70. This point should not be overstated. The labor market, as Peled shows, con-

tinued to be split along ethnic lines after 1967, in certain ways. See Peled, "Mizrahi Jews and Palestinian Arabs."

71. Spilerman and Habib, "Development Towns in Israel: The Role of Community in Creating Ethnic Disparities in Labor Force Characteristics," p. 200.

72. Ibid., pp. 203–7.

73. Ibid., pp. 211–17.

74. Shama and Iris, in *Immigration without Integration*, pp. 116–2, note the occupational concentration of Jews with Middle Eastern roots. The quote is from Yiftachel, "The Internal Frontier: Territorial Control and Ethnic Relations in Israel," pp. 39–67.

75. Shama and Iris, *Immigration without Integration*, pp. 137–38.

76. Swirski, *Israel*, p. 28.

77. Spilerman and Habib, "Development Towns in Israel," p. 222.

78. See Levy, *Trial and Error*, chap. 4, on the change in social structure after the 1967 war. Levy ties this change in strategy by Israel to a de-escalation of its conflict with the Arabs. In my view, he underestimates the impact of the war itself on both these processes.

79. Amir, *Divided We Stand: Class Structure in Israel from 1948 to the 1980's*, p. 62.

80. Haidar, *On the Margins*, chaps. 5–6, presents excellent data on the new mobility. Chapter 6 is titled "From Village to Dormitory Community."

81. For the relation between the two forms of protest, see Etzioni-Halevey, "Patterns of Conflict Generation and Conflict 'Absorption': The Cases of Israeli Labor and Ethnic Conflicts," pp. 231–54.

7

War as Leveler, War as Midwife
Palestinian Political Institutions, Nationalism, and Society since 1948

Yezid Sayigh

That war has had a repeated and massive impact on the evolution of Palestinian politics and society since the early twentieth century can hardly be denied. The most graphic example is the conflict accompanying the end of the British mandate over Palestine and the establishment of the state of Israel, which resulted in the exodus of around 55 percent of the Arab population (some 1.4 million people) and its dispossession of land and other properties and means of livelihood in the course of 1947–49.[1] What the Palestinians have referred to since then as *al-nakba* (the catastrophe) had far-reaching consequences. The loss of a shared economic "space" and the dispersal of the refugees to several places of exile compounded their social dislocation severely, as did their subjection (along with those Arab inhabitants of mandate Palestine who were not displaced) to the diverse political, administrative, legal, and economic systems and security controls of the various governments that now exercised authority over them.[2] No less important was the unwillingness of the Arab "frontline" states directly concerned—Jordan and Egypt—to sanction the establishment of a Palestinian state in those parts of Palestine that remained under their control, namely, the West Bank and Gaza Strip.[3] This not only impeded the construction of recognized and unitary Palestinian political institutions, and consequently of a common postcolonial national identity, but also fragmented the social and economic base for the conduct of "national" politics and for the emergence of distinct elite groups and corporate interests. Official Arab policy after 1948 thus consolidated the long-term effects of the absence of a Palestinian version of the colonial state and native (Arab) rule during the British mandate.

Indeed, the sheer scale of *al-nakba* and the complexity of the varied and often hostile environment in which the Arab former inhabitants of mandate Palestine subsequently found themselves only beg the question of how the Palestine Liberation Organization (PLO) was able to assert itself after the mid-1960s as a distinct political actor enjoying not inconsiderable autonomy and extensive recognition on the domestic, regional, and international stages. No other nonstate actor since 1945 has gained equivalent diplomatic status, while many other self-defined national communities have failed to assert their claims to self-determination and statehood with equal success.[4] Of course it is obvious that the PLO was neither a sovereign actor, enjoying full empirical and juridical statehood, nor the inheritor of a previous state, as the Palestinians had not formed an autonomous political entity under the British mandate or even a single administrative unit under the Ottomans.[5] However, as I have argued elsewhere, at issue was not "stateness" (actual possession of the key attributes of the state, such as exclusive control over population and territory) but rather "statist" character, as defined by "the emergence and maintenance of a particular set of political practices and institutional arrangements centred on the PLO; the processes through which it redefined its political relations with, and sought to co-opt, Palestinian society; and the manner of its interaction with sovereign members of the regional and international state systems. It is in this sense that the underlying logic of Palestinian national politics and organizational evolution . . . since 1948 has been one of state-building."[6]

The political ascendancy of the PLO is no less notable for the main features of the Palestinian state-society dyad (with the PLO standing in for the state) as it has developed since the mid-1960s. These can be summarized as its neopatrimonial character—typified by the use of rent, corporatism, and the tendency to populist nationalism and authoritarianism—and the political ascendancy of lower-middle-class strata, especially of rural-provincial background, thanks to their marked transition to salaried employment generally and to their direct engagement within the statist PLO framework more specifically. Moreover, this historical process went hand in hand with the promotion of a particularistic national identity that emphasized Palestinian-ness over wider Arab or Islamic affiliations, among others (even when these were acknowledged or co-opted). In short, the Palestinian experience has been remarkably similar to that of Arab states (particularly republican Egypt, Algeria, Syria, and Iraq, but also, arguably, monarchic Jordan in certain respects) in terms of organizational structure, political practice and culture, state nationalism, rent-based relations with society, and the social origins of the "new elites" who came to power at various points in the post-1945 independence period.[7]

This was hardly a predictable outcome in the aftermath of *al-nakba,* and so the question is, what brought it about nonetheless? In answer, the central argument of this chapter is that it was war that enabled the PLO to emerge as the nonterritorial equivalent of a state (paradoxical as the notion may be), assert its brand of nationalist discourse and practice, and structure its relations with Palestinian society accordingly. This is not to suggest that these were conscious aims or anticipated consequences of the much-vaunted "armed struggle," but simply to observe that war assisted the PLO both in acquiring such institutional autonomy as it did and in obtaining the resources (whether material, especially financial, or symbolic) that allowed it to occupy a statelike position in relation to its "domestic" constituents. War legitimated political leadership and helped decide the outcome of internal contests over political programs and the choice of military and diplomatic means, while in parallel altering the form, substance, and direction of relations with external actors. Similarly, it contributed unmistakably to the shaping of Palestinian nationalism, and exercised both direct and indirect influence on the political and economic fortunes of various social forces, affecting their access to key resources and impinging on paths of elite formation, and so shifting the relative balance between them.

That said, it is important to understand what war was, and what it was not. War explains *how* the Palestinians, having departed from so divergent a starting point, arrived eventually at a model of state-building and state-society relations close to that of many Arab countries, but it does not explain *why* they did so. This can be understood only by situating the impact of war within the broader context of the prevalence and power of two sets of factors that have affected state formation throughout the postcolonial world. The first consists of the models and norms of the international system— foremost of which are the "universalization of the territorial state format," along with nationalism and other legitimizing enterprises such as welfarism and development—and the politically motivated interventions of major global and regional actors that provided opportunities for local actors to secure material resources in the form of strategic and diplomatic support or financial and military assistance.[8] The second set comprises structural factors and secular trends affecting many postcolonial and developing countries worldwide, especially the expansion of state sectors, increase in salaried employment generally, spread of modern education, accelerated urbanization, and the rise of rentier politics financed by primary commodity exports and the rewards of superpower rivalry.

These are the factors that shaped the formation of modern Arab states and societies since World War I. They determined both the range of possible resources and images that could be brought to bear and the paths that Palestinian political and social transformation might actually take. War was a mechanism that brought certain of the external factors to bear and a midwife (to use Raymond Aron's expression) for shifts in internal political and social balances at key moments (such as 1948 and 1967), but the fact that it could deny or provide opportunities for political and social change should not encourage us to read backward and regard it as either a sufficient condition for such change or a determinant of its direction.[9] Indeed, whether it was even necessary is debatable: to belittle its role would be ahistorical and would seem to replace one monocausal explanation for another, but to posit that the transformation of Palestinian politics, institutions, nationalism, and society since 1948 would not have occurred as they ultimately did without its impact is to privilege it excessively and to confuse the contingency of its timely intervention for necessity. Indeed, given the additional knowledge that the PLO finally acquired qualified jurisdiction over a limited demographic and territorial base in the West Bank and Gaza Strip in 1994 through negotiation with Israel, it may be argued that war was not a necessary factor in its acquisition of what Barry Buzan terms the three components of the modern state, namely, the idea of the state, its physical basis, and its institutional expression.[10]

To the extent that it was a decisive factor at key moments in modern Palestinian history, war acted as an intervening or facilitating variable. That is, it was a variable that could accelerate social processes that were already under way (such as the transition of elites) and that Palestinian (and other) political actors could use to accomplish ends (such as the promotion of Palestino-centric nationalism or the centralization of the PLO's functional and symbolic authority) that might well have been achieved anyway through other means even if war had not occurred, albeit in somewhat different form or pace. After all, broadly similar political and social transformations took place in Egypt, post-1962 Algeria, Syria, Iraq, and Jordan in the same period without being driven by war; the militarization of politics and society in the Palestinian case was not fundamentally different in its political underpinnings and social consequences and did not require further war-waging once in place. Of course, there is a tension here between the seemingly incidental nature of war's intervention and its equally demonstrable centrality in certain respects, but this is explained largely by the manner in which other actors blocked or impeded alternative courses of Palestinian institutional, political, and social evolution.

The role of war in the Palestinian case therefore also diverges fundamentally from its historical role in state formation in Europe. In the latter case, as Charles Tilly has argued, war and the preparation for war acted as a central and necessary mechanism affecting the entire process of state formation.[11] Internally, it involved rulers in extracting the means of war ("men, arms, supplies, or money to buy them") from those who held them, in a process that led them to centralize state authority, to impose taxation and conscription, and to develop the administrative agencies to manage these and other expanding functions. This involved extensive struggles with existing social organizations, out of which arose durable political and administrative structures; these structures, moreover, varied from one country to another according to the relative strength of those social organizations, the nature of previous constitutional arrangements, and the degree of concentration of capital and coercive resources and their geographical distribution.[12] As Tilly, Gianfranco Poggi, and others have also noted, the eventual result of these negotiations and contests between statebuilders and other domestic actors was the rise of nationalism and notions of citizenship and democracy. At the same time, war was an important mechanism tying state formation to the external environment—which impinged on that process, assisting it in ways and limiting it in others—and helped develop common "rules of the game" among states. Thus "national states always appear in competition with each other, and gain their identities by contrast with rival states; they belong to *systems* of states."[13]

In the Palestinian case, only the external dynamic is really evident, and then only to a limited degree, in that the PLO was able to utilize war as a means of activating regional or international alliances and of generating needed political and material resources. In addition to helping the PLO carve out sanctuaries in three of the four Arab frontline states, external alliances also allowed it to acquire "strategic rent," much as Egypt, Syria, or Jordan did (whether as confrontation states with Israel or as peace brokers with it) from the oil-rich Arab states or from the superpowers. Crucially, the availability of financial and other assistance from external sources obviated the need for the PLO to engage in struggles with domestic social actors or to transform social relations in order to extract revenues for the purposes of war waging and state building. It further follows that the threat of war, and the *idea* of war as an image and even a norm, was more important than *real* war, the actual conduct of war. Indeed, most episodes of large-scale war waging in the Palestinian experience (as in the wider Arab-Israeli context more generally) are noticeable for their brevity, however seriously the Palestinians took their armed struggle and genuinely fought for the rights they claimed.

In most, if not all, of these respects the PLO followed the path of other postcolonial and national liberation movements in that war was not about the attainment of a desirable new political or social order (such as democracy or socialism), but rather was a means of creating a state in the Western image and a validation in itself.[14] Evidently this privileged external factors while marginalizing internal contests (during the struggle for national liberation) between the principal domestic political actors and social organizations over the extraction of material resources and the construction of structures embodying and governing their relations. This had several negative consequences. One was that war could do as much to undermine state building as to facilitate it; for example, the availability of external supporters engaged in their own rivalries encouraged competitive rent-seeking within the Palestinian movement and therefore fragmented it and impeded centralization. Second, the parallel marginalization of internal social contests meant that the "right to rule" was based almost exclusively on the conduct of armed struggle and on control of the state and military apparatus, leaving fundamental aspects of state-society relations, best represented by the notions of "social pact" and citizenship, unresolved for the postindependence phase. It follows, finally, that the enduring legacy of political institutions and practices put into place during armed conflict is a postcolonial polity that is fragile, fragmented, and contested internally.[15]

The role played by war in Palestinian political and social transformation, and the limits of that role, are revealed in four discursive areas in which identities, practices, and institutions were constructed in relation to international, regional, and local contexts. The first area is institutional and refers to the way in which the PLO was able, whether through conflict of its own making or that of others, to generate and maintain institutions and to obtain recognition as and relate as an autonomous political actor to the Arab and international state systems. The second area is political in the sense of praxis and refers to the manner in which the armed struggle enabled the PLO to acquire a "political class," establish a new political system with its own culture and "rules of the game," decide the outcome of programmatic contests (both political and ideological), and legitimize internal practices and modes of control. The third area is ideational and refers specifically to the connection between political violence, on the one hand, and the emergence and dominance of particular forms of Palestinian nationalism, on the other hand. The fourth, and last, area develops the notion of community by looking at the role of war in societal construction and, in particular, at its impact on social balances and elite formation. In all cases, the focus of this chapter is on those institutional, political, ideational, and social processes and forces that were promoted, enclosed, or otherwise represented by the PLO.

CARVING A REGIONAL NICHE, ACQUIRING INTERNATIONAL CHARACTER: INSTITUTIONAL AUTONOMY AND RECOGNITION THROUGH CONFLICT

To apply loosely to the PLO Theda Skocpol's observation about Third World social revolutions in general, "these revolutions have happened in settings so penetrated by foreign influences—economic, military, and cultural—that social-revolutionary transformations have been as much about the definition of autonomous political identities on the international scene as they have been about forging new political ties between indigenous revolutionaries and their mass constituents."[16] War, arguably, played its most significant role in this context, because the construction of statist political institutions required attainment of a key attribute—autonomy—as well as a territorial base (however modest), and therefore necessarily placed the

PLO in a position of direct contestation and negotiation with external actors and host states. Yet because this process also required attainment of a second key attribute—recognition—adopting the norms and "rules" of the dominant states system eventually became a more effective way of mobilizing external support than waging war, even if this imposed constraints on the use of violence and necessitated parallel changes in national objectives and internal political structure.[17]

The importance of autonomy from, and recognition by, established state actors in determining the form and purpose of Palestinian political institutionalization was evident especially in the thinking of Fateh, the mainstream nationalist guerrilla group formed in 1958–59 that was to win lasting control of the PLO a decade later. Fateh's founders were clear that recognition by others, attainment of internal unity, and assertion of a Palestinian national identity required an autonomous political entity with independent organizational structures. Indeed, they were convinced that the aftermath of *al-nakba* "would have been very different had the Palestinian leadership after 1948 continued to raise the banner of the government and entity."[18] The inability of the All-Palestine government (formed in the closing stages of the first Arab-Israeli war in October 1948) to assert itself in the face of the indifference of some Arab states and active obstruction by others had prevented the Palestinians from independently making decisions and had turned them into a "neglected mass."[19] From the outset Fateh argued that "the Palestinian entity is necessary in order to concentrate the efforts of our people and mobilize them" but believed equally that an entity could only come into being if a Palestinian vanguard imposed it on the Arab state system and forced recognition through armed revolution.[20]

Yet the need for recognition imposed its own logic. Fateh initially adopted an ambivalent, and then openly hostile, attitude toward the PLO, which was seen upon its establishment in 1964 as an overly bureaucratic and obedient instrument in the hands of the Arab states, which had formed it "with the express purpose of pre-empting the revolutionary process among the Palestinians."[21] For this reason many in the ranks at first opposed taking over or preserving the PLO structure once this became possible after the resounding Arab defeat at Israeli hands in June 1967. However, the Fateh founders were also aware that "the PLO enjoyed Arab legitimacy, and this was important," since it "embodied an official Arab commitment to the Palestinian people for the first time."[22] In any event, Fateh conducted a systematic takeover of the PLO and its constituent agencies and departments from 1968 onward, instituting what was to be a permanent symbiosis between itself and the latter's statist structures, much like that in Arab and non-Arab states dominated by a single or governing party.

The central issue here is that war played a pivotal role in the PLO's acquisition and maintenance of its institutional character, described by a senior official as "an ambition of all revolutions," above all by enabling it to "exercise significant autonomy in the face of other centers of state power."[23] The foremost instance of this dynamic was the 1967 war, which, by weakening the Arab host governments politically and militarily, enabled the Fateh-dominated PLO not only to establish guerrilla sanctuaries in rural areas but also, critically, to acquire an extensive political and administrative presence in the capital cities and other urban centers of Jordan, Lebanon, and (albeit to a lesser degree) Syria in the next two years. The extraterritorial status of the PLO was, moreover, recognized officially by the host authorities in these countries and enshrined in a variety of formal treaties and secret memoranda. Conscious of the immense moral and material advantages conferred by its ability to openly mobilize and direct its mass base, the PLO also resorted to force on several occasions between November 1968 and May 1973 to defend the arrangements sanctifying its public presence in Jordan and Lebanon, and formed a fully fledged state-within-the-state to protect its various institutions and consolidate its international diplomatic status following the disintegration (to which it had contributed heavily) of the Lebanese state in 1975–76.

At the same time it is necessary to note the limits of war as an instrument of Palestinian institutional development. The events of June 1967 and the following decade explain the ability of the PLO to obtain considerable extraterritorial privileges and institutional autonomy in specific host countries, where it became part of domestic power struggles and social conflicts, but are insufficient to explain why it came to enjoy regional and international recognition on a scale unprecedented for a nonstate actor. Here the answer lies primarily in the nature of the regional and international systems of states rather in the role of war as such, although the latter acted repeatedly as a mechanism connecting attitudes and developments at these levels with Palestinian institution-building. For example, it is true that the military conflict of 1948 triggered the collapse of Palestinian national institutions, but the conflicting agendas of the main Arab states were a major contributory factor throughout the 1947–49 period, as they opposed successive Palestinian proposals for the establishment of an Arab government and state in mandate Palestine and then disbanded Palestinian irregular forces.[24] Their rivalry moreover ensured the subsequent lack of all but the most nominal Palestinian representation in collective Arab fora, such as the League of Arab States, until the mid-1960s. The situation changed only when the escalation of inter-Arab rivalries made the Palestinian issue a potent "card" in regional politics from 1959 onward: it eventually became expedient to set up the PLO as a means of defusing the "Arab cold war" and deflecting the rising Palestinian nationalism that threatened an untimely war with Israel, a fear that PLO founder Ahmad Shuqayri and Fateh separately utilized to gain leverage and seek relative autonomy from the Arab states.

The latter example, moreover, shows that it was the threat of war, rather than its actual conduct or material results in the first instance, that was most potent in Palestinian hands. This potency was due to the tendency of the Arab states system to balance politics and mutual intervention and to the power of symbolic competitions based on shared norms among its members.[25] It was this that imbued the PLO with an influence far exceeding its physical capabilities after the 1967 war and, in following years, magnified the coercive power that the PLO could bring to bear in Jordan and Lebanon by mobilizing wider Arab backing for its extraterritorial status. The same characteristics could also render the PLO vulnerable to challenges from internal opponents who had outside backing—witness Syrian and Libyan support for the rebellion that split Fateh and the PLO in 1983. But more generally these characteristics enabled the PLO to mobilize regional resources and alliances to protect its institutional autonomy from external rivals—witness Arab support during the 1970 conflict in Jordan (extending to military intervention in the case of Syria) and Egyptian and Iraqi logistic backing against the Syrian intervention in Lebanon in 1976. Cold war politics further magnified the PLO's manipulative capability as a convergence of interest emerged in the 1970s with Soviet policy objectives in the Third World.[26] Indeed it can be argued, as Frantz Fanon did with regard to the Algerian war of independence, that the Palestinian armed struggle only had a serious impact and that the PLO was only able to win external recognition (at least from one superpower camp) in an environment in which international contradictions were "sufficiently distinct."[27]

Contradictions in the regional and international systems did not privilege war as a mechanism of political change, however, even though it provided the opportunity for ideological and programmatic changes. It was quite the reverse, as the evolution of PLO national objectives and strategies in the 1970s suggests. Thus the defeat of the guerrilla movement in Jordan in 1970–71 contributed to the mainstream PLO leadership's pragmatic shift from its objective of liberating the whole of mandate Palestine by force to the more modest goal of setting up a state in the West Bank and Gaza Strip by negotiation. In much the same way, the Arab-Israeli war of October 1973 provided the PLO with a critical political moment in which to develop a credible diplomatic option, based on the justifiable calculation that it was in the interest of the major regional and international powers to settle the conflict. In both instances the first need was to consolidate PLO standing in the Arab states system: having faced several challenges to its status as Palestinian national representative after the expulsion from Jordan, it won decisive Arab confirmation (and defeated the Jordanian political challenge conclusively) following the October war. This was the basis for securing the second need: Arab diplomatic and strategic support, greatly enhanced by the war and use of the "oil weapon," was critical in mobilizing international support for the Palestinians, leading over the next year to PLO membership in the Non-Aligned Movement and Islamic Conference Organization, observer status at the UN and Organization of African Unity, and official recognition from the Soviet bloc and other socialist countries.

The PLO could, and did, continue to use military means to advance its national agenda, but this occurred increasingly within a referential framework provided by the international state system. Even the use of terror in 1968–73, counterproductive as it was in terms of alienating Western public and government opinion, proved in the long run to have demonstrated the necessity of addressing the Palestinians as a distinct and separate strand in the wider Arab-Israeli conflict. However, the PLO also increasingly utilized more conventional military means to assert its political status and uphold its statist character. The transformation of its guerrilla forces after 1971 into semiconventional units with regular training, command and logistics structures, and heavy weaponry was as much a reflection of this concern ("soldiers, not bandits or terrorists") as was the provision of a guard of honor for foreign dignitaries visiting PLO headquarters in Beirut up to 1982. The PLO meanwhile cemented its diplomatic gains in some instances by supplying arms, training, and combat personnel to Arab and Third World countries or Soviet allies—such as Libya, Uganda, Zimbabwe, and Nicaragua—and in others gave military assistance to domestic opponents of governments deemed hostile—such as Pahlevi Iran—as a means of pressure. Conflict could also be used to engage outside powers in support of the PLO's political and diplomatic agenda: its military policy during the Israeli siege of Beirut in summer 1982 was calibrated to the diplomatic rewards it expected, and succeeded in prompting active Franco-Egyptian diplomacy on its behalf at the UN, while later its pursuit of the bitter "camps war" with the Lebanese shi'a Amal militia in 1985–88 helped it restore relations with certain Arab states and the USSR.[28]

The above account indicates that two, contradictory dynamics were in operation even as the PLO gained the autonomy and recognition it sought (both externally and internally). First, the fact that the PLO was obliged to observe certain norms (above all, that of sovereignty) in order to gain membership of the Arab states system, and to moderate its goals and means in the conflict with Israel in order to gain acceptance from the international community, demonstrates the limits of war as a means of acquiring recognition in the international system, at least so long as war does not come with exclusive control over territory and population. Indeed, the more noticeable trend was the substitution, by the mid-1970s, of the discourse of "guerrilla warfare" and "people's war" with a terminology drawn directly from United Nations resolutions that spoke of "legitimate" and "inalienable" Palestinian rights, including especially that of self-determination.

Second, and conversely, the quest for recognition could work to opposite effect. Important as Western acceptance was, the PLO's constant concern to combat any challenge to its status as the *sole* legitimate representative of the Palestinians and its determination, to that end, to secure the loyalty of its mass constituency and internal opposition, at times required it to adopt political stances (such as refusing to acknowledge unconditionally Israel's right to exist) or military tactics (such as Fateh's foray into international terrorism in 1971–73 and its "suicide" raids against Israeli civilian targets in 1974–78) that severely damaged or even derailed its diplomacy. Yet the overall trend was toward a redefinition of national goals and therefore, implicitly, of political constituency, culminating ultimately in the PLO-Israel Oslo Accords of September 1993. The ability of the Fateh-dominated mainstream PLO leadership to conduct this protracted transition, despite the deep rifts it produced and the fundamental challenges it posed to national identification, testifies to the durability of the political structures and practices developed over the preceding three decades of conflict.

WAR AND THE ORDERING OF POLITICS

Predictably, the transformation of Fateh and the other guerrilla groups into a mass movement after 1967 was accompanied by new contests over leadership, organization, and political agendas. Furthermore, the attempt to incorporate various social forces and build a secure constituency, acquire material resources, and institutionalize political practice led to intense competition and increasingly complex internal politics. In all cases armed conflict shaped the emergent political system, defining its sources of legitimacy, rules and norms, organizational structure, and balance of power. However, it did so in relation to two additional factors that exerted a determining influence on the evolution of Palestinian politics: "rent" and Arab intervention. The interplay of these factors can be assessed by examining the manner in which war impacted on three sets of political relations: between the various guerrilla groups, within their respective memberships, and between the PLO and its social constituency.

The cornerstone of the new political system was the legitimating function of armed struggle. This derived in part from the Palestinian "repertoire of contention," the stock of familiar forms of collective action going back, in particular, to what Palestinians call the Great Revolt of 1936–39, rather than from an ends-related calculation of the effectiveness of military means.[29] It also owed much to extraneous factors, not least the marginalization or outright suppression by Israel and Arab governments of alternative forms of Palestinian political mobilization, including nonviolent ones, that appeared initially in the aftermath of *al-nakba*.[30] The Palestine Refugee Congress was one such example: formed by middle-class figures who were not affiliated to the pre-1948 national leadership, it sought to represent the Palestinians at the 1949 Arab-Israeli armistice talks but was excluded by both sides. Similarly, although the communists were undoubtedly in the minority in calling for coexistence with Israel after 1948, government repression of both communists and the other, more militant opposition parties that Palestinians joined in significant numbers in the Arab frontline states (and Israel) in the 1950s further narrowed the scope for political mobilization within participatory frameworks provided by the host states. The subsequent preeminence of organized violence makes it difficult now to conceive that the Palestinian national movement could have adopted any form or means other than those it eventually did, but this was not a foregone conclusion then; a significantly different course of events might have arisen had Israel and one or more of its Arab neighbors come to agreement on any of the various peace proposals mooted in the early years after 1948, or had a Palestinian state been allowed to come into being in the West Bank and/or Gaza Strip with the authority to press its own claims in diplomatic fora.

In any case, the legitimating function of armed struggle was evident in its role in the political demise of the founding generation of the PLO, which had been established with Arab sponsorship in 1964. Unable to break free from the restrictions imposed by host governments and army commands on its political and military activity, the original PLO leadership headed by Ahmad al-Shuqayri was discredited both by its association with the organization's poor showing in June 1967 and by its own inability afterward to devise new strategies and resume the conflict with Israel. Conversely, the speed with which Fateh and other guerrilla groups responded to the occupation of the West Bank and Gaza Strip—by sending in hundreds of cadres in an (ultimately futile) attempt to mount an armed insurrection[31]—assured them majority support within the Palestine National Council (the PLO's unelected parliament-in-exile) and then formal control of its executive committee and conventionally structured liberation army by February 1969, when Fateh's Yasir Arafat was elected chairman. This seemed to validate the underlying Blanquism in Fateh's strategy, inasmuch as it had deliberately used the energetic and unrelenting action of a small number of resolute activists both to draw the mass of the people behind itself and to seize the helm of the quasi-state PLO, despite its own lack of the requisite organization and a revolutionary ideology.[32]

The imprint that the ethos of armed struggle left on the guerrilla movement as a whole also showed how successful Fateh had been in providing a "collective action frame," "inscribing grievances in overall frames that identify an injustice, attribute the responsibility for it to others and propose solutions to it."[33] After 1967 only those groups that demonstrably engaged in guerrilla warfare could compete with rival claimants to command a mass following, and only those individuals who actively espoused its tenets could join the ranks of the new "political class" that now formed. As George Habash, the secretary-general of Fateh's main rival, the Popular Front for the Liberation of Palestine (PFLP), put it, "The masses will not heed any group unless they feel that it continues its strikes against Israel and increases its effectiveness."[34] Additional confirmation of the validity and effectiveness of armed struggle, both as a norm and as a model, came from the recent experience of postcolonial national liberation movements: the Algerian was the closest in many respects, but the anti-British campaigns in the Suez Canal zone in the early 1950s and Aden in the mid-1960s were also influential, as of course were the successes of China, Vietnam, and Cuba. Cold war politics, Sino-Soviet rivalry, and the proliferation of new liberation struggles in sub-Saharan Africa and Latin America only emphasized this further.

However, despite being a necessary element, the legitimacy derived from the armed struggle is not sufficient to explain either the durability of the nascent Palestinian political system or the emergence of rules and norms that were understood and shared by all. Similarly, the system's rapid institutionalization provides an important part of the explanation but does not answer fully the question of why this proceeded in one form and not another or took place at all, nor why all the various guerrilla groups found it either desirable or unavoidable to join the statist, umbrella structure of the PLO, whether sooner or later. The political preferences of the group that had taken the lead in the armed struggle were of course influential, but Fateh hardly had a monopoly on military action and the legitimacy to be derived from it, and in any case its own ranks were initially divided over whether or not to retain the PLO structure and how to achieve national unity with other groups.

Two additional factors contributed significantly to the shaping of the emergent political system and, arguably, exerted a determining influence on it: rent and Arab intervention. These were interlinked, as it was both the huge popularity of the guerrilla movement after 1967 and consequently its appeal as an ally or proxy in inter-Arab disputes—especially among the countries of the Arab East—that secured financial, military, and other material assistance from Arab governments of all ideological persuasions. Much as was the case for attracting recruits and building a mass following, military action against Israel was the primary means to demonstrate credibility to Arab backers and ensure the continuity of external support. This only reinforced the fragmentation of the Palestinian arena by increasing the advantages to be obtained from forming new guerrilla groups and competing for rent flows. The other cost was the magnified vulnerability of the movement as a whole to the political agendas of the Arab states, which penetrated the PLO and threatened to entangle it in unwanted conflicts with host governments and to undermine the Arab consensus it strove to weave around its representation of the Palestinian cause. This "transnationalization" of domestic politics caused particular concern for Fateh, which, after the election of Arafat, strove to assert the authority of the PLO as the central decision-making body of the guerrilla movement as a whole, in keeping with its long-standing search for a unified Palestinian organization in order "to preserve identity and independence" from Arab control.[35]

The armed struggle was therefore open to all as a field for political contestation, no less so because external rent was equally available to all, often out of real proportion to military effectiveness or size of popular base. Indeed, the weakness of Palestinian social forces or corporate identities in exile only confirmed the bargaining power of the guerrilla groups, since effective alternative channels for contestation and negotiation did not exist, and encouraged political fragmentation and decentralization of authority. What permitted a single, centralized institutional structure to emerge nonetheless was the intervention of war initiated by external actors. This helped decide internal political contests, as well as reduce political penetration of the Palestinian movement by the Arab states (without necessarily reducing its physical vulnerability to them). A significant instance of this effect was the Jordanian civil war of 1970–71, which ended with the expulsion of the Palestinian guerrillas from the kingdom. Worst hit were the leftist PFLP and Democratic Front for the Liberation of Palestine (DFLP): not only had they suffered proportionately more casualties than Fateh but their provocative rhetoric and behavior were widely regarded as foremost causes of the confrontation, leading to an ebbing of public support and internal splits and defections. Fateh was therefore finally able to strip the Central Committee—the main consultative body of the guerrilla movement, which operated outside the PLO structure—of any policy- or decision-making power and subordinate it firmly to the PLO executive committee, which Fateh already dominated.

The ability of the Fateh-dominated PLO leadership to consolidate the Palestinian political system by capitalizing on the incidence of war demonstrates war's utility but does not mean that it was a necessary or determining factor, however. It continued to perform significant political functions, externally as well as internally, but these either took a highly instrumental form of limited military operations geared toward specific policy objectives or else related to the militarization of the PLO's civilian base and internal politics. The brief resort by Fateh to international terrorism in 1971–73 was an example of the instrumental approach, as it was partly an attempt to obscure the PLO's strategic dilemma in the wake of the defeat in Jordan, while its "suicide raids" on Israeli civilian targets in the mid-1970s were intended to spoil U.S. diplomatic initiatives to resolve the Arab-Israeli conflict that excluded the PLO. Similar effects obtained internally, as both the "rejectionist" guerrilla groups, on the one hand, and Fateh and its mainstream allies, on the other, conducted dramatic raids to assert their patriotic credentials and so lend weight to their respective political positions against and for the evolution of PLO diplomacy. The fact that military action also attracted substantial assistance from Arab backers and, increasingly, the Soviet bloc demonstrated both its utility as a means of generating strategic rent and the degree to which its functions had become institutionalized within the Palestinian political system.

The PLO leadership strove from 1973 onward to make its own exchange, in effect, of military bargaining cards in return for diplomatic recognition and participation in the Arab-Israeli peace process. The fact that it consciously sought objectives that ran counter to its founding principles, including nonrecognition of Israel and the total liberation of mandate Palestine, raises the question forcefully of how it was able to maintain internal control despite effecting such a fundamental ideological shift. Here, the second set of political relations, those within each guerrilla group, reveal that more immediate and tangible measures of internal control were the practices and organizational structures put into place in the early years of armed struggle and consolidated in the context of constant military preparation and conflict in the 1970s. It was virtually inevitable for a movement formed in clandestinity and engaged in guerrilla warfare to acquire an authoritarian character; but the durability and cohesion of its top echelons (if not its general membership) are no less striking for that, especially as these features were maintained in the context of a political system that was both highly competitive internally and highly penetrated externally.

Several factors account for this state of affairs. The legitimacy conferred on the founders of the various guerrilla groups by their initiation of the armed struggle was one factor, an advantage they translated, almost without exception, into permanent tenure as leaders. This might seem paradoxical given their inability to achieve their stated national objectives and their questionable military competence, but can be explained in part by their ability to manipulate the situation of perpetual crisis and external threat in which the PLO found itself. Thus the defeat in Jordan in 1970–71 may have caused serious internal splits, large-scale defections, and a marked contraction of the mass base, but it equally enabled the leadership to stifle dissent in the name of survival. The Fateh leadership's resort to international terrorism in this period was also partly a means to restore its internal credibility and distract the rank and file from pressing questions of accountability for recent defeats.

Another manifestation of the manner in which the idea, rather than reality, of war affected internal political relations was the transformation of Fateh guerrilla forces into semiconventional units in the early 1970s in a process described aptly as *tajyish* (making-into-an-army). Initiated in the wake of the expulsion from Jordan and bitterly resisted by many veteran guerrillas on political and ethical grounds, it served to assert the central leadership's control at a critical juncture and was later emulated by the other guerrilla groups. *Tajyish* was also driven partly by a fear of domination by Arab states, above all by Syria, which was host and conduit for a substantial part of Palestinian military manpower and supplies, and was reflected in, among other things, repeated tussles for control over the PLO's Palestine Liberation Army (formed in 1964 as a conventional force under Arab supervision), the bulk of which came under Syrian military command.[36] Of equal significance was the militarization of the civilian membership: responsibility for the self-defense militia in the refugee camps and other population centers was transferred from local civilian to central military commands, and local military commanders were replaced by outside appointees. As with *tajyish*, militarization also met with resistance, which was stifled, sometimes forcibly, and similarly was undertaken first in Fateh and then other groups.

Not surprisingly, both processes were also driven by internal power struggles: the manner in which the centralization and extension of military affairs proceeded in Fateh's case, for example, reflected Arafat's striving both to weaken rivals in the central committee and to assert his authority, following the leadership's wholesale transfer from Jordan, over the independent-minded civilian organization in Lebanon. The ability of the mainstream Palestinian national leadership to override opposition to these processes was, moreover, in inverse proportion to the power and authority of the host state: the PLO's political and military writ was strongest over refugee camps or other areas that were furthest from capital cities and other centers of host-state power or most marginalized socially and economically; it was weakest in the case of communities and strata that were closest, physically or in terms of socioeconomic integration, to those same centers. The result was a marked tendency to authoritarian control and, on occasion, military coercion in the former case, and to negotiation and greater tolerance of dissent in the latter, at least so long as the central government held sway.

Once in place, two factors led to a massive expansion of *tajyish* and militarization of the civilian base. First was the virtually constant state of conflict in Lebanon over the next decade—Israeli retaliatory raids in the early 1970s and attrition campaign in 1978–81, Syrian intervention in 1976, and Lebanese civil war in 1975–76 and intrafactional clashes in 1979–81—in which fixed front lines emerged and Palestinian population centers were frequently assaulted. The need to achieve a decision in local battles, defend refugee camps and other vital areas, and deter foes accelerated the buildup of PLO regular forces and the acquisition of heavy weaponry, as well as the deployment of PLO units in civilian areas and a marked increase in numbers, training, and armament of local militia forces.

Yet this would have been difficult without the second, crucial factor: namely, the externally derived rent reaching the PLO and its constituent guerrilla groups, especially following the meteoric rise of Arab oil revenues after 1973–74 and, albeit to a lesser degree, the commitment of substantial Soviet political and military support. This allowed probably a large majority of civilian members of the various guerrilla groups to be placed on the payroll, nominally in security and other paramilitary agencies, in a process known as *tafrigh* (making-into-full-timers). Their formal subordination to central military commands in this way eroded the civilian organization and undermined its political functions, and therefore ensured the domination of the central leadership, which controlled the allocation of posts and funds. *Tafrigh* was common to all the guerrilla groups, but its impact was reinforced most notably in Fateh (in 1980) by amending internal statutes to stipulate that, in a movement engaged in armed struggle, military personnel should hold a majority of seats on central policy- and rule-making bodies.

The convergence of conflict and rent gave rise by the late 1970s to a system of political management best described as neopatrimonial, characterized at one and the same time by nationalist co-optation and charismatic politics, concentration of decision-making and allocative power, clientalist internal relations, and organizational fragmentation.[37] It hardly needs to be said that this was moreover a male-dominated, in many ways patriarchal, system, no less so because it involved and even reinforced the built-in gender biases of war and nationalism.[38] The role played by war in the shaping of this system was largely instrumental, in that it helped Palestinian political actors to decide internal contests and to justify the militarization of internal relations. Much the same can be said of the third set of political relations, namely, those between the PLO and its mass base. This was vital given the Palestinian reality of collective uprooting and widespread dispersal, which not only prevented the extraction of resources from a defined social and economic base over which the PLO exercised physical control (for example, through taxation and conscription) but also meant that any attempt to instigate social transformations in order to generate resources, let alone employ them in war against Israel, would necessarily constitute a direct challenge to the political, social, and economic structures of the host Arab states, leading to undesirable conflict. One consequence was a general disregard (even on the Left of the guerrilla movement, for all its rhetoric) for purposive social transformation, to which the emphasis on "pure" national ist politics also contributed. Another was the absence in effect of autonomous social forces to which the PLO might be vulnerable or accountable in any meaningful way. The availability of rent undermined the necessity of social transformation, and indeed reversed the pattern of PLO-society relations, since the former was able to offer financial resources in the form of social services and material benefits to co-opt its target constituencies.

The PLO needed a credible social constituency nonetheless, whether to provide military manpower and secure its state-in-exile in Jordan (to 1970) and Lebanon (to 1982), or to confirm its claim to national and international status as sole legitimate representative of the Palestinians. As discussed earlier, the 1967 war caused the sweeping social and political dislocations that made Palestinian nationalism effective in general; but in a more immediate sense conflict did two further things: it created the insecurity and material dependency that reinforced the PLO's statist function as provider of basic social welfare and a modicum of economic stability, and, by using violence to generate "mass" politics, provided the dynamic that prompted people to accept the organizational structures promoted by the PLO and take active part in them.[39] This was obvious in the case of the communities most directly affected by war, such as the refugees in Jordan and Lebanon, but less so among those for whom it was not a constant experience, such as the Palestinian middle class in Jordan or expatriates in the Gulf. At the same time, it is instructive that the former category was less likely to contest the PLO politically or compel it to negotiate for the material and symbolic resources it needed, while the latter tended to be both more critical of the PLO and more amenable to alternative statist centers (such as that, primarily, of Jordan). The question, then, is to assess the impact of war on the emergence and consolidation of a shared nationalism that underlaid the mass politics of the PLO and its organizational structures.

CONSTRUCTING IDENTITY:
VIOLENCE, THE STATE, AND ETHNICITY

That violence and mass mobilization are intrinsically linked to nationalism is frequently, and rightly, asserted in the literature.[40] It is argued that this is due to, among other things, the impact of military conscription, which both exposes subjects to new experiences and ideas in unfamiliar settings and turns them into citizens with new political claims and material entitlements, and to the breakdown of traditional controls, "of which war is the ultimate expression," leading to "a search for alternative sources of authority."[41] What underlies these factors and explains their causal effect (what makes them "work," in other words) is the way in which they act simultaneously on two social constructs—identity and the state—that determine the access of individuals to needed resources (whether material or moral).[42]

A further implication is that identity is not fixed, especially in its political attachments, although nationalists and ideologues of other hues insist otherwise, despite the role of political, economic, legal-administrative, and cultural institutions in demarcating and reproducing specific identities. War makes certain of that, as its impact on identity is not independent of its impact on the state (and other social organizations): crucially, it affects how the two constructs relate to each other, altering their balance and generating the competitions and crises that may lead either to latent substate collectivities gaining new meaning as political communities or to the suppression of their challenges to the state.[43] The issue therefore becomes not one of how war alters the preformed identity of individuals or groups, but rather of how, through its intervention, they are "induced, persuaded, forced or cajoled into making identifications" that are profoundly political and that affect their relation to the state.[44] At the same time, as I will argue later, the nature and extent of war's impact is bound closely to the manner of its convergence with other contextual factors and underlying processes that exist both prior to, and independent of, war.

It is precisely these dynamics and patterns that are revealed in the case of the Palestinians, no less so because they are stateless. Here, too, the central question is not about the ontological reality or makeup of Palestinian national identity, but rather of how armed conflict prompted people to assert or change identifications, and how this necessarily involved statist structures of one type or another and led to nationalist reformulations. After all, the emergence of a distinctly Palestinian national identity was not a foregone conclusion, since it did not correspond to a defined state-society dyad. The Arab inhabitants of mandate Palestine may have had the historical experience of the British mandate and *al-nakba* in common, but it is not self-evident that they formed a "people" or "cultural community" (as a historically derived ontological reality) distinct from neighboring Arab populations with whom they broadly shared language, religion, and social custom. The ambivalent relationship of Palestinian and Jordanian identities is a case in point: a persistent, if minority trend in Palestinian national politics has argued at least since the 1930s for the inclusion of any Palestinian patrimony under the umbrella of the Jordanian state; the defeat of the guerrilla movement in 1970–71 similarly decided the issue of overt identification for local Palestinians in favor of Hashemite-led Jordan, even as the undeclared policy of "Jordanization" of the armed forces and civil service reinforced the unspoken ethnic stratification of political power in the kingdom. Thus, only the assertion of a specifically Palestinian statist ambition and the associated territorialization of national claims could give rise to a separate political identity.

It goes without saying that violence has been the chosen means of most postcolonial and national liberation movements, but the fact that it was directly linked to self-image and identity was specifically clear to the founders of Fateh. Borrowing from Fanon's writings on the Algerian revolution, in which he stressed the "cleansing" effect of violence on the psyche of the oppressed, they sought consciously to use it as a catalytic agent that could break through what they saw as the resignation of the Palestinian refugees.[45] More to the point, "revolutionary violence," as they termed it, was an expression of independent national will, proof of the existence of a distinct Palestinian people. It followed that armed struggle was required in order to cure "the worst diseases of dependency, division, and defeatism" that had afflicted the Palestinians since *al-nakba*, allowing them to take their fate into their own hands, achieve national unity, and "restore our people's self-confidence and capabilities, and restore the world's confidence in us and respect for us."[46]

Yet just because the integral relationship between identity, violence, and statist political institutions was central to Fateh thinking does not explain why Palestinians should have accepted its outlook and responded to its appeal, let alone done so with sufficient vigor and in numbers to make it dominant among the many guerrilla groups that appeared on the scene in the 1960s. After all, it was not inevitable that a majority of political activists among them should have coalesced at any point after 1948 into a single national movement with broadly agreed-upon objectives and strategies. No more inevitable, for that matter, were the use of organized violence (however likely in the long run) and the dominance of a particular mode of political mobilization or brand of nationalism over other alternatives. Indeed, in the first decade after *al-nakba* most Palestinian activists joined pan-Arab or pan-Islamist parties such as the Arab Socialist Renaissance Party (Ba'th), Movement of Arab Nationalists, and Society of Muslim Brothers, while Palestinians in general still looked to the Arab states, above all Nasir's Egypt, for salvation. In this context the pinprick guerrilla attacks that Fateh launched against Israel in 1965 drew attention to the inactivity of other Palestinian groups and of the Arab states but had only a modest effect otherwise.

For Fateh to be transformed into a mass movement characterized by the use of organized violence, and for its brand of Palestinian nationalism to become dominant when it did, reflected a set of three contingent factors or events: the prior emergence and experience of alternative, nonviolent modes of political mobilization; contextual conditions creating a social constituency potentially available for political action along the particularistic Palestinian lines that Fateh espoused; and a crisis that would both demolish the political and social certainties to which Palestinians clung and shake the physical, administrative, and ideological control of the state structures that held sway over them. Only in the latter instance was war directly a factor.

In the first instance, the experience gained by the activists who joined Arab political parties in considerable numbers after *al-nakba* was an important factor in the subsequent evolution of Palestinian nationalism. This was measurable not so much in terms of their acquiring organizational skills or political sophistication, as in limiting and eventually reversing the appeal of ideologies—from class-based ones to pan-Arabism, Islam, and pan-Syrian nationalism—that invoked broader objectives than Palestine. The parallel marginalization or closure of alternative options—such as the short-lived Palestine Refugee Congress of 1949—was key in the eventual emergence of what can be termed an ethnic form of nationalism, best embodied in Fateh's stress on Palestinian-ness. It also underscores the importance of Palestinian grassroots associations—such as the general unions of students, women, and teachers—which emerged or revived after 1948. These played a crucial role in enhancing a distinctive national consciousness and provided many members of the guerrilla leadership that was to come to the fore after 1967 (although the unions' experience of democratic internal practice was not to survive the takeover of the PLO by the guerrilla groups, most of which had paternalistic or authoritarian roots in Islamist and nationalist forerunner organizations.)

The second necessary factor was the marginality of Palestinians under Arab state control after *al-nakba* in terms of political entitlement, social mobility, and economic access.[47] This varied markedly from one government to another, but for refugees of peasant, worker, or petty trades and employee background in particular the mass migration and economic dispossession of 1947–49 were compounded by their sense of social uprootedness and of degradation resulting from the disintegration of their cultural environment.[48] Nor was marginality the result only of official policies; Palestinians ostensibly shared language, religion, and social culture with Arab host societies, but in reality there were numerous markers that could be used (by others or by themselves) to set them apart, including confessional denomination and socioeconomic mode (Sunni among Shi'a Muslims and Maronite Christians in Lebanon, sedentary agriculturalists among pastoral bedouins in Jordan, and peasants among townsfolk in the cities of West Bank, Gaza, and neighboring Arab countries), not to mention landlessness and refugee status. These became operative in competitions over labor markets and in differentiating access to state services, public employment (both civil and military), and political power, even in Jordan where the Palestinians were granted full citizenship in the course of the 1950s. So, not unlike rural migrants in urban settings, they may have yearned "for incorporation into some one of those cultural pools which already has, or looks as if it might acquire, a state of its own" but knew they had been spurned and would "*continue* to be spurned."[49]

The third necessary factor was an external crisis that would undermine the structural and normative contexts within which Palestinians operated. This happened to be provided by war in their case, specifically the devastating defeat of the Egyptian, Jordanian, and Syrian armies by Israel in June 1967. It shook not only the physical control of the frontline Arab states over their territory, allowing the Palestinian guerrillas to set up sanctuaries along the borders with Israel, but also their political credibility and moral standing. This was especially true of Nasir's Egypt, and of the pan-Arabism and Third World socialism that it, along with the Ba'thist regime of Syria, epitomized. The fact that Fateh now "engaged in a popular discourse that was heavily laced with religious imagery and well-entrenched within the framework of an Islamic-oriented value system," at a time when many Palestinians and other Arabs were turning to Islamic identification in response to the 1967 defeat, only enhanced its ability to draw support from most sectors.[50] However, while the changed external environment and loss of certainties made the Palestinians available for new forms of political mobilization, this was insufficient by itself either to guarantee their active, mass participation in politics or to determine the particular ideological direction and organizational shape their participation would take.[51] Besides the presence of a mobilizing agent, a demonstration of the effectiveness of the model it proposed as an alternative was crucial. This was provided in March 1968, when Fateh opted to confront a vastly superior Israeli punitive force at the refugee town of al-Karama in the Jordan Valley; its decision cost it half its trained manpower, but, aided by astute manipulation of the media, caught the imagination of a public starved of victories and turned the guerrilla movement overnight into a force to be reckoned with in Arab politics.[52] For Palestinians generally, "a revolutionary expectation of fundamental changes was now available as an alternative to the passive acceptance of destiny."[53]

The battle of al-Karama gave birth to a new self-image. "To declare Palestinian identity no longer means that one is a 'refugee' or second-class citizen. Rather it is a declaration that arouses pride, because the Palestinian has become the *fida'i* [self-sacrificer] or revolutionary who bears arms."[54] Armed struggle was the new substance of the "imagined community" of the Palestinians. Guerrilla literature developed this theme by emphasizing the continuity of conflict and the tradition of resistance from the turn of the century; peasant imagery (real or imagined) and folklore were the source for political posters, compilations by academics of proverbs and songs, and traditional embroidery workshops run by middle-class women in the refugee camps. As a PLO pamphlet later presented it, the 1967 war and

conscious action by the "various popular, political and military organizations" had "led to a reawakening of the people's sense of national identity.
. . . And so . . . the process of a Palestinian cultural renaissance began."[55]
Naturally this also came with a romanticized imagery of war and an ethos of
martyrdom; posters bearing the photographs and biographical details of
guerrillas killed in action appeared regularly in the streets, serving to ad-
vertise the military presence and nationalist zeal of the group to which they
belonged, and funerals turned into powerful political demonstrations.

The 1967 war and al-Karama therefore enabled the ascendance of Palestinian "proto-nationalism," to use Eric Hobsbawm's term for the "feelings
of collective belonging which already existed and could operate, as it were,
potentially on the macro-political scale which could fit in with modern
states and nations."[56] This ambition was connected in no small measure to
the rise of lower-middle-class and petty-salaried strata over the preceding
decades, which discovered after *al-nakba* that the social and economic opportunities provided by education and employment could not be translated
into tangible political assets under Arab or Israeli state control. As in other
newly nationalizing societies, the collective dislocation and migration of
1947–49, followed by education, mobility, and the growth of novel strata in
urbanized settings bred strong political discontent.[57] Constant "pilgrim-
ages" between places of study, work, and family residence in different Arab
countries confirmed the commonality of their experience, while the myr-
iad impediments to obtaining travel documents and visas emphasized their
marginality.[58] Little wonder that the marginalized wielded protonationalism as a response to their own middle class, which was perceived to have
"denied its Palestinianism and hastened to obtain the nationality of Arab
and non-Arab states, and which obscured its Palestinian features, for instance by deliberately changing accent or social customs."[59]

The relationship illustrated above between violence, nationalism, and
social change demonstrates the need once again to "unpack" the role of
war more precisely. To adapt Fred Halliday's discussion of Yemeni nationalism, war was one of "a set of contingent events and processes" that explain
the particular form that Palestinian nationalism took and the timing in
which it emerged; but emerge it would, given universal pressures that made
some form of nationalism inevitable by the middle of the twentieth century.[60] Of course the British decision not to establish a Palestinian colonial
state during the mandate period, compounded by the massive dislocation
and dispossession of *al-nakba*, severely impeded the emergence of a dominant form of Palestinian nationalism by or after 1948 and heightened its
fragmentation into varieties that emphasized pan-Arab, Islamist, or Jordanian components of identity (to mention the most salient), and so war can
be said to have played a more central role in the Palestinian case. Certainly
it played an important part in enabling the PLO to promote its own statist,

cognitive brand of nationalism. However, the precise nature or form of this nationalism was dependent on other factors, as discussed previously.

To take this argument further, the success of the PLO was intrinsically connected to the manner in which the Palestinian encounter with Arab host states and societies produced what we have come to think of as a specifically *ethnic* form of nationalism. War, or rather manifestations of armed conflict, were an integral part of its rise, but primarily by providing an additional "marker" to distinguish Palestinians from Arab counterparts. This is not to suggest the ontological reality of ethnie, but simply to stress that, as a relational construct, it was influenced by the lack of alternative political or institutional paths, on the one hand, and the use of violence against, or by, others, on the other hand. Though reflecting a particularly bitter view that was not representative of all Palestinians, the way in which Fateh's founding document described the encounter with the Arab environment and drew appropriate political conclusions is revealing: "Our people have lived, driven out in every country, humiliated in the lands of exile, without a homeland, without dignity, without leadership, without hope, without weapons. . . . With revolution we announce our will, and with revolution we put an end to this bitter surrender, this terrifying reality that the children of the Catastrophe experience everywhere."[61]

In short, the national and state-building project required the assertion of Palestinian difference, not from Israel but from other Arabs, as did the wielding of a specifically Palestinian (as distinct from pan-Arab, Islamic, or pan-Syrian) nationalism; armed struggle provided the means to this end. Equally, and not for Fateh alone, if it was the defeat of the Arab armies that "allowed the Palestinian people to grasp its cause in its own hands for the first time since 1948," then the appearance of an effective mobilizing agent that used conflict to establish symbolic and institutional alternatives to the *Arab* host authorities, produced what may be described as ethnic politics.[62] This implicit ethnicity was, moreover, to be maintained by the engraving in Palestinian official discourse and vicarious grassroots memory of massacres suffered at the hands of fellow Arabs—most notoriously in the Wahdat (1970), Tal al-Za'tar (1976), and Shatila (1982 and 1985–88) refugee camps—effectively creating collectivity through victimhood and death.

Ethnic politics, arguably, manifested itself at one level as "competition ethnicity," by which middle-class Palestinians initially sought in effect, through engagement in the PLO and use of their bicultural capital, to renegotiate their access to the political resources of host states. This was notably the case in Jordan, where they formed a major part of the population and private sector. At another level Palestinian protonationalism took the form of "enclosure ethnicity," as the economically deprived refugees, their numbers swollen by the three hundred thousand Palestinians displaced in 1967, replaced their previously "inward-looking strategy of collective self-definition" with membership in the paramilitary agencies of the various guerrilla groups.[63] Driven by class grievances and resentment of government treatment prior to 1967, the newly armed refugees vociferously displayed their contempt for middle-class sensibilities, reordered power relations with neighboring urban communities to which they had been socially or economically subordinate, and repeatedly assaulted members of the armed forces and security services and other agents of the state (including, not surprisingly, collectors for public utilities).

It can also be argued that, for its part, the Fateh-dominated PLO leadership effected a shift from enclosure to competition ethnicity, but did so in order to secure extraterritorial status in the host countries and negotiate Palestinian entry to the Arab state system, rather than to assimilate culturally and integrate politically within host states. To succeed, this shift further depended on manipulating the territorialization of Palestinian national claims. Having originally raised the slogan of "total liberation" of the whole of mandate Palestine, the PLO effectively reduced its territorial goal to the West Bank and Gaza Strip by the mid-1970s, implicitly at first but then explicitly by the end of the 1980s. The implied redefinition of national identity that this entailed was paralleled by a discernible and lasting shift in the social constituency that the PLO targeted: from the refugee communities of the diaspora, especially in frontline Arab states, to the inhabitants of the territories occupied by Israel in June 1967. This process eventually culminated in the transfer of the PLO's state-in-exile to its new territorial and social base in the West Bank and Gaza Strip following the start of Palestinian self-government under the terms of the Oslo Accords of 1993 with Israel. The question, then, is what role war played in constructing or deconstructing the social constituencies that correlated to these political transformations, and in particular in altering the balance between them and in shaping elite formation.

WAR, SOCIETY BUILDING, AND ELITE FORMATION

The legacy of the British mandate and *al-nakba* raises the question, even more forcefully than for other former Ottoman and former colonial peoples, of how the PLO could emerge and maintain itself as a statist actor despite, specifically, the absence of a single, functionally demarcated Palestinian society occupying a bounded territory and sharing a recognized political and bureaucratic-legal system (defining citizenship, among other things) and a distinct economy (or at least a common labor market). Indeed, to reverse the analytical focus, the Palestinian case provides a telling reminder that society is itself constructed and bounded through contingent factors and historical processes that have tied it intrinsically to the formation of the modern state and, therefore, to the construction of its institutions, political system, and national identity. Certainly in the Middle East, society as defined here is no more a unitary or preexisting sociological phenomenon than is the state—there can in particular be no "national society" without a "national state"—and it may also be deconstructed and restructured as a result of disintegrative trends in the state.[64]

There can be little doubt that war was an important factor affecting the nature and boundaries of Palestinian society in the twentieth century. Repeatedly since 1917 it has exerted a massive, direct impact on the Palestinians through physical interventions that have forcibly altered territorial borders, geographic distribution of population, and economic modes, thereby limiting or redirecting possible paths of social and political development. Much as the defeat of the Ottoman order in World War I and the imposition of the mandate system subsequent to the British military victory replaced one model of social and political community with another derived from the Western experience, so the 1947–49 war decided the outcome of the struggle to establish a modern Arab state in the whole of mandate Palestine and disarticulated local Arab society, removing the shared political framework and economic space within which distinctly Palestinian classes or social forces could form and compete. This role of war underlines the observation that the factors that shape state building have, necessarily, also intervened in society building.

By the same token, rump classes or fragmented social forces could seek to acquire particularistic corporate identities and interests in the aftermath of *al-nakba* by striving for a territorially defined statist structure that was specifically Palestinian, a process necessarily involving war in the Arab, Israeli, and international contexts of the period. This is by no means to accept the leftist DFLP's charge that the PLO was directed by "feudal elements, bank-owning millionaire money-changers, large merchants, and dyed-in-the-wool Palestinian reactionaries"—a view that grossly underestimated the autonomy of the PLO's statist political institutions and bureaucratic elite—nor to reduce Palestinian nationalism to the "chauvinism" of a bourgeoisie suffering constant Arab discrimination that prevented its political influence from matching its economic weight, as the communists argued.[65] But nonetheless there was much in the criticism directed against Fateh by one of its own ideologues, who noted the convergence between elements in the movement who "had suffered greatly from Arab policies" and "businessmen, small merchants, and craftsmen who wish to . . . compete with their counterparts in the Arab countries. Indeed, we can find shopkeepers in a town who will reveal a particularistic Palestinian prejudice. . . . They all want to be master in [government] departments."[66]

In all cases, the precise nature and outcome of social contests owed far more to secular historical processes—such as the spread of modern education, salaried employment, and urbanization—and to the way in which they derived from, or affected, the position of distinct social groups in relation to the state, than to war. There is therefore a fundamental difference between the role of war as an intervening or facilitating variable in Palestinian social transformation, especially as the result of external agency, and the indirect influence it exerted on the evolution of the national political institutions through which Palestinian social forces have competed and gained ascendancy since the mid-1960s. In neither case, it can be argued, was war a necessary or internal mechanism of social transformation; it may have provided the opportunity to translate potential into actual political mobilization and made possible new forms of collective action and discourse, but it did not fundamentally alter or enclose the processes of social change and mobilization that were unfolding continuously before, during, and after armed conflict. War weakened incumbent elites and social groups, but what is striking is how durable they proved to be and how persistent their retention of socioeconomic assets (especially networks); the decisive factor therefore was whether or not statist centers acted on them in ways that institutionalized any changes accentuated by war in their status and material conditions and thus made these advantages or disadvantages permanent.

The distinction is evident in the impact of war on the formation of Palestinian elites, altering the basis of their social status and economic wealth and, above all, contributing to their political decline or ascendancy. The 1947–49 conflict gave a stark manifestation of this dynamic: although some capital assets may have been transferred abroad, the loss of fertile agricultural land and external trade routes in coastal and low-lying regions of Palestine severely weakened the old landowning and merchant elite, much as land reform and the nationalization of industry, trade, and banking did in Egypt and Syria in the 1950s and 1960s. The lack of political and military preparedness in 1948 was, moreover, laid at the door of the old elite, further diminishing its prospects for regaining national leadership. Families whose assets lay outside the areas incorporated into Israel in 1948 were able to employ effective strategies of survival, especially in the West Bank, where they were aided by nominal incorporation of leading members into the Jordanian government; but any prospect of reemerging as a distinct social force, let alone playing a significant political role at either the national or local levels (such as their public support for union with Jordan in 1948–50), was effectively ended by the Israeli occupation of the West Bank in June 1967.[67] The modern middle class, which grew considerably in the mandate period and might have been expected to supplant the old elite in national leadership after 1948, was similarly discredited and fragmented by the exodus. Many of its members were active in Arab political parties in the 1950s and later joined with younger members of the pre-1948 national leadership to form the PLO in 1964, but were sidelined once more by their failure to provide effective national leadership and strategies after the 1967 war.

As suggested above, war could also affect the response of different social groups to the statist brand of nationalism and political institutionalization provided by the Fateh-dominated PLO from 1968 onward. On the one hand, the large number of refugees generated by the 1947–49 conflict broadly formed a natural constituency, whose desire to return to lost homes and properties and sense of collective injustice imbued the founding goals and strategies of the PLO and guerrilla groups alike and provided the armed struggle with much of its manpower. On the other hand, war also disempowered refugee communities, not least by depriving them of the economic basis to present demands, bargain over resources, and generally contest the PLO (or other statist centers) where relevant. The resultant overall political control of the PLO and the rivalry of its constituent guerrilla groups undermined what corporate identity the refugees had, as did the emphasis on nationalist politics rather than social agendas, and weakened them further. Of course the wide disparities in social, economic, and cultural capital that the refugees brought with them, coupled with the marked differences between them in access to social, economic, and political resources and networks in the various host countries or territories, led to significant variations in their relationship with the PLO. Lower-income or lower-status strata were generally more dependent on the social services and salaries it came to provide, as demonstrated in the refugee camps in Lebanon in 1969–82, but middle-class strata were not immune to the impact of war, as the forced exodus of some three hundred thousand Palestinians from Kuwait in 1990–91 showed. In the latter case, moreover, war dispersed a PLO constituency rather than create one, much as the 1970–71 conflict in Jordan and Israeli invasion of Lebanon in 1982 had done earlier.[68]

Comparison with the West Bank is instructive in this context. As indicated earlier, the Israeli occupation in June 1967 was a significant factor in the political (if not always economic) decline of old elite families; more pertinently it undermined the social control and political influence of the Jordanian state and provided the opportunity for the expansion of local civil society associations, media, universities, and other vehicles of potential political activism. Furthermore, Israel helped generate Palestinian nationalism and identification with the PLO by suppressing political expression at a time when Israel's integration and subordination of the local economy to its own was altering social balances and drawing the rural and refugee camp populations into urbanized and industrialized settings. However, the Palestinians of the West Bank differed from their counterparts elsewhere in an important respect: because they remained within their own social, territorial, and economic base (though subject to pervasive Israeli control), they were both less vulnerable to the physical and economic dislocations of war and better placed to negotiate with the PLO over political agendas and material resources, in return for lending credence to its demand for statehood. Their significance for PLO diplomacy explains their growing influence in the 1970s and especially after the PLO's expulsion from Beirut in 1982, leading to an almost exclusive concentration of its political attention and financial patronage on the occupied territories after 1987, and finally culminating in the Oslo Accords of 1993, which dramatized the abandonment of the diaspora refugee communities. At the same time their relative independence, reflected in, for example, the continuing political role of the "modernizing" second generation of old elite families (whether as mayors in the 1970s or as representatives of pro-PLO associations in the 1980s) also explains the PLO's fear of their potential challenge to its leadership and its protracted, if implicit, effort to marginalize them.

Yet these examples only underline the limits of war's role as a causal factor of social change, and instead privilege the policies of state actors and the various assets that different social forces were denied or could bring to bear. This is equally borne out by the manner in which the Palestinian armed struggle, by giving rise to institutional settings and organizational dynamics within which political mobilization and recruitment took place, enabled or limited various shifts in the social balance. Membership in the guerrilla movement could provide a social group with political influence and material resources greater than those of another group to which it had previously been inferior in social status and economic wealth. In the Burj al-Barajna camp near Beirut, for example, refugees from the village of Kabri altered the balance with their former landlords from the market town of Tarshiha (who also became refugees in 1948) by playing a leading role in the local Fateh branch once the camp came under PLO control in 1969.[69] However, because the PLO did not utilize its political authority to extract human and financial resources from these constituencies through conscription or taxation, such shifts in the social balance were neither radical and permanent nor translated into fundamental alterations of social status and economic wealth. The PLO's ability to pursue significant social transformation in the diaspora is moot in any case: even at the height of its physical control over defined populations and territories in Jordan and Lebanon, it exercised little of the legal and fiscal authority needed to alter the national systems of ownership and markets within which the bulk of its constituency operated on a daily basis. Nonetheless, the failure to institutionalize the situation of the refugees (that had been changed after 1948 or 1969) in ways that favored modern forms of solidarity or group consciousness (especially class and gender) meant that forms and sources of traditional authority not only survived but could easily adapt to, and even influence, the PLO neopatrimonial system.[70]

A more striking feature of the relationship between the PLO as a social corpus and the refugees in the camps was the relative stability of the social difference between them. This reflects the operation of both informal and structural impediments to the upward mobility of refugees within the ranks of the PLO's full-time salaried military, civilian, and security apparatus. Thus a majority within the PLO bureaucratic elite came from families deemed to be "resident" or "citizen" *(muwatin)*, that is, who did not become refugees or lose their immovable capital in 1948. (The same can largely be said, for that matter, of the Palestinians who formed the backbone of the political parties of the 1950s in the West Bank and Gaza, and of those who staffed much of the civilian and security apparatus of the Palestinian Authority after 1994.)[71] The vertical divide between refugees and nonrefugees reveals that, while nationalist conflict mobilized both sectors, the heightened existential insecurity of the former and their comparative lack of access, status, and key material assets made them less able to compete for political power. This confirms the importance of ownership of productive assets and property such as small landholdings for sustained political activism, in contrast to patterns of refugee activism. A related implication is that only where social forces had a distinct territorial base were they able to translate political assets into lasting, institutionalized advantage.

These implications appear to be further borne out upon inspection of the background of "resident" personnel in the PLO. Though incomplete, available data suggest a predominance within the bureaucratic elite of Fateh and the PLO, from 1967 onward, of members originating not from the main urban centers of mandate Palestine, which dominated nationalist politics until 1948, but rather from market towns and outlying villages of the West Bank and Gaza Strip.[72] Of all the effects of the armed struggle, this brought the Palestinians closest to the experience of social transformation in Egypt, Syria, Algeria, and Iraq, where new elites of similar social origin and political socialization came to power in 1952–68. Given that this social sector was not a class or group in the classical sense, what distinguished it was its access to, and hold over, state structures; as in other Arab cases, the expansion of state agencies enabled "dynamically autonomous" officers and bureaucrats drawn from previously subordinate social strata or peripheral regions to acquire control over major political and material (financial and coercive) resources and so displace established social forces.[73] Taken in the context of PLO institution-building after 1967, the rise of combined resident and rural elements offers a telling example of how social actors may, by responding to political opportunities with collective action, create new opportunities, in this case the statist bureaucratization and militarization that provided channels for elite recruitment and undergirded authoritarian and neopatrimonial modes of political management.[74]

It is evident that the determinant of these social transformations was not war, but rather the secular processes affecting all Middle East and Third World societies at much the same time. Not least of these were the spread of modern education and salaried employment, especially in government sectors that were rapidly expanding in the wake of independence, and state building and territorialization more generally. In the Palestinian case the expansion of the British-run civil service and wartime economy in mandate Palestine had already laid the basis, but of equal importance were near-universal access to modern education after *al-nakba,* leading, in line with developments in host Arab societies, to the transformation of a "people of small farmers, artisans and traders . . . into a people of clerks, accountants and administrators."[75] Moreover, these trends extended increasingly into the rural population, previously marginal or subordinate to urban sectors in terms of political power. After 1948 new political values and models were derived from the states in which Palestinians resided, worked, and moved—rentier politics and militarization being two salient features—and were further influenced by the international era in which they lived, one dominated by decolonization, cold war politics, and developmental or welfarist state models. The Palestinians were distinguished from fellow Arabs only to the extent that they strove to construct similar structures of their own—framed within the ubiquitous model of the national state—though in this case the enterprise was assisted by the timely intervention of war and the conduct of armed struggle.

To return to the discussion at the beginning of this section, only where a reiterative, recursive relationship has developed between Palestinian political and social organizations may a defined society be said in a real sense to exist or to be in the process of emerging, legitimizing claims to a wider national community and collective memory notwithstanding. In other words, although it is possible to speak of a Palestinian "people" (in the sense of national community) comprised of all the surviving inhabitants of mandate Palestine and their descendants, Palestinian "society" refers to those persons whose conduct of social, economic, and cultural relations is bounded in one manner or another by a political and institutional framework denoted specifically as Palestinian, with which they share a territory and which has successfully contested other statist centers for exclusive functional jurisdiction and a monopoly on symbolic representation. It is therefore the transfer of the PLO's statist political institutions from exile to the West Bank and Gaza Strip in 1994, coupled with its entry into new recursive relationships with local social forces and consolidation of its political power and social control, that heralds the emergence of a distinct, if truncated Palestinian society in those territories. It follows that Palestinian society remains as much "in the making" as the Palestinian state, so long as its institutional and territorial boundaries have not been determined and accredited internationally. Deep ambivalence about the fate of the refugees of 1948 and the relationship between the West Bank and Gaza Strip, on the one hand, and the diaspora, on the other, means that national identity will remain fluid and that "official" nationalism will be seriously contested, not least by political Islam. The foremost social legacy of war for the Palestinians, therefore, is to have generated "the territorial shape of a state, the character of the regime institutionalized within its borders, and the power position of incumbent elites."[76]

SUMMARY AND CONCLUSIONS:
THE PALESTINIANS BEYOND WAR

It is the singular success of the PLO that, while not forming a sovereign state as such, it came to occupy a broadly similar position in relation to its constituents. It sought, to borrow from Poggi's discussion of the state, "to entrust the conduct of political business to a single organisation, and to distinguish that from all other entities harbouring and ordering social existence."[77] It therefore conformed to a key feature of the state: namely, that its "organizational configurations, along with [its] overall patterns of activity, affect political culture, encourage some kinds of group formation and collective political actions (but not others), and make possible the raising of certain political issues (but not others)."[78] Much like a state, the PLO was the receptacle for political legitimacy and the main locus for Palestinian political processes; it was the central arena for the conduct of "national" politics. The fact that opposition groups or factions found interests to pursue within its framework, and gave primacy to political over social issues and clienteles, only reinforced its centralizing, statist character.[79] The sense of existential insecurity—rooted in *al-nakba* but reinforced by the mass dislocations caused by Israeli occupation in June 1967, Jordanian civil war in 1970–71, Lebanese civil war in 1975–76, Israeli invasion in 1982, Syrian intervention in 1976 and 1983, Lebanese "camps war" of 1985–88, and post–Gulf War expulsions from Kuwait in 1991—contributed heavily to this evolution. Underlying this process and binding its different elements together was the consolidation of a shared nationalism, shaped politically by conflict and defined discursively by the Fateh-dominated mainstream PLO leadership.

Ironically, by threatening the PLO's statist character and hard-won international status, war also propelled it to replace its original emphasis on military means with diplomatic ones (albeit backed by more occasional and selective military action). This was demonstrated graphically by the Israeli invasion of Lebanon in 1982, which deprived the PLO of its main institutional base and diplomatic "address" and rendered it dependent on the goodwill of its new Arab hosts in Tunisia and elsewhere to maintain its headquarters and public relations effort. War could also impose untenable choices between allies and the accepted political norms and institutional roles of the regional and international state systems: PLO support for Iraq during the occupation of Kuwait in 1990–91 was in keeping with the mood of its general public, but alienated the Gulf petro-monarchies and Western powers and cost it the sought-after seat at the Arab-Israeli peace talks. The ability of the PLO to survive in both cases underlines the importance of international political, strategic, and financial networks and the degree to which territoriality was only symbolically necessary, as the experience of the Kuwaiti government during the Iraqi occupation of 1990–91 also showed.[80] However, because the PLO was not a juridically recognized state to begin with, it was deprived of the advantages of "negative" sovereignty that Kuwait (and Cambodia, Somalia, and Liberia, for that matter) continued to enjoy even after losing the empirical attributes of "positive" sovereignty.[81]

A further implication is that when the PLO's evolving political and diplomatic agenda required a particular social constituency, it was relatively easy to abandon those segments of the mass base whose functional value had been superseded. This occurred demonstrably as the PLO directed its political and material resources increasingly toward the inhabitants of the West Bank and Gaza Strip after the 1973 war and especially after its expulsion from Lebanon in 1982; by the same token there was a diversion of resources away from the refugee communities of the diaspora, most evidently after the 1987 *intifada* and, especially, the 1991 Gulf War when the Arab-Israeli peace process finally seemed likely to bear fruit. This utilitarian, not to say opportunistic, relationship had long been reflected in the PLO's incorporation of the various trade and labor unions and mass organizations, some of which had previously played a critical role in maintaining a distinct Palestinian identity and politics in the first two decades after *al-nakba*. The corporatism, militarization, and bureaucratization that characterized the PLO in exile were, moreover, replicated in relations with grassroots organizations and social constituencies in the Israeli-occupied West Bank and Gaza Strip. There, Israeli economic and settlement policies and later the 1990–91 Gulf crisis created both the political conditions (generating nationalist sentiment) and those of social and economic crisis that drove people toward the PLO. So although the *intifada* initially appeared to reorder social relations, and thus to offer an alternative mode of politics and institution building and of nationalist identification, the combination of Israeli counter-measures and the co-optive and neopatrimonial policies of the PLO undermined any lasting transformative effect.[82] Local political or social actors could always disengage, of course, but the crucial point is that anyone wishing to conduct organized, mass-based activity found themselves obliged to do so in an established political, institutional, and symbolic field represented and dominated by the PLO and its constituent groups (and subsequently transposed into the Palestinian Authority in 1994).

Moreover, this summary suggests that rent, rather than war, was the indispensable factor in the particular form and path taken by Palestinian state building, nationalism, and "state"-society relations under the PLO. Though generated by the conduct of armed struggle, its effect was to obviate the need for social transformation as a means of extracting revenues for war waging or state building. The PLO merely followed a prevalent Arab political model in this regard, acquiring "strategic" rent much as Egypt, Syria, or Jordan did from the oil-rich Arab states or from one superpower or the other. In turn, the fact that the PLO was able both to wage war and to acquire such autonomy, recognition, and capital as it did without needing to engage purposefully in social transformation (including class and gender relations) emphasizes the shift in Third World state formation since 1945 from an internal dynamic to an external one, appropriating outward organizational forms, ideological norms, and policy discourses available in the international system.[83] War had an instrumental role in bringing the PLO into line with the regional and international systems of states, but because these systems (especially the latter) existed as a prior conditioning framework it was they that determined the structure and norms of the type of constituent unit that the PLO and other "latecomers" sought to construct.[84] Furthermore, although militarization may remain central to state consolidation and maintenance, the fact that the organization of emergent states reflects their adaptation to the requirements of establishing political control over their constituents, rather than to local social and economic conditions, only confirms the shift from internal to external determinants of state building.

To drive the point home in the Palestinian case, the function of war as an engine for political transformation ended conclusively once the PLO was locked into an internationally recognized institutional arrangement, in which capital and international relations conclusively eclipsed violence as vital resources. Even though the Palestinian Authority established in the Gaza Strip and West Bank in 1994 fell considerably short of being a sovereign state, its political and social dynamics differed sufficiently from the earlier phases of armed struggle and *intifada* as to reduce the utility of coercive capabilities to a largely internal function, the continued nationalist conflict with Israel notwithstanding. The Palestinians of the West Bank and Gaza Strip therefore moved into a phase in which the militarization of society and politics still applied to a significant degree (as in Arab states), reflected in a noticeable shift of political contestation to the arena of citizenship rights (including gender, labor, and civil rights). But the reverse trend of the "civilianization" of the military is at least as important, and in future key social contests will be waged without the intervening effects of war against external foes.[85] The forms and channels through which they will be waged owe much to the legacy of Palestinian political and institutional development during decades of armed conflict and of the conditioning contexts of cold war and Arab regional politics, but, from 1994 onward, inward flows of international capital and policy-related interventions of international actors have become the principal variables affecting the state-society relationship.

In closing, the relationship between past legacy and future course of Palestinian political and social development in the West Bank and Gaza Strip is evident in three main areas. First is the continuing tension between state and society (with implications for the instability of national identity) where each lacks clear or compatible definition, not least because of the way in which war previously combined with rent to shape state building without generating concomitant social transformations. Second, the emergence of a neopatrimonial system of political management during the period of armed struggle (and the accompanying lack of mechanisms linking the construction of state and society through contests and negotiations over resources) means that a key struggle since 1994 has been over the definition (or restriction) of civil society and citizenship rights, leading to deepening schisms not only over constitutional arrangements but also over formal and informal mechanisms of social dispute resolution, gender and labor issues, and religion.[86] Third, much as in neighboring Arab states and elsewhere, pressures to dismantle rentier politics and liberalize economics in the Palestinian arena have led, not to a fundamental renegotiation of state-society relations, but to the emergence of a new nexus of state "managers," senior security officials, and big businesspeople connected by overlapping, if variegated, commercial interests and heralding the rise of an authoritarian-liberal mode of governance in a globalizing world.[87] It is perhaps a fitting historical irony that war, which did so much in the first half of the twentieth century to prevent the Palestinians from following the same path of political and social development as other post-Ottoman and postcolonial peoples, should have enabled them ultimately to rejoin that path at a similar point.

NOTES

The author is grateful for comments on earlier drafts of this chapter received from Steven Heydemann, Paul Lalor, Michael Barnett, Rosemary Sayigh, Rex Brynen, Dimitris Livanios, Montserrat Guibernau, Roger Owen, and James Mayall.

1. The best documented account of the exodus is Morris, *The Birth of the Palestinian Refugee Problem, 1947–1949.*

2. The main concentrations of refugees were in Israel, Lebanon, Syria, Jordan, and the Jordanian-ruled West Bank and Egyptian-administered Gaza Strip, with smaller numbers in Egypt and Iraq.

3. United Nations General Assembly Resolution 181 of November 1947 called for the partition of mandate Palestine into two states, one Jewish and the other Arab. Britain, the League of Arab States, and the Palestinian national leadership in exile opposed the plan, albeit for different reasons.

4. The Kurds offer a particularly relevant example of the failure of other peoples to acquire recognition. Eritrea represents a success story, but prior to independence neither the Eritrean Popular Liberation Front, nor the Polisario in the Western Sahara, which gained membership in the Organization of African Unity (OAU), enjoyed status similar to that of the PLO, which was a full member of the League of Arab States, Non-Aligned Movement, Organization of Islamic Conference, and observer at the UN and OAU, and which won full diplomatic recognition from over one hundred countries by the end of the 1980s. In July 1998 the UN General Assembly moreover set a new precedent by voting overwhelmingly to upgrade the observer status of the Palestinian delegation, placing it on a par with sovereign member-states in all respects except the right to vote.

5. On the distinction between empirical and juridical statehood, see Jackson, *Quasi- States: Sovereignty, International Relations and the Third World.*

6. Yezid Sayigh, *Armed Struggle and the Search for State: The Palestinian National Movement, 1949–1993,* pp. viii–ix.

7. This is especially true of Egypt, Syria, Algeria, and Iraq between 1952 and 1968, but arguably also, albeit in varying degrees, of Tunisia, North and South Yemen, Sudan, and even Libya. For the parallels, see Batatu, *The Egyptian, Syrian, and Iraqi Revolutions: Some Observations on Their Underlying Causes and Social Character;* and Lisa Anderson, *The State and Social Transformation in Tunisia and Libya, 1830–1980.*

8. Term from Holsti, *The State, War, and the State of War,* p. 79.

9. Aron, *Peace and War: A Theory of International Relations,* p. 6. Cited in Bloom, *Personal Identity,* p. 60.

10. Buzan, *People, States, and Fear: An Agenda for International Security Studies in the Post-Cold War Era,* p. 65, fig. 2.1, and chap. 2 generally.

11. Tilly, *Coercion, Capital, and European States, AD 990–1992,* pp. 14–15.

12. On the importance of preexisting constitutional arrangements and their link to the social impact of war, see Downing, *The Military Revolution and Political Change: Origins of Democracy and Autocracy in Early Modern Europe,* pp. 3 and 9.

13. Tilly, *Coercion,* p. 23.

14. Holsti, *The State,* chap. 4, especially pp. 72, 77, and 79.

15. A similar argument is made in Frisch, *Countdown to Statehood: Palestinian State Formation in the West Bank and Gaza,* conclusion.

16. Skocpol, *Social Revolutions in the Modern World,* p. 288.

17. The link between autonomy and recognition in state formation is discussed in Buzan, *People, States, and Fear,* chap. 2.

18. Al-Wazir, *Fateh: Genesis, Rise, Evolution, Legitimate Representative—Beginnings,* pt. 1, p. 4.

19. "Fateh Starts the Discussion," p. 16.

20. Document reproduced in al-Wazir, *Fateh,* p. 66. On the need to impose recognition by force, see ibid., pp. 21–22; and *Filastinuna,* no. 36 (April 1964).

21. Al-Wazir, *Fateh,* p. 99.

22. Ibid., p. 99; and [Buha'uddin,] *Dialogue about the Principal Issues of the Revolution;* interview with Salah Khalaf, published in *Al-Tali'a* (Cairo) (late 1969): 9.

23. First quote from 'Umar, "The Palestinian Ramadan War: Position and Results," p. 78. The second quote, in relation to a different context, is from Migdal, *Strong Societies and Weak States: State-Society Relations and State Capabilities in the Third World,* p. 269.

24. An excellent account of Palestinian disarray is Nevo, "The Arabs of Palestine, 1947–48: Military and Political Activity." The best account of Arab policy toward the Palestinians remains Shlaim, *Collusion across the Jordan: King Abdullah, the Zionist Movement, and the Partition of Palestine.*

25. For an extended argument on the power of norms and symbolic exchanges, Barnett, *Dialogues in Arab Politics: Negotiations in Regional Order,* especially chap. 1.

26. For a discussion of Soviet-PLO relations in the cold war context, see Yezid Sayigh, "The Palestinians."

27. Fanon, *Wretched of the Earth,* p. 62.

28. The best account of the link between PLO military policy and diplomacy in 1982 is Khalidi, *Under Siege: PLO Decisionmaking during the 1982 War.*

29. Term taken from Charles Tilly. Cited in Tarrow, *Power in Movement: Social Movements, Collective Action, and Politics,* p. 19.

30. Idea of alternative options taken from John G. Cockell, "Ethnic Nationalism and Subaltern Political Process: Exploring Autonomous Democratic Action in Kashmir," *Nations and Nationalism* 6, no. 3 (2000).

31. The attempt is reconstructed in Yezid Sayigh, "Turning Defeat into Opportunity: The Palestinian Guerrillas after the June 1967 War."

32. This description of Blanquism is from Wolf, *Peasant Wars of the Twentieth Century,* p. 269.

33. Tarrow, *Power in Movement,* p. 123.

34. Popular Front for the Liberation of Palestine, *The Proletariat and the Palestinian Revolution* (two speeches by George Habash in May 1970), pp. 53–54.

35. Quote from Fateh, "Birth and March," pp. 32–3. The notion of transnationalization in this context is from Brynen, *Sanctuary and Survival: The PLO in Lebanon,* p. 15.

36. On the PLO-Arab negotiations that accompanied the formation of the Palestine Liberation Army, Yezid Sayigh, "Escalation or Containment? Egypt and the Palestine Liberation Army, 1964–1967."

37. For further discussions of this system, see Brynen, "The Neopatrimonial Dimension of Palestinian Politics"; and Yezid Sayigh, *Armed Struggle and the Search for State,* particularly chap. 19.

38. Although there is a growing body of excellent studies on the subject, a particularly useful discussion of gender bias in PLO nationalist discourse is Massad, "Conceiving the Masculine: Gender and Palestinian Nationalism," *Middle East Journal* 49, no. 3 (summer 1995).

39. The link between violence and mass politics is derived from the discussion in Arendt, *On Violence*, p. 67.

40. For instance, in Tilly, ed., *The Formation of National States in Western Europe;* Howard, *The Lessons of History;* and Smith, *The Ethnic Origins of Nations.* "The mobilization of the masses, when it arises out of the war of liberation, introduces into each man's consciousness the ideas of a common cause, of a national destiny, and of a collective history." Fanon, *Wretched of the Earth*, p. 73.

41. Breuilly, *Nationalism and the State*, p. 20.

42. Indeed it can be argued, following on Hannah Arendt, that it is only when violence, through wars and revolutions, acts on the construction of identity and the state that it enters the political realm and so becomes something more than violence. See *On Revolution*, p. 19. Also making the link between nationalism, on the one hand, and identity and the state, on the other, is Bloom, *Personal Identity, National Identity, and International Relations*, p. 61.

43. On the relation between collectivity and community, see Martin, "The Choices of Identity," pp. 10–11 and 12–13.

44. Finlayson, "Psychology, Psycho-Analysis, and Theories of Nationalism," p. 157.

45. Fateh published an abridged translation of Fanon in "Revolution and Violence Are the Way to Liberation."

46. Fateh, "The Memorandum Submitted by the General Command of Asifa Forces to the Chairman and Members of the Palestinian National Council in Cairo in Its Second Session" (in Arabic), 28 May 1965, p. 20; al-Wazir, *Fateh: Genesis, Rise, Evolution, Legitimate Representative—Beginnings Part One*, p. 71; and Fateh, "Structure of Revolutionary Construction," pp. 102–3.

47. For an excellent study of the relationship between Palestinian identity, institutionalization, and marginality, see Brand, *Palestinians in the Arab World: Institution Building and the Search for State.*

48. On the impact of social uprootedness, Fred C. Bruhns, "A Socio-Psychological Study of Arab Refugee Attitudes" (manuscript, October 1954), p. 31; on cultural environment, Polanyi, *The Great Transformation*, cited in Block and Somers, "Beyond the Economistic Fallacy: The Holistic Social Science of Karl Polanyi," p. 67.

49. Gellner, *Nations and Nationalism*, p. 46.

50. Quote from Budeiri, "The Palestinians: Tensions between Nationalist and Religious Identities," p. 201.

51. This borrows from the discussion of the role of mobilizing agents in the politicization of Lebanon's Shi'a in Norton, *Amal and the Shi'a: Struggle for the Soul of Lebanon*, chap. 2.

52. The bulk of Israeli casualties were in fact inflicted by the Jordanian army, but Fateh claimed the credit almost wholly for itself. The example of Karama runs counter to the view expressed by Ernest Renan, that "sorrows have greater value than victories; for they impose duties and demand common effort." Renan, *What Is a Nation?* cited in Miller, *On Nationalism*, pp. 22–23. Perhaps the difference is that defeats and sorrow are needed for nation building, whereas victories were more suited to the pragmatic concern of establishing the legitimacy of state building.

53. From the discussion of class conflict and nationalism in Hobsbawm, *Nations and Nationalism since 1870: Programme, Myth, Reality*, p. 128.

54. Yusif, *Palestinian Reality and the Union Movement.*

55. Palestine Liberation Organization, *Palestinian Popular Culture Faced with Zionist Attempts at Arrogation,* p. 6.

56. Hobsbawm, *Nations and Nationalism,* p. 46.

57. I have adapted an argument based on European experience, from ibid., p. 109.

58. I have borrowed a notion from Anderson, *Imagined Communities: Reflections on the Origins and Spread of Nationalism.*

59. Former member of the Fateh central committee and then PLO executive committee member, al-Khatib, "Whither the Palestinian Revolution?"

60. Halliday, "The Formation of Yemeni Nationalism: Initial Reflections," p. 40.

61. Fateh, "Structure of Revolutionary Construction."

62. Quote from Nayif Hawatma, *Action after the October War to Defeat the Surrenderist Liquidationist Solution and Seize the Right of Self-Determination,* pp. 37–38.

63. Terms from Pieterse, "Deconstructing/Reconstructing Ethnicity," pp. 375–76.

64. The term *national* state is used here rather than *nation*-state, based on the distinction made by Tilly, *Coercion,* pp. 2–3.

65. DFLP quote drawn from "The Basic Political Report of the PFLP," p. 664. DFLP cadres drafted the report before breaking away from the PFLP. The communist text cited is *Ten Years after the Re-establishment of the Palestinian Communist Party* (in Arabic) (n.p., n.d.), p. 48.

66. This was the left-leaning pan-Arabist, Naji 'Allush, in "Is the Palestinian Revolution an Arab Nationalist Movement?" pp. 52–3.

67. On survival of old elite families, see Lamia Radi, "La famille comme mode de gestion et de controle du social chez les élites traditionelles Palestiniennes" (manuscript, May 1996). On their political support for the Hashmite throne and union with Jordan, see Ma'oz, *Palestinian Leadership in the West Bank: The Changing Role of the Mayors under Jordan and Israel.*

68. The significance of the multiplicity of Palestinian migrations is discussed in Rosemary Sayigh, "Dis/Solving the 'Refugee Problem.'"

69. Case-study in Jallul, *A Critique of Palestinian Arms: People, Revolution, and Camp in Burj al-Barajna,* pp. 33 and 48.

70. A point made with reference to Iraq in Isam al-Khafaji, "Always One War away from Revolution," *Civil Society* (Cairo) (September 1998): 15.

71. These patterns discussed in my "Social Origins and Political Paths of Palestinian Nationalism: Refugees, Residents, and Bureaucrats" (manuscript, April 1998).

72. Inevitably there are exceptions, though these do not seem to challenge the basic proposition presented here. For example, PLA personnel recruited before 1967 were predominantly refugees rather than residents, but even then probably an overwhelming majority came from rural backgrounds. Similarly, many of the refugees who joined PLA units based in the Gaza Strip came from nearby villages and sedentarized clans that had previously been part of Gaza's agricultural and marketing network.

73. Term from Trimberger, *Revolution from Above: Military Bureaucrats and Development in Japan, Turkey, Egypt, and Peru,* p. 5.

74. On social movements and political opportunities, see Tarrow, "States and Opportunities: The Political Structuring of Social Movements," pp. 48–9.

75. Rosemary Sayigh, *Palestinians: From Peasants to Revolutionaries,* p. 121.

76. Lustick, *Unsettled States, Disputed Lands: Britain and Ireland, France and Algeria, Israel and the West Bank-Gaza,* p. 441.

77. Poggi, *The State: Its Nature, Development, and Prospects,* p. 20.

78. Theda Skocpol, "Bringing the State Back In: Strategies of Analysis in Current Research," p. 21.

79. This borrows from Zartman, "Opposition as Support of the State."

80. Idea from Timothy Luke, cited in Murphy, "The Sovereign State System as Political-Territorial Ideal: Historical and Contemporary Considerations," p. 288.

81. Jackson, *Quasi-States,* pp. 1 and 26–31.

82. In this I disagree with the argument that posits a more fundamental reordering of social relations in the occupied territories during the *intifada,* as presented in Robinson, *Building a Palestinian State: The Incomplete Revolution.*

83. On the role of war and the shift from internal to external state-building, see Tilly, *Coercion,* pp. 195–6; and Tilly, *As Sociology Meets History,* p. 45.

84. This point derives from the argument that only rarely is there a fundamental "reordering of the constitutive units of the international system." Spruyt, *The Sovereign State and Its Competitors,* pp. 186–88.

85. Civilianization in this context refers to the increased role of former military or security personnel in public political and economic life, and to the involvement of active personnel and of the armed forces as an institution in commercial and other business ventures.

86. Examples of the areas of citizenship rights under contestation are discussed in Giddens, *The Nation-State and Violence,* pp. 201–9.

87. The rise of an authoritarian-liberal mode in the Middle East is discussed in Yezid Sayigh, "Globalization Manqué: Regional Fragmentation and Authoritarian-Liberalism in the Middle East."

8

War in the Social Memory of Egyptian Peasants

Reem Saad

The purpose of this chapter is to explore the ways in which Egyptian peasants remember wars.[1] Peasants, who constitute almost half the Egyptian population, have been largely excluded from both academic literature and public political discourse dominated by the urban middle class. This situation is not unique to Egypt or to peasants. Recent studies of "resistance" and "voice" reflect the concern that the dominant classes in various parts of the world have denied representation to marginal social groups such as peasants, women, and blacks. My approach is primarily motivated by my belief that it is important to explore the opinions of social groups whose voices are politically inconsequential. Despite the romantic and patronizing overtones that characterize much work on "voice," it remains a useful concept. In this chapter I do not intend to "give voice to the voiceless" or to celebrate the fact that the powerless have a voice, as much as to investigate what the "content" of such voice can tell us about the contemporary Egyptian village. More specifically, I would like to examine the ways in which war memories both structure and reflect an attitude toward the state that is more complex than is often implied in much of the recent literature on "peasant resistance."[2]

Although official narratives tend to exclude peasants, peasant memories are not a direct or mechanical response to this exclusion, nor are their voices necessarily ones of resistance. Peasants do not define themselves against the state whenever a national issue is at stake, and wars are matters that involve the nation perhaps even more than the state. In the issue of war, as in that of labor migration to oil-rich countries, peasants perceive themselves primarily as Egyptians rather than peasants. The terms in which memories are expressed, however, are still largely related to the world of the village.

The state's (and its allied classes') claim to the monopoly of representing the nation is far from being uncritically accepted or taken for granted. When it comes to issues involving the nation, this claim is ignored rather than resisted. Therefore although the official discourse dominated by the state and the urban middle class tends to exclude peasants and not regard them as complete citizens, peasants have no doubt that they are citizens who speak for themselves in matters of importance to their nation. This is true regarding national issues but not where economic or class issues are concerned. In the latter case, peasants do see themselves as excluded, powerless, and victimized, and this is the area where voices of resistance (everyday forms and otherwise) find expression. On the other hand, the state's attitude regarding peasants is not just one of bias and exclusion. Official discourse about the war shows particularly clearly the importance of the idea of "the people." State and intellectuals glorify the idea of "the people" primarily represented by the peasants who are the "soul of the nation," to use Salim Tamari's expression.[3]

In looking at memories of wars, my main purpose is to examine aspects of the contemporary Egyptian village especially in its relationship to the state. Addressing the events of the recent past is important for the study of the present, especially since many present-day problems are often compared with, or related to, events or conditions witnessed or experienced in the recent past. This interest in the present and how peasants speak of the "now" and the "then" is related to the idea of social memory. What peasants remember or forget informs us about their identity and situates the contemporary Egyptian village within the broader framework of social, economic, political, and discursive relations. The village is linked to the state through various administrative structures and institutions, and the village economy is inseparable from the larger economy. The various levels on which village and nation are articulated shape the experiences of particular individuals and determine their perceptions in major ways.

A basic assumption of this chapter, therefore, is that peasants' perceptions of history are inseparable from their personal experience and participation in the making of such history. Peasants not only know about particular historical and political developments taking place "outside" of the village but are themselves historical actors who have taken part in the making of events and in the general processes of social transformation. This issue is particularly evident regarding peasants' participation in wars as soldiers or their witnessing these significant events as members of the Egyptian nation. There is a corresponding link at the level of narrative between autobiographical and historical accounts. Peasants' reminiscences about recent political events and social transformations are very closely related to their reminiscences about their own life histories. This chapter focuses on the link between the local and national levels by examining the relationship between personal reminiscences and perceptions of the national past. Rather than being a source of facts or data, perceptions of the past illuminate the relationship between past and present, and between a village subordinate discourse and a dominant official discourse. This is not to deny, however, that a better understanding of recent Egyptian history can be achieved by considering villagers' reminiscences and recollections as historical sources.

The study of peasant social memory should be examined in its relation to a dominant official discourse. Peasant discourses concerning public political issues are not a simple byproduct of a dominant discourse nor are they an antithetical image of it. This close link with the official discourse is not only due to effects of the state's political hegemony but is more importantly linked to the multiple identities to which the villagers subscribe. Village dwellers do not only define themselves as peasants but equally they possess a sense of Egyptian-ness that often coincides with the official view of "who we are."

MEMORIES OF WARS AS POLITICAL EVENTS

Before I begin a discussion of war narratives, two preliminary general observations are in order. The fact that Egypt fought its last war with Israel in 1973, coupled with the signing of the Camp David Accord in 1979, places war in the domain of the past. War is not normally a subject of everyday conversation in Imam, although fragments of the events find their way into discussions of current political developments. One resilient memory related to war is the false reports of victory that preceded the shock of defeat in 1967. The state remains unforgiven for this incident that serves as the major evidence for the state's deception and lack of credibility. Official reports of "good news," which are usually met with mistrust and apprehension, often trigger the memory of this incident. Another context in which war is mentioned is related to the personal experience of village men who took part in the fighting. War and labor migration are two major sources of direct contact with the world outside the village. Dispersed anecdotes drawn from the military experiences of peasant conscripts who took part in the fighting find their way into everyday conversation in the village and contribute significantly to ideas about and perceptions of the outside world.

Furthermore, and the second major point, war stories concern the marked generational divide that exists along lines of "war" and "peace." Virtually all males have to perform military service. However, the military experience of present-day conscripts is very different from that of the previous generation who fought in wars. For members of the present generation who serve in the army in peacetime, military service is regarded as a "sentence" rather than as national service. The difference between the two generations is not only due to the change in the general historical circumstances but also to the difference in their respective age concerns. The youth link their military service to apprehensions about the future rather than memories of the past. They particularly stress the element of anxiety, whereby "the army" *(el-geish)* means no more than a two-year delay "in the start of one's life." Seen in this light, the army for the present generation is also linked to the value of the official military discharge papers for pursuing the work opportunities open to this generation, especially those that involve migration. A man cannot obtain a passport or a job in the private or public sector without having performed or been exempted from military service. The generational divide, therefore, applies not only to the very different army experience but also to the perception of wars as political events. This is particularly the case for the 1967 war—members of the younger generation are largely ignorant of it or they lack the passion with which the events of this war are remembered by those who witnessed them as "present."

The following is mainly based on narratives that were recounted for my benefit and upon my request during field work in 1989–90, although I was never the sole audience, as others were always present.

THE GENERAL ABSTRACT NOTION OF WAR

In his book *The Great War and Modern Memory*, Paul Fussell discusses the influence that World War I has had on modern European thought.[4] He also deals with the way the war has survived in modern memory, by looking at the literature and memoirs of the period. Fussell's book is particularly relevant in this context, as many of his insights are helpful when looking at peasants remembering the Egyptian wars.

Fussell shows how World War I influenced people's perceptions of World War II in a way that "is enough almost to make one believe in a single continuing Great war running through the whole middle of the twentieth century" (317). People came to think of the two world wars "as virtually a single historical episode" (318). This is an accurate way of describing how peasants view the Egyptian wars.[5] In retrospect, people came to treat the frequent wars in which Egypt participated in a relatively short period of time as a "single historical episode."

There is no unified, consistent view of war as an abstract concept. However there is talk of war as an important component of Egyptian history. War, in this sense, is not really regarded so much as an event or a number of similar events but rather as a feature of contemporary Egyptian history.

In general, peasants' view of war in this sense coincides greatly with the official view. In this context, peasants back the state and almost never challenge its role as representative of the nation.

Narratives of wars as political events are characterized by what Hayden White calls "a discourse that narrativizes," that is "a discourse that feigns to make the world speak itself and speak itself as a story."[6] This is particularly the case regarding the 1967 war but is also true for talk of war in general. In its abstract dimension, war is often used to express concern about problems of the present rather than traumas of the past. War is linked to other contemporary political issues as part of an attempt to make sense of a present situation.

The most common association here is that of war and debt, the latter being a very contemporary concern. Linking war and debt comes as part of the "conspiracy" theme that is often used whenever an "explanation" is needed. Inflation and deteriorating living standards are the main concerns of the peasants today, and these are always associated in the official rhetoric with the debt problem. The debt problem (and economic hardships in general) and the wars Egypt fought are inseparable in the official rhetoric, especially during the time of Sadat, when they were used in order to justify the peace treaty with Israel. The views peasants express on this matter are heavily influenced by the changing political rhetoric of the different regimes.

In a general interview with Fathi, the mention of wars in this sense links past and present:[7] "The only thing that is annoying people nowadays is the high prices. Also war has affected us to a very great extent. It affected us financially and otherwise. Financially, you and me and everyone has been contributing. The country's economy itself has been contributing. And because I did not have [money] and was fighting I had to borrow. The state borrowed money from abroad, and perhaps, I don't know but I imagine that since the days of the war and until this day there are still debts—long-term debts—for weapons and other things."

The tendency to perceive and narrate certain events in terms of a coherent plot is especially evident when the purpose is to answer a "why" question. Toward the end of an interview with Sayed, who fought in the wars in Yemen and the wars of 1967 and 1973, I asked him, "But why did all these wars happen?" His answer was: "War is like a *fitna* [discord]. The big nations like to *tiftin* [create discord among] the other states in order to benefit. For example, when we fight Israel we need arms; where are we going to get them? Either from America or from Russia. We use these weapons and bring others. We get the most advanced weapons they have got, and with hard currency. They drag us into debt."

Fitna is a key word in the discourse of conspiracy. In the everyday usage it is almost exclusively used in its substantive form, *fattān*, meaning someone who tells on others or who stirs up people in general, thus causing them harm intentionally. As a noun, *fitna* has a strong Islamic connotation and is usually used in situations pertaining to the wider community: Egypt, the Arabs, or Muslims. It refers to a much higher level of evil and manipulation by a person or a group who is not part of that moral community. It is used to explain defeat in wars and the underdevelopment of Egypt and the Arab world.

One important way in which war influenced peasants' views on politics is that it provided them with a concrete reference point regarding the wider world of politics in which they live. Villagers are aware that they are part of a political arena that extends far beyond the boundaries of Egypt. One reason why peasants often resort to official interpretations is that these provide convenient formulations that serve to impose some order on matters that influence their lives but which they have no access to or control over. Peasants, like most other Egyptians, are well aware of Egypt's dependent and often vulnerable position in world politics. The theme of conspiracy expresses a recognition of Egypt's dependent and weak position without, however, compromising the nation's integrity or honor. The conspiracy explanation essentially says that things could not have turned out otherwise. In that sense, "conspiracy" is more of an explanation for Egypt's present state of dependency than it is an explanation of the occurrence of wars.

It is important to note, though, that the conspiracy explanation coexists with other ways of talking about war. The view of war as caused by *fitna* applies mainly in a general and abstract sense but does not hold when applied to concrete cases where the issue of will and initiative is more prominent. When each war is analyzed in its own context, it is justified, usually on the grounds of defending "land" and "house." These are metaphors that are very commonly used to describe the Arab-Israeli conflict. Although this could be taken as an example of how themes from peasant culture bring the abstract closer to everyday concerns, we should also remember that "land" and "house" are powerful metaphors even in urban-based official discourse. The following description of the Arab-Israeli conflict by Sayed is typical: "We are fighting for our land only. Imagine there are people who want to take this house from us. If they came and stood in front of the house and we did not do anything, they would come to sit with us. If we went to sleep and left them there, they would take the whole house for themselves and we will not be able to drive them out of it. Our war is like this. We are fighting for our house and land only."

Even in the case of the Yemen war, however, when Egypt was not defending its land, it was never said that this war was a mistake in principle. Also Fathi's mention of war in the abstract in the general interview is different from the view reflected in a second interview, which was based on his military experience.

WAR AS A CONCRETE EVENT

In contrast to the abstract notion of war, reference to specific wars brings out a tension between peasant and state versions of events. It is true that peasants are willing to go along with certain official justifications for Egypt's present state of dependency, and that they do acknowledge the principle that the state represents the nation and is responsible for regulating and mediating relationships with the outside world. This, however, does not mean that they extend the logic of conspiracy to absolve the state of all responsibility. Peasants' memories of the concrete events show wars as events that belong to the nation as much as, if not more than, the state. Not only are they part of people's personal memories but they are also part of their perception of a collective national past. Memories of wars as concrete events play a major part in structuring perceptions of the national past, producing a view that is not easily influenced by state political rhetoric.

There are two important points here. First, peasants' reminiscences about many issues may not be very different from those of other social groups. The narratives reveal a high degree of knowledge, interest and concern regarding public political issues that are of importance to the whole nation. The fact that their social memory reveals a strong sense of belonging to the nation runs contrary to widespread assumptions that they are ignorant and parochial. A striking example of this biased view can be seen in Richard Adams's observation: "As has been noted by a number of keen observers[,] . . . peasants tend to have an ontology that stresses the concrete and immediate character of social reality. In the eyes of the average Egyptian fellah, the world consists of a series of very concrete social units: his immediate family, his extended family and a group of families known as a village. On the whole, Egyptian peasants remain quite incapable of abstracting beyond these concrete units in order to perceive groups of people who act together on the basis of shared political beliefs or economic conditions."[8]

Second, perceptions of wars as concrete events are linked to peasants' attitudes toward particular regimes rather than to "the state" as an abstract authority. As will be shown later, this especially applies to memories of 1967 and the issue of Nasser's responsibility. This is one of the areas where it is possible to discern a view that may be specific to peasants and where the narratives express the peasant as well as the Egyptian identities.

In discussing the surviving memories and the relative significance accorded them, one should look into the extent to which a national or political event is perceived or narrated in autobiographical terms. A certain degree of participation in any given event allows it to be narrated as autobiographical. The 1967 war offers a good example. Apart from the memories of those who actually took part in the fighting, 1967 is remembered in autobiographical terms by those who witnessed the nationwide demonstrations of June 9–10, 1967, that followed Nasser's resignation. Those who fought, however, possess an added dimension to their involvement in the events, namely the direct experience of the war situation as concretely and physically felt. Elements of this experience enter into the 'izba's repertoire of anecdotes, besides forming an important component of their abstract notion of war. These two types of participation will be termed simply the physical and the political.

Physical descriptions of battles, and repeated references to death, are common to all war narratives. They form part of a definition of war in general and are not related to any particular war. The individual concrete experience of war—the battle situation—is the same in all wars regardless of whether the overall result was victory or defeat. Each battle is as bad as every other. In three separate cases, the description of the physical aspect of war as experienced by the soldiers carries the same message. One such incident is recounted by Abu Assad when a mine exploded during a routine training maneuver in 1953. The other is recounted by Sultan during 1967, and the third by Sayed in 1973. Despite the very different macro context of each of the three incidents, the descriptions of the particular cases are almost identical.

Abu Assad relates his story:

> After we finished our training we were performing a maneuver to make sure that our training had been successful. We were thirty soldiers in a truck, and we stopped at a certain spot in order for them to divide us so that some would simulate the Egyptians and some would simulate the enemy. We went down from the truck and were almost three hundred or four hundred meters away. But that particular spot was mined, and a mine exploded suddenly and turned the ground upside down. It turned the ground, and I fell. I got up after the dust had settled. I got up and looked around this way and that way. The dust had settled. This is God's predestined fate. They were thirty or more. Those whose heads had been separated from their bodies, and he whose body was divided in two, and another whose leg was separated: they resembled a group of pigeons that had been shot at by a machine gun. There was no one standing up in their midst except me. I was running frantically among them, but all of them, they were shattered by the mine.

Sultan tells his story from 1967:

> The aircraft started strafing us. People were flying in the air, in pieces, tents were burning and cars were burning. I hid inside a hole in the ground until the dust settled. The sight was horrible. The cars were burnt and the people dead. Separate legs and separate arms and human heads. We did whatever we could do. One of us would collect some legs and bury them, and another would collect a human being and bury him.

Sayed's account of the 1973 October war begins with the crossing of the Suez Canal, which he recounts with pride and joy; but the bulk of the narrative is devoted to a description of the siege of his squadron in Suez, their physical suffering, and the hardships encountered:

> We were besieged. Aircraft, tanks, and cars were hitting at us and sweeping us like with a broom. . . . I don't know for how many days I had not seen bread in the hands of anyone. When the night came we used to crawl to look for anything we could eat. If I found a small palm tree I would cut its fronds and eat them. In the night. In the morning, no—we could not come out in the morning. I would cut the frond and eat it, and it would taste like honey in my mouth. We would look for the grass—that which people tread on with their feet—and eat it, and it would taste like honey in my mouth.

This type of participation is, naturally, restricted to those who fought in the wars. However, as it is a general feature of all wars, it is not related to a particular time or place. In this sense it does not enter into the process of formulating a political statement about specific historical events.

Because these are examples of universal atrocities that are not restricted to 1967, they cannot be the reason why this particular war is clearly remembered by peasants. Not only was the 1967 defeat a huge blow to the whole Egyptian (and Arab) nation, but it was also a landmark event at the personal and local levels, mainly due to popular "political" participation during the events of 9–10 June. It is worth noting that these demonstrations are known locally as "the revolution" (el-sawra), and almost everybody who was old enough at that time remembers vividly what happened then.

The 1967 war is unique in the way it is perceived and narrated. What Hayden White describes as "emplotment" in narrative historical discourse applies particularly aptly to peasant narratives of the 1967 war.[9] This war is narrated as a coherent, tragic drama, and the causal links are particularly stressed in an attempt to make sense of what happened. When the political events of June 1967 are narrated, the elements of a tragedy are discernible (hero, villain, treason, conspiracy, fate), the tragic hero being, of course, Nasser.

Peasants' memories of 1967 are drastically different from contemporary official representations of this war. A transformation in official rhetoric about 1967 took place after 1973, a transformation that was not paralleled in the peasants' narratives. The defeat of 1967 constituted a huge blow both to the Nasser regime and to the Egyptian people. Euphemism characterized the official presentation of 1967, in which the defeat came to be called el-naksa (the setback; lit. relapse). It is in this light that the 1973 war came to be hailed as a great victory. The "crossing" of the Suez Canal by the Egyptian army (el-cubur) has been imbued with tremendous moral significance, with the metaphor of crossing itself often used to represent a shift to a new age of triumph and dignity *(karama)*. The contrast between the two wars was also heavily employed by the Sadat regime to establish the superiority of Sadat over Nasser. With the 1973 war, euphemism disappeared and 1967 came to be described in very harsh language. To say that 1967 "dragged [the] pride of the Arab nation through the mud" in a school textbook would have been unthinkable before 1973.[10] It is as if stressing the "humiliation" and "shame" brought about by the *naksa* was a prerequisite for hailing 1973 as a victory. In short, "1973 has wiped out the shame of 1967."

Peasant narratives reveal that they do not share this view of events. But the fact that peasants' views on this issue contradict the official version promoted by the post-Nasser regimes cannot be adequately described as peasants' resistance to the state. For one thing, accounts of the events themselves reveal a high degree of identification with the state. When the nation's interests are at stake the state is never undermined. Peasants' backing of the state points to aspects of the complex relationship between peasants and the state that cannot be captured if we rely solely on the "resistance" model. Points of convergence and divergence between state and peasant narratives do not follow the class-based antagonistic polarity that characterizes peasant-state relations in other domains. It is true that, in their subordinate class position, peasants feel powerless and antagonistic toward the Egyptian state and its allied classes, and state policies are invariably blamed for economic hardship and much of the problems of everyday life that peasants face. However, peasant-state relations involve much more than collecting taxes and extracting surplus. Peasants do not perceive themselves only as members of a powerless class, but they also identify themselves as members of the Egyptian nation. It is their national belonging that partly explains the overlap between their own interpretations of events and certain official interpretations.

In addition to this, the need to maintain the memory of 1967 is by no means unique to peasants but is largely shared by a generation of Egyptians who witnessed the events. This can be seen in Ahdaf Soueif's autobiographical novel set against the background of Egypt's political history in the years 1967–1980. In the novel, the mother sends her daughter who is studying in England a letter dated 6 June 1975 in which she mentions the reopening of the Suez Canal: "They opened (re-opened) it yesterday amid much fanfare as you can imagine—on the anniversary of sixty-seven: *that* is supposed to be quite wiped out by the Heroic Crossing."[11]

The humiliation of the defeat was taken personally not just by peasants but by the great majority of Egyptians who witnessed these events. Specifically, the memory of 1967 has a strong generational aspect. The leftist weekly *Al-Ahali* chastises members of the new generation for their ignorance of this event. In the 3 June 1992 portion of a two-part series on "5

June 1967 in the memory of the 90's generation," the journal claims that "this generation's awareness of Egypt's national history is in danger" and questions whether there is "a gap in consciousness between this generation of the future and the generations which preceded it."

In Imam, a need to "make sense" of an incomprehensible event persists, and the 1973 war seems to have had no effect on a retrospective appraisal of 1967. Except for the people who fought in the 1973 war, it is a pale memory whose contents differ very little from the official media presentation and interpretation. There are a number of factors that could explain this. First, there was no popular sense of participation in the 1973 war, and therefore the personal aspect of reminiscence is largely eliminated. Second and more important, there has been so much official emphasis on this "victory" that it has become an event that belongs completely to the state; there is nothing left to be expressed by the people, nor is there a "need to remember." Rather, people almost are ordered to do so. The following passage from the introduction to a school textbook on the October 1973 war illustrates this point: "The Ministry of Education places great importance on the present events, which are decisive in the life of this nation, and is concerned that our sons, the students, be completely knowledgeable about (these events) and that they possess a deep understanding of all the elements of the conflict which decides their present and future. Therefore it was only natural that the Ministry directs its attention to teaching the October War to all students at all stages and requires them to understand it and write about it in their school journals and their speeches and their composition pieces."[12]

With the 1967 war it is very difficult to establish the exact link between the conspiracy scenario as political opinion, on the one hand, and the personal experience of participation in or witnessing of the 9–10 June demonstrations, on the other. Participation explains interest and a need or perhaps a feeling of duty to know what happened and why. The personalized quality of this matter is evident in the passionate and authoritative manner in which these events are recounted. In the course of a general interview with Hagg Wahba, I asked him what happened during Nasser's time. He answered:

> Abdel Nasser was called "the war hero," and then when the states let Abdel Nasser down, namely Syria, Libya, Iraq and Algeria, when they all joined forces against him he failed in 1967, when he entered the Palestine war. In 1970 he had a heart attack and died. Abdel-Nasser died *'ahran* (of distress) at the time of *naksa el-balad etnakasit minnu* (the country was defeated while he was in charge). . . . We wanted to liberate Palestine. The reason for *el-naksa* was that we wanted to liberate Palestine. So we entered into an agreement with Palestine, Jordan, and Syria to become one state. So when Nasser came to power he kicked out the English. So who joined him? Russia. He wanted to

kick out Russia from the country; Russia wanted to create a military base and I don't know what in this country and that state, so he told them, No, we don't want you. Then Russia tricked him. . . . Russia entered Palestine.

When asked to elaborate on how Russia came to enter Palestine, Wahba responded:

Listen carefully. Russia enticed Israel to take Palestine. That was in 1965. Things started to escalate until 1967. Abdel Hakim Amer kept saying let us strike first; by God, we are going to strike first. But Russia who wanted to trick Nasser told him, No, let Israel strike first. So Israel, when she started, instead of striking at the country she hit the airports. We stopped. She hit our airports. We were hindered. Israel came in.

Gamal Abdel-Nasser presented his resignation. Three days, no more, and he presented his resignation. He presented his resignation but of course the country did not accept. They said, "No, do you think you can throw us in the fire like this and then resign? Impossible. You are going to stay like this until you figure out how to rescue the country." Then, people from all governorates went and surrounded Nasser's house. They formed a circle around his house in Cairo and said, "You either let him look to see us or we are going in to see him. . . . If he is dead, tell us, but he shouldn't throw us into the fire and then leave us. We are not going to accept a resignation from him."

In the morning he had said, "I gave up the presidency in this day, and I will not be the president of the republic in this day." The people revolted and they rose from all over the governorates and filled Cairo. Transportation was free. People made a revolution here in Fayoum and they were forcing the drivers to go to Cairo. Ten or fifteen men would hold the driver and hit him to force him to go to Cairo.

I did not [go to Cairo]. We went to Fayoum when this revolution took place, but I did not go to Cairo. Those who went to Cairo were saying, "You either let him look to see us or we are going in to see him. . . . If he is dead, tell us, but he shouldn't throw us into the fire and then leave us." The next day he said, "I withdraw yesterday's declaration according to the demand of the people, because I am at the service of the people," and he cried.

A similar view is expressed by Abu Maghrabi, the chief guard of the village: "The reason for *el-naksa* is the treason of Amer.[13] They said he took bribes and some people said he used to get drunk. Each person says a different thing. But there was treason, anyway. And this treason was American because of Russia and the High Dam. They say Russia built the High Dam and so jealousy developed on the part of the U.S. or the other states, so a *fitna* happened and treason took place, and that led to the defeat of Egypt."

For those who fought, the military aspect of their participation has no direct bearing on their political analysis. They share the same political views as the rest of the community. Sayed adopts the same interpretation for the reasons behind *el-naksa*: "The cause of what happened is treason. We Egyptians are kind-hearted. We were fighting against an enemy not a friend—it's an enemy. The big states told Egypt, 'Don't start with the attack, don't start with war.' When they said that, we did not do anything. So they started first. The aircraft came, and then the tanks, and they stood at the Suez Canal. Everyone who was in the Sinai Desert was killed or taken as captive. It was treason."

And Sultan too:

> They started by hitting the airports at zero hour. It is true that we had good weapons, but we were paralyzed by the hitting of the airports. So when the leadership tried to get in touch with the airports, they did not find airports. . . . We would have won the war were it not for the matter of treason. As I told you, we were just soldiers, so we don't know, but people were saying that Abdel Hakim Amer was having a party with Warda [a famous singer] in the airports, and it was a plan agreed upon between Amer and the Israelis. Nasser said, "We will attack first," but Amer told him no we are not going to attack until they do." . . .
>
> The soldiers were not to blame at all, and the officers' morale was very low, and I admit there was nothing wrong with them. The problem was with the leadership. No one knows exactly what it was. Was it embezzlement, or was it that Amer became too bigheaded?
>
> If we had an air force to cover us, we would have taken Israel in 1967 because [the size of] Israel then was less than this 'izba. It was photographed. Nasser photographed it and also Amer did, and they determined its area and the size of forces that were there. Treason. Yes, treason. And also America was helping Israel, and at that point we could not stand in the face of America.
>
> When Nasser felt this pressure he declared defeat and resigned from the throne [sic]. Of course people did not agree, so he went back to the throne. Of course the people did not agree. They said he should not bring us to 1967 and then resign. They told him you have to go on and bring back this land. People revolted against him and went to his palace. . . . He resigned on the radio and TV. Everybody was very sad when this happened. People were committing suicide in the army. Soldiers and officers were committing suicide by shooting themselves. How could he resign and leave them at this stage! The army revolted. At that time also there were problems between him and Amer. But we were not present when these things happened, and we did not talk about them either. And then he went back to the throne.

From the above narratives on the *naksa* we notice that priority is given to having a coherent plot formed of elements of a tragedy. Treason is seen as the main cause of the defeat, but it does not seem to matter much who committed it. Amer, Warda, Russia and America are almost interchangeable in that respect. It is just "treason," with no overtones of inefficiency or weakness. In a similar way, Fussell speaks of the spread of myths and rumors during World War I mainly for the purpose of providing explanations for events that were too shocking to accept. It is useful to compare peasants' explanation of *naksa* with Fussell's comment on a Canadian artillery sergeant Reginald Grant's book *S.O.S. Stand To!* Fussell says:

> We can now see that the book is a virtual anthology of fables, lies, superstitions, and legends, all offered as a sober report. Sergeant Grant's problem is simple: he simply can't believe that Huns can be skilled at counter-battery location through sound and flash calculations. Seeing his own battery constantly hit by accurate counter-battery fire no matter how cleverly it moves or hides itself, he must posit some explanation. This he does by conceiving of the Belgian landscape as swarming with disloyal farmers who signal the Canadian artillery locations to the Germans. . . . [This] fantasy of folk espionage Grant projects in a frantic search for some way of explaining the disasters suffered by the Canadian artillery which will not have to acknowledge the enemy's skill in observation, mathematics, and deduction.[14]

The main purpose of such explanations is "to 'make sense' of events which otherwise would seem merely accidental or calamitous."[15]

It is important to note that, as mentioned earlier, this interpretation of the 1967 war may be specific to peasants and should be read in light of their attitude toward Nasser. Nasser is appropriated by the peasants and regarded as a local hero especially for issuing the Agrarian Reform laws in 1952 (locally known as the Law of Freedom). Agrarian Reform (in its association with Nasser) forms a break point between past and present. The "age of freedom" (as opposed to "the age of feudalism") is how they characterize the political and moral order of the community at present. The issue of Nasser's responsibility regarding the defeat of 1967 offers an interesting case of how peasants maintain a version of national history that ensures the survival of Nasser, even as a defeated hero. The importance of Nasser for the community's self-image could explain why they cannot just disown him and blame the defeat on "the state." Also these memories show us the way in which "the state" is neither homogenized nor reified as far as they are concerned. The state of Nasser is certainly not that of Sadat or Mubarak.

The treason explanation is thus linked to the ambivalence concerning the question of Nasser's responsibility for the defeat. On the one hand, he is portrayed as the tragic hero who was let down by his friends and tricked by his enemies, and these are portrayed as almost acts of fate that, naturally, entail no responsibility. On the other hand, the events of 9–10 June are portrayed less as an expression of love and support than as a protest against Nasser's seeking to evade his responsibility. The phrase *el-balad etnakasit minnu* (the country was defeated while he was in charge) used by Hagg Wahba is, I think, a key phrase as it signifies that the *naksa* took place while he was in charge of the country but does not place direct blame on him. This form of the preposition *min* is rendered in Hinds and Badawi (1986) as "lack of control over a circumstance." A common example of the usage of this form in the Egyptian vernacular is the phrase *el-'ayyil mat minha*, meaning the child died on her [his mother]. It is a situation of formal responsibility but also of helplessness in the face of uncontrollable forces.

The dramatic or plotlike nature of this topic is also accompanied by the use of rhetoric and incidents pertaining to other times. Familiar clichés borrowed from official rhetoric are also employed but are taken out of their original contexts. There is a repertoire of what are considered to be serious political phrases that are often arbitrarily matched with subjects deemed to be of the same order of importance. For example, the account of Hagg Wahba is colored by rhetoric of the Sadat era, such as calling Nasser "the hero of war," which is a favorite phrase used by the media to describe not Nasser but Sadat. Using this phrase in this context to describe Nasser adds to the dramatic effect of the narrative. Nasser, rather than Sadat, is also given the role of driving the Russians out of Egypt, adding even more dramatic effect to the plot. Also, when talking of the Arab states who let Nasser down, he mentions Libya, Syria, Iraq, and Algeria. These were among the Arab states that were most opposed to the Camp David Accord signed in 1979. They were frequently mentioned and criticized in the media at that time, which may justify the choice of these particular states for the role of the friend who behaves basely. In Abu Maghrabi's account most of the references are borrowed directly from the Suez war of 1956.

Those who fought in the war did not participate in the 9–10 June demonstrations, because they were in the army. Sayed's account of the events of 9 June provides a particularly powerful expression of a bitter memory:

> On June 9 I was supposed to be transferred to another position where I had to pave the ground with a bulldozer. A special car took me to that position and left me there. I came to start the bulldozer but it wouldn't start. Then I told myself I am going home—I am going back home. I went on the main road and waited. I saw the Fayoum bus coming, so I changed into a *galabiyya* I had in my bag and went into the bus.
>
> When the bus reached Kum Ushim there was an inspection point there. There they arrested anyone who they discovered belonged to the army. The officer asked me where I have just come from, and I said that I was coming from Qanater. He asked me what my job was and I told him I was a driver and showed them my I.D. card. Then they searched me, and for my bad luck they found the army letter in my pocket. So they asked me to leave the bus. I found myself the only person leaving the bus, and I began to wonder what they were going to do to me. Then I told myself the worst thing they can do is send me back to war, and I am used to that.
>
> They took me to the police station at Kum Ushim, and when I entered I found almost four hundred persons in the same position as me. So I thought, well, if we die, we die together; and if we live, we live together. Then they

brought a huge truck, which transferred us to the police station at Fayoum city. When we arrived there a police officer came to us. He was not wearing a cap and his hands were in his pockets. He pointed to us and said, "Are these the sons of bitches who brought the *naksa* on us? They are deserting! They should all be shot dead." Then one of us shouted, "We are not sons of bitches. You are the ones who are sons of bitches," and he jumped at his throat and we all joined until the officer disappeared under us.

Then the *ma'mur* [officer] came out and ordered that we should be locked up in the school and not in the police station. They took us to the school and put us in the classrooms. We broke the windows. Then the *ma'mur* came and asked us what our demands were, and we said we do not want anything except our families. We asked them to bring our families to the school. Then a policeman entered each classroom to ask us what our villages were in order to call our families. . . . My family came and brought with them the stove and the tea and food and the cooking pots and everything. If you had seen this sight in the night—the school courtyard was like a *mawlid* [saint's birthday], with each group of people coming to see their relative. It was like a *mawlid* and we stayed until the morning.

This was a situation where military discipline was totally meaningless, and alienation from the institution total. The defeat withdrew from the army its raison d'être. Order collapsed and the peasant soldier became only a peasant. This was a moment when the village and the army confronted each other as two distinct worlds, divorced by the defeat. What, for Sayed, simply meant "going home" was, in military terms, desertion. He only wanted his family, and so did everybody else: "the school courtyard was like a *mawlid*."

Mawlid is the key word here. Being an occasion for visiting and socializing, it evokes the familiar world of the village. The word *mawlid* is also used to denote chaos. The example that Hinds and Badawi (1986) cite for this usage is *"mafish nizam ya 'amm da mulid"*[16] (There's no organization [order], my good man, it's complete chaos!). It was.

CONCLUSION

Peasants are concerned with events outside the boundaries of their own village, but they perceive and remember these events on their own terms. The merging of personal and national history and the use of themes and symbols from peasant culture are major ways in which these events are perceived and remembered.

Peasant discourse cannot be easily disentangled from official discourse. There are tensions but no clear-cut rupture. Consequently, I do not hold the view that a distinctive peasant social memory exists, at least not one that is primarily based on a discourse of resistance. In terms of identity, peasants generally define themselves vis-à-vis the state, the elite(s), and city dwellers.

However, they possess a sense of Egyptian-ness that largely coincides with the official view. Where the issue of nationalism is concerned, there is a large degree of identification with the state. This is one reason why the concept of everyday forms of resistance does not adequately describe or explain the particular way wars are remembered. Moreover, this way of remembering 1967 and forgetting 1973 (to put it very crudely) is not exclusive to peasants but is shared by a wide range of Egyptians, especially the generation whose members actually witnessed the events of 1967. War memories are important mainly for those who witnessed the actual experiences of war. Members of the younger generation are largely unaware and uninterested in this matter. The "peace generation" has other concerns.

Peasants' memories of wars as political events constitute part of their attempts to attach themselves to national history and show that their discourse is integrative rather than separatist. They possess a sense of peripheralization and attempt to seek a place for themselves within national history. Peasants' experiences in, and reminiscences of, war reflect such attempts.

NOTES

This work is mainly based on one year of fieldwork in a hamlet in the governorate of Fayoum, which is denoted here by the pseudonym "Izbet Imam." The population of Izbet Imam is made up of a little over eight hundred inhabitants. The bulk of the fieldwork was carried out in the year 1989; I made subsequent short visits, the last of which was in March 1995. I am grateful to Steven Heydemann for his valuable comments on various drafts of this paper.

1. *Peasant* and *village* are problematic terms, and their analytic utility is increasingly being questioned. However, though they may not be adequate in strict political economy terms, their persistence as meaningful and evocative cultural categories make them indispensable for this discussion.

2. For an inspiring approach to the study of the relationship between resistance and power, see Abu-Lughod, "The Romance of Resistance: Tracing Transformations of Power through Bedouin Women," pp. 41–55.

3. Tamari, "Soul of the Nation: The Fallah in the Eyes of the Urban Intelligentsia," pp. 74–83.

4. Fussell, *The Great War and Modern Memory.*

5. The Egyptian army participated in six wars in the period extending from 1948 to 1973. The 1948 war, which ended with the creation of the state of Israel, was followed by the Tripartite aggression of Israel, France, and Britain in 1956; the Six-Day War in 1967; and the October War in 1973. There was also the "War of Attrition" (1969–70), which involved a series of military operations conducted by both the Israelis and the Egyptians. Apart from the Arab-Israeli armed conflict, Egypt took part in the Yemeni civil war on the side of the Republicans against the Royalists from 1962 until 1967.

6. White, "The Value of Narrativity in the Representation of Reality," p. 2.

7. I conducted two interviews with Fathi. One was a general interview on recent Egyptian history, and the other was specifically on his military experience.

8. Adams, *Development and Social Change in Rural Egypt,* p. 163.

9. White remarks, "Since no given set or sequence of real events is intrinsically tragic, comic, farcical, and so on, but can be constructed as such only by the imposition of the structure of a given story type on the events, it is the choice of the story type and its imposition upon the events that endow them with meaning." "The Question of Narrative in Contemporary Historical Theory," p. 44.

10. El-Shorbagi, *Mudhakkarat 'an harb Octobar li-Gami' al-talaba* [Notes on the October War for all students], p. 14.

11. Soueif, *In the Eye of the Sun,* p. 412.

12. El-Shorbagi, *Mudhakkarat 'an harb Octobar,* p. 6.

13. Field Marshal Abdel Hakim Amer was commander in chief of the armed forces at that time. The regime held him responsible for the defeat in 1967. He allegedly committed suicide as he was being arrested in his Cairo home.

14. Fussell, *The Great War and Modern Memory,* pp. 120–21.

15. Ibid., p. 121.

16. This quotation is adapted to my system of transliteration.

9

War as a Vehicle for the Rise and Demise of a State-Controlled Society

The Case of Ba'thist Iraq

Isam al-Khafaji

INTRODUCTION: IS WAR REALLY AN EXCEPTIONAL PHENOMENON?

A general assumption underlies most writings on wars and societies: namely, that war is an exceptional event, one that introduces qualitatively new and disruptive elements into the routine functioning of state structures, civil society organizations, and the daily life practices of citizens. Unfortunately, this assumption has all too often been challenged by the reality of long-term conflict, notably in various parts of the developing world. And in few regions have such conflicts been more prominent, or their effects more significant, than the Middle East.[1] The distinction between war and peace becomes even more blurred when one tries to apply it in regions or periods where national states have not taken their final shape yet; that is, where the boundaries of an existing state are contested by noncitizens belonging to the nation that forms the majority within the given state, or by citizens that do not belong to the majority nation in that state. This phenomenon has also been painfully apparent across the contemporary Middle East, Indian subcontinent, and Africa.

On one level, therefore, Iraq's experience of near constant war making since 1980 might seem entirely in keeping with other cases of protracted conflict in the Middle East and perhaps elsewhere. The situation in Iraq can be viewed as yet another example of the kind of hypermilitarism and aggressive nationalism so evident in cases like Syria and Israel. In all three countries, the current regime inherited but also deepened and consolidated extensive national security states that rely on war preparation as a principal mechanism of mobilization and control, of regime legitimation and rent seeking.

Iraq's experience is nonetheless distinctive from other cases discussed in this volume in significant respects. First and foremost, Iraq is not a case in which preparation for war has been pursued without the intent to actually fight a war—which, as Perthes argues in his chapter in this volume, was the case for Syria after 1973. Instead, war preparation has been inextricably linked to repeated and extended episodes of war making that have, in turn, had pervasive effects on the dynamics of Iraqi politics, the organization of state and economy, and on state-society relations. In addition, war making—the projection of organized violence *outside* of Iraq's borders—has been augmented in unique ways by the extraordinary routinization of *internal* violence as an everyday form of governance. The sheer pervasiveness of coercion as an instrument of governance has, for Iraq's regime, erased the boundary between external and internal threats. War making is now channeled in all directions as a logical extension of the regime's war-based system of rule. War preparation, war making, and *raison d'état* have become thoroughly and disastrously integrated in Iraq, in ways that differ both qualitatively and quantitatively from any other Middle East state. What is critical in the Iraqi case, therefore, is to explain how a familiar constellation of features coalesced in a set of forms and practices that are exceptional in their force and intensity.

To develop such an explanation, this chapter explores the trajectory of hypermilitarization in Iraq and its political, social, and economic dynamics. It also demonstrates how war making has achieved such extraordinary social, cultural, ideological, and political centrality in Iraq. The chapter traces the effects of shifts in Arab nationalist ideology on the formation of Iraqi political identity in ways that increasingly legitimated Iraq's self-perceived mission as defender of the Arab nation and valorized Iraq's military prowess. It explores how this aggressive form of nationalism interacted with and helped shape a centralized and ultradictatorial system of rule, paving the way for the increasing compression of Iraq's political arena around the personality of Saddam Hussein. Further securing the consolidation of a war-based system of rule were the normalization of war as a social condition and system of governance, the construction of a war-driven political economy, and the use of war as a basis for the redefinition of Iraqi national identity. As will become evident, the first Iran-Iraq War (1980–88) proved to be a crucial episode in the consolidation of these dynamics.

Finally, this chapter puts the specific Iraqi experience of war preparation and war making within the wider context of theories of state formation and consolidation, whereby the state asserts its supremacy over society by monopolizing the means of coercion and by asserting its legitimacy as the sole agent capable of preserving the unity of a social formation. Had they not won their contests with various armed groups within their populations concerning who could best defend their interests, state makers in Europe, as in the Arab Mashreq, could not have proceeded to practice their violence internally, to homogenize their populations culturally, religiously, and linguistically in the name of nation building.[2]

WAITING FOR SADDAM

Saddam Hussein's Iraq has been a long time in the making. This is not to imply that Iraq has been destined by some fault of nature to suffer under dictatorship, or that Saddam's rise to power was somehow predetermined by Iraqi political culture. Indeed, Saddam's rule has profoundly altered Iraqi political culture and transformed social relations in general, as I argue below. Instead, the intense compression of the Iraqi political field around the personal authority of Saddam Hussein resulted from a long-term trajectory of state formation in which a network of "received" political institutions—monarchical and later republican—were emptied of substance, authoritarian political practices were consolidated, and a dramatic process of state expansion undertaken. Throughout this process, the careful cultivation of threats, war preparation, and actual conflict reinforced and legitimated the efforts of successive ruling elites to centralize political authority and control the accumulation and distribution of national income. These legacies of Iraqi state formation made available to Saddam Hussein a style of governance that was well suited to his domestic political ambitions. Yet Saddam's regime has not only appropriated an existing set of political resources, it has also vastly expanded and applied the politics of war making across a wide range of social, cultural, ideological, and economic domains, leading to wholesale shifts in the structure of Iraq's society and economy and promoting the rise of a state dominated society.

The Erosion of Monarchic Institutions

During the period of Iraq's monarchy (1921–58), parliamentary democracy was anything but representative of the majority of the population. This was not mainly the product of the malevolent will of the ancien régime nor of imperialism, as many Arab writings imply, but has to do with the virtual absence of civil society, which is the necessary condition for the rise of a pluralistic democracy.[3] The parliamentary system that existed in Iraq and elsewhere in the Arab Mashreq was based on a set of rules whereby representation, political solidarities, and alliances reflected not the voluntary choices of individuals, but rather the various "primordial" associations that characterize a prebourgeois community. Thus the relative weight of each ethnic, sectarian, and tribal association in the country's politics, economy, and society was delicately preserved by assigning parliamentary seats to absentee tribal sheikhs or big landlords, religious leaders, urban merchants, and notables.

Even prior to its violent demise in 1958, however, processes of social and, in particular, economic transformation were eroding the social foundations of the monarchy. These include the exodus of Iraqi Jews after 1948, permitting Shi'i merchants to strengthen their positions vis-à-vis the dominant Arab Sunnis, and the 1952 agreement between the Iraqi government and the Iraq Petroleum Company that began Iraq's transformation into a rentier state. Related to both these developments was the breakdown of the semifeudal system in agriculture, causing massive migration from rural areas and provincial towns to the big cities, notably Baghdad. While the population of Iraq rose almost fourfold between 1919 and 1968, that of Baghdad jumped eightfold during the same period.[4] During these years, a small coterie of first- or second-generation immigrants to Baghdad from impoverished provincial towns acquired modest education or training. Through networks formed around notables from their own towns of origin, they entered schools and gradually made their way into the expanding state apparatus (civil, military, or paramilitary). Yet their assimilation into urban life was at best partial: new migrants to Baghdad confronted significant barriers to professional mobility and were looked upon with disdain by established urbanites.

These urban newcomers expressed an ambivalence typical of ambitious immigrants confronting a rigid social order. For them, Baghdad was both a place where they could enhance their social and economic conditions, and one that deprived them of the means to participate in the comfortable lifestyles of longtime residents. No wonder they viewed their positions within such societies in terms of provincial-metropolitan antagonisms and regarded existing political arrangements as corrupt. One of the great contemporary Arab poets, Badr Shakir al-Sayyab, himself a migrant from a humble village near Basra, described Baghdad as a "grand brothel." Over time, animosity developed against city dwellers among the better off immigrants, who saw their chances of promotion blocked by Baghdadis.

Limits on the expansion of urban economic structures added to the sense of marginality among provincial immigrants. What little expansion occurred in these structures drew first from the larger pool of rural unskilled migrant workers. Ironically, these poorer immigrants, mostly from the Shi'i regions of southern Iraq, were more integrated into the structures of urban life than their lower-middle-class counterparts, but this should not be read as suggesting a deeper commitment to existing social or political arrangements. They too shared in the sense of alienation and marginality that shaped the worldviews of other newcomers to the city. Occupying subordinate positions as laborers and servants, however, they tended to view their oppression more in terms of class antagonisms than those of region, tribe, or sect. This may partially explain the relative success of the Iraqi Communist Party in mobilizing poorer immigrants.

Authoritarianism and the Rise of Revolutionism, 1958–68

In general terms, the political environment of Iraq in the 1950s was marked by a growing gap between the monarchy and its social base of big landowners, who were losing touch with the rapidly expanding groups of social, economic, and political "marginals" who made up an ever larger share of the urban population, and who hoped that the tremendous rise in state revenue after the 1952 agreement with the Iraq Petroleum Company would improve their miserable standard of living. The 1958 revolution that overthrew Faisal's monarchy, under the leadership of Abdul Karim Qassim, grew out of these tensions and was explicitly reformist in character. It sought, at least publicly, the restoration of civilian democratic government, and a more inclusive strategy of national development. It promised a new era of economic opportunity and depicted itself as a reaction against both the widespread corruption that prevailed under Faisal and the monarchy's collaboration with the British.

Yet in opening up the possibility of renegotiating the status of marginal urban populations, Qassim's "revolution" was rapidly captured by more radical and transformational political forces that undermined its original intent and dramatically altered the trajectory of Iraqi state formation. Because the elite of Qassim's regime was composed largely of urban Baghdadis and Mossulites, or high-ranking professionals and military officers who had already been incorporated into urban institutions, new actors championing the causes of marginalized strata came to challenge Qassim's more moderate outlook, and placed tremendous pressure on the regime to move in more radical directions.[5] In response to urgent demands for more job opportunities and for programs to alleviate the misery of the population, a reformist project that originally sought modernization and industrialization was replaced by a more radical developmental project based on expanding the state apparatus and increasing state intervention. Thus, Iraq's cabinet expanded from fourteen ministers in 1958 to some thirty portfolios a decade later, with each of these new ministries requiring its own bureaucracy.

In an oil-rich economy, state expansion proved to be a relatively easy task. Yet its consequences were disastrous in the long-term. The growth of state institutions dramatically altered the balance of power between state and society, to the detriment of the latter. It also significantly recast the state elites' conception of themselves and their relationship to society. As modernization gave way to revolutionism, state elites were transformed into a vanguard, their privileged positions justified, in part, by the sense of vulnerability and threat they created surrounding the revolution, and their subsequent (self-interested) determination to attack counterrevolution whether from within or from without. This increasingly politicized atmosphere served as justification for the vast expansion of the internal security apparatus, and what began in 1958 as a popular revolution against "a handful of traitors" turned into a nightmare for thousands and thousands who could be accused at any moment of conducting activities against the revolution. Moreover, with the multiplication of "revolutions" during the volatile years of the 1960s, few could escape being labeled as hostile to at least one of them. Not only was the General Directorate of Security (al-Amn al-'Ammma) active in this field, but the Directorate of Military Intelligence (al-Istikhbarat al-'Askariyya) also played an increasingly pronounced role in harassing so-called opponents of the regime. With the intensification of terror after the fall of Qassim, more and more public buildings were turned into prisons and torturing places, including Qasr al-Rihab, the former royal house and the Olympic Club.[6]

These developments were sharply at odds with the proclaimed intent of the Qassim government to restore parliamentary rule, a contradiction that became ever more transparent. When the monarchy was overthrown in 1958, the Qassim regime routinely stressed the exceptional and temporary nature of the revolutionary period. Time and again Qassim, whether wholeheartedly or out of sheer opportunism, spoke at length to assure audiences that a national assembly and a permanent constitution would come into being once the "feudal and [pro-British] agents' regime was uprooted." The official discourse, borrowed from the Egyptian revolution of 1952, denounced an already popularly discredited parliamentary regime, but stressed the need for a "healthy" political system in which political parties, civil rights, and personal freedoms would thrive once the corrupt elements in society had been eliminated. To keep up formal appearances Qassim instituted a totally powerless "Sovereignty Council" to act as the executive authority of the state, while preserving for himself the posts of prime minister, minister of defense, and the supreme commander of the armed forces.

In this way, the formal separation of legislative, executive, and judicial powers was preserved—in the sense that executive power, the cabinet under Qassim, was acting temporarily under the supervision of a council that held sovereignty in its hands. And despite the cynicism of these arrangements, this was not entirely a matter of appearances. Legal-bureaucratic formalities were respected in some areas, including regulations governing military promotions.[7] Yet the overall erosion of democratic and meritocratic practices was too pervasive to be papered over through modest and highly circumscribed observance of the rule of law. And even these feeble attempts at legalism soon broke down under the weight of increasingly authoritarian practices. The war in Kurdistan and the attempts of Nasser's Egypt to overthrow the nascent republican regime gave Qassim and his allies the pretext to extend the interim period.[8] And by 1968, with the multiplication of coups d'état, each claiming to rectify the errors of its predecessors, the proclaimed goal of returning to constitutional rule was abandoned.

Not all Iraqis were saddened by the regime's retreat from a commitment to restore some form of political pluralism, at least at the time. Revolutionism found fertile soil in the Iraq of the 1950s and 1960s. People who cheered the revolution in 1958 were expecting radical improvements in their life conditions and in the status of their country. The remedy at the time seemed quite simple. The backwardness of Iraq, as of all the colonies, semicolonies, and former colonies, was attributed to the imperialists and their local agents who plundered the wealth of their former imperial possessions and implemented policies that were deliberately aimed at hindering their industrialization. Thus all that was needed was a good patriotic government to permit these countries to catch up with the developed world.

This anti-imperialist euphoria was shared by major sections of the population. The belief that imperialism would try to forestall any attempt to overcome underdevelopment, whether through direct intervention as in the Suez aggression of 1956 or through local agents as in Iran in 1952, reinforced the perception that a strong state with a strong army was an essential prerequisite for genuine development. Hence the easiness with which liberal and even reformist ideas were dismissed or discredited among the populace. The call for pluralistic democracy was synonymous with advocating the right of reactionary ideas and groupings to find a legal platform from which they could combat the revolution. By the second half of the 1960s, the general atmosphere was so radicalized that it was fashionable to talk about parliamentary democracy, even among those who suffered most from despotism, as a corrupt and bourgeois form of rule.

Revolutionism and the Military.   Throughout the 1950s and 1960s, Iraq's military was a major beneficiary of the complementary trends toward state expansion and the use of revolutionism to bring about the compression of the political field around a military-authoritarian ruling elite. As in many late-developing states, military officers dominated Iraqi politics throughout the period from 1958–1968. Officers held the posts of president, prime minister, minister of defense, director general of security, and director of military intelligence, as well as various ministerial posts.[9] The role of the military during the first decade after the 1958 revolution was further enhanced by the nationalization acts of 1964, when newly nationalized public sector establishments were put under the direction of military officers. Moreover, the size of the armed forces increased enormously and the budget of defense and security more than quadrupled, from ID 31.2 million in 1958 to ID 142.1 million in 1969—though in relative terms this raised the military's share of the national budget by only 10 percent, from 39 to 49 percent of expenditures.[10]

In part, the military's good fortune can be understood as the routinization of political protection payments. From 1958 onward, a primary concern of all Iraqi regimes became the foiling of coup attempts, appeasing and buying off the military, and giving it more and more privileges to stem its discontent and secure the loyalty of the officer corp. It was not surprising then that youth who had no chance of pursuing a career in such prestigious fields as medicine or engineering would look to the officer corps for their future. In the 1960s, Madinat al-Dhubbat, an exclusive suburb on the outskirts of Baghdad, was built for army officers; special shops were established to supply the military with expensive goods at cheap prices; and the second Iraqi radio station was established under the name Armed Forces' Radio. Hanna Batatu estimates that in one decade after the 1958 revolution the number of army officers jumped by 250 percent, from four thousand to ten thousand.[11]

The drive for a strong state, identified as a highly centralized and monolithic body with a strong and efficient army, reached its peak in the 1960s, when the Iraqi regime as well as its major opponents where competing to prove that they were the ones most committed to these ideals. But apart from isolated urban groups, no one was challenging the validity of these ideals themselves, or whether the goals of development, anticapitalism, anti-imperialism, and building a highly centralized and despotic state were compatible with each other. The political field, composed of numerous Nasserite groupings and parties, two rival factions of the Ba'th Party, and two rival factions of the Communist Party, was thus undergoing a process of compression around an ever-smaller spectrum of ideological positions, none of which accepted the legitimacy or desirability of political pluralism.

Thus, the officers who undertook a revolution to serve the "cause of the people" ended up creating a monstrous state apparatus that compelled the people to serve it and its bureaucrats. By the end of 1967, political life in Iraq was in a deep crisis, to the point that periodic meetings were organized by former president 'Arif with pan-Arab and Nasserite movements "to discuss the future of Iraq," a move unheard of during the republican period, when every regime claimed that it had the correct answers and remedies to all the problems facing the country. Moreover, all the major political trends were suffering from numerous setbacks. The Ba'th Party had badly tarnished its reputation during its bloody nine-month rule in 1963, to the point that its own officers, including al-Bakr, Hardan al-Tikriti, and 'Ammash, joined hands with the Nasserite 'Arif to remove their own party from power. The Iraqi Communist Party—which was then the most popular political force in Iraq—was still recovering from damage inflicted during the brutal 1963 massacre of party members and sympathizers by the Ba'th when it splintered as a result of differences over how to respond to shifts in the policies of the U.S.S.R. toward nonsocialist, nationalistic regimes in the Third World.[12] The Nasserites, never a popular group in Iraq, had ruled for five years under 'Abdul Salam and Abdul Rahman 'Arif, and had plunged the country into a deep crisis.

POLITICAL TRANSFORMATION UNDER THE BA'TH

It was in this highly tense and radical atmosphere that the Ba'th seized power on July 17, 1968, overthrowing 'Arif's regime. The success of the coup, which has since been recast in official rhetoric as the glorious realization of Iraq's destiny, was hardly a foregone conclusion. Bitter internal struggles splintered the party after 1963, which, together with harassment of the party by the 'Arif regime, brought about its near demise in Iraq.[13] The radical atmosphere of Arab politics in the mid-1960s made any effort to rebuild the official "right wing" party all the more difficult. Whatever militant Ba'thists were there chose either to join newly formed Marxist groups or to be within the "left," pro-Syrian wing of the party.[14] It should be no surprise, then, that when the Ba'th Party seized power in July 1968 it had no more than a few hundred full members.[15]

For Iraqis, exhausted by a decade of bloody coups and the rule of corrupt military juntas, this was yet another in a series of palace settlements of scores. The indifference with which the new regime was met is evident from the fact that no curfew was imposed after the coup and not a drop of blood was shed during the seizure of power from 'Arif. In an effort to appease fears of a new blood bath à la 1963, the Ba'th continued to emphasize this last aspect in their propaganda to show the uniqueness of their "revolution" and to remind those 1960s youth who clamored for radical changes in society and politics that this swiftly implemented coup d'état was indeed the legitimate heir to Iraqi revolutionism.

At the time of the Ba'thist coup, the predominant mood among politically articulate sections of the population was quite contradictory. On the one hand, people were weary of military rule and the bloodshed associated with it. The defeat of Arab armies in 1967 had undermined the appeal of pan-Arabism, although, as will become evident below, the Ba'th Party skillfully managed to articulate this idea with a strong sense of Iraqism and thus kept it a powerful force in Iraqi politics. On the other hand, the second half of the 1960s witnessed a resurgence of radicalism in both the developed and the developing worlds. The Ba'th played quite skillfully on both sentiments to transform the institutional structures of the Iraqi state and the cultural-ideological norms of Iraqi society. War, in particular the Iran-Iraq War, and the growing convergence of revolutionism and militarism, played critical roles in this process. How this dynamic unfolded must be explained with some elaboration, since it brought forward the crucial elements of the Iraq we see today.

Party-Military Relations after 1968

One of most significant areas in which Ba'th elites pushed Iraqi politics in new directions concerned the relationship between the Ba'th Party and the military. While appropriating many of the practices introduced during the period of military dominance, and while continuing to expand the military apparatus, Ba'thist elites nonetheless moved rapidly to assert the supremacy of the party over the military.[16] Under the Ba'th, the size of Iraq's army doubled from six divisions in the mid-1960s to twelve in 1980, and then to forty-four divisions during the eight-year war with Iran.[17] By the first year of that war, military expenditure constituted some 70 percent of Iraq's GDP.[18] Yet even while continuing to pour resources into the expansion of Iraq's military capacity, the Ba'thist regime skillfully worked to neutralize that huge institution politically.

Nowhere is this shift more evident than in the Ba'th's efforts to marginalize the military as a channel of elite recruitment. Under the Nasserist regime in Egypt and long periods of Ba'thist rule in Syria, those who headed the rapidly growing apparatus of state security and intelligence, ideological indoctrination, and propaganda, as well as the economy, were mainly professional army officers. Algeria and the former South Yemen, two other "postcolonial" Arab states, manned such posts with cadres drawn from the liberation fronts that fought the French and British colonial powers, respectively. In contrast, the leadership of Ba'thist Iraq—which built the biggest armed force of all the Arab countries and went into the longest and bloodiest wars that the Arab world has witnessed in its contemporary history—was largely civilian.

With the exception of former president al-Bakr (1968–79) none of the top officials of Iraq under the Ba'th, including those who held the post of minister of defense, had a high military rank before the Ba'th came to power.[19] As president of Iraq, the civilian Saddam Hussein assumed the post of the supreme commander of the armed forces. His deputy chairman of the Revolution's Command Council, also a civilian, is the vice-commander of the armed forces. The defense portfolio in the Iraqi cabinet has twice been given to noncommissioned officers. The major personalities responsible for decision making on matters concerning the armed forces—that is, the members of the Military Bureau of the Ba'th Party, most of whom were assigned high posts in the military in addition to their membership in the bureau—were either noncommissioned officers or civilian party activists with no higher education.[20]

To further ensure the subordination of the military, the Ba'thist government resorted to other forms of control as well, including the creation of a praetorian guard within the army itself (the Republican Guards). Moreover, it placed the armed forces under the surveillance and supervision of people with no background in the officer corps, producing a decline in the prestige and influence of career officers. As arbitrary promotions and the awarding of military ranks (even staff ranks) to such people became a routine practice in the Iraqi army, seniority ceased to play a significant role in commanding loyalty or obedience among the rank and file. To counter the negative impact of these changes on the morale and loyalty of the professional army officers, Ba'thist authorities heaped generous material incentives on them, especially after the outbreak of the Iran-Iraq War.[21] Through such measures the Ba'th sought to balance its need for a professional and functioning officer corps with its determination to subordinate the military politically by whatever means necessary: surveillance, repression, or bribery.

By thus routinizing and trivializing the military as a career, it was possible for the Ba'th to enlarge the professional army without enhancing its social and political weight. As a result, the party was able to appropriate popular appeals to patriotism and militarism, without concern that such rhetorics would promote the political influence of the military as an institution. And having tamed militarism, the Ba'th celebrated manifestations of militarism as indicators of its own achievements. As noted in the chapter on "social and cultural transformation" in the political report of the ninth Ba'th Party congress: "By affirming the values of patriotism and courage . . . in the new society, another important value spread and took firm roots, namely the affection toward militarism. Military dress has become fashionable among the youth. Military toys have become the most attractive to Iraqi children. And military expressions are being widely used in society."[22]

Aggressive Arabism and a New Iraqism

A second mechanism through which the Ba'th transformed not only political institutions but also social norms was the construction of a new, hypermilitarized and aggressive form of Arab nationalism in the period leading up to the Iran-Iraq War. Moreover, and in contrast to what came earlier, Ba'thist constructions of Arabism were grounded in and legitimated by a rigid narrowing of Iraqi identity. Like other transformations wrought by the Ba'th, these changes drew on the legacies of earlier shifts in Iraqi politics and society. Yet the Ba'th invoked these legacies to advance ideas and policies that were profoundly transformative, and ultimately, deeply destructive. They would have devastating consequences for Iraqi society as the Iraq-Iran War and the second Gulf War wound on.

As early as the 1950s, and accelerating over time, a new concept of Arabism emerged to compromise the pan-Arabist raison d'être of such ruling elites as the Ba'thists and the Nasserists with the *raison d'état* of such solid states as Egypt and Iraq. As Nasser achieved his victories in nationalizing the Suez Canal and bringing Syria under his rule, and as the Iraqi Ba'th succeeded in nationalizing Iraq's oil industry, a distinction began to emerge between the "liberated base" of the Arab Nation, which denoted the countries that had been under Nasserist or Ba'thist rule, and all the other parts of the Arab world. This distinction had far-reaching consequences, because, from then on, partisans were expected to treat the "liberated bases of Arab Revolution" as eternal entities, the defense of which was the criterion for their loyalty to the ideals of pan-Arabism. Moreover, any attempt to achieve Arab unity, or other goals of this vaguely defined Arab Revolution, had to be conducted on behalf of the liberated base.

Thus, Arab unity was no longer viewed as a fusion between equally artificial entities, but rather as a newly liberated zone obediently joining the leading core, with all that this implies concerning a new sense of hierarchy and superordinate versus subordinate Arab states. To complicate matters more, the concept of liberated bases was formulated by each of the major pan-Arabist trends in such a way as to exclude all the others from claiming an equal or superior status compared to the original "liberated base." Hence, Nasserism never recognized the Ba'thist experiences in Syria or Iraq as achieving what it had achieved in Egypt; Ba'thists in turn mocked the failures of Nasserism to achieve the goals of "Arab revolution"; and Syrian and Iraqi Ba'thists enthusiastically denounced one another's legitimacy and authenticity.

Rather than devolve toward an angry stalemate, as seemed likely by the end of the 1960s, the regional environment that prevailed in the 1970s led the Iraqi Ba'th to feel much more confident in representing themselves as the sole representatives of the Arab cause. Nasserism had already died with the coming of Sadat in Egypt, and Syria was no longer engaged in the ultraradical rhetoric of the 1950s and 1960s. Many Egyptian Nasserist and leftist intellectuals and politicians were moving to Iraq, where lucrative jobs were waiting for them. Syria's competition with the Iraqis was of no significance; Syria had tarnished its Arabist credentials, in the eyes of Arab pannationalists, as a result of its deals with the Israelis after the 1973 war and its bloody intervention against Palestinians and the Lebanese left in the Lebanese civil war in 1976. Sadat's visit to Israel and the subsequent Camp David agreements further enhanced Iraq's drive to assert itself as the sole remaining legitimate defender of Arabism.[23]

To understand how the Ba'thist appropriation and transformation of Arabism took place, and to understand the kind of policies it made possible during and after the Iran-Iraq War, it is necessary, above all, to examine the connections between the Ba'th's redefinition of Arabism and its redefinition of what would henceforth constitute Iraqi national identity. One critical aspect of these shifts can be traced through the Ba'th's use of language. During the 1970s, the discursive reification of such concepts as "Iraq" and "the Arab Nation" by Ba'thist elites played a central role in the process of elevating Iraq as the leading defender of Arabism. This reification not only accounted for the existence of separate state structures but also insulated Ba'thist policies from any Arab interference or criticism. In the meantime, it helped to legitimize the aggressive attitude of the Iraqi leadership toward Arab countries and its own citizens in the name of defending the nation's will.

The regime's new emphasis on Iraq's special character, and its promotion of an aggressive notion of "Iraqism," could have been interpreted as a Ba'thist drive to foster collective awareness of a common identity and equality among Iraqis were it not associated with a troubling redefinition of "true Iraqism" and the regime's willingness to impose this definition through the coercive restructuring of Iraqi society. The main features of the Ba'thist formula for restructuring ethnic and sectarian relations in Iraq are not found simply in its extreme reliance on violence. Rather they can be seen in the new norms and practices of governance and social mobilization created by the Ba'th that found little resistance from a political culture impoverished as a result of the previous republican regimes.

As Ba'thist rule brought a radical improvement in the economic conditions of Iraqis, including a vast network of public education and health institutions and the construction of a wide range of infrastructural facilities, the party's claims to be fulfilling the "will of the nation" grew bolder and bolder. The metaphors frequently used in the Ba'thist discourse are of great significance here, because the concept of representation of the interests of the people or of "the Nation" were totally absent. The reification, or the subjectification of both the nation and the political leadership, which was always given the name "the Revolution," was intended to completely identify one with the other in such a way as to present those who dared to criticize or oppose the regime as enemies of the revolution, that is, the nation. Since the nation was a subject with a will, it could not be hostile to itself, naturally. Thus the only source of hostility could come from forces outside the nation that infiltrated it through local opposition elements, making any critic, no matter how moderate and no matter how strong his or her claim to Iraqi or Arab identity, an outsider and thus someone who could legitimately be repressed.

To romanticize the "Arab cause" and portray the Iraqi leadership in an inflated image, it was necessary to view the latter as fighting on behalf of the Arabs as whole, on the one hand, and to overdramatize the challenges it was facing, on the other. Even when Iraq was enjoying significant support in its war with Iran from both the West and the Soviet Union, as well as most Arab governments, the founder and secretary general of the Ba'th Party, Michel 'Aflaq declared, "The real and profound nature of the battle fought by the Ba'thist Iraq is revealed by its facing of an alliance grouping *the Christian West, Jewish Zionism, and atheist communism.*"[24] In this spirit, whenever hostile acts were uncovered, the Ba'thist ideological machine did its best to prove that their perpetrators had non-Arab blood running in their veins.[25]

These factors help explain why the Kurds were easily targeted whenever they demanded recognition of their national rights. The degradation of Iraqi politics under the monolithic rule of the Ba'th further explains how it was possible to move from the first interim constitution of 1958, which stated that Arabs and Kurds were partners in Iraq, to the resolution passed by the Tenth Pan-Arab Congress of the Ba'th Party, twenty years later, stating that Iraqi soil is Arab land. Thus whenever autonomy was granted to a minority, it was to be understood as an autonomy for people and not for land.[26]

The tensions with Iran that climaxed in the eight-year war were the catalyst that speeded and facilitated this redefinition, to the detriment of urban Iraqis in general and the Shi'i and Kurdish communities in particular. It was in association with these tensions that, for example, the Ba'th launched, for the second time in the modern history of Iraq, the practice of deporting a significant proportion of a specific Iraqi community on the grounds that they were not "true citizens."[27] In 1970 some sixty-five thousand Faili Kurds were deported to Iran because the Ba'th leadership considered them to be of "Persian origin."[28]

Increasingly as the 1970s wore on, Ba'thist slogans emphasized the "special role that the Nation had assigned to Iraq and the Iraqis to achieve its goals." Seen from this vantage point, the war with Iran—a conflict undertaken with the sole purpose of securing a hegemonic position for the Ba'thist leadership in the region—is all too easily portrayed as a defense of the "Eastern Flank of the Arab Nation," a role for which Iraq claimed singular responsibility and expected to reap singular rewards.

WAR AND THE FORMATION OF A STATE-DOMINATED SOCIETY AFTER 1980

By the outbreak of the Iran-Iraq War, therefore, the trajectory of Iraqi state formation had produced a political context with tremendous capacity for violence, both outward and inward. Institutionally this took shape through the formation of a massive military apparatus, now under the control of the civilian elite of the Ba'th, and through the deepening and extension of the internal security apparatus throughout Iraqi society. Politically, this context manifested itself through the institutionalization and sharpening of revolutionist politics under the Ba'th and the decisive rejection of pluralist or republican practices as antipathetic to the organic unity of Iraqi society. Ideologically, and perhaps the most significant element in a combustible mix, this context was shaped by the consolidation of an Arabism that depicted aggression as necessary to protect a beleaguered Arab nation—now embodied in a vision that presented Iraq, regime, and nation as a seamlessly integrated whole—from threats. What made this even more potent, of course, was the ability of the Ba'th to exploit the "betrayals" of Egypt and Syria both to monopolize this role for itself and to attach to it a new and frightening urgency. For a regime intent on maximizing its own power both domestically and regionally, this context provided all the necessary ingredients for war. It served up the symbolic, discursive, and institutional material the Ba'th used in initiating and managing its war with Iran and later the invasion of Kuwait.

At the same time, and of crucial importance, it also provided the ingredients for a tremendously brutal approach to the management of the Iraqi economy, society, and political system during the course of almost twenty years of near constant conflict. Still, if the availability of these ingredients made *possible* a distinctively coercive, aggressive, and militaristic strategy of governance and resource extraction, their presence did not make this strategy *inevitable*. The Iran-Iraq War was the trigger. And what brought these ingredients together in such a destructive and volatile combination was, among other things, the economic effects of the war, notably the impact of Iraq's postwar economic crisis on the Ba'th's strategy of rule.

To fully explain the importance of transformations brought about under Saddam's auspices, this section elaborates on four specific mechanisms through which war and domestic politics interacted to shape the political, social, and economic character of Saddam's regime. First is the shift from oil rents to strategic rents as the basis of Iraq's political economy, and the role of war in the construction and breakdown of Iraq's rent-seeking strategy. Second is the cynical and dangerous manipulation of social violence as a basis for stabilizing the regime politically. Third is the redefinition of Iraqi identity as the basis for the coercive reorganization of Iraqi society, and the violent marginalization of Kurdish and Shi'a communities. The final mechanism is the deinstitutionalization of Iraqi politics and formation of an even narrower and more intensely personalized notion of political authority—embodied in the physical person of Saddam Hussein—than had ever previously existed in Iraq.

Rent-Seeking and War Making in Ba'thist Iraq

Thanks to the oil boom of the 1970s, Iraq under the Ba'th had become virtually a textbook form of rentier state, dependent financially on the revenues accruing to it from its natural resources.[29] It was through the massive influx of oil revenues during the 1970s that Iraq was able to pursue a policy of guns and butter, spending lavishly on both social development and military expansion. By 1982–83, however, the costs of the conflict with Iran forced a dramatic change. Iraq remained dependent on external resources, but now military power rather than oil became the source of rents. Strategic rents—that is, sums of money received from other countries in exchange for political support or military protection against adversaries— now became a critical source of foreign exchange.[30]

During the first two years of the war, Iraq's comfortable economic situation did not prompt its leadership to ask for rents from neighboring states.[31] Iraq entered the war with a fully utilized oil export capacity of 3.5 million barrels per day and an annual income from oil of close to $30 billion. It had already accumulated liquid reserves equal to a year's annual income from oil exports. This gave the Iraqi leadership an additional chance to present itself as the dedicated savior of its weak brethren to the south, sacrificing its wealth and sons without asking for any advantages or benefits. As the war dragged on, however, confounding Saddam's expectations of a blitzkrieg, and as Iran began to absorb the shock of the Iraqi attack, turn to the offensive, and recapture its occupied territories, Iraq's economic situation began to deteriorate. Its oil-export facilities in the Gulf (Mina'a al-Bakr and Khawr al-'Umayya) were heavily damaged by Iranian air attacks; Syria closed a pipeline passing through its territory to the Mediterranean; and oil prices began a downward slide. From 1983 until 1989, the Iraqi economy was kept afloat through regular infusions of cash and oil exports made on its behalf by Saudi Arabia, Kuwait, and the UAE. As a result, most Iraqis did not suffer real hardship during this period of the war. Army officers and technicians employed in military industries were arguably better off than during the prewar period.

It is quite interesting to note that the official discourse of the Iraqi leadership was very cautious not to overestimate the vital role of these rents in preventing Iraq's defeat. Whenever an acknowledgment was made of support received from Arab states or through "donations" from wealthy Iraqis, it was always accompanied by a reminder that without Iraq's war Arab rulers would not be sitting on their thrones, their wealth would have disappeared, and their territories would have been occupied by the Iranians. In addressing wealthy Iraqis, the regime added an additional note: that they had been barefoot before the revolution made it possible for them to accumulate their fortunes.[32] In the official reports of the Ba'th Party, the boldness of the discourse did away with external support altogether, praising the heroic Iraqi leadership for its ability to stand alone against a bigger Iran that had "suspicious" international connections with the enemies of the Nation.[33]

This aspect of the mechanism of strategic rent extraction is quite essential for understanding why the Ba'thist leadership was so confident at the time that Iraq would not face economic hardship once the war was over, and to make ever bolder demands for support, touching upon the sovereignty of its neighbors after the cease-fire with Iran. Saddam's regime, in other words, took it for granted that it was doing the hardest and most costly part of a job whose rewards would be shared by all the monarchies of the Gulf. Hence its insistence that no official debt arrangements through financial institutions should be made to account for their contributions toward the costs of their own joint venture. Unlike the case in cash-strapped Syria (or Nasser's Egypt), squeezing financial gains from Iraq's neighbors was not in and of itself a rationale for prolonging its military adventures. Rather, the Ba'thist regime felt that securing military supremacy or hegemony in the region would be economically rewarding in its own right, because, once that objective had been achieved, Iraq would be able to implement its plans to export 8 million barrels of oil per day without fear of competitors blocking its tiny outlet to the sea or threatening to shut Iraqi pipelines passing through other countries. Indeed, throughout the war, Iraqis were told that they would reap the fruits of their suffering once the war was over, that they were viewed by their Arab brethren with high admiration, and that Iraq had acquired a unique place in the Arab nation thanks to the war.[34]

By the end of the war, however, the harsh realities of everyday life cast a gloomy shadow over what Iraqis had been told they should expect. Iraq's economic difficulties began to show directly after the cease-fire with Iran. Three quarters of a million soldiers, mostly conscripts, had been waiting eagerly for demobilization to go back to normal life. But the war had redefined the terms of normality in Iraq. For one thing, the state was simply no longer capable of securing jobs and welfare services for every citizen. In 1986–87 a huge privatization campaign had been launched under the rubric of "the administrative revolution." Within two years, this campaign led to more wide-ranging economic restructuring in Iraq than had been accomplished in Egypt in the ten years following the Infitah.[35] Draconian measures were taken to amend the labor act, giving private entrepreneurs the right to dismiss their workers and lengthen the workday. For the first time in more than a decade, Iraqis began to feel the pinch of unemployment. Far from creating a bright economic future, the war confronted young Iraqis with the most dismal of economic prospects, while the postwar economic crisis posed a significant political challenge for the regime.

In response, the regime once again deployed the techniques and practices it had developed during the prewar period, but this time with even more devastating consequences for Iraqi society and political culture. Reaffirming its identity as the defender of the Arab nation, Saddam's government now turned its energies inward, cynically and strategically manipulating the politics of inclusion and exclusion to focus popular discontent on targets other than the regime—notably the weakest and most vulnerable populations within Iraq.

Discharging Violence

The mood of despondence and disillusion among the youth had far-reaching repercussions for the regime. Throughout the war, and especially during its last three years, Iraqis were exposed to high levels of paranoid indoctrination, told that because of their superior qualities and traits they had been subject to all sorts of external conspiracies intended to hinder their progress and their opportunity to assume their natural role in leading the Arab nation. Now that the war was over, there was no foreign enemy to blame for local difficulties. What sense of national pride and unity the war had fostered among Iraqi youth could disrupt into unpredictable violence once the demobilized fighters, who had been through all the atrocities of the war, discovered that the rewards of the war went into the pockets of others, especially the nouveaux riches who had benefited from the privatization campaign and war contracts.

The regime was quite aware of this potential violence among many Iraqis.[36] Two episodes that took place between 1989 and 1990 could well have been intended to discharge this potential and direct it toward two targets: Egyptian workers in Iraq and Iraqi women. In the first case, more than one thousand Egyptian workers were brutally slaughtered in various "vague accidents."[37] Though the Iraqi authorities, including Saddam Hussein, were forced to acknowledge the existence of such murders only after an uproar in the Egyptian press, no official account has been given as to why they took place or who the perpetrators were.[38] However, since the murders were carried out immediately following the cease-fire with Iran and reflected similar if not identical forms of violence (smashed or pierced skulls)—and given the intensity of surveillance in Iraq—it seems likely that this violence was tolerated and perhaps encouraged by Iraqi authorities to stem the discontent of unemployed Iraqi citizens by implying that Egyptians had taken Iraqi jobs and were thus legitimate targets of violence. Indeed, the Ba'thist regime had additional motives to encourage these brutal acts. Egyptians working in Iraq were allowed to transfer half of their earnings abroad in hard currency, at the highly inflated official exchange rate of the Iraqi dinar. And while it was highly embarrassing officially to rescind past decrees concerning Arabs working in Iraq—simply because the presence of Arab workers had never been cast in terms of economic need but as a reflection of Iraq's commitment to the principle of Arab unity—these Egyptians represented a clear drain on Iraq's already depleted foreign currency reserves.[39] The exodus of Egyptians as a result of the massive violence directed against them, whether officially sanctioned or not, was therefore an outcome the regime can be expected to have greeted with a measure of relief.[40]

Militarism and Hypermasculinity.   The other act aimed at discharging violence was directed against women. It took concrete form in a Revolution's Command Council (RCC) decree that empowered Iraqi male citizens to murder their female relations if they were found to have committed adultery.[41] The significance of this decree, however, goes far beyond discharging violence and can be seen as an attempt to reaffirm the supremacy of Iraqi males over females after eight years of war, which, for all intents and purposes, had widened the scope of freedoms enjoyed by Iraqi women. Throughout the war years, Iraqi women, as well as immigrant workers, had filled the gap between supply and demand for labor in civilian sectors of the Iraqi economy. The rate of women's participation in the total workforce rose from 17 percent in the late 1970s to some 25 percent in the mid-1980s.[42] While the Ba'thist regime exploited these developments to show how secular it was and how committed—in contrast to Islamist Iran—to building a modern state, its ideology and the provincial origins of the Ba'th's leadership and rank and file were heavily imbued with a stress on masculinity, strength, and manhood.[43]

The symbolism of Ba'thist discourse succeeded in reconciling these two contradictory aspects of the need for women's participation, on the one hand, and the male chauvinist ideology, on the other, through a heavy emphasis on what was turned into the true criterion for real manhood and, hence, for promotion and respect in Ba'thist Iraq, namely, the fighting experience. As the war dragged on, the prewar division of labor within Iraq, whereby most of the Egyptians would work in agriculture and the construction sectors of the economy, underwent a profound change. Iraq was becoming like an Athenian society of citizen-warriors and slave-workers. The ratio of armed forces to the total workforce leaped from about 12 percent in 1981 to 21.3 percent in 1988.[44] Those who were too young to participate in the war directly or who occupied civilian jobs were expected to join the People's Army (al-Jaish al-Sha'bi) and spend a few weeks each year at the front. Intellectuals were brought to the front, as well, to provide material for a "battle literature" and to underscore the "softness" of their everyday lives.[45]

In such an atmosphere, it was natural to look upon those who could not or did not participate in the fighting as inferior. Women, intellectuals, and non-Iraqis working in Iraq belonged in this category. They were routinely reminded that they were able to live their ordinary lives only because of the heroes defending their honor. The repeated references in official discourse to the concept of honor served to reiterate the subordinate role of women in Iraqi society while valorizing the masculinity of the Ba'th. Time and again, Saddam Hussein would remind his (male) audiences that, were the Iranians to invade Iraq, they would *rape* their wives and kinswomen. The tribal norm, in which the honor of a kinship group resides in the sexual conduct of its womenfolk, was invoked repeatedly by Iraq's leadership. Thus, in defending the honor of Iraqi women, male fighters were at the same time defending their own honor, because dishonoring women sexually was a powerful means of attacking social cohesion and humiliating their male kin. In order to preserve the honor of war widows, who were left without a man to protect them, "grants were introduced which were payable to men as financial incentives to marry war widows. This was supposedly to protect the honor of martyrs' wives who might otherwise be forced into prostitution. . . . Women without men clearly could not be trusted and there was a need to increase the population."[46]

> In exchange for being defended by the male fighters, Iraqi women were expected to serve national security by raising their birth rates. Under the slogan "we promise you a cradle in every home," contraception that had previously been freely available was made illegal, as was abortion. Every family should have five children. . . . Women in their forties and even fifties were pressured into giving birth. . . . "We hope," Saddam Hussein told leaders of the General Federation of Iraqi Women "that a woman's inclination to go out to work will not take her away from her family or from giving birth along the lines set by our slogan."[47]

Whether these developments helped in discharging the violent mood among discontented Iraqis is not entirely clear. Yet in manipulating and directing social violence toward vulnerable communities within Iraq, and by reintroducing traditional, gendered norms of social cohesion and hierarchy into its strategy of governance, the Ba'th had tapped into two very powerful veins of political mobilization it could exploit to enhance its own stability.

Forging National Identity

Foreigners and women were not the only two social groups affected by the war. In addition, the Iran-Iraq War served to redefine the borders between Arab Sunnis, Shi'is, and Kurds in Iraq, putting the latter two communities on the defensive by questioning their "true Iraqism." This process brought into the open what no previous government dared to acknowledge publicly. Moreover, a new hierarchy of privileged subcommunities was established even within the Sunni community to the extent that it would be incorrect to talk about whole sects in a generalized form. In some respects, Ba'thist practices can be seen as the reinvention and reconstruction of a long-standing tribal practice, Dakhala, that established differing degrees of participation and entitlement among members of a given community.

During the Ottoman period, a *dakheel* (the word can be translated as "stranger" or "guest") individual, family, or clan would seek the protection of a stronger tribe or clan. The granting of this right is the sole prerogative of the chief of the tribe. In exchange for his protection, the *dakheel* is then expected to work for the tribe as would any of its members. Theoretically, the *dakheel* can gradually acquire the same rights as the tribe's members, including marriage rights, if he proves his loyalty to the host tribe through fighting or hard work. But in practice, a *dakheel* is always considered inferior since he has been cast out by his kinsmen. In the context of the contemporary Ba'thist regime, what might be called a system of neo-Dakhala has emerged in which individuals who prove themselves loyal to the regime are permitted to occupy senior posts in its decision-making bodies, but on the condition that they act as faithful individuals and not as representatives of any non-Ba'thist group. Once such individuals lose favor with the regime, however, their families or even their tribes are subject to reprisals.[48]

Moreover, this neo-Dakhala has important implications in determining the boundaries of social inclusion and exclusion. From the point of view of a tribe, its territory is that land that it had conquered or settled in, and which it can protect from the incursions of rival groups or tribes. When we say that the Ba'thist attitude toward the different associations of Iraqis is a modern version of Dakhala practice, therefore, it implies that centuries of Kurdish presence on their own land is viewed by the Ba'th as irrelevant in determining whether the Kurds should be included or excluded from Iraqi society. In fact, the Ba'th always looked upon the Kurds as *dakheel,* or at best as guests in Iraq who were expected to behave as such, including providing customary forms of service to the regime in exchange for its protection.[49]

The Kurdish leadership, however, did not live up to the expectations of the Ba'th during the Iran-Iraq War. For the Kurds, this was a war between two alien and hostile regimes. The longer it lasted the better. War would distract and weaken both Iran and Iraq, so that the Kurds ultimately could hope to force more concessions from both regimes.[50] For the Ba'thist leadership, this posture represented a severe violation of the basic principles of membership in Iraqi society. It called into question the authenticity of the Kurdish commitment to Iraqism and thus exposed the Kurds to horrifying retribution. Indeed, under conditions of war, and with the benefit of its intense nationalist agitation, the Iraqi regime could play on this feeling of betrayal so cleverly that atrocities committed against the Kurds were met with a degree of complicity, or at least acquiescence, on the part of many non-Ba'thists and even some anti-Ba'thists.[51] In fact, by the mid-1980s the pursuit of Iraqism as a core "raison de revolution" had become so embedded that it could justify almost any act without fear of a public outcry against the excesses committed in its name. Brutality and despotism alone cannot explain the silence that met such acts as the use of nerve gas against Kurdish villagers.

While it was relatively easy to single out the Kurds as traitors, given their history of antistate revolts and the bitter memories of two generations of military conscripts in fighting them, dealing with the Shi'i opposition to the Ba'th proved to be a thornier problem. With the Shi'a and Kurds constituting some 75 percent of the Iraqi population, it obviously was not possible to question the Arab origin of all the Shi'a in Iraq, otherwise one would risk making ridiculous Iraq's claim to be an Arab country.[52] Nor was it possible to attack Shi'ism as an heretical sect, for that would automatically lead the Iraqi Shi'a to defend their identity through an alliance with Iran and create the conditions for a civil war in Iraq. In the meantime, the war with Iran had to be cast first in terms of defending "authentic" Islam, because Iranian propaganda had put great emphasis on the secular aspect of the Ba'thist regime, branding it as corrupt and atheistic. The ideological legitimization of the war was of tremendous importance during the first years, when Iran enjoyed great popular sympathy among many Arabs and Iraq was unquestionably an aggressor. Iraq thus adjusted its discourse in a way that put heavy emphasis on the Arab character of Islam, so that anyone who opposed the Arabs became as a matter of course an enemy of Islam. Moreover, the Persians, it was stressed, had never been faithful to Islam. They pretended to accept Islam when they were defeated by the Arabs, but they in fact simply disguised their continued commitment to heresies such as Zoroastrianism, hence the almost daily use by Iraqi officials and media of the term "al-Furs al-Majus," the Zoroastrian Persians, to refer to Iranians.

Following this logic, the Ba'th proceeded to show that there had always been Iranian agents and infiltrators in Iraqi society who benefited from the weakness of the past governments to control Iraq's domestic trade and markets, and who were using their economic power to bring the Shi'i of Iraq under Iranian influence. The rise of Iraqi nationalism, and the atmosphere of war preparation in 1980, made it possible for the regime to deport no less than a quarter of a million Iraqi Shi'a to Iran, confiscate their properties, and resell them to favorites of the regime for a fraction of their value.

By the mid-1980s, the relations and borders between and among the various Iraqi communities had taken their new shape. Not only were Kurds and Shi'a redefined as marginal communities, but a gradual transformation of Arab Sunni society was also achieved, whereby urban Sunnis lost influence in Iraqi politics and society to the benefit of those with provincial backgrounds. Except for General Husham Sabah al-Fakhri from Mosul, no one from Baghdad, Basra, or Mosul was present in the higher levels of the Iraqi political apparatus. The main beneficiaries of this change—the continuation of a process that had been under way since the days of the first

Ba'thist government in 1963—were not only Tikritis but also newcomers to the Iraqi business community originating from the so-called Sunni Arab triangle in north-central Iraq. While the Jubour tribe, whose lands extend from the south of Mosul to Tikrit, had its sons staffing the main military and intelligence posts, Kubaisis from a town west of Baghdad, acquired a quasi monopoly of the textile industry and trade after the deportation of Shi'ites in 1980 and the confiscation of their properties.[53]

Through this process, a new hierarchy of powerful tribes and elites emerged during the Iran-Iraq War in which certain clans, families, and individuals found their places not because of their a priori sectarian or ethnic affiliations but because they proved their loyalty to the hard core of the regime. Within this power block were Kurdish, Christian, and Shi'i individuals who had not lost favor with the regime despite its outbursts against their respective communities, while there were Sunni Arab towns or clans that had been subject to the regime's wrath.[54] Obviously, the chances of a whole Shi'a or Kurdish tribe or town occupying a privileged position in the power block has always been slim and became even slimmer following the uprising after the second Gulf War, in which Shi'a played a prominent role. However, in the economic sphere, the Kurdish tribes that cooperated with the regime and constituted the mercenary Juhoush troops to combat the Kurdish movement, along with the Shi'a families and tribes that supported the regime during the Iran-Iraq War, enjoyed a considerable improvement in their economic situation. Their leaders were incorporated into the elite of the Iraqi bourgeoisie, even though they were prevented from occupying sensitive or executive positions in decision-making bodies of the regime.

Thus, by the end of the Iran-Iraq War, Iraqi society seemed to have developed a new structure, whereby the most decisive political and administrative functions were fulfilled by Tikritis, followed by Samarra'is, Douris, and Jubouris, all of whom belong to the region north of Baghdad and south of Mosul. The economic elite came mostly from the Ramadi region west of Baghdad, besides those from Tikrit and Mosul. However, there were many affluent and influential Kurdish, Shi'ite, and Christian businessmen and families who had close relations with the regime and reaped tremendous fortunes through their connections. The Shi'ites, Kurds, and Christians were more prevalent in the lower echelons of the state hierarchy and the business community.[55]

The Deinstitutionalization of Iraqi Politics

Iraqi society was not the only target of the regime's policies. If the Ba'thist regime proved all too willing to use the worst forms of demagoguery to reshape Iraqi society and to marginalize communities it perceived as threatening, the dangers of potential rivals among the ruling elite were eliminated through an artful use of carrot-and-stick techniques combined with a radical populism aimed at encroaching upon the authority of even the Ba'th's own institutions to the benefit of the presidential office. This aspect of Saddam's rule has been overlooked by the vast majority of writers on Iraq, who tend to lump the entire Ba'th period under the rubric of "dictatorship" or "fascism." While this has elements of truth, it does not allow for an understanding of variations in internal political dynamics of the regime over time.

The changing course of the Iran-Iraq War since 1984, and Iraq's position as a defender of its sovereignty once Iran turned to the offensive, gave a significant boost to Saddam Hussein's bid to distance himself from the existing institutions and take upon himself the role of the patron of the nation. In this way, he could turn the war with Iran into Saddam's Qadisiyyah (a seventh-century battle in which Arab Muslim forces defeated Persian troops), harness military and administrative institutions, give them strictly executive and professional tasks, and erode the power of other Ba'thist institutions.[56] Thus the mid-1980s witnessed the eclipse not only of the Revolution's Command Council and the Regional Command of the Ba'th Party but also of organizations that the Ba'th had designed to mobilize supporters, such as the National Union of Students and Youth and the Federation of Peasants' Associations. The Federation of Labor Unions was abolished altogether, and workers in the state sector, comprising a majority of wage earners, were henceforth banned from joining unions.

The drive to crush associational life and to cut intermediary links (or buffers) between the patron and his atomized subjects culminated in the 1986 Bai'a, Saddam's call for a march by Iraqis to show confidence in him, in retaliation for Iran's denunciation of the Iraqi regime as illegitimate. In one of the largest political spectacles of our time, millions of Iraqis poured into the street to show their support—not for the Ba'th Party, the RCC, or any other institution—but for Saddam himself.[57]

DEPRIVATION, REPRESSION, AND THE RENEWAL OF IDENTITY POLITICS AFTER KUWAIT

Saddam's bid to create a personalized dictatorship, putting the single leader above the nation and establishing some sort of a Francoist regime, was going more or less smoothly in the period between the cease-fire with Iran and the invasion of Kuwait. However, the economic factors that facilitated this same process were at the heart of the problems that ultimately led to the breakdown of the whole endeavor. Indeed, Saddam's drive into Kuwait, motivated by his concern to provide the economic resources to stabilize his system of rule, led instead to its collapse and the emergence of a bitter and polarizing identity politics. The importance of this shift cannot be overemphasized. What resulted from Saddam's efforts to construct a new vision of Iraqi identity based on a glorification of the Iraqi nation produced the deep fragmentation of Iraqi society along subnational lines. It would be a mistake, however, to see anything primordial in the struggles that gripped Iraq following its defeat in Kuwait. These conflicts can in fact be understood as the culmination of more than twenty years of policies which, by denying the legitimacy of ethnic, regional, and sectarian identities, only reinforced their centrality as frameworks of opposition and dissent. With the near-destruction of Iraq's national sovereignty in 1991, it is not surprising that cracks in the brittle armor of "true Iraqism" would reveal a very different political dynamic at work underneath.

As the economic situation began to deteriorate following the 1988 cease-fire with Iran, as inflation and unemployment increased, and as disparities between the flagrantly rich and the poor became more visible—with the nouveaux riches belonging mostly to the Tikrit-Ramadi Sunni Arab region—people were driven more and more to search for security in their towns of birth or among their extended family relations or tribes. Hatred toward the newly rich took regional or sectarian dimensions. The 1991 Intifada following the end of the second Gulf War was an expression of the strength of subnational identities in Iraq. As the Islamist agitation began to take charge of the Intifada, breaches not only between the various groups but also within each group began to surface, such that it would be misleading to use general categories (Sunnis, Shi'a, or Kurd) to describe the attitudes of the various communities toward the present regime or their perceptions of the future of Iraq.

Since the invasion of Kuwait, and particularly after the Iraqi defeat, Sunnis, whether sheikhs of tribes such as the powerful Shammar tribe or secular former Ba'thists, Nasserists, liberals, or leftists have shown their opposition to the regime and their willingness to overthrow it. Many of those opposing the existing regime posed alternatives that were, in fact, mirror images of the Ba'thist model, such as authoritarian forms of Islamic rule, or lived in hope of yet another coup d'état that would bring a new junta to power.[58] The regime itself, once faced with the mounting opposition of the population, gave up its pretensions of building a new Iraq. The tanks of the Republican Guard that were sent to crush the 1991 Intifada were painted with graffiti reading "No Shi'a from Now On." A series of editorials in *Al-Thawra,* the daily organ of the Ba'th Party, tried to "explain" the Intifada through an explicitly racist and sectarian discourse: "A certain sect [i.e., the Shi'a] has historically been under the influence of the Persians. . . . they have been taught to hate the Arab Nation." As for the Iraqis in Nasiriyya and Samawa, known for their secularism, *Al-Thawra* dismissed them as "the marsh people, so accustomed to breeding buffaloes that they have become indistinguishable from them. When they migrated to big cities like Baghdad they made their living through begging, prostitution, and robbery, not out of poverty but because of their intrinsically degraded nature. A true Arab, of course, cannot be so degraded. These are not Arabs. They were brought with their buffaloes from India by Mohammed al-Qassim" (the Abbasid leader who conquered India in the ninth century).[59]

In this context, the terms "Arabs," "non-Arabs," and "anti-Arab" were gradually detached from their ethnic substance and came to play a role equivalent to that of "anti-Sovietism" in the former Soviet Union; that is, they became terms used to defend one's ghetto in the face of mounting opposition and criticism. It was not the fact of being an Arab that entitled a citizen to the full rights of citizenship, but his faithfulness to the "spirit of Arabism." Being a highly subjective criterion, this could well favor a certain region, clan, or even non-Arab Ba'thists (such as the Chaldean Tariq 'Aziz or the Arabized Kurd Taha Yassin Ramadan) while acting against whole Arab communities.

The sanctions imposed by the United Nations Security Council on Iraq following the invasion of Kuwait, the devastation of the infrastructure during the war and the deprivation and immiseration of Iraqis since then, have drastically altered the relations of power between the various Iraqi communities. The fragile equilibrium of the social pyramid that took shape during the 1980s has been fatally weakened because of the regime's incapacity to defend its own proclaimed goals politically and economically.

The fall in the standard of living of the vast majority of the population came in a sudden and shocking manner. At its height, per capita GDP in Iraq (in constant 1980 prices) reached about $4,200 in 1979. By 1988, at the close of the Iran-Iraq War, this figure was $1,756. But in 1990, per capita GDP had fallen to less than half of these depressed levels, slumping to $868. The fall has continued since then, reaching an estimated $485 in 1993, a figure comparable to the standard of living of Iraqis in the 1940s.[60] Such a drastic decline within such a short span of time left Iraqis with no viable options for adapting to new economic realities. Moreover, those classes and communities that had acquiesced in the 1980s status quo to secure some small measure of their benefits were becoming economically marginal. The pie had simply shrunk to a degree that the regime monopolized it and distributed the bulk of it to close allies in order to keep their loyalty.

Indeed, the 1991 Intifada and the regime's response to it, was an outright acknowledgment by both the regime and its opponents of the breakdown of the social pyramid of the 1980s. The rebellion took sectarian and regional dimensions, while the regime responded by making its regional and clannish nature more explicit.[61] For this reason the short-lived Iraqi Intifada was more of a civil war than a revolution, because a civil war implies that a major component of society has withdrawn its obedience to the existing political regime and entrusted its leadership to others that it judged more representative or capable of defending its actual or mythical cause. The military or quasi-military course that the Intifada took clearly showed that both warring parties took their communal identities with the utmost fanaticism.

From the above, one can see that if the Ba'thist brutal dictatorship is facing its *quart d'heure,* this will by no means give way to a Jeffersonian democracy. Any reorganization of political life in Iraq through the institutional forms of parliamentary democracy would almost inevitably reproduce a configuration of power that is already taking shape, in which political organizations would tend to operate as interest groups of their respective regions, clans, sects, or ethnicities.[62] Yet even this outcome is unlikely. For the more sophisticated urban middle and working classes, severe economic pressures will probably undermine the appeal of a social democratic or liberal alternative, because the solutions that such alternatives profess are too slow to come into effect. Thus one should not be surprised that a people that have suffered so much from tyranny and populism might search for its own Zhirinovski, opening up the possibility that the demise of Saddam Hussein will simply pave the way for some new Iraqi dictator to take his place.

NOTES

1. Even in the majority of major industrialized countries, however, more than 10 percent of this century has been spent in a condition of war. If one includes civil wars, colonial wars, and wars that have not been fought on the territories of the advanced countries themselves but have nevertheless mobilized at least part of their armed forces, the ratio might well surpass 20 percent.

2. Of course, attempts to impose homogenous forms of political identity often serve to reinforce all kinds of particularities, as happened in Iraq as well as dozens of other cases, from the former Soviet Union to the United States.

3. The widespread notion that colonial powers imposed Western-style parliamentary regimes in the Arab Mashreq is simply unfounded, because it was the urban movements that pressed for constitutional democratic monarchies, while the former colonial powers preferred more direct and authoritarian forms of rule. See Pool, "From Elite to Class: The Transformation of Iraqi Political Leadership," pp. 72–73. This discussion of democracy and civil society draws from my "Beyond the Ultra-Nationalist State," pp. 34–39.

4. Najm al-Din, *Ahwal al-sukkan fi al-'Iraq* [Conditions of the population in Iraq], pp. 11–15.

5. Defining a rural person as someone who was born and raised in a community of fewer than two hundred thousand, Tikriti found that only 36 percent of cabinet seats were occupied by Iraqis of rural origins under Qassim (1958–63), while the proportion jumped to 63 percent under the Brothers 'Arif (1963–68), and 75 percent in the first decade of the Ba'thist rule (1968–76). Mwafaq Haded Tikriti,

"Elites, Administration, and Public Policy: A Comparative Study of Republican Regimes in Iraq, 1958–1977" (Ph.D. diss., University of Texas at Austin, 1976), p. 276. According to Amatzia Baram, around 60 percent of Qassim's ruling elite were Baghdadis with an urban background. See Amatzia Baram, "The June 1980 Elections to the National Assembly in Iraq: An Experiment in Controlled Democracy," p. 411.

6. It should be recalled that the institution of political police in Europe was perfected by the French Revolution and the drive of the other European countries toward direct rule. See Chernyak, "The French Revolution: 1794," pp. 65–84.

7. One such aspect of particular relevance here is that regulations governing the military were respected. For example, promotion guidelines requiring that a senior officer had to wait four years before being promoted to a higher rank were upheld even in the case of General Qassim himself, who was promoted to the rank of lieutenant general in 1959 but could not be promoted to brigadier general until 1963, one month before his execution by the Ba'th.

8. At the time, Egypt and Syria had merged to form the United Arab Republic. This gave Nasser the chance to use the long border between Syria and Iraq to encourage and support coup attempts against Qassim's regime with the aim of getting Iraq into this united republic.

9. For one short period in 1966, a civilian, Dr. 'Abd al-Rahman al-Bazzaz, served as prime minister.

10. Figures for 1958 are from Jalal, *The Role of Government in the Industrialisation of Iraq, 1950–1965*, p. 74. For 1969 figures, see Central Bank of Iraq, *Bulletin*, n.s. (October-December 1971): 26.

11. Batatu, *The Old Social Classes and the Revolutionary Movements of Iraq*, p. 1126.

12. The Soviet government announced a new policy of support for such regimes and extended new legitimacy to what it called the "noncapitalist" path to socialism, acknowledging the unlikelihood of a "true" socialist revolution in the developing world.

13. Among the most prominent of these internal conflicts were struggles between the civilian and military wings of the party that led to 'Arif's coup against the Ba'th in late 1963. Subsequent splits in the party—first by a faction led by the secretary of the party, 'Ali Salih al-Sa'di, then by the formation, after the sixth pan-Arab congress (in 1966), of two hostile wings of the Ba'th, a Syrian ("left") wing and Iraqi ("right") wing—further weakened the Ba'th in Iraq.

14. Thus there was the Trotskyite al-Munathamma al-'Ummaliyya (the Workers' Organization), led by Qais al-Samarra'i; the Hizb al-'Ummal al-Thawri al-'Arabi (the Revolutionary Arab Workers Party), led by 'Ali Salih al-Sa'di; and the Arab Ba'th Socialist Party—Left Wing, led by Fu'ad Shakir Mustafa; in addition to the Ba'th Party, which would be reorganized under the leadership of Ahmed Hassan al-Bakr and 'Abdallah Salloum al-Samarra'i.

15. Figures ranging from 170 to 400 were obtained through interviews with several Ba'thist former leaders. These seem reasonable, given the illegality of all political parties in Iraq during the 1960s and the multiple splits within the Ba'th, as well as its elitist organizational structure, whereby full membership was acquired after passing successfully through many preliminary steps as "supporter" and "partisan." It seems that the five-thousand-member estimate quoted by the *Economist* from

Ba'thist sources and endorsed by Phoebe Marr is highly exaggerated. Marr, *The Modern History of Iraq*, p. 213. In fact, by the early 1980s, after sixteen years in power, party officials told a source then considered to be "friendly" to the regime that there were only 2,500 full party members. See Helms, *Iraq: Eastern Flank of the Arab World*, p. 87.

16. In large measure this move grew out of deep and long-standing tensions between the Ba'th and the Iraqi military. The Ba'th's short-lived rule in 1963 witnessed the creation of a paramilitary militia aimed at terrorizing the populace and offsetting any potential threat of a countercoup by army officers. This led to serious friction between the Haras al-Qawmi, the Ba'thist militia, and regular army troops. Nine months later, it was the president and his prime minister, both senior army officers, who organized a new coup that ousted the Ba'th from power and dissolved the "National Guard." The Ba'th Party that seized power in 1968 was even more estranged from the officers corps than the 1963 party.

17. Al-Zaidi, *Al-Bina'a al-ma'nawi li al-quwwat al-musallaha al-'Iraqiyya* [The moral structure of the Iraqi armed forces], p. 261.

18. U.S. Arms Control and Disarmament Agency, *World Military Expenditure and Arms Transfers* (Washington, D.C.: ACDA, 1982).

19. The Ba'th relied on two key officers of the 'Arif regime to achieve their goals, Colonel 'Abdul Razzaq al-Nayef, head of military intelligence, and Lt. Colonel Ibrahim 'Abdul Rahman al-Daoud, chief of the Republican Guard. The two were appointed prime minister and minister of defense, respectively, only to be removed from office thirteen days later in a second coup.

The Revolution's Command Council, which was formed after the first coup as the supreme ruling body in Iraq, had seven members, all of whom were officers. These were General Ahmad Hasan al-Bakr, president of the republic; al-Nayef; al-Daoud; Marshall Salih Mahdi 'Ammash, minister of interior; Gen. Hardan 'Abdul Ghaffar al-Tikriti, chief of staff; Lt. Colonel Hammad Shihab, head of Baghdad's military garrison; and Lt. Colonel Sa'doun Ghaidan, chief of the Republican Guard. See, *Al-Waqai' al-Iraqiyya* [The official gazette], 1602 (August 7, 1968), Communiqué No. 23. As for the fate of these officers, 'Ammash and Hardan were removed from their posts by 1971. Shihab was killed in a coup attempt in 1973. Ghaidan was relegated to the secondary post of minister of communications until his expulsion in 1982.

20. By the late 1980s, five of the seven members of the Military Bureau of the Ba'th Party were originally NCOs: 'Ali Hasan al-Majid, Hussein Kamil al-Majid (killed in 1996 following his return from a period of exile in Jordan), Kamil Yaseen al-Tikriti, Ahmad al-'Azzawi, and Hamid al-Biragh. See al-Zaidi, *Al-Bina'a al-ma'-nawi li al-quwwat al-musallaha al-'Iraqiyya*, p. 385.

21. Early in 1980, military salaries were increased by 25 percent. Earlier, Law 43 of 1979 decreed that all nonconscripts should be given parcels of land "at reasonable prices." According to the same law, officers would be given ID 5,000, while other nonofficers would receive ID 3,500, to help them build personal homes (ID 1 was then equivalent to $3.30). According to Resolution 1275 of 9 September 1980, a nonconscript is entitled to the rights granted by the latter law even if he or his wife already have a house of their own. Resolution 240 of 26 February 1981 authorized all members of the armed forces to buy a personal car without payment of customs duties. Al-Zaidi, ibid., pp. 324–25, adds that the families of those killed in the war

with Iran were given ID 3,000 in compensation for the deaths of their sons; any soldier who killed more than 25 Iranians would be presented with a gift of ID 500–1,000; and army commanders were regularly presented with luxurious Mercedes and Oldsmobile cars, while junior officers received Toyotas.

22. The report, however, reminds us that "this love for militarism does not express any aggressive tendencies in the new Iraqi society." *Al-Thawra,* 29 January 1983.

23. As in most ultranationalist ideologies, concepts are reified and turned into subjects. Thus it is quite familiar to find in Ba'thi writings phrases like "the Nation wants" or the "spirit of the Nation." Though this is not the appropriate place to analyze nationalist ideologies, one aspect of this reification attracts attention here; namely, that it gives those speaking about the nation in such a manner a free hand to appropriate the representation of the nation in a subtle way. A similar case could be made about the way avant-guardist movements, such as the communists or the Islamists, reify concepts like the proletariat or Islam.

24. Speech on the anniversary of the founding of the Ba'th Party. *Al-Thawra,* 8 April 1981.

25. In addition to its racist discourse, Ba'thism relates more to Nazism than to Italian fascism, in that it considers the state as the ultimate embodiment of the will of the race, while fascism emphasized the role of the masses at the expense of the state. See Macciocchi, ed., *Elements pour une analyse du fascisme.* In a speech published in 1957 and never reprinted (even though the original text was withdrawn from libraries and bookshops), 'Aflaq admits, "We should emphasize here how grateful we are to *German philosophy* in directing our thoughts to that which is most profound. . . . Our thoughts aimed at something deeper than material phenomena and economic relations in explaining history and the development of society. This has rectified the influence of materialist philosophy on us and protected us from being deceived by the abstract view upon which socialism rests and which radically negates nationalism." Michel 'Aflaq, "Nahnu wa al-shiuy'iyya qabla khamsat 'ashara 'aman" [We and communism fifteen years ago], in Aflaq and al-Din al-Bitar, *Mawqifuna al-siyasi min al-shiuy'iyya* [Our political position toward communism], pp. 3–15.

26. *Al-Thawra,* 11 October 1978.

27. The first wave concerned the bulk of the Iraqi Jewish community, whose deportation en masse occurred between 1948 and 1954. According to the 1947 population census, Jews constituted 2.6 percent of the total population of Iraq and 7 percent of the urban population. Ironically, if one were to apply the term "deportation" to the Jewish migration from Iraq, it would be contested from two contrasting, though both nationalistic, points of view: on the one hand, official Israeli discourse considers the Jews to have joined their homeland; while the Arab nationalist view, on the other hand, never treated Iraqi Jews as real citizens. For an excellent account of the episode of Iraqi Jews see Shiblaq, *The Lure of Zion.*

28. For the number of deported Faili Kurds, see Khadduri, *Socialist Iraq: A Study of Iraqi Politics since 1968,* p. 152. Even at the time, it was evident that neither the deportation of Faili Kurds nor the execution of a handful of Iraqi Jews was aimed at weakening a foreign enemy. The Iraqi leadership took pride that it had been the first state to recognize the rights of the Kurdish population in self rule. The auton-

omy declaration came at a crucial time for the new Ba'thist regime, because the tensions with the shah's Iran were reaching alarming dimensions. The shah had abrogated a 1937 treaty and demanded equal access to the Shatt al-Arab waterway, the only river linking Iraq to a sea outlet. Exchange of artillery shelling took place on the southern borders between Iraq and Iran, and just two months before the declaration of Kurdish autonomy, a coup attempt assisted by the Iranians had been uncovered. Out of this sense of vulnerability, the Iraqi regime was eager to conclude a deal with the Kurdish leadership, to free the Iraqi army from the Kurdish quagmire, and to ensure that the Iranians would not use Iraqi Kurdistan as an outlet for their attempts to topple the Ba'th.

29. The concept of the rentier state was first applied to the Middle East by Mahdavy, "The Patterns and Problems of Economic Development in Rentier States: The Case of Iran," pp. 428–67. See also Beblawi, "The Rentier State in the Arab World," pp. 383–94. On Iraq's dependence on oil see al-Khafaji, *Al-dawla wa al-tatawwur al-ra'smali fi al-'Iraq, 1968–1978* [The state and capitalist development in Iraq, 1968–1978]; and al-Khafaji, "The Parasitic Base of the Iraqi Economy," pp. 73–89.

30. Strategic rent should be distinguished from economic aid for political allies. Aid implies support for an economically weaker party. Strategic rent, on the other hand, presupposes a country exploiting its strategic location or its politico-military strength, either to protect vulnerable allies or to create political problems for those same "allies," thus forcing them to pay what is, in effect, protection money.

31. The economic dimension of the Iran-Iraq War is discussed in my "Al-Iqtisad al-'Iraqi ba'd al- harb ma'a Iran" [The Iraqi economy after the war with Iran], pp. 177–223.

32. See, for example, all Iraqi papers, 2–3 May 1983.

33. Thus when Iran pushed Iraqi troops from its territory in 1982, the political report of the ninth congress of the Ba'th Party ascribed the defeat to "Iran's allies, who utilized all their means to support it . . . otherwise it would have been impossible for [Iran] to move our troops from their positions." *Al-Thawra,* 28 January 1983.

34. Nor was this entirely a construction of the Ba'th. During the war, Kuwaiti and Jordanian press and mass media parroted the official Iraqi line. Iraqi Embassies in both countries acted almost like the offices of a high commissioner, and Iraqi businessmen and employees in the Gulf and Jordan and especially in Kuwait were accorded special privileges.

35. See Chaudhry, "On the Way to Market: Economic Liberalization and Iraq's Invasion of Kuwait," pp. 14–23.

36. In the post-Iran-Iraq War period, frequent news and reports about highly organized crimes appeared in Iraqi papers. Saddam Hussein himself addressed the issue in his public meetings with Ba'thist cadres (even while escalating his practice of bribing public employees). See, for example a speech he made in Babylon, reported in *Al-Thawra,* 14 February 1990, in which he responds, "The comrade says that crimes have increased after the war. I cannot confirm or deny that before seeing the statistics of the Ministry of Interior. . . . Bribery has increased in 1989 compared with 1987 and 1988."

37. Egyptian and Iraqi authorities have not made public the exact number of massacred Egyptians. In the late 1980s, Egypt's prime minister did say that 1,000 corpses had been returned to Egypt by September 1989, a figure he expected to in-

crease to 1,200 by the end of the year. "As for those corpses buried in Iraq," he added, "neither we nor the Egyptian Embassy know anything about them." *Al-Safir,* 8 December 1989. According to figures published recently in the Egyptian press, the figure of Egyptians killed in Iraq is a staggering 5,996. *Al-Mussawwar,* 4 January 1999.

38. Iraq's Deputy Prime Minister Taha Yassin Ramadhan, for example, declared that "the increase in the numbers of Egyptians killed in Iraq does not reflect an exceptional phenomenon." *Al-Nida',* 19 November 1989.

39. Note that these murders overlapped with the creation of the Arab Cooperation Council, which included Iraq and Egypt, as well as Jordan and Yemen.

40. The Egyptian prime minister revealed that thirty-six thousand Egyptians had returned from Iraq following the massacres. *Al-Safir,* 8 December 1989.

41. RCC resolution no. 111, 28 February 1990. *Al-Safir,* 13 March 1990.

42. Excluding women working in agriculture, where the percentage rises to 43.7 percent. *Al- Thawra,* 25 July 1986.

43. Many observers and scholars on Iraq have failed to notice this aspect of Ba'thist discourse, because of their overemphasis on the modern state building project of the Iraqi regime. In fact, one of the first acts of the Ba'th in power was sending police patrols into the streets with scissors and paint to cut the long hair of male youth and paint the legs of women who wore miniskirts. It is also worth emphasizing that the Ba'th Party has never had a woman in its leading positions, nor are there any women in senior positions within the Iraqi state. This should be contrasted with 'Abdul Karim Qassim's policy, for example, who appointed the first woman cabinet minister in the Arab world twenty years before the Ba'th takeover. The Ba'th did have a non-Ba'thist woman minister during their first years in office, but soon abandoned this practice.

44. Abbas Alnasrawi, "Economic Devastation, Underdevelopment, and Outlook," p. 89.

45. The leading Ba'thist poet and chief editor of the daily *Al-Jumhuriyya* writes in one his poems, "the spoiled write about love and war, and the lazy write too. But the homeland is not what they describe. It is in the forward barrack, in the mouth of the barrel, in sand and blood." *Kul al- 'Arab,* 27 February 1982.

46. Omar, "Women: Honor, Shame, and Dictatorship," p. 64.

47. Ibid., p. 65

48. An example of such a case is the so-called 1979 conspiracy against Saddam Hussein, after which a decree was passed that even fourth-degree relatives of a "conspirator," i.e., brothers- and sisters-in-law of an accused, were to be dismissed from their jobs.

49. Besides the Ba'th's concept of Kurdish autonomy, in which rights are granted to people while land belongs to the regime, the Ba'thist concept of "true" citizenship also implies loyalty to the regime. When the deportation of Shi'a began in 1980, the general director of security declared that "deportation procedures apply to any Iranian family whose loyalty to the homeland and revolution is not proven *even if it has Iraqi nationality,*" *Alif Ba,'* 25 June 1980, emphasis added.

50. This view is reinforced by the opposition of the Kurdish leadership to the call by their only non-Kurdish ally, the Communist Party, to bring the Iran-Iraq War to an immediate end and overthrow the dictatorship in Iraq. The Kurds feared,

rightly, that as soon as the war was over the Iraqi army would turn its attention to the suppression of Kurds.

51. Iraqi nationalist sentiments ran so high in the mid-1980s that the Iraqi Communist Party, which had since 1979 endorsed the overthrow of the Ba'thist regime, experienced a split because of a demand from some cadres that the party shift to a position of support for the "homeland" in view of the threat from Iran.

52. However, when the opposition activities of the al-Da'wa Shi'ite party were on the rise, the minister of interior declared that "of the estimated one thousand active members [who had not fallen in the hands of the authorities] 90 percent are of Iranian origin." *Al-Majalla,* 10 May 1980.

53. Iraqi authorities have not released official data concerning the number of people deported in 1980 or the fate of their property. However, a book written by the then general director of security, Fadhil al-Barrak, provides an indication of the regime's interest in (and concern for) the level of "Iranian," i.e., Shi'i, participation in the Iraqi economy:

> The number of Iranian merchants in Baghdad alone was 3245, more than 1177 of whom were wholesale merchants. [Iranian] industrialists owned 258 factories and 35 goldsmith shops. . . . In real estate they owned 36 percent of al-Kadhmiyya district and its surroundings, as well as 32 percent in various districts of Baghdad. . . . in Najaf's Chamber of Commerce they constituted almost one-third [of the members]. . . . in Karbala, 75 out of 1160 merchants were of Iranian origin, but there were 20 Iranian industrialists out of 32 industrialists in that city. In Basra, 20 percent of all the merchants were of Iranian origin.
>
> Al-Barrak, *Al-madaris al-yahudiyya wa-al-iraniyya fi al-Iraq: dirasa muqarina* [Jewish and Iranian schools in Iraq: A comparative study], pp. 150–55.

Ironically, al-Barrak was himself subsequently executed by the regime as an accused KGB agent.

54. As early as 1980, for example, a Sunni Arab town northeast of Baghdad, al-Dijayl, was wiped out and many of its townsmen executed because of an assassination attempt against Saddam Hussein that had taken place there.

55. See Isam al-Khafaji, "The State and Infitah Bourgeoisie in the Arab Mashreq: The Case of Egypt and Iraq" (manuscript, 1991).

56. One example of political deinstitutionalization was Saddam's efforts to construct an unmediated relationship between himself and the Iraqi people, through such symbolic means as the opening in the mid-1970s of a direct telephone line that ordinary people could use to reach him to discuss and resolve problems.

57. Saddam Hussein has been careful not to employ the term "election" when faced with the need to renew his mandate. *Bai'a* is a term that came into use following the rise of Islam and refers to a unanimous expression of support by the faithful in the rule of a single leader, who would guide the community of Islam, the *umma,* until his death.

58. Isam al-Khafaji, "State Terror and the Degradation of Politics in Iraq," 15–22.

59. *Al-Thawra,* 1–3 April 1991.

60. See Abbas Alnasrawi, "The Economy of Iraq," p. 152.

61. The Iraqi regime's reliance on family ties was acknowledged publicly as early as Saddam's first months in power, when his press secretary wrote an article titled

"Kinship in a Revolutionary Society," in which the author complains, "If the relative is the son of the Party and Revolution, would occupying the position that he merits negatively affect the revolutionary march?" Sabah Yassin, *Al-Thawra*, 13 November 1979.

62. I have elaborated on this in "Repression, Conformity, and Legitimacy: Prospects for an Iraqi Social Contract," in *The Future of Iraq*, ed. John Calabrese (Washington, D.C.: Middle East Institute, 1997), pp. 17–30.

10

The Political Economy
of Civil War in Lebanon

Elizabeth Picard

In the comparative study of the political economy of war, the case of Lebanon permits endless and rich insights. Yet unlike other cases of war making discussed in this volume, Lebanon's experience between 1975 and 1990 shifts our attention to the political economy of *civil* war, a form of violence that implies the collapse of the state and thus breaks the causal chain that has linked war making to state consolidation in much of the literature on this topic.[1] What Lebanon's descent into civil war reveals, however, is not the eruption of disorganized, anarchic violence as a byproduct of the state's collapse. Just the opposite proved to be the case.

Largely through the activities of various militia groups, pervasive and wide-ranging networks of social organization emerged in the course of the war as competing militias struggled to construct and defend institutional arrangements that would permit them not merely to survive but to manage the organizational, material, and human demands of war making; maximize the economic opportunities created by the war; and compensate for the absence of the state in the provision of essential social services to specific communities. Militias provided an institutional framework—organized largely around the interconnected tasks of coercion and predation—that nonetheless aspired to consolidate practices of economic and political governance that would have the legitimacy, predictability, and integrity of the Lebanese state whose collapse they had brought about. Ultimately this effort failed, but in the process it profoundly influenced the shape of Lebanon's postwar political economy.

In addition, the civil war reveals a tremendous diversity in the responses devised by Lebanese militias in their modes of social domination and extraction of resources, their linkages with sources of external support, and, most important, their relation to the residual structures of the state, as well as their mode of access to the material and symbolic resources of its institutions.

Lebanon thus provides a fascinating window into the institutional and organizational logics that shape the strategic choices of those who take part in a distinctive form of war making. Almost inevitably, these are logics that produce high levels of fragmentation—territorial, social, economic—and Lebanon's experience provides ample evidence of this. Yet here too, the image of fragmentation needs to be tempered by a recognition that, in the economic realm in particular, markets in wartime Lebanon operated not only within but across newly created territorial boundaries, producing forms of interaction, even interdependence and collaboration, that seem almost out of place given the intensity of the violence between (and sometimes within) Lebanon's highly polarized communities.

After first situating the genesis and development of the wartime economy in a general framework characterized by a shift from clientelism to predation, I will focus on the redistributive dimensions of what I have called the "militia economy" and explore in detail the dynamics of these economies within specific territories under militia control. I will, moreover, go beyond an analysis of the formation of what might be called a "militia system" and begin to elaborate a typology of these militia economies in a comparative perspective. Finally, I will discuss various modes of adaptation of these militia economies to the end of the war and to the initial years of the postwar era.

THE GENESIS AND TRAJECTORY OF THE MILITIA ECONOMY

The birth of a militia economy during the Lebanese war was marked by the transition from the local mobilization of armed defense groups in villages or neighborhoods that operated within the framework of a unified state to the monopolization of resources and means of coercion by large, organized, and hierarchical militias that gradually carved up Lebanese territory after 1976. These militias consisted primarily of the Lebanese Forces (LF), which united into a Christian stronghold between 1975 and 1980; Kamal Jumblatt's Progressive Socialist Party (PSP), which ruled over the Druze community from its stronghold in Chouf; and 'Amal, which garnered support among the majority of the Shi'ite population until its radical competitor, Hizballah, gained momentum after 1982. There were, in addition, other less influential militias, such as the South Lebanon Army (SLA) in the zone occupied by Israel, the Popular Nasserite Organization (PNO) in Sidon, and the Marada Brigade in Zghorta. The consolidation and territorialization of the militias unfolded under the financial and military influence of the Palestine Liberation Organization (PLO) in the regions with a

Muslim majority, and in the shadow of Syrian hegemony in all of Lebanon starting in 1976.

In a general sense, the notion of a militia economy refers to various modes of adaptation to destruction, shortages, and more broadly, to a situation of deep social and institutional fragmentation. In other words it refers to the economy of Lebanon as it evolved during the war. However, it also refers to the various strategies the belligerents developed to turn the wartime economy into a strategic resource.[2] In establishing the periodization of the transition to a militia economy, it should be pointed out that there was a lag between various phases in the development of this economy and the military trajectory of the conflict due to the greater inertia of economic processes relative to military operations, on the one hand, and the strong external dimension of the Lebanese economy, on the other. Broadly speaking, however, the militia economy took shape during two distinct phases in the course of the civil war.

During the first phase, from 1975 to 1983, the prewar liberal economy subsisted on the margins of the civil war, showing a certain measure of resilience. Prewar economic arrangements were reconstructed to a considerable extent following the destruction of the commercial infrastructure in the center of Beirut and of the industrial infrastructure in the eastern and southern suburbs of the city in the period 1975–76. However, this resilience was soon exhausted as the militias became an increasingly powerful economic force. Even in this first phase of the conflict, armed militias operated as predators in the communities in which they had sprung up during the earliest days of the fighting. Throughout this first phase of militia accumulation, these groups attempted to concentrate the means of coercion and administration within the confines of each community so as to maximize their own resources. The result was the emergence of more efficient "survival units" within the territory of Lebanon which represented, in effect, "ministates" in formation.[3] In other words, this first phase represents a shift in the militias' operating practices from banditry to organized forms of extraction and exploitation.

The militias' mode of operation during the first phase of the war illustrates several important paradoxes associated with the political economy of civil war. First among them is that militia fighters were relentlessly seeking to destroy the very infrastructures they also sought to appropriate for themselves. All of the souks (markets) in the city center and half of the factories in the suburbs were either shelled or burned down. In Beirut's port, militia members "sold" goods simply on the basis of their volume rather than their value; and through continued fighting they prevented any activity at the port during nine months in 1976. The logic behind the destruction of fixed capital assets was in fact twofold. First, it destroyed the physical infrastructure that constituted the material basis of the coexistence between communities to legitimize the militias' bellicose project. And second, it deprived their adversaries of resources such as oil and electricity so as to secure a monopoly over them. The effect of this destruction was brutal, since Lebanon's GDP fell by 30 percent in 1975 and by an additional 40 percent in 1976. As a result, populations and armed groups were quickly forced to turn to external actors, and especially to expatriates, to secure financial resources; the revenues obtained from diaspora sources were estimated at the time to be $1.5–2.5 billion per year.[4]

Another paradox is that the maintenance of an overvalued exchange rate characterized by a strong pound relative to the dollar and to the money supply fostered overconfidence concerning the strength of the Lebanese economy even while the political system disintegrated.[5] Among other things, the overvalued currency provided opportunities for speculation that earned Lebanese some $300 million per year. More important, however, and somewhat ironically, it provided the means for the besieged Lebanese state to retain some capacity to manage macroeconomic policy. Governments like Selim Hoss's (1978–79) explicitly sought to alleviate the war's effects on lower income wage earners. Salaries of civil servants were paid regularly, including those of soldiers who had deserted the armed forces to join militias as fighting intensified. And the government established price controls on oil products, flour, beets, and other essential commodities.

In the second phase, 1983–90, the state finally collapsed. Following the 1984 split within the army the state lost its means of coercion, controlled less than a tenth of Lebanon's territory, and no longer controlled any of its financial resources. Whereas in 1980, the Ministry of Finance was still able to collect 90 percent of revenues from tariffs, this percentage dropped to 60 percent in 1983 and to a mere 10 percent in 1986. Worse, military goods worth several billion dollars, which had been bought from the United States to rebuild the army, fell into the hand of militias when the army rebelled in the western part of Beirut and split in February of 1984. The collapse of the army undermined confidence in the pound and resulted in a massive devaluation.[6] Finally, the international context, especially the drying up in 1982–83 of the resources contributed by the PLO and the repercussions of the 1984 oil crisis, accelerated the decline of state revenues and contributed to a general condition of economic crisis.[7]

The militia economy subsequently expanded on the ruins of a national economy that was falling back on agriculture as its leading sector. While agriculture's share of GDP was only 10 percent in 1974, it grew to 33 percent by 1985. However, this was a larger share of a much smaller GDP; indeed, GDP had been halved between 1984 and 1987 and further reduced by a third between 1987 and 1990. Fixed capital assets that had suffered two waves of destruction in 1982–84 and 1989–90 were no longer replaced. Massive capital flight took place following the collapse of the pound. Civil servants and salaried workers in the service sector were the hardest-hit victims of a crisis that polarized Lebanese society, dividing it into a minority who benefited from the militia economy and a pauperized majority. This situation led to the long-term emigration of skilled and even unskilled workers. And as a result, Lebanon ended the war with a population of nearly 3 million people, no more than fifteen years earlier.[8]

During the early postwar period, from 1990 to 1995, the restoration of state sovereignty remained partial, and it unfolded in ways that preserved many of the political prerogatives of the militias. One-tenth of the country remained under Israeli occupation in the south. The remaining 90 percent was under tight Syrian control following the signing of the Treaty of Brotherhood, Cooperation, and Coordination in May 1991. Moreover, both the Lebanese Forces and Hizballah successfully resisted an April 1991 law that mandated the disarming of militias. The LF complied with the law only in June 1995, while Hizballah still retains its military autonomy. The legitimacy of the regime resulting from the Ta'if accords of October 1989, as well as that of the legislature elected in August of 1992, was contested. The government and the bureaucracy incorporated militia leaders, and their participation renewed political communitarianism by bringing brute force to bear on the competitive relations between communities.[9]

Nor did the end of the war and the partial reassertion of state sovereignty mean the breakdown of the militia economy. In the economic as in the political realm the government sought to mobilize and engage militias rather than to control them. In its effort to rebuild the country it gave priority neither to public services nor social infrastructure. Rather, it privileged land and real estate operations such as Solidere in the center of Beirut and Elyssar in the southern suburbs, as well as rampant privatization (for example, of Lebanon's state-run telephone company). By so doing the government sought to attract the participation of the businesses created under the militias—as well as to attract the capital they had accumulated—in support of its efforts to reconstruct the Lebanese economy. Given that reconstruction was estimated to require between $15 and 20 billion, the global needs of the economy constituted a perfect opportunity for the state to rein in the militia economies by facilitating their integration into leading sectors of Lebanon's reemerging, postwar national economy.

FROM CLIENTELISM TO PREDATION

Wartime economies, of course, are not born sui generis. In the case of Lebanon, they can be traced back to widespread clientalist practices that consisted of exchanging personal loyalty (such as a vote during the legislative elections that take place every four years) for protection, a job, or various material or financial advantages.[10] But new phenomena would grow out of these long-standing practices. At the outset of the war, most local militias were self-defense organizations formed in response to a real or imagined threat, and they had a symbiotic relationship with the populations in which they originated. The first militia fighters did not receive wages. Unlike those of the "professional" fighters of the PLO, their initial arms purchases were financed by local entrepreneurs, and administrative tasks were performed by neighborhood volunteers. These early militias thus shared certain features with citizen-based vigilante movements that arise in other contexts, and even with such volunteer organizations as the neighborhood watch groups found in the United States. At this stage one cannot yet talk of a militia economy. Although the destruction and interruptions of economic activities had an impact on the resources of households, they did not really have structural effects on the overall economy of the state. Nor did localized economic hardship have an effect on popular perceptions and official representations that blamed the fighting on insidious foreign elements.

Next, the proliferation of defense units and the eclipse of regular forces encouraged petty criminality among urban gangs that lived off the looting of territories under their control—both those they protected and those they captured. Such petty criminality took the form of stealing cars, hijacking for ransom, squatting, and racketeering either at roadblocks or by patrols plundering neighborhood buildings. The resulting insecurity gave rise to new activities such as locksmithing, armor plating, and private security services. Meanwhile, activities such as the setting up of the large souk organized in 1975 by the Lebanese Forces in the port of Beirut, or the salvage of furniture by the Mourabitoun in the part of the city where the big hotels were located, constituted implicit modes of payment for the fighters whose allowances ranged from very meager to nil.

It was only later, during the 1980s that the big militias (primarily the Lebanese Forces, the Druze PSP, and later, Hizballah) turned into professional organizations whose members were paid a wage. This evolution, however, was enormously important, transforming the status of the militias. From then on, militia fighters were less "neighborhood youths" than servicemen in uniform. Their salaries were often the only resource for families hit by unemployment and the paralysis of the economy. Yet, this contribution was probably less important than the "extraordinary" resources that were available to militia fighters as a result of their new status. It was these new "professional" militia members who had ready access to rationed resources such as flour and gas, to "free" goods obtained by looting (even Israeli soldiers looted private homes during their 1982–85 occupation), and to profitable illicit activities such as the smuggling of cigarettes and drugs. In a fragmented social field, where the old aristocratic and commercial elite kept a low profile (those who had not emigrated), these new actors acquired prestige based not only on their weapons but also on their command of economic resources. They had the capacity to create a clientele for themselves even if the population condoned neither their project nor their practices. It is noteworthy that the members of Hizballah, who were notoriously the best paid, also had the reputation of being the least corrupt and least predatory with respect to the populations they controlled.[11] And yet they too knew how to manufacture artificial shortages (in water and electricity, for example) in the southern suburbs of Beirut so that the aid they offered would be appreciated to a greater extent.

Compared to the ultraliberal clientalist system that characterized the boom years of the prewar era, the militia economy operated on a different scale, with a different character, and through different spatial arrangements. It operated on a new scale because criminal activities such as smuggling, which had been a low-level activity in the 1970s, became systematized as the war dragged on. The harbors of Tyr and Tripoli thus became centers for the import of vehicles (often stolen in Europe) by private operators.[12] Militias also engaged in the export of goods that were subsidized in neighboring countries: a quarter of the gas imports, sold cheaper in Lebanon than in the Gulf oil-producing states, was smuggled into Syria, Turkey, Jordan, and even Cyprus.[13] Further, the militia economy operated on a new scale because Syrian troops inserted themselves into Lebanese social and economic networks through their own participation in looting, taxing and reexporting gas, wood, iron, tires, and medicine. In fact, the value of merchandise that passed through Syrian hands in these various ways was estimated to be $5 million per day in 1985.[14]

The militia economy also exhibited a different character than prewar economic arrangements because economic management was quickly perceived as an intrinsic part of the war between militias. In a country that imported more than 50 percent of its consumption goods, securing access to resources without having to rely on the mediation of an enemy, even if this enemy was the state administration, quickly became a priority. As early as 1976, Jumblatt's Druze PSP began to engage in the all-out import of petroleum products in the improvised ports of Jieh and Khaldeh because they did not have access to the refineries of Zahrani and Tripoli, and even less to the oil storage tanks in Dora. The Lebanese Forces that took control of the Christian regions to the north of Beirut also violated the state monopoly on oil: a crony of Camille Chamoun, the head of the National Liberal Party (NLP), became the first importer of smuggled goods in these regions through the port of Dbayeh. Here and there, various people called on businessmen who were sympathizers or members of their community. The first institutionalization of a parastatal economic structure was that of the Gamma groups that emerged in 1978 around the Lebanese Forces, the armed branch of the Kata'ib led by Bachir Gemayel. The groups were constituted of tens of academics but also entrepreneurs who mastered the functioning of the banking and commercial economy and became responsible for supply and distribution activities on the territory dominated by the Christian LF militia.

This, however, was only a first step. These entrepreneurs working for their community realized, and persuaded their patrons, that even though the war was destructive it could also produce economic wealth. And so they lobbied politicians and military men to organize wartime activities that were "economically oriented," to use Max Weber's formula. Asked to participate in the war effort by supplying the armed forces and the civilian population in the region with necessary civil and military equipment, but subject at the same time to new and significant taxes established by the militias, entrepreneurs applied a capitalist logic to their activities: they had to profit from them. They thus became accomplices of the fighters whose interventions affected the value of their goods and services. The ferryboat ride from Jounieh to Cyprus, which represented the way out of the country for the inhabitants of the eastern region who could not reach the Khaldeh airport to the south of Beirut, offers a telling example. On the one hand, no agreement was sought with the other militias in 1986–87 to reopen a safe passage to Khaldeh, because the Lebanese Forces were at the time completing construction of an alternative airport in Halate near Jbail with the cooperation of the banker Roger Tamraz. And, on the other hand, exchanges of artillery between militias around Jounieh as ferryboats departed were invoked by the transport companies as a reason to increase the cost of the fare.

Another example is provided by the inordinately high benefits that were reaped by the private companies that supplied the Christian town of Deir el-Qamar with flour and heating oil during the prolonged siege to which it was subjected by the PSP from mid-September until Christmas of 1983. The clientelism that had prevailed before the war shifted to practices of political and military extraction of social resources and to the development of mafia-like processes that supported not only the survival of the group but tremendous capital accumulation. If we take seriously several consistent estimates, the looting of Beirut's port allegedly generated some \$1–\$2 billion, as did the looting of Beirut's city center.[15]

In the 1980s, having secured control of the economy's key sectors (such as petroleum imports and cement production), militia leaders invested in new activities, including communications, computers, and maritime transport. They crossed, unhindered, the boundary between the legal and criminal economy by taking up drug production and trafficking. These activities quickly led to the emergence of new economic actors who were distinct from politicians and militiamen. These new actors worked both for the militia and themselves, reexporting short-term profits made in Lebanon to

Western banks, or investing in Lebanese real estate. One should nevertheless not underestimate the discreet but continuous participation of the largest fortunes from the prewar era in these new profitable ventures, nor the complex financial ties that formed between nonmilitary economic elites and the new entrepreneurs who prospered in the shadow of the militia system.

Finally, the intervention of militias produced a restructuring of Lebanon's economic space. It fragmented this space into territories where each militia sought exclusive control of resources.[16] This, for example, was the effect of the 1978 confrontations between the Lebanese Forces and the Maradas from Zghorta for the control of ports and cement works in the north. The division of territory that resulted from this confrontation lasted until 1990 and gave Samir Geagea, who took over leadership of the LF in 1986, a financial foundation based on the internal "customs" of Barbara on the coastal route. The desire to control resources was also the goal behind the crushing of Chamoun's NLP militia, its annexation by the Lebanese Forces under Bachir Gemayel in 1980, and Gemayel's takeover of the collective finances of the Lebanese Front, the coalition of Christian parties and militias.

However, the formation of quasi-statist political and economic spaces does not at all imply that each militia existed in a condition of autarky; quite the contrary. Not only was it necessary for militia economies to maintain a relation with "the outside," but trade between them was also central to their prosperity by making it possible to avoid shortages in certain goods such as flour or gas, or by feeding internal customs, or even sustaining illicit activities such as the drug trade from the Beka'a. Because the banking system also continued to operate within transcommunal and transterritorial networks, the breakup of the Lebanese mosaic was not a process in which boundaries between the communities became rigidified, but one that exhibited a dynamic quality that facilitated the accumulation of capital. Thus, militias were not only the agents of Lebanon's fragmentation, they were also the managers and immediate beneficiaries of territorial divisions in ways that combined economic and military-strategic logics.[17]

THE MICRO-DYNAMICS OF THE MILITIA ECONOMY

Can the militia economy in Lebanon be captured in its specific dimensions? Before analyzing four of its major characteristics, I will first offer a quantitative, though necessarily cautious, overview of the scale and composition of the impact of the militias on Lebanon's economy. The need for caution is not hard to understand, given the poor quality of the available data. Indeed, estimates of the total economic impact of the war differ considerably, ranging from $150 million to $1.5 billion per year, depending on the period in question—whether one focuses on relatively peaceful years or on those in which major battles took place—and whether calculations take only direct military costs into account or include broader economic effects as well. Even zeroing in on direct militia expenditures, however, does little to improve one's confidence in available data. For example, Roger Dib, the Lebanese Forces' second in command, announced in 1989 that the cost of his militia's equipment and salaries amounted to $40 million per year.[18] The cost in arms, ammunition, and salaries of the "liberation war" waged by General 'Aoun from March to July 1989 is estimated to be $1 billion.

It is even more interesting to break down the military and civilian resources of the militias, which have been estimated to have amounted to approximately $2 billion per year.[19] Half of this sum was alleged to have come from nonmilitia sources, either from patron states or from individuals or institutions belonging to the same community. By opening "embassies" in countries to which Lebanese had emigrated (in western Europe, the Americas, West Africa), militias tapped into diaspora resources that had previously been channeled into Lebanon through personal and family networks. Because the militias were the producers of economic insecurity and criminality, only they were able to guarantee emigrants access to their assets, whether in the form of bank deposits or fixed assets such as land or real estate. As for the militias' patron states (virtually every state in the region funded one armed group or another), they spent some $700 million per year to secure the superiority of their various local allies. After the war, Israel disclosed that it had given $25 million per year in subsidies between 1976 and 1982 to the Lebanese Forces. In addition, the looting of regular armed forces, including international monitoring groups, was a primary source of weapons for all the militias. The United Nations Truce Supervision Organization (UNTSO) estimated that it lost nearly $500 million between 1975 and 1978 as a result of looting, including what was lost at the hands of Palestinians.[20] Similarly, the storage facilities of the Lebanese army were looted on many occasions: between March 1976 and February 1977, when the Lebanese Arab Army units withdrew from the Lebanese Army; in 1984, when three of six operational brigades seceded after having been incited to do so by 'Amal and the PSP; and finally in October of 1989, when there was a division between two legal armies, those of Generals 'Aoun and Lahoud.

When it comes to the economic functioning of the militias, it is more useful to identify their specific modalities rather than to assess their overall resources as distinct from the global economy that they literally cannibalized. Four specific modalities stand out. First is the capture by militias of state functions for private gain. Second is the collapse of the state's monopoly over the legitimate use of force and the privatization of public security functions. Third is the criminalization of the Lebanese economy as militias increasingly expanded their activities in the economic domain. And fourth is the role of the militias in financial speculation.

The militia economy rested above all on the capture and appropriation of state functions. While the state administration was ever less capable of collecting land and real estate taxes and trading dues, or of exacting payment for the provision of electricity and water, armed groups enjoyed two strategic advantages in undertaking such tasks: their power to intimidate and their control over territory. Even if the services offered by the militias were of inferior quality compared to those provided by the public offices and ministries, society's dependence on them was greater. This dependence even took on totalitarian overtones when the most ordinary activities, such as going to movies or restaurants, using public transportation, traveling to other countries or, more simply, passing through a roadblock, became grounds for the exercise of control and the exaction of payment.[21]

The dramatic proliferation of ports offers a telling example of this phenomenon. Indeed, the expansion of militia-controlled ports during the war did not simply reflect the central administration's decline as a regulator of trade but also signaled the privatization of the country's maritime relations. The fifteen piers or so that sprang up were not accessible to average citizens who wanted to engage in trade or travel. The use of these piers was, instead, contingent on membership in the community networks of the militias that each controlled specific port facilities. And, as in other economic domains, the interweaving of financial interests and political tactics led to paradoxical decisions in the management of these facilities. Between 1985 and 1987, for example, a few hundred Palestinian fighters were clandestinely brought into the country through the Jounieh port—then controlled by the Christian and anti-Palestinian Lebanese Forces—to return to West Beirut to participate in the war of the camps against the Shi'ite militia, 'Amal. While the political objective of the LF in helping their enemy was to weaken their rival, it also generated a financial profit that was far from trivial.

The erosion of legal control over the militias' economic activities unfolded in a series of steps. Militias exploited breakdowns in communication occasioned by the fighting to justify their increasing economic autonomy. They permitted what little remained of official functions to subsist for a time, but simultaneously compelled the ever less viable public administration to acknowledge and eventually legalize criminal practices that were linked to the provision of essential economic services. The import of crude oil for the Tripoli and Zahrani refineries and the import of oil derivatives for the Dora reservoir escaped state monopoly as early as 1976, when the Ministry of Energy began to tolerate the emergence of private importation. State bureaucrats tolerated, for instance, an overland import network with which the Syrian president's brother was associated, as well as a seaborne import network that operated via Greece and Bulgaria. Still, the state oil monopoly continued to grant import licenses. More important, the Caisse des Carburants (the Fund for Fuel), whose accounting books disappeared after a battle in 1977, subsidized oil products until 1986 even while militias were collecting taxes from consumers and illegally reexporting oil to neighboring countries.[22] To make up for the subsequent shortage of oil, the government accepted the de facto deregulation of petroleum trade, causing the number of importers to rise from five before the war to several dozen by the middle of the 1980s. Finally, during the last months of the war, the Conseil supérieur des douanes (the Higher Council of Customs) granted official status to the dozens of private oil terminals that had been established along the coast. Although this recognition allowed the government to tax fuel once again, it also legalized the transformation of a state monopoly into a nonstate oligopoly consisting of five or six holding companies of importers—a situation that has become consolidated since the end of the war.

The case of tobacco is both less complicated and more telling, since it was the state agency itself that negotiated the terms according to which its monopoly was to be dismantled. The Régie de tabac, Lebanon's state tobacco monopoly, which at one time imported two thirds of local consumption and oversaw the marketing of South Lebanon's tobacco crop, was no longer able to suppress massive smuggling despite pitched battles between the Forces de sécurité intérieure (FSI, the state police) and smugglers in 1977 and again in 1983. In September 1987, the government signed an agreement with the six leading militias (the Lebanese Forces, the Progressive Socialist Party, 'Amal, the Marada Brigade, the Popular Nasserist Organization from Sidon, and the South Lebanon Army), whereby it granted them the right to sell cigarettes in their respective territories. The agreement produced an 8 percent increase in the price of tobacco, which went to the militias who had committed themselves to confiscating "contraband" cigarettes in the areas they controlled.[23] Yet, as in the case of oil, it would be a mistake to assume that the coerced appropriation of public resources implied the formation of alternative public services. In the two most developed cases of a militia economy, the Jumblatt's PSP in the Chouf and the Lebanese Forces, revenues were more than ten times greater than investment and social expenditures.[24] Such predatory structures are far from the kind of state modernity discussed by Tilly, who assumes that redistribution and legitimacy are linked.

Second, the shift from the state's monopoly over the legitimate use of force to unbridled private violence gave rise to a demand for security that the militias avidly exploited. As the army and state police withdrew from the provision of security, urban populations very quickly established agreements with fighters—a practice in the tradition of the *khuwa*.[25] Contrary to common representations, the main source of danger to populations other than unpredictable events such as car bombs or air raids did not come from enemy territory—since frontiers had been drawn between the militias' respective areas of control by the fall of 1976. Instead, the danger came from within, from the routine exercise of intimidation and criminality by the very people who represented themselves as providers of security. In this environment, the private provision of public order was a booming business. Security and armored transport companies proliferated, as did firms manufacturing and selling electric and electronic material and martial arts clubs run by paramilitary men. Not incidentally, these kinds of activities also served as a safety valve against unemployment, mirroring the role of public enterprises in many countries throughout the Middle East. Some 20 percent of the salaried employees in the cement works of Chekka were "protector-guards," according to local terminology. At the Khaldeh airport in the southern suburb of Beirut, the number of people close to 'Amal who were holding security-related jobs was estimated to be around five hundred, and it has not decreased much in the ten years since the war ended. The privatization of public order did more than generate profitable businesses that would remain in place after the end of war. It also kept social groups from constructing their collective security through shared norms or through public and enforceable rules. Instead, it promoted aggressive self-defense and the proliferation of weapons.

The third type of economic activity that the militias performed is also the most interesting because it locates militia activities at the intersection of the political and military realms, on the one hand, and sheer criminality, on the other. Indeed, militias did not simply take advantage of their physical domination in order to extract resources. They also invoked the needs of the population in the areas they controlled, and used established businesses and criminal networks to carry out their activities. Thus, by hijacking goods transported by their own regular companies, they were able to require an insurance premium on these goods while selling them to consumers at higher prices on the black market. In another case, the installation of a telephone switchboard by a militia in Zahleh that bypassed the public network's paralyzed lines, or the installation of pipes that made it possible to "hijack" the equivalent of a twenty-ton fuel tanker per week for five years from the refinery in Tripoli.[26] Between such activities and straightforward criminal endeavors motivated purely by profit there was a fine line. This line was swiftly crossed with the unregulated traffic in toxic waste from Italy, which has been circulating within Lebanon since 1987 with complete disregard for the humanitarian consequences. The development of drug-related activities including the production, extraction, and commercialization of hashish and heroin illustrates the distortions of an economy that

fulfilled immediate financial needs by involving various social groups without, however, taking their long-term interests into account. The area used
for growing hashish doubled between 1976 and 1984, and did so again in
1988. Likewise, the area where poppy fields were cultivated increased from
60 to 3,000 hectares between 1984, when poppy cultivation was introduced
by Kurdish experts under the protection of the Syrian army, and 1988. As a
result, drugs gave rise to a sudden and ostentatious prosperity in the Hermel and the Beka'a and peasants abandoned the production of food crops
in these areas.[27] The severe reduction of poppy cultivation in these areas,
which was imposed by Syria starting in 1990 at the request of the U.S. Drug
Enforcement Agency, produced a long-term economic crisis. Whether
Christian or Muslim, many peasants from the hinterland chose to leave
rather than to revert to the unprofitable cultivation of cereals or face competition from Syrian imports of vegetables and fruits. Meanwhile, neither
the reconstructed Lebanese administration nor the international community was able to come up with a rescue plan.

As for drug production, transport, and commercial networks protected
by militia members, their net profit was immeasurable.[28] Drugs were, in
some respects, a direct response of militias to the extraordinary financial
demands of war making, yet their sale also provided for massive capital accumulation among militia leaders, riches whose full scale will never be fully
known. Perhaps most important, however, the interruption of poppy production around 1990 did not cause the death of the networks feeding upon
the external production zones and bank circuits of northern countries; far
from it. The dismantling of the militia organizations that gave rise to and
protected local drug networks was followed by their long-term integration
into international drug marketing circuits.

The fourth type of economic activity that constituted the militia economy was the militias' involvement in financial speculation. This activity actually grew out of the need to launder drug money through means other
than real estate operations, but was fueled by the increasing volatility of the
Lebanese pound. Until 1982, the impressive stability of the pound helped
the militias purchase all kinds of goods outside the country. Following the
decline of oil prices in 1984 and the depletion of the state's foreign exchange reserves from which the militias benefited, however, this tendency
was brutally reversed. The fiscal crisis was such that in 1985 the value of the
Lebanese pound dropped by 30 percent per month: $1 was worth 2 £L in
1975, 50 in 1985, 500 in 1987, 1,500 in 1990 and 2,000 in 1992. Many
Lebanese and others speculated on the currency's devaluation, but militia
leaders had a definite advantage at this game. They obtained fictitious bank
guarantees for their loans, insisted on using short-term deposits to obtain
long-term credits, and exerted pressure on the Société financière du Liban,
the official body responsible for allocating liquid assets among banks, to ap-

propriate available foreign exchange. Moreover, certain banking institutions were created solely for managing the finances of militias, including the Prosperity Bank of Lebanon, which was linked to the Lebanese Forces. The protection of profits was also facilitated by the presence of big Western banks in Lebanon.[29]

On the whole, the relation of the militias to the Lebanese state remained ambiguous. This ambiguity dismisses the oversimplifying thesis analyzing the militias' onslaught against the state as part of a large plot aimed at dismantling the Near Eastern states (Syria, Lebanon, and possibly Jordan) to the benefit of communitarian statelets. Such a plot, depicted as an Israeli scheme, as the ultimate goal of extremist Lebanese Christians, as well as the secret vow of the Syrian 'Alawite minority, could never be implemented during fifteen years of war, even if several militia groups, among them the Lebanese Forces and the Druze PSP, envisioned at some stage being able to do without the Lebanese state and to create their own set of institutions, including a central bank and foreign relations department.

What the dynamic of the militia economy shows, on the contrary, is the complexity of the relationship between the state and the militia entrepreneurs. The state, with its central administration, its national institutions, and its sovereignty, remained an asset and a stake. The militia took greater advantage from their complementarity to the state economy than in its destruction and replacement. Even while despised, weakened, and delegitimized by the militias which concurred in its destruction, it was still their common good, as witnessed during the "reconciliation meetings" of Geneva (November 1983) and Lausanne (March 1984), when the warlords summoned by their Syrian "patron" competed in "national loyalty." Finally, by denying each other the right to secede or to take hold of state power the militias acted collectively as the warrant of the perenniality of the state.

ALLOCATION AND LEGITIMACY

The militia economy's predilection for criminality worked hand in hand with the militias' role as redistributive agents. As the war went on, militias came to play a growing role as economic patrons. Indeed, by the second half of the 1980s, one-third of Lebanon's population received income from the militias.[30] A comparison of various estimates indicate that one-sixth of men old enough to carry a weapon actually joined the militias at one time or another, and another sixth joined the militias' administrative organizations. The monthly salaries paid to the militants ($65–350 in the LF, $75–150 in the Maradas in rural area, and $60 to the part-time volunteers of the PNO) were not particularly attractive compared to salaries in the public sector, especially after the rapid devaluation of the Lebanese pound after 1984.[31] This situation partially explains the petty criminality of low-

level militia members who were inclined to engage in criminal forms of resource extraction at the expense of the surrounding community.[32]

What we might add to these figures, however, is that the rest of the population was also becoming increasingly dependent on the militias for their
security and material well-being. Indeed, the militias became the main
providers not only of salaries but also of material goods, health care, and
education. And they were more interventionist in the performance of these
functions than had been the prewar "laissez faire" state. Quite apart from
the economic scale of their operations, moreover, it was the militias' hegemonic control of collective and individual strategies in the economic realm
that was important. Indeed, their economic centrality in the everyday lives
of Lebanese helps explain the sense of confusion and helplessness that the
Lebanese population experienced when faced with the organizational-in-
stitutional vacuum of the immediate postwar era. It also explains the intensity of the expectations they imposed on the new billionaire Prime Minister
Rafiq Hariri.

Among Lebanon's social groups, displaced populations were the most
dependent on the militias, leaving them vulnerable to various forms of exploitation. So while displaced persons were provided with welfare support
by militias, and were resettled in facilities the militias had either requisi-
tioned (in the case of the Lebanese Forces) or forcibly and illegally appropriated (in the case of 'Amal), they were also kept in precarious conditions
so that militias could appeal to charitable organizations for support and exploit the presence of these displaced populations to secure political and financial advantages in any future peace negotiations. When the reconstruction projects Solidere and Elyssar were launched, in 1991 and 1995
respectively, 'Amal and Hizballah were thus able to increase the number of
applicants eligible to receive government indemnities. As for the leaders of
the eastern region who succeeded the Lebanese Forces, an accumulation of
obstacles to the return of displaced Christians from the Chouf was at the
core of their grievances against the postwar republic. It was, in turn, among
the young generation of these displaced populations, cut off from their
roots and animated by a spirit of revenge, that militias recruited the core
group of their fighters. The reorganization of the Lebanese Forces after
1985 under Samir Geagea offers the most telling example of this recruitment pattern, since his shock troops were made up of fighters and new recruits driven out of their villages in the north, the Chouf, and the Iqlim-el-
Kharroub.

And yet, having acknowledged the extraordinary range of economic activities in which militias engaged and the extent to which they were effective
in fashioning militia organizations into mechanisms of predation, it must
nonetheless be said that the militias by and large failed in the tasks of institutionalizing and legitimating their economic and political roles. In spite of

their intention to formalize their economic status and undertake projects of social transformation that would alter Lebanon's balance of social power, their economic activities never provided a stable regulatory framework and continued to reflect the interests of individual militia members in self-enrichment—interests they persistently advanced through tactics that were entirely at odds with their concern for legitimacy or the formation of lasting institutional structures.

Examples abound of the gap between the militias' aspirations and the rather tawdry character of their activities. The enthusiasm manifested toward the end of the 1970s by some intellectuals in the Lebanese Forces for a collective agriculture inspired by the model of kibbutz was short-lived and was rapidly overtaken by a form of speculative agroindustry. In Hizballah, a Research and Documentation Center was founded in 1988 with a mandate to promote urban development projects for the poor southern suburbs. At the execution stage, however, private offices and unsupervised real estate projects prospered and became sources of individual profits even, and especially, for the most pious of the local shaykhs.[33]

The development of social and medical services in all the militia regions, on the other hand, took place in the context of a growing cost of living and competition between militias or armed groups within each community. Among the Maronites, this conflict was between the LF and President Gemayel in 1984–88, and then between the LF and General 'Aoun in 1988–89. Among the Shi'ites, the conflict was, starting in 1987, between 'Amal and Hizballah. The provision of social services operated, therefore, as an instrument in the hands of the militias to mitigate the disaffection of populations tired of destruction and high handed methods. Hizballah illustrates this situation best. It invested in social and medical services through local branches of foundations headquartered in Iran: the *Jihad el-Bina'* for housing, the Martyrs' Foundation, the Foundation for the Wounded and a similar institution created to support orphans. Such investment was politically profitable among the populations of the Baalbek region and those of the southern suburbs of Beirut. Generally speaking, the legitimizing function of social programs, and the attraction of foreign private humanitarian aid (estimated at $10 million per year) which their adoption brought about were more important to the militias than the social objective itself.[34]

THE TERRITORIAL ILLUSION

After an initial period of political paralysis, followed by the collapse of the Lebanese Army and the beginnings of territorial fragmentation, the territories controlled by militias underwent a three-stage process marked by the increasing consolidation of autonomous sectarian "statelets" in the period from 1976 to 1983. These phases were characterized by the coercive unification of populations within the same communal space; the forced homogenization of those populations, causing the displacement of several hundred thousand Christians and Shi'ite Moslems; and physical separation along sectarian lines. Through this process of territorialization of militia control, the militias sought to establish their legitimacy and authority as sovereign entities. Ultimately, this quest was no less illusory than their pursuit of social or economic legitimacy. Yet it provides further insight into how the militias hoped to parlay their military capacity into a longer-term political role in Lebanon.

In the economic realm, this process of territorialization had three consequences. First, it favored the emergence and development of alternative urban and commercial centers whose economic circumstances fluctuated depending on the economic climate of the moment;[35] some of these centers would later suffer from the postwar reemergence of Beirut as Lebanon's financial capital. Second, the construction of internal frontiers generated revenues in several ways: the levying of custom duties, the artificial creation of local scarcities leading to skyrocketing prices and windfall profits, and even the lengthening of transportation distances (Beirut-Zghorta via Hermel, Homs, and Tripoli), that increased transport fees. As the state retreated, the partitioning of Lebanon among militias reproduced the old Ottoman divisions of military and fiscal domains *(iqtâ')*, each with their borders and customs checkpoints; Bater or Monteverde for the PSP, the Awali north of Sidon for the PNO, the Qasmieh bridge for 'Amal, and Barbara for the LF. Each of these crossing points generated significant revenues for the militias that controlled them.

Beside extracting taxes, militias took advantage of price differentials and the creation of artificial monopolies. As early as the first year of the war the refineries of Zahrani and Tripoli (located in Shi'ite and Sunni zones, respectively) were destroyed by shells fired from the Christian zones. The minister of industry and petroleum, who had close links to the Kata'ib, deemed it technically impossible to bring the refineries back into use quickly. Almost overnight, coastal storage units in the Christian regions between Beirut and Jounieh (Dora, Nahr el-Mott, Dbaye) became the country's main supply centers for fuel, and they provisioned other regions on the basis of intermilitia agreements.[36] Moreover, the SLA threatened several times to shell the ports of Tyr and Sidon in order to replenish its coffers, and received an allowance for abstaining from such action, thus collecting "taxes" from its enemies, 'Amal and the PNO. Finally, territorial divisions fueled real estate speculation through the expulsion of populations (for example, the Palestinians and Shi'ites from the shanty town of the Quarantine and the Christians from the region north of and around Sidon), through the massive arrival of refugees in southern Lebanon or in the northern suburbs of Beirut, or even through the development of a new political center such as Bikfaya, President Amin Gemayel's "capital" from 1984 to 1988.[37]

The territorial illusion, or the militias' quest for some status comparable to sovereignty, rested on an ideological construction concerning the importance of territory that was very much at odds with the way the militias were organized and actually operated. First, while the militias attached symbolic and even military importance to what the Lebanese Forces called the "liberated" territory, and while they also marked these territories with all the iconography of sectarian struggle, especially Hizballah, the majority of the militias had lost contact with the areas from which their fighters largely originated: the high mountains in the north and the remote villages in the Beka'a or the south. Moreover, most militias took as their main military objective the conquest of Beirut, an economic and social space far too vast and complex to be dominated by a single militia. Similarly, a principal economic aim was to use their military apparatus to seize control of the service sector, though this, too, defied any neat spatial division.

In fact, the militias had no need for a territorial "homeland" to engage in war making, to assert their control over populations, or even to enrich themselves. All of them, including the openly anticapitalistic Hizballah, shared the desire to be part of the "Hong Kong of the Middle East," if not to control it.

Second, the obsession with territory expressed in the militias' discourse of communal unity was continuously undermined by internal rivalries and conflicts among militia leaders. Such conflicts were usually based on personal or regional issues rather than programmatic ones, and their stakes were in most cases economic. The 'Amal movement in South Lebanon, for example, started fragmenting after 1982. Each warlord controlled a village and aspired to monopolize the benefits of traffic between zones occupied by the Israelis, the Shi'ite southern suburbs of Beirut, and the two ports of the region, Tyr and the illegal port of Zahrani. At the leadership level, the rift between 'Amal and Hizballah was more the result of competing interests than the product of ideological or strategic disagreements,[38] although such factors were nevertheless significant since Hizballah's sponsor, Iran, funded several Shi'ite charitable foundations. In the Christian regions, this logic of economic competition produced territorial divisions and a series of fratricidal confrontations. Christians in the north, for example, set themselves apart from the majority of the community when they sided with the Syrians as early as 1978, following a succession of pitched battles for the control of the ports and the distribution of gasoline and cement. There was also a series of coups to remove Fuad Abou Nader (1985), Samir Geagea (1985), and Elias Hobeika (1986), from the leadership of the Lebanese Forces. The expulsion of Hobeika was the final stage of a fierce struggle for the control of the Sunduq al-Watani, the "national fund" that was in fact the private bank of the LF, and for the control of revenues generated by illegal ports. Following his overthrow, Hobeika retreated to Zahleh, where he and his "finance minister," Paul Aris, continued to ransom enterprises and traders from the eastern part of Beirut. At this stage, they were no longer pursuing a political or economic project but merely using force, albeit from a distance, to extract resources.

THE MILITIA SYSTEM

The territorial divisions and economic conflicts among the six, and later the seven, major militias (Maradas, LF, PSP, PNO, SLA, 'Amal, and, after 1982, Hizballah) did not undermine the presence of a national market within which the militias were forced to cooperate in order to maximize their revenues. Even while Lebanon was divided politically and militarily into communal territories, transcommunal and interregional networks were diffused throughout the country, creating a dense web of interconnections across militia lines. As a result, despite the militias' rhetorical commitment to economic autarky, the interdependence created by the persistence of a "national" economic space imposed a degree of collaboration on the warring forces. These connections are revealed through the timing, type, and duration of military operations in which the militias engaged.

Cooperation between militias started as early as the autumn of 1975, when the souks and port of Beirut were being sacked. At that time it took the form of various mechanisms of compensation and supervision between regions, mechanisms which depended, ultimately, on personal trust. Occasionally, this cooperation was also broadened and institutionalized, as in the case of natural gas, whose import was entrusted to a single dealer. The £L 2,000 or $3 paid by consumers for each gas container in 1988 included a £L 360 tax that was not collected by the Ministry of Finance but was, rather, distributed among the militias according to negotiated agreements.[39] Narcotics trade provided a second example of cooperation between militias, this time organized around multiple, cross-militia economic networks, which negotiated specific divisions of labor. For purposes of drug trafficking, 'Amal was associated with the PSP; Hizballah was associated with the 'Alawite militia of Tripoli and the LF, or with individual members of the Kata'ib party and even with officers of the Israeli Golani brigade in the occupied south. Each militia performed its share of the operation and took its share of the profits. Likewise, in the aborted project to construct the new Halate airport near Jbail in 1987, the LF received the support of Walid Jumblatt, then minister of public works as well as the LF's sworn enemy since their confrontation in the Chouf war. Together, the different militias created a profit network at the expense of their population, thereby rendering obsolete the state principles of res publica such as equity and rationality.

TOWARD A TYPOLOGY OF MILITIA ECONOMIES

The interwoven character of the militia economy system that crisscrossed the Lebanese "territories" and produced organized networks of militias did not, however, diminish organizational differences among the militias. Besides their conflicting ideologies and political projects, the militias also differed in the methods they used for carrying out the various tasks involved in building the economy in the zones under their control: acquiring resources, particularly external resources, exploiting the state apparatus as an economic tool and source of wealth, accumulating capital, cooperating with entrepreneurs and, finally, formulating explicitly or implicitly an ethos that would complete their political doctrine in the economic sphere. In order to analyze and understand the diversity of the militias' economy-building strategies while taking into consideration the main two phases of their evolution (1975–82 and 1983–90), we can identify four ideal types corresponding to the four main militias dominating the Lebanese arena.

The Lebanese Forces: Between Business and Corporatism

From September 1976 until 1983 the economy of the Christian regions under the control of the Lebanese Forces (East Beirut, the North Metn, and Kisrwan) was characterized by the persistence of prewar economic structures and types of activity, and enjoyed a certain prosperity. Except for confrontations with the Syrian army in July and October 1978, the Lebanese Forces sustained a measure of order. The Christian zone enjoyed relative security and benefited from the relocation of a number of enterprises and from the arrival of Christians fleeing West Beirut.

The various military groups constituting the Lebanese Forces profited from land speculation. They also benefited from the wartime enrichment of various types of entrepreneurs such as carriers, importers, and middlemen, by levying protection taxes on economic activities and smuggled imports.[40] Foreign support, which was for the most part military and to a lesser extent humanitarian, remained marginal.[41] The transfer of activities abroad in Cyprus or Europe, on the other hand, as well as subsidies from the Christian Lebanese diaspora, helped to maintain a reasonable standard of living. The LF's main resources came from the levying of external customs and taxes ($60 million per year), from the organization of transport and internal customs ($15 million), and from the activities of the fifth dock in Beirut's port ($15–25 million). Together, these resources provided some $300 million annually.[42]

In the 1980s, several factors, including the impoverishment of wage earners following the collapse of the Lebanese Pound, the arrival of more than one hundred thousand displaced persons in the Christian zone, and the intensification of the struggle for power, led the LF's military leadership to tighten its control over the economy by multiplying parastatal institutions, increasing taxes, and establishing relief and social services, especially for the "displaced" population. The economic apparatus which the LF established under the name of Sunduq al-Watani was by far the most developed and up-to-date financial organization created by a militia. No civil activity, whether lawful or unlawful, could escape the control of the LF, which proved far more efficient than the state had been in collecting taxes. The scope of their takeover of the economy in the Christian regions is evidenced by the long list of enterprises belonging to the holding company they founded in 1989, and which encompassed virtually all fields of activity.[43] The militia was thus showing signs of a move toward authoritarian corporatism.

The last period of the war, starting in 1988, was characterized by a sharp shift in the balance of power between armed forces and businessmen. Taking advantage of the militia's lack of legal standing, economic actors emancipated themselves from military and territorial logics. Businessmen did this in part by exploiting intercommunal networks and playing on internal rivalries within the Christian regions.[44] They also undertook to reprivatize and civilianize properties that the militia had registered in its name.[45] While it was powerful, when it was holding a besieged population under its control, the Lebanese Forces had created exceptional and favorable conditions for accumulation that would allow enterprises and individuals to outlive the militia after the war. But its domination of economic activity nonetheless eroded as the war came to a close.

The Druze PSP: The Autonomous Principality

During the first phase of the war, the Druze regions of the Chouf, Aley, and the upper Metn, as well as the mixed bordering regions such as Iqlim el-Kharroub, were controlled by the PSP, Walid Jumblatt's Druze militia. The PSP was at the time one of the many militias that made up the National Movement. While the militia claimed to abide by the law, it was making the most of its militant position, smuggling gas at Jiyeh, obtaining supplies of ammunition from the PLO and Syria, and receiving financial aid from Libya.

A radical change occurred in 1983. After the Israeli withdrawal and the defeat of the LF in the Chouf, the PSP discarded the trappings of legality—notwithstanding Walid Jumblatt's participation in the national conferences of Geneva and Lausanne and his continuous presence as a cabinet minister

in Lebanese governments. The militia established the "Mountain administration," the PSP's public service operation, which gave Jumblatt and a few
of his close associates control over the region's main economic activities:
ports, cement works, a power station, and the maintenance of public infrastructure. The economic logic of the PSP was thus clearly more predatory
than productive. Its main resources came from taxes levied at the domestic
customs houses of Jiyeh, Bater, and Monteverde. Civil servants, while still
on the payroll of the state, fell under the authority of the PSP. The militia
was thus simultaneously complementing and substituting for the state, with
the result that the region emerged from the war as the best controlled and
the best kept in the country. With a civil budget of approximately $200 mil-
lion, the Mountain administration was a privileged instrument of communal control.[46]

In some respects, the Mountain administration exhibited an apparent
historic continuity with the Druze principality of the seventeenth century.
Indeed, Jumblatt controlled relations between the Druze community and
other Lebanese communities and shared with the leaders of 'Amal the monopoly on hydrocarbon products importation and distribution in the south
through the oil company COGECO. On a personal level, Walid Jumblatt
symbolized the symbiosis of the charismatic leader, the warlord, and the
businessman exercising personal control over a clientalist form of redistribution. After the war he retained his role, despite the resumption in Druze
areas of a state of legality, and his mediation remained decisive in every economic and political decision concerning the Chouf. As minister of displaced
populations in Rafiq Hariri's government (1992–98), he handled a budget
of several hundred million dollars, more than two-thirds of which came
from foreign aid. This position greatly facilitated his control over the Druze.

'Amal, the State, and Diaspora Networks

The budget of 'Amal, the largest Shi'ite militia, was less than the PSP's and
only half that of the LF, even though the territories and population under
its control were much greater (in 1984 'Amal's leader claimed to have one
million Shi'ite followers).[47] 'Amal was, moreover, a loose organization built
upon a variety of local self-defense groups controlling small territories such
as villages or individual streets in the southern suburbs of Beirut as well as
in southern Lebanon. Yet, the weakness of 'Amal's chain of command and
military organization does not in and of itself account for the type of economy that was developed in the areas it controlled. Two other factors must
be considered. The first is that since the 1950s and thus long before the
war, the Shi'ite population of Lebanon had been deeply concerned about
securing its position in the state bureaucracy and economy. This reinforced
the militia's capacity to infiltrate the bureaucracy and public services, and

to appropriate the revenues from the Zahrani refinery or the customs of Khaldeh airport. Its political power enabled the militia to keep the revenues it derived from the state and even to increase them, in spite of its open insubordination—Shi'ite soldiers of the Sixth Brigade, for example, continued to be paid by the government even after they rebelled in 1984. Linking the government and the militia, Nabih Berry, minister of the southern region after 1980, and Mohammed Beydoun, president of the Council for the South, ordered public (and even private) infrastructure works in the regions dominated by 'Amal, at the expense of the state. They also supervised the distribution of public funds to displaced Shi'ites and to victims of Israeli attacks. Beside facilitating the misappropriation of public funds, its links to the state enabled 'Amal to place a large number of its followers in the regular armed forces and, following the demobilization of April-June 1991, in the civil service.[48]

The second critical factor is that 'Amal collaborated with networks of diaspora Shi'ite investors eager to bring prosperity to their villages of origin in southern Lebanon, and just as eager to shield themselves from political tensions in their countries of emigration, particularly in West Africa. Responding to such concerns, 'Amal took over the role formerly performed by the traditional Shi'ite bourgeoisie of Beirut, such as the Beydouns and the 'Awdis, of capturing diaspora investment flows. These included real estate investments at Ras Beirut and Rue Verdun as well the industrial investments of the newly recommunalized bourgeoisie that was collaborating with Iraqi Shi'ite or Syrian entrepreneurs such as Ahmad Shalabi, who controlled Petra Bank in Amman, and Sa'ib Nahhas, a Syrian representative of Peugeot and Volvo and the owner of a luxury hotel chain. The most visible representative of these "African Shi'ite" associates of 'Amal was the Sierra Leone billionaire Jamil Sa'id, a rice and diamond wholesaler who mined sand off the beaches of Tyr and sold gasoline smuggled from Zahrani throughout all of southern Lebanon.[49]

After the war, however, the economic power of 'Amal eroded as a result of three factors. First, senior party officers neglected the movement as they became more interested in their positions within the state: Berry became speaker of the Lebanese parliament; Beydoun was made minister, and so on. Second, new, private Shi'ite banks took over from 'Amal the ability to capture the capital flows originating within the Shi'ite diaspora. Last, and perhaps most significant, Hizballah supplanted 'Amal within the main Shi'ite stronghold, namely, the southern suburbs of Beirut.

Hizballah and the Islamic Welfare State

Besides its leading role in the resistance effort against Israeli occupation in the south, and the clever adaptation of its religious doctrine to popular culture in the regions under its control, Hizballah owed the rapid growth of its legitimacy within Shi'ite areas to the expansion of its charitable, medical, and educational activities. Unlike 'Amal, whose strategy rested on its relationship to the state, Hizballah undertook to distance itself from the state as a way to enhance both its organizational autonomy and its popular legitimacy as an independent alternative to 'Amal. To solidify its popular appeal, Hizballah established local branches of numerous Iranian foundations created during the Iran-Iraq War to provide aid to various groups of the injured (orphans and the wounded) and for reconstruction, or for the support of social services such as the Imam al-'Uzma hospital and many professional schools founded after 1987 in deprived areas such as the Beka'a and Beirut's southern suburbs. Known for relative integrity of its leaders, and for paying its fighters salaries that were three times higher than those of other militias, Hizballah had little difficulty establishing its hegemony in a region where the state had been totally absent since 1983.

With what resources did Hizballah operate? Various Iranian subsidies, even if they diminished in the postrevolution period following Khomeini's death, constituted a decisive factor of Hizballah's influence. One should not underestimate either the party's participation in the development of poppy farming in the Hermel and Baalbek, or in the preparation and the marketing of drugs in a region where Hizballah became the dominant force, with the full knowledge and agreement of the Syrian army. In addition, the party was locked in a sharp struggle with Shaykh Fadhlallah and his important Mabarrât Foundation, as well as with the Shi'ite Higher Council, directed by Shaykh Chams ed-Din, to collect and secure control over the money produced as a result of *zakât* and *khoms*—the alms that hundreds of thousands of Shi'ite believers are obligated to give. The diaspora, in particular, was the target of rival appeals from missionaries dispatched from Beirut by these three competing religious authorities.

Born in adversity and preoccupied with armed struggle, Hizballah had to deal with an economy of destitution and assistance during the war. Yet the party demonstrated a remarkable ability to adapt to the challenges of the post-Ta'if period. To begin with, Hizballah was perceived as outdoing the government in various operations of popular assistance in Shi'ite areas. These included a dangerous mountain rescue during a snowstorm in the spring of 1992, rapid reconstruction following the shellings that accompanied Israel's July 1993 operation, and the distribution of water to the entire southern suburbs of Beirut. With twelve members elected in the 1992 parliamentary elections, the party asserted itself as Rafiq Hariri's unavoidable interlocutor in the development and execution of the Elyssar project in 1995, whose goal was to rehabilitate the southern suburbs. Although Hizballah continued to hesitate between the tempting strategy of deepening its autonomous control over the areas it dominated, on the one hand, and a strategy of collaboration that could bring it recognition at the highest level, on the other, many of Hizballah's leaders chose the latter approach. In this instance too, however, collaboration often took an economic form that secured significant benefits for the participants. Hizballah leaders established engineering design and private construction firms, for example, some of which became involved in shady real estate deals in a suburb of Beirut that was expected to become an area of urban renewal and tourism. The party of God demonstrated, if proof was at all necessary, that in Lebanon the conversion of a fundamentalist militia member into an ultraliberal businessman was not merely a hypothetical possibility.[50]

ENTERING THE POSTWAR ECONOMY

This typology, though perhaps overly rigid in the distinctions it draws between modes of militia operations, can nonetheless serve as a starting point for identifying the trajectories of actors irrespective of their communal differences, and for disentangling the shifting patterns of economic activities that rose and fell under both the pressure and the protection of various militias. In short, it can help to understand the functioning of a system restructured by a culture of war in an ultraliberal economic environment.

In the years following the war, continuity was secured by the presence on the economic scene of firms that had been launched through the illegal accumulation of capital. Far from being marginalized when their militia partners were disarmed or even, in some cases, ostracized, wartime entrepreneurs had no difficulty finding new protectors among senior Syrian officers stationed in Lebanon. Nor was it difficult for them to share in the joint public-private consortium headed by Rafiq Hariri. Even those who voiced their hostility toward the Second Republic and the pervasive presence of armed Syrian forces in Lebanon took part in the speculative transactions that accompanied "reconstruction" by purchasing Solidere shares and Lebanese Eurobonds. Despite the amnesty law's provisions regarding economic and financial offenses committed during the war, no action was taken against the perpetrators because the needs of "reconstruction" were great and diaspora resources, together with international aid, were far from sufficient to meet them. While the Lebanese political system was restored with few modifications and the Second Republic inherited many of the flaws of the First, the war forced open financial and economic domains to new actors and new practices.[51] The relationship between political and economic arenas also underwent a significant shift. Before the war, that relationship was patrimonial and characterized by political patrons presiding over economic redistribution. After the war, the practices of the militias enabled the financiers and the big businessmen to establish themselves as protectors and sponsors of a weak state and a declining public sector.

What was the place of militia members themselves in the postwar Lebanese scene? They had to convert their military power into economic power by taking advantage of the demobilization and amnesty laws. The compromise solution reached in Ta'if allowed them to make a transition toward full participation in the political system. Having become ministers, parliamentarians, and top-ranked civil servants, they established their influence over economic matters in general and over the vast project of national reconstruction in particular. Their control over public and private foreign aid gave them exceptional leverage to broaden their clientele and thus to renew their legitimacy. Existing specialized agencies like the Reconstruction and Development Council, the Fund of the Displaced, and the Council of the South provided new sources of redistribution and patronage for former militia leaders.

The most tangible effect of the militias' economic practices is precisely to have reduced the notion of public good and to have crippled the legal and financial instruments of a state whose autonomy had already been curtailed by ultraliberalism. After the war, one-third of the population lived below the poverty line as a direct consequence of wartime destruction of Lebanon's infrastructure and the ongoing currency crisis.[52] In spite of this, the government refused to tax financial profits, terminated the remaining subsidies on essential commodities (such as flour) in July of 1995, and gave up the state's monopoly in strategic sectors, such as communications and the importation of petroleum products. Since the government did not consider itself accountable to citizens and lacked political independence, it was nothing more than the representative of financial interests and militias who now had an opportunity to pursue their military objectives by other economic means. This is how Prime Minister Rafiq Hariri, who participated in the war by financing successively or simultaneously each of the protagonists, became the symbolic figure of the postwar private entrepreneur who took over from the militia leaders and contributed to the marginalization of the state while financing huge reconstruction works, including a national telephone grid, road network, electric power grid, and the rebuilding of Beirut's city center, in which he was the most important investor.

To conclude, while the civil conflict in Lebanon did not generate a war economy in the classical sense of the word, it did facilitate the birth and development of certain specific characteristics that have not disappeared with the return of peace—far from it. The new role played by the former militia leaders and the importance of militia resources (such as physical violence and illegal fortunes) in the postwar political and economic reconstruction showed that the civil war was not a parenthesis but contributed to the shaping of lasting new social activities and identities.

Moreover, the endurance of militia activities after the war found legitimacy and support in the globalization process and the existence of a "bifurcated" world, to quote James Rosenau. First, a variety of nonstate actors operating along transnational networks dominated the reconstruction economy. According to a postmodern logic, many of their activities and hierarchies remained out of state control and regulation policies.

Second, the Lebanese administration had to take into account the segmentation of the national territory by the militia powers during the war. While the decentralization provided by the Ta'if Accord intended to take this reality into account and contribute to restoring local security and confidence in public services, it could hardly prevent the deepening of communal specificities and regional inequalities.

Finally, beyond the dramatic years of 1975–90, the Lebanese civil war has thus to be considered in light of the modern history of the Near East. For many of the logics at work during the war both revealed and exacerbated the weaknesses of the Lebanese state.

NOTES

1. However, the condition of stateness, i.e., the power to supplant, destroy, replace, and conquer, is implicitly present in civil war. See Tilly, "War Making and State Making as Organized Crime," pp. 169–91.

2. Debates over the economic aspects of the war, its cost and revenues, have been prominent throughout the Middle East. Whether the issue is the mobilization of recruits, of material resources, or the search for financial support, these debates entail a necessary domestic dimension. See Barnett, *Confronting the Costs of War: Military Power, State, and Society in Egypt and Israel.*

3. On the dynamics of this concentration process and the statist model underlying it, see the chapter "La loi du monopole," in Elias, *La dynamique de l'Occident,* pp. 61–82.

4. See Starr, "Lebanon's Economy: The Cost of Protracted Violence," p. 72. The Lebanese GDP was $8 billion in 1974.

5. See Guttentag and Herring, "Disaster Myopia in International Banking." Cited by Gayle Baker in "The Role of Political Events and Political Expectations in Exchange Rate Movements: The Case of Lebanon" (Ph.D. diss., University of Pennsylvania, 1993).

6. The dollar was worth around 2 Lebanese pounds in 1975, 50 in 1983, and 2,000 in 1990. See Dagher, *La crise de la monnaie Libanaise, 1983–1989.*

7. The PLO's budget in the Middle East was generally estimated to be around $1 billion per year.

8. This does not take into account those who were displaced, potentially unemployed, and a burden on their communities—especially Christians from West Beirut and the Chouf and Shi'ites from the northern suburbs and South Lebanon.

9. In October 1989, summoned to a conclave in Ta'if and generously subsidized, fifty-eight of the seventy surviving Lebanese deputies approved the Docu-

ment of Reconciliation, which contains various amendments to the constitution. See Maila, "The Document of National Reconciliation: A Commentary."

10. Hottinger, "Zu'Ama' and Parties," pp. 85–105. Lebanon is one of the countries where the cost of a vote in an electoral campaign is high.

11. In the middle of the 1980s, members of Hizballah received $300 per month, compared to $100–150 in other militias, including the South Lebanon Army.

12. See *L'Express,* 30 April-7 May 1987; *Libération,* 6 June 1992; *L'Événement du Jeudi,* 11–17 March 1993.

13. Personal interviews, Beirut, April 1995.

14. Sadowski, "Cadres, Guns, and Money: The Eighth Regional Congress of the Syrian Ba'th," p. 6.

15. See Corm, "The War System: Militia Hegemony and Reestablishment of the State," pp. 215–30. See also the series of reports in *Al-Hayat,* 31 January-8 February 1990.

16. See Bourgey, "Beyrouth, ville éclatée," pp. 5–32.

17. See Moore, "Le système bancaire libanais: les substituts financiers d'un ordre politique," p. 30–47.

18. See Roger Dib, interview in *Le commerce du Levant* (June 26, 1991).

19. See Corm, "Hegemonie milicienne et le problème du rétablissement de l'Etat," 13–25.

20. See Le Peillet, *Les bérets bleus de l'ONU à travers 40 ans de conflit israélo-arabe.*

21. See "Liban: l'Argent des Milices," 271–87.

22. Personal interviews, Beirut, April-May 1995. The oil bill represented roughly 10 percent of nonmilitary imports during the war. Even after oil was no longer subsidized, the price of gas was still lower than in neighboring countries, including Syria and even the Gulf states.

23. See *Le commerce du Levant* (5 October 1987).

24. See Harik, *The Public Services of the Militias.* See also *Al-Kitab al-aswad* [The black book] published by the Army monthly *Al-Jaysh* (June 1990): 8–13. This document, supposedly seized by General 'Aoun's army when it took over the headquarters of Samir Geagea in January of 1990, provides details of the alleged budget of the Lebanese Forces.

25. The protection tax that armed nomads exacted from city dwellers in the Middle Ages.

26. The 26 June 1991 article from *Al-Safir,* which discusses this story, specifies that the pipes vent "on the Beddawi side," which is the stronghold of the 'Alawi militia of Ali'Id.

27. For a description of this reconversion, see Makhlouf, *Culture et commerce de drogue au Liban.* See also, "Face à la mafia de la drogue," *Le commerce du Levant* 5703 (20 May 1993): 63, 74–76; U.S. Department of State, *International Narcotics Control Strategy Report,* 1990 (Washington, D.C.: U.S. Government Printing Office, 1990), quoted by *Le commerce du Levant* (April 18, 1988): 47. Salim Nasr gives some numbers, without citing sources, in "Lebanon's War: Is the End in Sight?" *MERIP* 162 (January-February 1990): 8; the same numbers appear in *L'Express,* 30 April-7 May 1987, which cites the U.S. Drug Enforcement Administration.

28. According to Corm, "Hegemonie milicienne et le problème du rétablisse-

ment de l'Etat," the figure is $700 million per year. *Le commerce du Levant* (July 11, 1988): 10, gives a figure of $1 billion.

29. Simone Ghazzi, "Les entrepreneurs et l'Etat dans la crise libanaise: interaction du politique et de l'économique" (Ph.D. diss., Institut d'Etudes Politiques, 1992).

30. Corm, "Hegemonie milicienne et le problème du rétablissement de l'Etat."

31. Nasr, "Lebanon's War: Is the End in Sight?"; Kari Karamé, "Miliciens farouches et fils pleins d'égard: la question de la réinsertion des miliciens libanais" (manuscript, 1994); Picard, *Demobilization of the Militias: A Lebanese Dilemma; Al-Hayat*, 31 January-8 February 1990.

32. Another explanation invokes the criminality of the leadership of the military structure, which made it difficult to impose legal behaviors on lower level militia members and led to the toleration of daily lootings by fighters in the spirit of both "redistributing" war returns and involving the militants in the spoil system.

33. Harik, *The Public Services of the Militias;* Harb el-Kak, *Politiques urbaines dans la banlieue-sud de Beyrouth;* al-Khazin and Salem, eds., *Al-Intikhabat al-ula fi Lubnan ma ba'd al-harb* [The first Lebanese elections after the war].

34. Kasparian, Beaudouin, and Abou, *La population déplacée par la guerre au Liban.* The Foundation for Social Solidarity, for example, does not represent more than 15 percent of the budget of the LF.

35. Longuenesse, "Guerre et décentralisation urbaine au Liban: le cas de Zghorta," pp. 345–61; Harris, "The View from Zahleh," pp. 270–86.

36. In 1984, one of the private importers operating since the first years of the war wanted to discharge a tanker at the Dbaye port without paying the militia tax. His residence was attacked.

37. The Quarantine occupied land at the northern entrance of Beirut belonging to the order of Maronite monks. Luc de Bar estimates that in the early 1970s the real estate of the Maronite church represented 15 percent of Lebanese territory (40 percent in the Kisrwan). See de Bar, *Les communautés confessionnelles au Liban.*

38. 'Amal exhibited a more accommodationist and pragmatic Shi'ism, compared to the militant Shi'ism of Hizballah. In terms of strategic differences, 'Amal was closer to Syria and Hizballah to Iran.

39. At the time, £L 100 each for the LF, the PSP and Amal, and £L 60 for the Sunni *zaqât*.

40. These taxes amounted to approximately $100 per month per company, according to Fouad Abou Saleh, president of the Chamber of Industry. Personal interview, Beirut, May 1995.

41. Military equipment received as aid was supplied by Jordan with the consent of Syria, by Israel starting in 1976, and by some NATO countries.

42. *Al-Hayat*, 2 February 1990, and 13 March 1989; Corm, "Hégémonie milicienne."

43. *Al-Kitab al-aswad.*

44. The most striking example is also the most complicated. The banker Roger Tamraz took advantage of his connections to President Amine Gemayel to get hold of 51 percent of the revenues from the Casino du Liban through the Intra Bank. From 1987 onward, the greatest part of gambling revenues were collected by the LF

and no longer by the state. The militia therefore became his principal partner. In 1988, Tamraz broke with the LF and bet on Danny Chamoun in the upcoming presidential elections. He then had to take refuge in the Druze Chouf, and eventually departed for the United States, leaving the Casino with a deficit of $4 million. See "Le casino malade de la guerre," *Le commerce du Levant* (August 7, 1989): 14.

45. The most successful example is the Lebanese Broadcasting Corporation, the first Lebanese private television station. Its postwar president, Pierre Daher, succeeded after a legal dispute in separating it from its founders and rival sponsors, the Kata'ib party and the LF. He made it the country's first television channel by adopting a position of moderate opposition to the Second Republic. Personal interview, Beirut, May 1995.

46. *Al-Hayat,* 3–4 February 1990.

47. US$150 million per year according to *Al-Hayat,* February 2, 1990.

48. Around four thousand former militia members. See Picard, *Demobilization.*

49. Personal interviews, Beirut, April-May 1995.

50. Harb al-Kak, *Politiques urbaines dans la banlieue-sud de Beyrouth.*

51. Picard, "Les habits neufs," 49–70.

52. From the report "Poverty in Lebanon," prepared for the UN-ESCWA in March 1995 by Antoine Haddad; personal interview, April 1995.

PART THREE

Conclusion

11

The Cumulative Impact
of Middle Eastern Wars

Roger Owen

Wars of one kind or another have been a regular feature of twentieth-century Middle Eastern life. They have included not only the century's two world wars but also the briefer periods of intense fighting among Israel, the Palestinians, and their Arab neighbors; a variety of civil wars with outside participation like those in Yemen, Sudan, Oman and Lebanon; and the long, drawn-out war between Iraq and Iran during the 1980s. All this was enough, as these chapters amply demonstrate, to create a situation in which not just the wars themselves but also the cumulative effects of the memory of past wars and the ever present threat of new ones became important factors in their own right, influencing policy and the distribution of national resources in ways that had profound effects on political institutions, economic and social arrangements, and the general exercise of power.

Whether this central impact of repeated wars can be taken either as a defining feature of Middle Eastern political life or as something that distinguishes the Middle East from the other regions of the non-European world remains to be explored. But certainly the chapters in this book make a good case for the argument that this impact was sufficiently important to be treated as a basic part of any serious account of modern Middle Eastern history, just as it is in modern European history. The question then becomes: how should this be done? And how can such a process of factoring in be accomplished so as to make use of insights developed in the European context without being dominated by them?

The organizers of this project, Professors Steven Heydemann and Joel Migdal, set limits on what might otherwise have been an open-ended inquiry by asking contributors to concentrate on the impact of war on Middle Eastern institutions and social change. This was a good idea in principal but, like most such exercises in boundary setting, it created a number of problems of its own. For one thing, it confined the discussion within the compass of state making and national development while allowing less attention to significant aspects of the larger subject such as the regional context or the cumulative impact of repeated conflict. The discussion raised, but could not provide a definitive answer to, the question of whether when we focus on war per se we are dealing with a single, unified object of analysis.

The general approach yields best results when focused on the local impact of the twentieth century's two world wars. Fought largely by outside powers—with the exception of the Ottomans in the first—these wars subordinated local polities and economies to the dictates of forces largely beyond local Middle Eastern control. In the Middle East, the world wars lasted more or less the same length of time as in Europe itself: that is, four to six years for World War I, depending on the region in question, and nearly six years for World War II. They involved many of the same techniques of mobilization and demobilization, although with certain local adjustments. And they followed somewhat the same trajectory, from a slow start as far as their impact on the noncombatants was concerned, through increasing hardship and privation to a short postwar period marked by inflation fueled by pent-up consumer spending, as well as by boundary changes, enforced movements of population, and the emergence of often radically new political forces. All this allows useful comparisons to be made between the Middle Eastern and European experience, with students of the former being able to draw on, and benefit from, some of the vast literature generated apropos of the latter.

One useful by-product of this same perspective is that it calls into question the usual systems of periodization imposed on Middle Eastern history, which, by using the world wars themselves as dividing lines, tends to ignore or to minimize their impact. Many of these systems make a break in 1914 before beginning again in 1918 or, in the case of Anatolia, 1923. Studies of Arab history often seem to jump from 1939 to the creation of the Arab League in 1944–45, as though, for example, the Wafdist government in Egypt simply acted as Britain's loyal wartime agent from 1942 to 1944, or, more generally, as though political life simply closed down for the duration. And yet wars have their own powerful dynamic that often has little to do with what caused them in the first place while creating powerful new forces that continue to affect individual national polities and economies for many years after.

To begin with World War I, fighting itself took place over many parts of the Fertile Crescent during the four years of the war itself and then continued, on and off, in the form of armed resistance to foreign intrusion both in the former Arab provinces and in Anatolia and parts of Iran for several years more. This in turn involved large parts of the civilian population, many of whom were subject to various forms of mobilization—either of their husbands and sons or of their labor, crops, and animals—and most of whom suffered from one form of deprivation or another, including, in the case of the Anatolian Armenians, Assyrians, and later, Greeks, forced removal accompanied by massacre and disease. And while World War II involved less actual fighting inside the region itself, it affected just as many, perhaps more, members of the local populations, given the fact that attempts to allocate scarce resources and mobilize new ones was carried out by administrations that had developed since 1918 a much greater capacity for intervention.

These are large subjects that cannot possibly be given their full due in a work this size. Nevertheless, the three chapters devoted to them here (by Tell, Thompson, and Heydemann and Vitalis) are full of significant and, in many cases, novel suggestions about how the subject of the impact of the two world wars on the Middle East can most usefully be treated. I will highlight four: the choice of period, the contrasts drawn between the experience of the two world wars in the Middle East and between the Middle East and Europe, the particular importance of methods of wartime mobilization, and finally, the way in which the wars themselves gave rise to particular modes of action, as well as developed new resources that played a significant role once the wars had come to an end.

The choice of period is a simple but often neglected matter. Clearly, any discussion of the impact of wars has to be placed in its proper historical context. This usually means beginning the analysis some years before the event itself and then going on for some years after. Only then is it possible to sort what was truly new about wartime experience from those processes that were already in place and which simply received encouragement from a war in such a way as to accelerate their further development. Tell does this particularly well in his study of the impact of World War I on the power and positioning of the various elements of what was to become Transjordanian society.

As to the question of useful comparison, Thompson and Heydemann and Vitalis make use of the differences in the intensity between wartime mobilization in the two world wars, as well as address the significant question of why the British and French used methods for managing the Middle Eastern economies that were different from those they employed at home. This at once provided space for the entry of Middle Eastern society, which these three authors see as having been not only an object to be managed and, if possible, kept docile while the war was at its most dangerous but also as an actor in its own right, one that made use of prewar patterns of mobilization, resistance, and dissent to press its own demands upon the Allied administrators. The consequent relationship was, as Heydemann and Vitalis nicely demonstrate, one of trial and error in which, once the main priorities were established, the means to achieve them were left very much to circumstance and to what did or did not prove effective. The use of gold sales to mop up surplus purchasing power in the interest of controlling inflation was one very good example of this. Against this, efforts to introduce an effective income tax were much less successful, as was the use of anything but the most selective form of food rationing. In addition, Thompson has analyzed particularly well the different contexts in which Syria's wartime regulation took place: first that of the Vichy French, then that of the British and Free French, and finally that of the local nationalists.

Central to successful wartime management was the control of both local resources and those transported in from outside. Here, in World War I, the British and French benefited greatly from their control over the sea-lanes that connected the region with the outside world, as well as from their ability to blockade the coastal ports in the Mediterranean and the Red Sea, thus reducing Ottoman access to the cereals and other foodstuffs it needed to maintain the loyalties of the local Arab populations. In Tell's account, this becomes a powerful factor in explaining why some tribes joined the Anglo-Hashemite revolt against the Turks and some did not. Much the same situation obtained during World War II, with the British and the French, now joined by the Americans, engaged in a largely successful battle to ensure that food shortages, as well as falling real wages, did not turn the Arab peoples against them in such a way as to hamper the general war effort.

Lastly, both world wars served as incubators for ideas, practices, and new forms of legitimation that proved important at war's end. When it comes to the impact of ideas, previous historians have generally contented themselves with questions associated with the weakening of British and French imperial power, combined with the fillip that such wartime declarations as Wilson's Fourteen Points, the Balfour Declaration, and the North Atlantic Charter provided to various Middle Eastern nationalisms. But, as Tell ably demonstrates, local factors such as the legitimation derived from the successful wartime leadership of someone like the Amir Faisal are also an important part of the equation. Thompson makes a different point with her argument about the way the French ingratiated themselves with parts of the Syrian population, as well as the international community represented by the League of Nations, by being so obviously involved in the postwar relief effort after 1918. The continuing impact of some of the policies and practices initiated by the Anglo-American Middle East Supply Centre is somewhat better known. Nevertheless, Heydemann and Vitalis take the general argument many steps further by demonstrating the Supply Centre's precise links with both increasing state interventionism in Egypt and Syria and the consolidation of a state-sponsored import-substituting industrialization regime.

All this is nicely suggestive of many new avenues for further research. As far as World War I is concerned, there are still many important links to be made between the suffering endured by the civilian populations and their reactions to the choices they faced in the highly charged months just after its end. Are the wartime deprivations endured by the Egyptian peasants, with their crops forcibly purchased and their menfolk and cattle forcibly conscripted, enough to explain the nationwide outburst in response to the travel ban imposed on the members of the Wafd trying to make their way to the Paris Peace Conference? Or did this also call up a mode of thought and of political action that had been in the making for some years before 1914? By the same token, what role did the increasingly anti-Ottoman feelings of the suffering Syrian population play in their attempts to define new identities for themselves in 1919–20? We also know little of the spur given to the growth of wartime industry, and of the industry's sudden collapse when trade began again in conditions of rapid inflation and a huge consumer spending boom in Egypt just after 1918. Conditions for the Jewish settlers in what was to become Palestine are also not well understood. How many stayed? How many moved temporarily, or permanently, to safer spots such as Alexandria? And then what forces impelled some of them to create or defend positions on the ground in the somewhat anarchic conditions in the months after the war when boundaries were still to be defined?

As for World War II, there are just as many areas where the historical record seems either wholly inadequate or simply nonexistent. Even as far as the two countries Syria and Egypt are concerned, we still know very little about the war's impact on the civilian population. And what we do know tends to be biased in terms of their suffering from shortages or, in the case of the Egyptian malaria epidemic of 1942, actual illness and disease, as against the opportunities that the wars provided for some groups to earn higher wages or become one of the war profiteers *(ghani al-harb)*, as described in Naguib Mahfouz's novel *Midaq Alley*. There are also useful contrasts to be drawn between the various regions under Anglo-French and American control. On the basis of present evidence, it would seem that in Palestine the British administrators attempted to replicate most closely the type of institutionalized controls and systems of wartime mobilization and redistribution in place in London but found that these could work effectively only with a population that was as committed to the war effort as the British themselves. This then necessitated various shifts and compromises in the direction of more flexible rationing (using a points system rather than fixed allocations of particular foodstuffs) and more creative attempts to mop up excess purchasing power, including the introduction of a government lottery. Finally, as is well-known, the encouragement given to the Jewish sector of the economy by government contracts created a firm material base for the Zionist drive for statehood as the world war came to an end. The situation in Transjordan, Iraq, and the Gulf was different again, as it most certainly was different in southern Iran and areas beyond Allied control, like Turkey.

The role of war, once the majority of Middle Eastern states had gained their independence after 1945, was wholly different and is much more difficult to pin down. In the first place, war began to involve sovereign states with their own ability to prepare for and initiate, and perhaps hope to benefit from, armed conflict with their neighbors. In the second place, war affected one part of the region, the area consisting of the new state of Israel and its immediate neighbors, much more in the first decades after independence than in either the Gulf or North Africa. There is also a question of the great disparity between the short duration of the fighting itself—less than a week in June 1967 and not much longer than two weeks in 1956 and 1973—and the huge consequences for regime authority, interstate relations, and the day-to-day lives of large sections of the civilian populations. By contrast, the Iraq-Iran war of the 1980s, and the long periods of civil war in Yemen, Lebanon, and Sudan, were bound to have quite different effects simply by virtue of the time they allowed for basic changes to take place.

As far as the history of the eastern end of the Mediterranean was concerned, it began with a bang: the intermittent fighting between Israel and its Arab neighbors from May 1948 to the Rhodes Armistice agreements of the spring and early summer of 1949. This, as many have pointed out, was one of the defining events of the postcolonial era: the fighting lasted long enough to allow the expansion of Israel's borders to the north and south, the flight of three-quarters of a million Palestinian refugees, the establishment of Jordanian control over the West Bank, the development of pressure on the Jewish communities in the Arab east and North Africa to migrate to Israel, and the beginning of seismic shifts in power in a number of Arab states, starting with Zaim's military coup in Syria in March 1949 and continuing through to the Free Officers' coup in Egypt in July 1952, which, as Nasser and his colleagues were quick to point out, had its origins in their defeat in Palestine. This in turn began a process of escalating hostility involving cross-border raids, an arms race fueled after a while by the two superpowers, and four more wars, until tensions gradually began to wind down again as a result of the Camp David Peace Agreement between Israel and Egypt, followed nearly fifteen years later by the Oslo Agreement between Israel and the Palestinians.

Paradoxically, although most of the later wars were of relatively short duration, they are the ones that remain fixed in every local person's memory, and which had a cumulative impact on policy, the conduct of interstate relations, and the creation of new political actors, like the PLO, so large as to still defy proper historical accounting. Indeed, for the time being, one gets a better sense of all this from personal testimony in novels, anthropological fieldwork, and films than from the scholarly literature itself. Reem Saad's chapter provides a very good example, with its emphasis on the central role of war "as a feature of contemporary Egyptian history" burned into the memories of the peasants she studied. What is also important in her account is the fact that wars, and the immediate impact of wars, are seen as part of the common national experience of all the people of Egypt, to be remembered and shared as part of a process of communal recollection. Another way of making the same point is to note the fact that the Egyptian novelist Rhada Ashour, who as a girl heard the air force planes flying overhead toward the Israeli border in 1948, says that her work is a prolonged attempt to cope with what she calls "defeat."

Consequences of this central role played by war, the expectation of war, and its use in support of a variety of powerful Middle Eastern political agendas comprise the subject of the chapters by Perthes, Migdal, and Sayigh on Syria, Israel, and the Palestinians. Each author comes at the subject from a somewhat different direction. For Perthes, the subject is not war itself, although that is lodged firmly in Syrian historical memory, but the use of preparation for war to manage society—to justify the existence of a large security establishment and to obtain a high level of strategic rent from the oil states of the Gulf in support of Syria's self-proclaimed role as the defender of the Arab heartland against Israeli aggression. For Migdal, however, the subject is the consequences of war, notably the expansion of Israel's boundaries following its victories against the Egyptians, Jordanians, and Syrians in 1967, and the impact this had on the unraveling of the system of leadership and national consensus built up by the Labor Party over the previous two decades. For Sayigh the focus is on the systematic employment of Palestinian defeat and forced dispersal to create statelike institutions, which allowed a fractured community to rally behind a single political leadership with access, like the Syrian government, to another form of strategic rent.

There were, however, two types of situations in which war itself played a much more permanent role in national life. One was where states of roughly commensurate military strength fought themselves to a standstill over many years, as in the case of Iraq and Iran. The other was a long-lasting civil war in which the local combatants were encouraged, and then thwarted, by a variety of outside powers. In both cases the conflict itself went on for sufficient time to allow the creation of new structures and the emergence of new forces with significant consequences for the political, economic, and social order. As noted in Isam al-Khafaji's account of Iraq in the 1980s, this took the form of the deliberate militarization of much of Iraqi society, which in turn led to regime-sanctioned violence, as well as the marginalization of the two communities branded as disloyal or said not to be proper Iraqis, that is, the Shi'is and the Kurds. Meanwhile, in Lebanon, the militias and their business allies adopted methods of maximizing the resources under their control, which undermined what was left of state authority and state regulation while paving the way for the creation of new economic centers of power after the war's end.

The chapters dealing with the second half of the twentieth century are also enormously suggestive of further lines of research. But rather than make a list of such topics on a country-by-country basis, it would be useful to step back and pose the larger question of how this same material might be employed to define our subject, "war, institutions, and social change," in such a way as to emphasize the coherence that the essays in this volume, implicitly or explicitly, suggest. I will begin by examining the transnational context before moving on to comments on the state and certain comparative issues, and then will return to the question of cumulative impact.

Of all the perspectives involved in the study of the impact of Middle Eastern war, it is the transnational that has so far received the least attention. This is odd, given the huge amount of literature devoted to general questions of war and peace and to the peculiar character of the regional subsystem. Nevertheless, it is rare to find more than passing reference to the notion of a Middle Eastern arms race or to the relationship between local military expansion and outside suppliers of either aid or equipment. And yet, clearly, in the state of no-peace between Israel and its neighbors—which existed in one form until the Camp David Agreement and continues, in another, until the present day—rival notions of the size and composition of the forces needed either to deter or overcome one or more potential enemies were crucial to the military buildup on all sides. In the light of such calculations, force levels and general strength were constantly ratcheted up through the 1970s before beginning to level off and then decline from the 1980s on. This much can be said in general, even though much about the exact nature of the process itself remains unexplored.

The felt need to maintain an increasingly large and competitive military establishment in Israel, Syria, Iraq, Jordan, and Egypt necessitated, in turn, access to outside aid and arms. And while in general terms this was greatly affected by the changing relationship between each government or regime and the United States, the Soviet Union, the European arms exporting states and, in the case of the Arabs, the rulers of the oil-rich Gulf sheikdoms, the full range of consequences has, again, never been adequately explored. These consequences include the influence of suppliers over the size and deployment of the military equipment in question, the impact of imported weapons systems on local systems of command and control, the strategies needed to influence foreign suppliers, and the creation of ever-increasing opportunities for self-enrichment by middle men, entrepreneurs, and freelance suppliers. To give just one of the most obvious examples, there is a very close correlation between the major supplier of battle tanks to the Arab armies—which was first the Soviets and now, for the Egyptians at least, the Americans—and the supplier's influence on the organization of local command structures designed to deploy them to best effect.

It can also be argued that the question of the size and nature of Middle Eastern armies had, in turn, a significant impact on the nature of the state. While state structures were different enough to make comparison difficult, it remains obvious that their sheer size alone made the militaries influential actors whose demand for local resources and a share in some of the most important decision-making processes concerning matters of security had to be fitted into the larger system of political management and control. To begin with the question of size: the expansion of a typical Arab army from a few thousand men at independence to several hundred thousand after the series of Arab-Israeli wars moved the military from a position of being too weak to control the whole state apparatus to one in which it could create and support powerful regimes; it grew so large that coups by disaffected colonels—or even generals—became a thing of the past. Another important trajectory was one that took armies into certain key sectors of the civilian economy, first in connection with military equipment itself, then into a host of peripheral activities as well. This in turn had the most important consequences for the relationship between the public and private sectors and was, in the case of the Israeli economy, partly responsible for the change in structure that took place after the 1967 war, which many economists blame for the marked slowdown in economic growth that continued for most of the next twenty years. By the same token, the present reduction in military size and spending, as the threat of another all-out Arab-Israeli war declines, will also have its own impact on the allocation of domestic resources and on the relationship between the military and other powerful economic actors.

Ideally, the situation as it developed at the center of the Middle East should be compared from the point of view of the salience of war and of preparations for war with that in North Africa and the Gulf, where, for different reasons, cross-border fighting was less important and armies remained much smaller. This is more like the Third World norm, where armies were kept mainly for internal security purposes and where few military organizations had much ability to project power outside their own territory or could do much damage to a neighboring army. By and large, wars had fewer long-lasting effects, arms races were less significant, and the nature of civil-military relations was likely to be different too. Indeed, it might be possible to imagine the situation in North Africa as constituting a useful example counterfactual to conditions in the Levant, and which allows us to at least speculate on what might have happened if Israel and its neighbors had managed to make peace shortly after 1948.

This brings me back to the central question of the cumulative impact of Middle Eastern wars and of the best way to gauge their impact on states, state making, and the development of the economy and society. The impact of one war, large or small, is clearly one thing; the impact of repeated wars, and so of an atmosphere in which new wars are both feared and expected, is quite another. Analysis of the latter represents a challenge, which the editor and contributors to this volume have begun to address. They are to be congratulated for posing so many new questions and for opening up so many new channels for research and debate. I am also confident that they have succeeded in one of the most important aims of this project, which was to transcend the limits of the Middle East itself and show the general blurring of the boundaries between war and peace, the study of which will have relevance for many other parts of the non-European world as well.

SELECTED BIBLIOGRAPHY

Abu Lughod, Janet. *Cairo: 1001 Years of the City Victorious.* Princeton: Princeton University Press, 1971.

Abu-Lughod, Lila. "The Romance of Resistance: Tracing Transformations of Power through Bedouin Women." *American Ethnologist* 17, no. 1 (1990): 41–55.

Abu Nowar, Ma'an. *The History of the Hashemite Kingdom of Jordan.* Vol. 1: *The Creation and Development of Transjordan, 1920–1929.* Oxford: Ithaca Press, 1989.

Adams, Richard. *Development and Social Change in Rural Egypt.* Syracuse University Press, 1986.

Aflaq, Michel, and Salah al-Din al-Bitar. *Mawqifuna al-siyasi min al-shiuy'iyya.* Cairo: n.p., 1957.

Aharoni, Yair. *The Israeli Economy: Dreams and Realities.* New York: Routledge, 1991.

Ake, Claude. "Modernization and Political Instability: A Theoretical Exploration." *World Politics* 26, no. 4 (July 1974): 576–91.

'Allush, Naji. "Is the Palestinian Revolution an Arab Nationalist Movement?" In *The Palestinian Revolution: Its Dimensions and Issues* (in Arabic). Beirut: Dar al-Tali'a, 1970.

———. *The Palestinian Revolution: Its Dimensions and Issues* (in Arabic). Beirut: Dar al-Tali'a, 1970.

Alnasrawi, Abbas. "Economic Devastation, Underdevelopment, and Outlook." In *Iraq since the Gulf War: Prospects for Democracy,* ed. Fran Hazelton. London: Zed Books, 1994.

———. "The Economy of Iraq." In *Iraq since the Gulf War: Prospects for Democracy,* ed. Fran Hazelton. London: Zed Books, 1994.

Alt, James E., and Kenneth A. Shepsle, ed. *Perspectives on Positive Political Economy.* New York: Cambridge University Press, 1990.

Amir, Ben-Porat. *Divided We Stand: Class Structure in Israel from 1948 to the 1980's.* New York: Greenwood Press, 1989.

Anderson, Benedict. *Imagined Communities: Reflections on the Origins and Spread of Nationalism.* London: Verso Editions and New Left Books, 1983.

Anderson, Lisa. *The State and Social Transformation in Tunisia and Libya, 1830–1980.* Princeton: Princeton University Press, 1986.

Anhoury, Jean. "Les reprecussions de la guerre sure l'agriculture Egyptienne." *L'Egypt contemporaine* (March-April 1947).

Antoun, Richard T. *Arab Village: A Social-Structural Study of a TransJordanian Peasant Community.* Bloomington: Indiana University Press, 1972.

Antoun, Richard T., and Donald Quataert, eds. *Syria: Society, Culture, and Polity.* Albany: State University of New York Press, 1991.

Arendt, Hannah. *On Revolution.* Reprint, London: Penguin Books, 1973.

———. *On Violence.* New York: Harcourt, Brace, and World, 1969.

Arms Control and Disarmament Agency. *World Military Expenditures and Arms Transfers.* Washington, D.C.: Arms Control Disarmament Agency, 1996.

Armstrong, James. "The Search for Israeliness: Toward an Anthropology of the Contemporary Mainstream." In *Critical Essays,* ed. Russell A. Stone and Walter P. Zenner.

Aron, Raymond. *Peace and War: A Theory of International Relations.* Malabar, Fla.: Krieger, 1981.

Aronoff, Myron J. *Israeli Visions and Divisions: Cultural Change and Political Conflict.* New Brunswick, N.J.: Transaction, 1989.

———, ed. *Cross-Currents in Israeli Culture and Politics: Political Anthropology.* Vol. 4. New Brunswick, N.J.: Transaction Books, 1984.

Asfour, Edmund Y. *Syria: Development and Monetary Policy.* Harvard Middle Eastern Monograph Series 1. Cambridge: Harvard University Press, 1959.

Ashford, Douglas E. *The Emergence of the Welfare States.* New York: Basil Blackwell, 1987.

Avineri, Shlomo. "Political Ideologies: From Consensus to Confrontation." In *The Impact of the Six-Day War: A Twenty-Year Assessment,* ed. Stephen J. Roth. New York: Macmillan, 1988.

Azar, Edward, ed. *The Emergence of a New Lebanon: Fantasy or Reality?* New York: Praeger, 1984.

Al-'Azm, Khalid. *Mudhakkirat Khalid al-'Azm.* Beirut: Dar al-Muttahida lil-Nashr, 1972.

Badran, Margot. *Feminists, Islam, and Nation: Gender and the Making of Modern Egypt.* Princeton: Princeton University Press, 1995.

Baldwin, Peter. "The Welfare State for Historians." *Comparative Studies in Society and History* 34, no. 4 (October 1992): 695–707.

Baram, Amatzia. "The June 1980 Elections to the National Assembly in Iraq: An Experiment in Controlled Democracy." *Orient,* no. 3 (1981).

Baram, Philip J. *The Department of State in the Middle East, 1919–1945.* Philadelphia: University of Pennsylvania Press, 1978.

Barnett, Michael. *Confronting the Costs of War: Military Power, State, and Society in Egypt and Israel.* Princeton: Princeton University Press, 1992.

———. *Dialogues in Arab Politics: Negotiations in Regional Order.* New York: Columbia University Press, 1998.

Al-Barrak, Fadhil. *Al-madaris al-Yahudiyya wa-al-Iraniyya fi al-Iraq: dirasa muqarina.* 2d ed. Baghdad: n.p., 1985.

Barzilai, Gad. *Wars, Internal Conflicts, and Political Order: A Jewish Democracy in the Middle East.* Albany: State University of New York Press, 1996.

Batatu, Hanna. *The Egyptian, Syrian, and Iraqi Revolutions: Some Observations on Their Underlying Causes and Social Character.* Washington, D.C.: Center for Contemporary Arab Studies, Georgetown University, 1983.

———. *The Old Social Classes and the Revolutionary Movements of Iraq.* Princeton: Princeton University Press, 1978.

Bates, Robert H. "Macropolitical Economy in the Field of Development." In *Perspectives on Positive Political Economy,* ed. James E. Alt and Kenneth A. Shepsle. New York: Cambridge University Press, 1990.

Bates, Robert H. et al. *Analytic Narratives.* Princeton: Princeton University Press, 1998.

Beblawi, Hazem. "The Rentier State in the Arab World." *Arab Studies Quarterly* 9, no. 4 (fall 1987): 383–94.

Beinin, Joel, and Zachary Lockman. *Workers on the Nile: Nationalism, Communism, Islam, and the Egyptian Working Class, 1882–1954.* Princeton: Princeton University Press, 1987.

Ben-Eliezer, Uri. *The Making of Israeli Militarism.* Bloomington: Indiana University Press, 1998.

Bidwell, Robin. *Arab Personalities of the Early Twentieth Century.* Cambridge: Archive Editions, 1986.

Biersteker, Thomas J., and Cynthia Weber, eds. *State Sovereignty as Social Construct.* Cambridge: Cambridge University Press, 1996.

Bill, James A. "The Study of Middle East Politics, 1946–1996: A Stocktaking." *The Middle East Journal* 50, no. 4 (autumn 1996): 501–12.

Binder, Leonard. *Islamic Liberalism: A Critique of Development Ideologies.* Chicago: University of Chicago Press, 1988.

Blin, Louis, and Philippe Fargues, eds. *L'Économie de la paix au Proche-Orient.* Paris: Maisonneuve et Larose, 1995.

Block, Fred, and Margaret R. Somers. "Beyond the Economistic Fallacy: The Holistic Social Science of Karl Polanyi." In *Vision and Method in Historical Sociology,* ed. Theda Skocpol. Cambridge: Cambridge University Press, 1984.

Bloom, William. *Personal Identity, National Identity and International Relations.* Cambridge: Cambridge University Press, 1990.

Bourgey, André. "Beyrouth, ville éclatée." *Hérodote* 17 (January-March 1980): 5–32.

Boustany, Fouad L. *Introduction à l'histoire politique du Liban moderne.* Beirut: Editions FMA, 1993.

Brand, Laurie. *Palestinians in the Arab World: Institution Building and the Search for State.* New York: Columbia University Press, 1988.

Breuilly, John. *Nationalism and the State.* Manchester: Manchester University Press, 1995.

Bromley, Simon. *Rethinking Middle East Politics.* Austin: University of Texas Press, 1994.

Brynen, Rex. "The Neopatrimonial Dimension of Palestinian Politics." *Journal of Palestine Studies* 25, no. 1 (autumn 1995).

————. *Sanctuary and Survival: The PLO in Lebanon.* Boulder, Colo.: Westview, 1990.

Brzoska, Michael. "Militarisierung als analytisches Konzept." In *Militarisierungs-und Entwicklungsdynamik: Eine Exploration mit Fallbeispielen zu Algerien, Iran, Nigeria, und Pakistan.* Hamburg: Deutsches Überseeinstitut, 1994.

————, ed. *Militarisierungs-und Entwicklungsdynamik: Eine Exploration mit Fallbeispielen zu Algerien, Iran, Nigeria, und Pakistan.* Hamburg: Deutsches Überseeinstitut, 1994.

Budeiri, Musa. "The Palestinians: Tensions between Nationalist and Religious Identities." In *Rethinking Nationalism in the Arab Middle East,* ed. James Jankowski and Israel Gershoni. New York: Columbia University Press, 1997.

[Buha'uddin, Ahmad.] *Dialogue about the Principal Issues of the Revolution* (in Arabic). Kuwait: Qabas for Fateh, n.d.

Burke, Victor Lee. *The Clash of Civilizations: War-Making and State Formation in Europe.* Cambridge: Policy Press, 1997.

Burley, Anne-Marie. "Regulating the World: Multilateralism, International Law, and the Projection of the New Deal Regulatory State." In *Multilateralism Matters: The Theory and Praxis of an International Form,* ed. John G. Ruggie. New York: Columbia University Press, 1993.

Buzan, Barry. *People, States, and Fear: An Agenda for International Security Studies in the Post–Cold War Era.* Hempstead: Harvester Wheatsheaf, 1991.

Calabrese, John, ed. *The Future of Iraq.* Washington, D.C.: Middle East Institute, 1997.

Campbell, John L. "The State and Fiscal Sociology." *Annual Review of Sociology* 19 (1993).

Castles, Frances, ed. *The Comparative History of Public Policy.* New York: Oxford University Press, 1989.

Catroux, Georges. *Dans la bataille de Méditerranée.* Paris: René Julliard, 1949.

Chartouni-Dubarry, May, ed. *Le couple syro-libanias dans le processes de paix.* Paris: Institut français des relations internationales, 1998.

Chaudhry, Kiren A. "Myths of the Market and the Common History of Late Developers." *Politics and Society* 21, no. 3 (September 1993): 245–74.

————. "On the Way to Market: Economic Liberalization and Iraq's Invasion of Kuwait." *Middle East Report,* no. 170 (May-June 1991): 14–23.

————. *The Price of Wealth: Economies and Institutions in the Middle East.* Ithaca: Cornell University Press, 1997.

Chernyak, Effim. "The French Revolution: 1794." *Social Sciences* (Moscow) 2 (1990): 65–84.

Chesnoff, Richard Z., Edward Klein, and Robert Littell. *If Israel Lost the War.* New York: Coward-McCann, 1969.

Clarkson, Jesse D., and Thomas C. Cochran, eds. *War as a Social Institution.* New York: Columbia University Press, 1941.

Cockell, John G. "Ethnic Nationalism and Subaltern Political Process: Exploring Autonomous Democratic Action in Kashmir." *Nations and Nationalism* 6, no. 3 (2000).

Cohen, Erik. "The Black Panthers and Israeli Society." In *Studies of Israeli Society.* Vol. 1: *Migration, Ethnicity, and Community,* ed. Ernest Krausz. New Brunswick: Transaction Books, 1980.

————. "Ethnicity and Legitimation in Contemporary Israel." *Jerusalem Quarterly* (summer 1983).

Cohen, Erik, Moshe Lissak, and Uri Almagor, eds. *Comparative Social Dynamics: Essays in Honor of S. N. Eisenstadt.* Boulder, Colo.: Westview Press, 1985.

Cohen, Miriam, and Michael Hanagan. "The Politics of Gender and the Making of the Welfare State, 1900–1940: A Comparative Perspective." *Journal of Social History* 24, no. 3 (spring 1991): pp. 469–84.

Cohen, William B. R. "The French Colonial Service in French West Africa." In *France and Britain in Africa: Imperial Rivalry and Colonial Rule,* ed. Prosser Gifford and William Roger Louis. New Haven: Yale University Press, 1971.

Collier, David, and James E. Mahon Jr. "Conceptual 'Stretching' Revisited: Adapting Categories in Comparative Analysis." *American Political Science Review* 87, no. 4 (December 1993): 845–55.

Collings, Deirdre, ed. *Peace for Lebanon: From War to Reconstruction.* Boulder, Colo.: Lynne Rienner, 1994.

Committee against Repression and for Democratic Rights in Iraq, ed. *Saddam's Iraq: Revolution or Dictatorship?* London: Zed Books, 1986.

Connor, Walker. *Ethnonationalism: The Quest for Understanding.* Princeton: Princeton University Press, 1994.

Conseil supérieur des intérêts communs. *Receuil de statistiques de la Syrie et du Liban, 1944.* Beirut: n.p., 1946.

————. *Receuil de statistiques de la Syrie et du Liban, 1945–47.* Beirut: n.p., 1948.

Cook, M. A., ed. *Studies in the Economic History of the Middle East.* London: Oxford University Press, 1970.

Corm, Georges. "Hegemonie milicienne et le problème du rétablissement de l'Etat." *Maghreb-Machrek* 131 (January-March 1991): 13–25.

————. "The War System: Militia Hegemony and Reestablishment of the State." In *Peace for Lebanon: From War to Reconstruction,* ed. Deirdre Collings. Boulder: Lynne Rienner, 1994.

Couland, Jacques. *Mouvement syndical au Liban, 1919–1946.* Paris: Editions sociales, 1970.

Curtis, Michael, and Mordecai S. Chertoff, eds. *Israel: Social Structure and Change.* New Brunswick: Transaction Books, 1973.

Dagher, Albert. *La crise de la monnaie libanaise, 1983–1989.* Beyrouth: Fiches du Monde Arabe, 1995.

Danet, Brenda. *Pulling Strings: Biculturalism in Israeli Bureaucracy.* Albany: State University of New York Press, 1989.

Dann, Uriel. *Studies in the History of Transjordan, 1920–49: The Making of a State.* Boulder, Colo.: Westview, 1984.

Dawisha, Adeed, and I. William Zartman, eds. *Beyond Coercion: The Durability of the Arab State.* London: Croom Helm, 1988.

Dawn, Ernest. *From Ottomanism to Arabism: Essays on the Origins of Arab Nationalism.* Urbana: University of Illinois Press, 1973.

de Bar, Luc. *Les communautés confessionnelles au Liban.* Paris: Recherches sur les civilisations, 1983.

DeNovo, John. "The Culbertson Economic Mission and Anglo-American Tensions in the Middle East, 1944–1945." *Journal of American History* 63 (1977): 913–33.

Deshen, Shlomo. "Political Ethnicity and Cultural Ethnicity in Israel During the 1960s." In *Studies of Israeli Society*. Vol. 1: *Migration, Ethnicity, and Community*, ed. Ernest Krausz. New Brunswick: Transaction Books, 1980.

Al-Disuqi, 'Asim. *Misr fi al-harb al-'alamiyya al-thaniyya, 1939–1945*. Cairo: Ma'had al-Buhuth was al-Dirasat al-'Arabiyya, 1976.

Divine, Donna Robinson. "Political Legitimacy in Israel: How Important Is the State?" *International Journal of Middle East Studies* 10 (1979): 205–24.

Diwan, Ishac, and Nick Papandreou. "The Peace Process and Economic Reforms." In *The Economics of Middle East Peace*, ed. Stanley Fischer, Dani Rodrik, and Elias Tuma. Cambridge: MIT Press, 1993.

Dominguez, Virginia. *People as Subject, People as Object: Selfhood and Peoplehood in Contemporary Israel*. Madison: University of Wisconsin Press, 1989.

Downing, Brian M. *The Military Revolution and Political Change: Origins of Democracy and Autocracy in Early Modern Europe*. Princeton: Princeton University Press, 1992.

Dowty, Alan. *The Jewish State: A Century Later*. Berkeley and Los Angeles: University of California Press, 1998.

Drake, Paul. *The Money Doctor in the Andes: The Kemmerer Missions, 1923–1933*. Durham: Duke University Press, 1989.

Eichholtz, Dietrich. *Geschichte der deutschen Kriegswirtschaft, 1939–1945*. Vol. 1 (1939–1941). Berlin: Akademie-Verlag, 1984.

Eisenstadt, S. N. *The Transformation of Israeli Society: An Essay in Interpretation*. London: Weidenfeld and Nicolson, 1985.

Eley, Geoff. "War and the Twentieth-Century State." *Daedalus* 124, no. 2 (spring 1995): 155–74.

Elias, Norbert. *La dynamique de l'Occident*. Paris: Payot, 1996.

Esman, Milton J., and Itamar Rabinovich, eds. *Ethnicity, Pluralism, and the State in the Middle East*. Ithaca: Cornell University Press, 1988.

Etzioni-Halevey, Eva. "Patterns of Conflict Generation and Conflict 'Absorption': The Cases of Israeli Labor and Ethnic Conflicts." In *Studies of Israeli Society*. Vol. 1: *Migration, Ethnicity, and Community*, ed. Ernest Krausz. New Brunswick: Transaction Books, 1980.

Evans, Peter, Dietrich Rueschemeyer, and Theda Skocpol, eds. *Bringing the State Back In*. Cambridge: Cambridge University Press, 1985.

Evron, Yair. *War and Intervention in Lebanon: The Israeli-Syrian Deterrence Dialogue*. London: Croom Helm, 1987.

Fanon, Frantz. *Wretched of the Earth*. 1967. Reprint, London: Penguin Books, 1969.

Fateh. "Birth and March" (in Arabic). Text originally published in early 1967 and reproduced in *Revolutionary Studies;* reprint, n.p.: Thawra Publications, n.d.

———. "Revolution and Violence Are the Way to Liberation" (in Arabic). In *Revolutionary Studies and Experiences*. No. 3. N.p., n.d.

———. "Structure of Revolutionary Construction" (in Arabic). In *Revolutionary Studies*. Reprint, n.p.: Thawra Publications, n.d.

"Fateh Starts the Discussion." In *Some Tenets of Guerrilla Action* (in Arabic). Kuwait: n.p., n.d.

Fieldhouse, David K. "The Economic Exploitation of Africa." In *France and Britain in Africa: Imperial Rivalry and Colonial Rule*, ed. Prosser Gifford and William Roger Louis. New Haven: Yale University Press, 1971.

Finlayson, Alan. "Psychology, Psycho-Analysis, and Theories of Nationalism." *Nations and Nationalism* 4, no. 2 (April 1998).

Fischer, Stanley, Dani Rodrik, and Elias Tuma, eds. *The Economies of Middle East Peace: Views from the Region.* Cambridge: MIT Press, 1993.

Flora, Peter, and Arnold J. Heidenheimer, eds. *The Development of Welfare States in Europe and America.* New Brunswick: Transaction Books, 1981.

Frisch, Hillel. *Countdown to Statehood: Palestinian State Formation in the West Bank and Gaza.* Albany: State University of New York Press, 1998.

Fromkin, David. *A Peace to End All Peace: The Fall of the Ottoman Empire and the Creation of the Modern Middle East.* New York: Avon Books, 1989.

Fussell, Paul. *The Great War and Modern Memory.* London: Oxford University Press, 1975.

Galnoor, Itzhak. "Israeli Society and Politics." In *The Impact of the Six-Day War: A Twenty-Year Assessment,* ed. Stephen J. Roth. New York: Macmillan, 1988.

———. *The Partition of Palestine: Decision Crossroads in the Zionist Movement.* Albany: State University of New York Press, 1995.

Gates, Carolyn L. "The Formation of the Political Economy of Modern Lebanon: The State and the Economy from Colonialism to Independence, 1939–1952." Ph.D. diss., Somerville College, University of Oxford, 1985.

———. "The Historical Role of Political Economy in the Development of Modern Lebanon." Papers on Lebanon 10. Oxford: Centre for Lebanese Studies, September 1989.

———. *The Merchant Republic of Lebanon: Rise of an Open Economy.* London: Centre for Lebanese Studies, in association with I. B. Tauris, 1998.

de Gaulle, Charles. *The Complete Memoirs of Charles de Gaulle.* New York: Simon and Schuster, 1972.

Gellner, Ernest. *Nations and Nationalism.* 1983. Reprint, Ithaca: Cornell University Press, 1993.

Gelvin, James L. "Demonstrating Communities in Post-Ottoman Syria." *Journal of Interdisciplinary History* 25, no. 1 (1994).

———. "The Social Origins of Popular Nationalism in Syria: Evidence for a New Framework." *International Journal of Middle East Studies* 26, no. 4 (1994).

Gereffi, Gary, and Donald L. Wyman, eds. *Manufacturing Miracles: Paths of Industrialization in Latin America and East Asia.* Princeton: Princeton University Press, 1990.

Giddens, Anthony. *The Nation-State and Violence.* Berkeley and Los Angeles: University of California Press, 1987.

Gifford, Prosser, and William Roger Louis, eds. *France and Britain in Africa: Imperial Rivalry and Colonial Rule.* New Haven: Yale University Press, 1971.

Gillis, John R., ed. *The Militarization of the Western World.* New Brunswick, N.J.: Rutgers University Press, 1989.

Godard, Jean. "Etude statistique de la situation économique en Syrie et au Liban." *L'Egypte contemporaine,* nos. 212–13 (April-May 1943).

———. *L'Oeuvre politique, économique, et sociale de la France Combattante en Syrie et au Liban.* Beyrouth: Ecole française de droit de Beyrouth, 1943.

Goldberg, Ellis, Resat Kasaba, and Joel Migdal, eds. *Rules and Rights in the Middle East: Democracy, Law, and Society.* Seattle: University of Washington Press, 1993.

Gongora, Thierry. "War Making and State Power in the Contemporary Middle East." *International Journal of Middle East Studies,* 29 no. 3 (August 1997): 19–50.

Gordon, Linda, ed. *Women, the State and Welfare.* Madison: University of Wisconsin Press, 1990.

Gorny, Yosef. *The State of Israel in Jewish Public Thought: The Quest for Collective Identity.* London: Macmillan, 1994.

Guazzone, Laura, ed. *The Middle East in Global Change: The Politics and Economics of Interdependence versus Fragmentation.* London: Macmillan, 1997.

Gubser, Peter. *Politics and Change in al-Karak, Jordan: A Study of a Small Arab Town and Its District.* Oxford: Oxford University Press, 1972.

———. "The Zu'ama' of Zahlah." *Middle East Journal* 27, no. 2 (1973).

Guttentag, Jack, and Richard Herring. "Disaster Myopia in International Banking." *Essays in International Finance.* No. 164. Princeton: Princeton University International Finance Section, 1986.

Haidar, Aziz. *On the Margins: The Arab Population in the Israeli Economy.* New York: St. Martin's Press, 1995.

Al-Hakim, Yusuf. *Suriya wa al-intidab al-Faransi.* Beirut: Dar al-Nahar lil-Nashr, 1973.

Hall, Peter, ed. *The Political Power of Economic Ideas: Keynesianism across Nations.* Princeton: Princeton University Press, 1989.

Halliday, Fred. "The Formation of Yemeni Nationalism: Initial Reflections." In *Rethinking Nationalism in the Arab Middle East,* ed. James Jankowski and Israel Gershoni. New York: Columbia University Press, 1997.

Hammel, Eric. *Six Days in June: How Israel Won the 1967 Arab-Israeli War.* New York: Charles Scribner's Sons, 1992.

Hanna, Abdullah. *Al-Haraka al-'ummaliya fi Suriya wa Lubnan 1900–1945.* Damascus: Dar Dimashq, 1973.

Harb el-Kak, Mona. *Politiques urbaines dans la banlieue-sud de Beyrouth.* Beirut: CERMOC, 1996.

Harik, Judith. *The Public Services of the Militias.* Oxford: Centre for Lebanese Studies, 1994.

Harris, William. "The View from Zahleh: Security and Economic Conditions in the Central Bekaa, 1980–1985." *Middle East Journal* 39, no. 3 (1985): 270–86.

Hassan, Najah Qassab. *Jil al-shaja'a hatta 'amm 1945.* Damascus: Alif Ba' al-Adib, 1994.

Hawatma, Nayif. *Action after the October War to Defeat the Surrenderist Liquidationist Solution and Seize the Right of Self-Determination* (in Arabic). N.p.: DFLP, 1974.

Hazelton, Fran, ed. *Iraq since the Gulf War: Prospects for Democracy.* London: Zed Books, 1994.

Helms, Christine Moss. *Iraq: Eastern Flank of the Arab World.* Washington, D.C.: Brookings Institution, 1984.

Herbst, Jeffrey. "War and the State in Africa." *International Security* 14, no. 4 (spring 1990): 117–39.

Herzog, Hanna. "Political Ethnicity as a Socially Constructed Reality: The Case of Jews in Israel." In *Ethnicity, Pluralism, and the State in the Middle East,* ed. Milton J. Esman and Itamar Rabinovich. Ithaca: Cornell University Press, 1988.

Heydemann, Steven. *Authoritarianism in Syria: Institutions and Social Conflict, 1946–1970.* Ithaca: Cornell University Press, 1999.

Hilan, Rizqallah. "The Effects on Economic Development in Syria of a Just and Long-Lasting Peace." In *The Economies of Middle East Peace: Views from the Region,* ed. Stanley Fischer, Dani Rodrik, and Elias Tuma. Cambridge: MIT Press, 1993.

———. *Al-thaqafa wa-l-tanmiya al-iqtisadiyya fi Suriya wa-l-buldan al-mukhallafa.* Damascus: Dar Maysaloun, 1981.

Himadeh, Raja S. *The Fiscal System of Lebanon.* Beirut: Khayat's, 1961.

Hinds, Martin, and El-Said Badawi. *A Dictionary of Egyptian Arabic.* Beirut: Librairie du Liban, 1986.

Hinnebusch, Raymond A. *Authoritarian Power and State Formation in Ba'thist Syria: Army, Party, and Peasant.* Boulder, Colo.: Westview, 1990.

———. "State Formation in a Fragmented Society." *Arab Studies Quarterly* 4 (1982): 177–97.

Hobsbawm, Eric J. *The Age of Extremes.* New York: Vintage Books, 1994.

———. *Nations and Nationalism since 1870: Programme, Myth, Reality.* 2d ed. 1990. Reprint, Cambridge: Cambridge University Press, 1994.

Holsti, Kalevi J. *The State, War, and the State of War.* Cambridge: Cambridge University Press, 1996.

Hottinger, Arnold. "Zu'Ama' and Parties." In *Politics in Lebanon,* ed. Leonard Binder, 85–105. New York: Wiley, 1966.

Hourani, Albert. "The Arab Awakening Forty Years Later." In *The Emergence of the Modern Middle East.* Berkeley and Los Angeles: University of California Press, 1981.

———. *The Emergence of the Modern Middle East.* Berkeley and Los Angeles: University of California Press, 1981.

Hourani, Hani. *Al-tarkib al-iqtisadi al-ijtima'i li sharq al-Urdunn: muqaddimat al-tatawwur al-mushawwah.* Beirut: Palestine Liberation Organization Research Center, 1978.

Howard, Michael. *The Lessons of History.* Oxford: Oxford University Press, 1991.

Hudson, Michael. "After the Gulf War: Prospects for Democratization in the Arab World." *Middle East Journal* 45, no. 3 (summer 1991): 407–26.

———. *The Precarious Republic.* New York: Random House, 1968.

Hull, Adrian Prentice. "Comparative Political Science: An Inventory and Assessment since the 1980s." *PS: Political Science and Politics* 32, no. 1 (March 1999): 117–24.

Hunter, Guy. "Economic Problems: The Middle East Supply Centre." In *The Middle East in the War,* ed. George Kirk. Royal Institute of International Affairs. London: Oxford University Press, 1952.

Ingram, Edward, ed. *National and International Politics in the Middle East: Essays in Honour of Elie Kedourie.* London: Frank Cass, 1986.

Iskandar, Adnan G. *Bureaucracy in Lebanon.* Beirut: American University of Beirut, 1964.

Issawi, Charles. *Egypt: An Economic and Social Analysis.* London: Oxford University Press, 1947.

———. *The Fertile Crescent, 1800–1914: A Documentary Economic History.* New York: Oxford University Press, 1988.

Jackson, Robert H. *Quasi-States: Sovereignty, International Relations, and the Third World.* New York: Cambridge University Press, 1990.

Jackson, Robert H., and Carl G. Rosberg, "Why Africa's Weak States Persist: The Empirical and the Juridical in Statehood." *World Politics* 35 (October 1982): 1–24.

Jalal, F. *The Role of Government in the Industrialisation of Iraq, 1950–1965.* London: Frank Cass, 1972.

Jallul, Faysal. *A Critique of Palestinian Arms: People, Revolution, and Camp in Burj al-Barajna* (in Arabic). Beirut: Dar al-Jadid, 1994.

Jankowski, James, and Israel Gershoni, eds. *Rethinking Nationalism in the Arab Middle East.* New York: Columbia University Press, 1997.

Janoski, Thomas, and Alexander M. Hicks. *The Comparative Political Economy of the Welfare State.* New York: Cambridge University Press, 1994.

Jarvis, Claude Scudmore. *Arab Command: The Biography of Lieutenant Colonel F. G. Peake Pasha.* London: Hutchinson, 1942.

Kasparian, Robert, Andre Beaudouin, and Selim Abou. *La population déplacée par la guerre au Liban.* Paris: L'Harmattan, 1995.

Katznelson, Ira. "The State to the Rescue? Political Science and History Reconnect." *Social Research* 59, no. 4 (winter 1992): 719–37.

Kaufman, Robert. "How Societies Change Developmental Models or Keep Them: Reflections on the Latin American Experience in the 1930s and the Postwar World." In *Manufacturing Miracles: Paths of Industrialization in Latin America and East Asia,* ed. Gary Gereffi and Donald L. Wyman. Princeton: Princeton University Press, 1990.

Kazziha, Walid W. *The Social History of Southern Syria (TransJordan) in the Nineteenth Century.* Beirut: Jami'at Bayrut al-'Arabiyya, 1972.

Keen, B. A. *The Agricultural Development of the Middle East: A Report to the Director General, Middle East Supply Centre, May, 1945.* London: HMSO, 1946.

Keen, David. *The Economic Functions of Violence in Civil Wars.* International Institute for Strategic Studies, Adelphi Paper 320. Oxford: Oxford University Press, 1998.

Kelidar, Abbas, ed. *The Integration of Modern Iraq.* London: Croom Helm, 1979.

Keren, Michael. *The Pen and the Sword; Israeli Intellectuals and the Making of the Nation-State.* Boulder, Colo.: Westview Press, 1989.

Khadduri, Majid. *Socialist Iraq: A Study of Iraqi Politics since 1968.* Washington, D.C.: Middle East Institute, 1978.

Al-Khafaji, Isam. "Always One War away from Revolution." *Civil Society* (Cairo) (September 1998): 15.

———. "Beyond the Ultra-Nationalist State." *Middle East Report,* nos. 187–188 (March-June 1994): 34–39.

———. *Al-dawla wa al-tatawwur al-ra'smali fi al-'Iraq, 1968–1978.* Tokyo: UN University and Cairo: Third World Forum, 1983.

———. "Al-iqtisad al-'Iraqi ba'd al-harb ma'a Iran." *Al-fikr al-istratiji al-'Arabi,* no. 32 (April 1990): 177–223.

———. "The Parasitic Base of the Iraqi Economy." In *Saddam's Iraq: Revolution or Dictatorship?* ed. Committee against Repression and for Democratic Rights in Iraq. London: Zed Books, 1986.

———. "Repression, Conformity, and Legitimacy: Prospects for an Iraqi Social Contract." In *The Future of Iraq*, ed. John Calabrese. Washington, D.C.: Middle East Institute, 1997.

———. "State Terror and the Degradation of Politics in Iraq." *Middle East Report* 176 (May-June 1992): 15–22.

Khalaf, Samir. *Lebanon's Predicament*. New York: Columbia University Press, 1987.

Khalidi, Rashid. *Under Siege: PLO Decisionmaking during the 1982 War*. New York: Columbia University Press, 1986.

Khalidi, Rashid, Lisa Anderson, Muhammad Muslih, and Reeva Simon, eds. *The Origins of Arab Nationalism*. New York: Columbia University Press, 1991.

Al-Khatib, Husam, "Whither the Palestinian Revolution?" (in Arabic). *Shu'un Filastiniyya*, no. 4 (September 1971).

Al-Khazin, Farid, and Paul Salem, eds. *Al-Intikhabat al-ula fi Lubnan ma ba'd al-harb*. Beirut: Dar al-Nahar, 1993.

Khoury, Philip S. *Syria and the French Mandate: The Politics of Arab Nationalism, 1920–1945*. Princeton: Princeton University Press, 1987.

———. "Syrian Political Culture: A Historical Perspective." In *Syria: Society, Culture, and Polity*, ed. Richard T. Antoun and Donald Quataert. Albany: State University of New York Press, 1991.

———. *Urban Notables and Arab Nationalism: The Politics of Damascus, 1860–1920*. New York: Cambridge University Press, 1983.

Kimmerling, Baruch. "Between the Primordial and the Civil Definitions of the Collective Identity: Eretz Israel or the State of Israel?" In *Comparative Social Dynamics: Essays in Honor of S. N. Eisenstadt*, ed. Erik Cohen, Moshe Lissak, and Uri Almagor. Boulder: Westview Press, 1985.

Kingston, Paul W. T. *Britain and the Politics of Modernization in the Middle East, 1945–1958*. Cambridge: Cambridge University Press, 1996.

Kirk, George, ed. *The Middle East in the War*. Royal Institute of International Affairs, London: Oxford University Press, 1952.

Klieman, A. S. *Foundations of British Policy in the Arab World: The Laird Conference of 1921*. Baltimore: Johns Hopkins University Press, 1970.

Korany, Baghat. "The Old/New Middle East." In *The Middle East in Global Change: The Politics and Economics of Interdependence versus Fragmentation*, ed. Laura Guazzone. London: Macmillan, 1997.

Korany, Baghat, Paul Noble, and Rex Brynen, eds. *The Many Faces of National Security in the Arab World*. London: Macmillan, 1993.

Kostiner, Joseph. "The Hashemite Tribal Confederacy." In *National and International Politics in the Middle East: Essays in Honour of Elie Kedourie*, ed. Edward Ingram. London: Frank Cass, 1986.

———. *The Making of Saudi Arabia, 1916–1936: From Chieftancy to Monarchical State*. New York: Oxford University Press, 1993.

Koven, Seth, and Sonya Michel. "Womanly Duties: Maternalist Policies and the Origins of Welfare States in France, Germany, Great Britain and the United States, 1880–1920." *American Historical Review* 4 (October 1990): 1076–108.

Kraus, Vered, and Robert W. Hodge. *Promises in the Promised Land: Mobility and Inequality in Israel*. New York: Greenwood Press, 1990.

Krausz, Ernest. *Studies of Israeli Society*. Vol. 1: *Migration, Ethnicity, and Community*. New Brunswick: Transaction Books, 1980.

Laqueur, Walter Z. *Communism and Nationalism in the Middle East.* 3d ed. London: Routledge and Kegan Paul, 1961.

Lee, J. M. *Colonial Development and Good Government: A Study of the Ideas Expressed by the British Official Classes in Planning Decolonization, 1939–1964.* Oxford: Clarendon Press, 1967.

Le Peillet, Pierre. *Les bérets bleus de l'ONU a travers 40 ans de conflit israélo-arabe.* Paris: France-Empire, 1988.

Lerner, Daniel. *The Passing of Traditional Society: Modernizing the Middle East.* New York: Free Press, 1958.

Levy, Yagil. *Trial and Error: Israel's Route from War to De-escalation.* Albany: State University of New York Press, 1997.

Lewis, Arnold. "Ethnic Politics and the Foreign Policy Debate in Israel." In *Cross-Currents in Israeli Culture and Politics: Political Anthropology.* Vol. 4, ed. Myron J. Aronoff. New Brunswick: Transaction Books, 1984.

"Liban: l'Argent des Milices." *Cahiers de l'Orient* 10 (1988): 271–87.

Lichbach, Mark I., and Alan S. Zuckerman, eds. *Comparative Politics: Rationality, Culture, and Structure.* New York: Cambridge University Press, 1997.

Liebman, Charles S., and Eliezer Don-Yehiya. *Civil Religion in Israel: Traditional Judaism and Political Culture in the Jewish State.* Berkeley and Los Angeles: University of California Press, 1983.

Liebman, Charles S., and Elihu Katz, eds. *The Jewishness of Israelis: Responses to the Guttman Report.* Albany: State University of New York Press, 1997.

Liron, Yocheved. *Deprivation and Socio-Economic Gap in Israel.* Jerusalem: Israel Economist, 1973.

Lipset, Seymour Martin. *Political Man: The Social Bases of Politics.* New York: Doubleday, 1960.

Lissak, Moshe, ed. *Israeli Society and Its Defense Establishment: The Social and Political Impact of a Protracted Violent Conflict.* London: Frank Cass, 1984.

Lloyd, E. M. H. *Food and Inflation in the Middle East, 1940–45.* Stanford: Stanford University Press, 1956.

Lobmeyer, Hans-Günter. *Opposition und Widerstand im ba'thistischen Syrien.* Hamburg: German Orient Institute, 1995.

Longrigg, Stephen Helmsley. *Syria and Lebanon under French Mandate.* 1958. Reprint, Beirut: Librairie du Liban, 1968.

Longuenesse, Elisabeth. "Guerre et décentralisation urbaine au Liban: le cas de Zghorta." In *Petites villes et villes moyennes dans le monde arabe.* Tours: Urbama, 1986.

Lustick, Ian S. "The Absence of Middle Eastern Great Powers: Political 'Backwardness' in Historical Perspective." *International Organization* 51, no. 4 (autumn 1997): 653–83.

———. *Arabs in the Jewish State: Israel's Control of a National Minority.* Austin: University of Texas Press, 1980.

———. *Unsettled States, Disputed Lands: Britain and Ireland, France, and Algeria, Israel and the West Bank-Gaza.* Ithaca: Cornell University Press, 1993.

Macciocchi, Maria Antoinetta, ed. *Elements pour une analyse du fascisme.* 2 vols. Paris: Edition 10/18, 1976.

Madi, Munib, and Suleiman Musa. *Tarikh sharq al-Urdunn fi al-qarn al-'ishrin.* Amman: n.p., 1958.

Mahdavy, H. "The Patterns and Problems of Economic Development in Rentier States: The Case of Iran." In *Studies in the Economic History of the Middle East,* ed. M. A. Cook. London: Oxford University Press, 1970.

Maila, Joseph. "The Document of National Reconciliation: A Commentary." *Prospects for Lebanon.* No. 4. Oxford: Centre for Lebanese Studies, 1992.

Makhlouf, Hassan. *Culture et commerce de drogue au Liban.* Paris: L'Harmattan, 1994.

Al-Malla, Ziad. *Safhat min tarikh al-hizb al-shiyu'i al-Suri (1924–1954).* Damascus: Al-Amali, 1994.

Mann, Michael. "The Autonomous Power of the State: Its Origins, Mechanisms and Results." In *States, War and Capitalism: Studies in Political Sociology.* Oxford: Blackwell, 1988.

———. "State and Society, 1130–1815: An Analysis of English State Finances." In *States, War, and Capitalism,* ed. Michael Mann. Oxford: Blackwell, 1988.

———. *States, War, and Capitalism.* Oxford: Blackwell, 1988.

Ma'oz, Moshe. *Palestinian Leadership in the West Bank: The Changing Role of the Mayors under Jordan and Israel.* London: Frank Cass, 1984.

———. *Syria and Israel: From War to Peacemaking.* Oxford: Clarendon Press, 1995.

Marr, Phoebe. *The Modern History of Iraq.* Boulder, Colo.: Westview Press, 1985.

Martin, Bernd, and Alan S. Milward, eds. *Agriculture and Food Supply in the Second World War.* Ostfildern: Scripta Mercaturae Verlag, 1985.

Martin, Denis-Constant. "The Choices of Identity." *Social Identities* 1, no. 1 (1995).

Massad, Joseph. "Conceiving the Masculine: Gender and Palestinian Nationalism." *Middle East Journal* 49, no. 3 (summer 1995).

Matthews, Roderic D., and Matta Akrawi. *Education in Arab Countries of the Near East.* Washington, D.C.: American Council on Education, 1949.

McAdam, Doug, John D. McCarthy, and Mayer N. Zald, eds. *Comparative Perspectives on Social Movements: Political Opportunities, Mobilizing Structures, and Cultural Framings.* Cambridge: Cambridge University Press, 1996.

McNeely, Connie L. *Constructing the Nation-State: International Organization and Prescriptive Action.* Westport, Conn.: Greenwood Press, 1995.

Meyer, John W. "The World Polity and the Authority of the Nation-State." In *Institutional Structure: Constituting State, Society, and the Individual,* ed. George M. Thomas, John W. Meyer, Francisco Ramierez, and John Boli. Neubury Park, Calif.: Sage Press, 1987.

Migdal, Joel. "Civil Society in Israel." In *Rules and Rights in the Middle East: Democracy, Law, and Society,* ed. Ellis Goldberg, Resat Kasaba, and Joel Migdal. Seattle: University of Washington Press, 1993.

———. *Strong Societies and Weak States: State-Society Relations and State Capabilities in the Third World.* Princeton: Princeton University Press, 1988.

———. "Studying the State." In *Comparative Politics: Rationality, Culture, and Structure,* ed. Mark I. Lichbach and Alan S. Zuckerman. New York: Cambridge University Press, 1997.

Migdal, Joel, Atul Kohli, and Vivienne Shue, eds. *State Power and Social Forces.* New York: Cambridge University Press, 1994.

Miller, David. *On Nationalism.* Oxford: Oxford University Press, 1995.

Millspaugh, Arthur C. *Americans in Persia.* Washington, D.C.: Brookings Institution, 1946.

Milward, Alan A. "The Second World War and Long-Term Change in World Agriculture." In *Agriculture and Food Supply in the Second World War,* ed. Bernd Martin and Alan S. Milward. Ostfildern: Scripta Mercaturae Verlag, 1985.

———. *War, Economy, and Society, 1939–1945.* Berkeley and Los Angeles: University of California Press, 1979.

Ministère des affaires étrangères (France). *Rapport à la Société des Nations sur la situation de la Syrie et du Liban (Année 1928).* Paris: Imprimerie nationale, 1929.

Mitchell, Timothy. *Colonising Egypt.* Cambridge: Cambridge University Press, 1988.

Moore, Clement Henry. "Le système bancaire libanais: les substituts financiers d'un ordre politique." *Maghreb-Machrek* 99 (February-March 1983): 30–47.

Morris, Benny. *The Birth of the Palestinian Refugee Problem, 1947–1949.* Cambridge: Cambridge University Press, 1987.

Moualem, Walid. "Fresh Light on the Syrian-Israeli Peace Negotiations." *Journal of Palestine Studies* 27, no. 2 (1997): 81–94.

Murphy, Alexander. "The Sovereign State System as Political-Territorial Ideal: Historical and Contemporary Considerations." In *State Sovereignty as Social Construct,* ed. Thomas J. Biersteker and Cynthia Weber. Cambridge: Cambridge University Press, 1996.

Musa, Suleiman. "The Rise of Arab Nationalism and the Emergence of Transjordan." In *Nationalism in a Non National State,* ed. William Ochsenwald and William W. Haddad. University of Ohio Press: Columbus, 1977.

Najm al-Din, Ahmed. *Ahwal al-sukkan fi al-'Iraq.* Cairo: Jami'at al-Duwal al-'Arabiyya, Ma'had al-Buhouth wa al-Dirasat al-'Arabiyya, 1970.

Nettl, J. P. "The State as a Conceptual Variable." *Comparative Politics* 20, no. 4 (July 1968): 559–92.

Nevo, Joseph. "The Arabs of Palestine, 1947–48: Military and Political Activity." *Middle Eastern Studies* 23, no. 1 (January 1987).

North, Douglass C. *Institutions, Institutional Change, and Economic Performance.* New York: Cambridge University Press, 1990.

Norton, Augustus Richard. *Amal and the Shi'a: Struggle for the Soul of Lebanon.* Austin: University of Texas Press, 1987.

Ochsenwald, William L. *The Hijaz Railway.* Charlottesville: University Press of Virginia, 1981.

———. "Ironic Origins: Arab Nationalism in the Hijaz, 1882–1914." In *The Origins of Arab Nationalism,* ed. Rashid Khalidi et al. New York: Columbia University Press, 1991.

———. "Opposition to Political Centralisation in South Jordan and the Hijaz." *Muslim World* 63 (October 1973): 297–306.

Ochsenwald, William L., and William W. Haddad, eds. *Nationalism in a Non National State.* Columbus: University of Ohio Press, 1977.

O'Donnell, Guillermo. *Modernization and Bureaucratic Authoritarianism: Studies in South American Politics.* Berkeley: Institute of International Studies, University of California, 1973.

Office Arabe de presse et documentation (Syria). *Receuil des statistiques syriennes comparées (1928–1968)*. Damascus: n.p., 1970.

Omar, Suha. "Women: Honor, Shame, and Dictatorship." In *Iraq since the Gulf War: Prospects for Democracy,* ed. Fran Hazelton. London: Zed Books, 1994.

Palestine Liberation Organization. *Palestinian Popular Culture Faced with Zionist Attempts at Arrogation.* N.p., 1976.

Parker, Geoffrey. *Military Innovation and the Rise of the West, 1500–1800.* New York: Cambridge University Press, 1996.

Peake, Frederick G. *A History of Jordan and Its Tribes.* Coral Gables, Fla.: University of Miami Press, 1958.

———. "Transjordan." *Royal Central Asian Society Journal* (1939).

Pedatzur, Reuven. *The Triumph of Embarrassment: Israel and the Territories after the Six-Day War* (in Hebrew). Tel-Aviv: Bitan, 1996.

Peled, Yoav. "Ethnic Democracy and the Legal Construction of Citizenship: Arab Citizens of the Jewish State." *American Political Science Review* 86 (June 1992).

———. "Mizrahi Jews and Palestinian Arabs: Exclusionist Attitudes in Development Towns." In *Ethnic Frontiers and Peripheries: Landscapes of Development and Inequality in Israel,* ed. Oren Yiftachel and Avinoam Meir. Boulder: Westview Press, 1998.

Peleg, Ilan. "The Arab-Israeli Conflict and the Victory of Otherness." In *Critical Essays on Israeli Social Issues and Scholarship: Books on Israel,* vol. 3, ed. Walter P. Zenner. Albany: State University of New York Press, 1994.

Peres, Yochanan. "Modernization and Nationalism in the Identity of the Israeli Arab." *Middle East Journal* 24 (autumn 1970): 479–92.

Perthes, Volker. "From War Dividend to Peace Dividend? Syrian Options in a New Regional Environment." In *L'Économie de la paix au Proche-Orient,* ed. Louis Blin and Philippe Fargues. Paris: Maisonneuve et Larose, 1995.

———. "Kriegsdividende und Friedensrisiken: Überlegungen zu Rente und Politik in Syrien." *Orient* 35, no. 3 (1994): 413–24.

———. *The Political Economy of Syria under Asad.* London: I. B. Tauris, 1995.

———. "Scénarios syriens: Processes de paix, changements internes et relations avec le Liban." In *Le couple syro-libanias dans le processes de paix,* ed. May Chartouni-Dubarry. Paris: Institut français des relations internationales, 1998.

———, ed. *Scenarios for Syria: Socio-Economic and Political Choices.* Baden-Baden: Nomos Publishers, 1998.

Picard, Elizabeth. *Demobilization of the Militias: A Lebanese Dilemma.* Oxford: Centre for Lebanese Studies, 1999.

———. "Les habits neufs du communautarisme libanais." *Cultures et conflits,* nos. 15–16 (1994): 49–70.

———. "State and Society in the Arab World: Towards a New Role for the Security Services?" In *The Many Faces of National Security in the Arab World,* ed. Bahgat Korany, Paul Noble, and Rex Brynen. London: Macmillan, 1993.

———. "La Syrie et le processus de paix." *Monde arabe Maghreb Machrek* 158 (October-December 1997): 56–69.

Pieterse, Jan Nederveen. "Deconstructing/Reconstructing Ethnicity." *Nations and Nationalism* 3, no. 3 (November 1997).

Pipes, Daniel. *Greater Syria: The History of an Ambition.* New York: Oxford University Press, 1990.

―――. "Syrie: l'après-Assad." *Politique internationale* 59 (spring 1993): 97–110.

Plessner, Yakir. *The Political Economy of Israel: From Ideology to Stagnation.* Albany: State University of New York Press, 1994.

Poggi, Gianfranco. *The State: Its Nature, Development, and Prospects.* Cambridge: Polity Press, 1990.

Polanyi, Karl. *The Great Transformation.* Rev. ed. 1944. Reprint, Boston: Beacon Press, 1957.

Pool, David. "From Elite to Class: The Transformation of Iraqi Political Leadership." In *The Integration of Modern Iraq,* ed. Abbas Kelidar. London: Croom Helm, 1979.

Popular Front for the Liberation of Palestine. "The Basic Political Report of the PFLP." In *Palestinian Arab Documents 1968* (in Arabic). Beirut: Institute for Palestine Studies, 1970.

―――. *The Proletariat and the Palestinian Revolution* (two speeches by George Habash in May 1970; in Arabic). Beirut: n.p., n.d. [1970].

Porter, Bruce D. *War and the Rise of the State.* New York: Free Press, 1994.

Powell, Walter W., and Paul J. DiMaggio, eds. *The New Institutionalism in Organizational Analysis.* Chicago: University of Chicago Press, 1991.

Prest, A. R. *War Economics of Primary Producing Countries.* Cambridge: Cambridge University Press, 1948.

Puaux, Gabriel. *Deux années au Levant.* Paris: Hachette, 1952.

Putterman, Louis, and Dietrich Rueschemeyer, eds. *State and Market in Development: Synergy or Rivalry?* Boulder, Colo.: Lynne Reinner, 1992.

Qasimiyyah, Khayriyyah. *Hukumah al-'Arabiyyah fi Dimashq, 1918–1920.* Beirut: Al-mu'assasa al-'arabiyya lil-dirasat wa al-nashr, 1982.

Qurtas, Wadad al-Maqdisi. *Dhikrayat, 1917–1977.* Beirut: Mu'assasat al-Abhath al-'Arabiya, 1982.

Ranis, Gustav. "The Role of Governments and Markets." In *State and Market in Development: Synergy or Rivalry?* ed. Louis Putterman and Dietrich Rueschemeyer. Boulder: Lynne Reinner, 1992.

Remba, Oded. "Income Inequality in Israel: Ethnic Aspects." In *Israel: Social Structure and Change,* ed. Michael Curtis and Mordecai S. Chertoff. New Brunswick: Transaction Books, 1973.

Richards, Alan. *Egypt's Agricultural Development, 1800–1980: Technical and Social Change.* Boulder, Colo.: Westview Press, 1982.

Richards, Alan, and John Waterbury. *A Political Economy of the Middle East: State, Class and Economic Development.* Boulder: Westview, 1990.

Rivlin, Paul. *The Israeli Economy.* Boulder, Colo.: Westview Press, 1992.

Robinson, Glenn E. *Building a Palestinian State: The Incomplete Revolution.* Indiana: Indiana University Press, 1997.

Rock, David, ed. *Latin America in the 1940s: War and Postwar Transitions.* Berkeley and Los Angeles: University of California Press, 1994.

Rogan, Eugene. "Bringing the State Back: The Limits of Ottoman Rule in Transjordan, 1840–1910." In *Village, Steppe and State: The Social Origins of Modern Jordan,* ed. Eugene Rogan and Tariq Tell. London: British Academic Press, 1994.

Rogan, Eugene, and Tariq Tell, eds. *Village, Steppe, and State: The Social Origins of Modern Jordan.* London: British Academic Press, 1994.

Rosen, S. McKee. *The Combined Boards of the Second World War: An Experiment in International Administration.* New York: Columbia University Press, 1951.

Rosenau, James N. "The State in an Era of Cascading Politics: Wavering Concept, Widening Competence, Withering Colossus, or Weathering Change?" *Comparative Political Studies* 21 (April 1988).

Rosenthal, Jean-Laurent. "The Political Economy of Absolutism Reconsidered." In *Analytic Narratives,* ed. Robert H. Bates et al. Princeton: Princeton University Press, 1998.

Roter, Raphael, and Nira Shamai. "Social Policy and the Israeli Economy, 1948–1980." In *Economic and Social Policy in Israel: The First Generation,* ed. Moshe Sanbar. New York: University Press of America, 1990.

Roth, Stephen J., ed. *The Impact of the Six-Day War: A Twenty-Year Assessment.* New York: Macmillan, 1988.

Rothwell, Charles Easton. "War and Economic Institutions." In *War as a Social Institution,* ed. Jesse D. Clarkson and Thomas C. Cochran. New York: Columbia University Press, 1941.

Rudolph, Lloyd I., and Susanne Hoeber Rudolph. *The Modernity of Tradition: Political Development in India.* Chicago: University of Chicago Press, 1967.

Ruggie, John G. *Multilateralism Matters: The Theory and Praxis of an International Form.* New York: Columbia University Press, 1993.

Sadowski, Yahya. "Cadres, Guns, and Money: The Eighth Regional Congress of the Syrian Ba'th." *MERIP Reports,* no. 134 (July-August 1985).

———. "Political Power and Economic Organization in Syria: The Course of State Intervention, 1946–1958." Ph.D. diss., University of California, Los Angeles, 1984.

Said, Edward. *Orientalism.* New York: Vintage Books, 1979.

Salibi, Kamal S. *The Modern History of Lebanon.* New York: Frederick A. Praeger, 1965.

Sanadiki, Chafik. "Le Mouvement syndical en Syrie." Ph.D. diss., University of Paris, Faculty of Law, 1949.

Sanbar, Moshe, ed. *Economic and Social Policy in Israel: The First Generation.* New York: University Press of America, 1990.

Savir, Uri. *The Process: 1,100 Days That Changed the Middle East.* New York: Random House, 1998.

Al-Sayigh, Anis. *Al-hashimiyyun wa al-thawra al-'Arabiyya al-kubra.* Beirut: Dar al-Tali'a, 1966.

Sayigh, Rosemary. "Dis/Solving the 'Refugee Problem.'" *Middle East Report,* no. 207 (summer 1998).

———. *Palestinians: From Peasants to Revolutionaries.* London: Zed Books, 1979.

Sayigh, Yezid. *Arab Military Industry: Capability, Performance, and Impact.* London: Brassey's, 1992.

———. *Armed Struggle and the Search for State: The Palestinian National Movement, 1949–1993.* Oxford: Clarendon Press, 1997.

———. "Escalation or Containment? Egypt and the Palestine Liberation Army, 1964–1967." *International Journal of Middle Eastern Studies* 30, no. 1 (February 1998).

―――. "Globalization Manqué: Regional Fragmentation and Authoritarian-Liberalism in the Middle East." In *The Third World beyond the Cold War*, ed. Louise Fawcett and Yezid Sayigh. Oxford: Oxford University Press, 1999.

―――. "The Palestinians." In *The Cold War and the Middle East*, ed. Yezid Sayigh and Avi Shlaim. Oxford: Clarendon Press, 1997.

―――. "Turning Defeat into Opportunity: The Palestinian Guerrillas after the June 1967 War." *Middle East Journal* 46, no. 2 (spring 1992).

Sayigh, Yezid, and Avi Shlaim, eds. *The Cold War and the Middle East*. Oxford: Clarendon Press, 1997.

Schatkowski-Schilcher, Linda. "The Famine of 1915–1918 in Greater Syria." In *Problems of the Modern Middle East in Historical Perspective: Essays in Honour of Albert Hourani*. St. Antony's Middle East Monographs, ed. John P. Spagnolo. No. 26. Reading: Ithaca Press, 1992.

Scott, James C. *Weapons of the Weak: Everyday Forms of Peasant Resistance*. New Haven: Yale University Press, 1985.

Seale, Patrick. *Asad of Syria: The Struggle for the Middle East*. London: I. B. Tauris, 1988.

Sen, Amartya K. *Poverty and Famines: An Essay on Entitlement and Deprivation*. New York: Oxford University Press, 1981.

Shalev, Michael. *Labour and the Political Economy in Israel*. New York: Oxford University Press, 1992.

Shama, Avraham, and Mark Iris. *Immigration without Integration: Third World Jews in Israel*. Cambridge, Mass.: Schenkman, 1977.

Shaw, Martin, ed. *War, State, and Society*. New York: St. Martin's Press, 1984.

Shiblaq, Abbas. *The Lure of Zion*. London: Al-Saqi Books, 1987.

Shlaim, Avi. *Collusion across the Jordan: King Abdullah, the Zionist Movement, and the Partition of Palestine*. Oxford: Clarendon Press, 1988.

El-Shorbagi, S. *Mudhakkarat 'an Harb Octobar li-gami' al-talaba*. Cairo: al-Mu'assassa al-Arabiyya al-Haditha, 1974.

Sikkink, Kathryn. *Ideas and Institutions: Developmentalism in Brazil and Argentina*. Ithaca: Cornell University Press, 1987.

Skocpol, Theda. "Bringing the State Back In: Strategies of Analysis in Current Research." In *Bringing the State Back In*, ed. Peter Evans, Dietrich Rueschemeyer, and Theda Skocpol. Cambridge: Cambridge University Press, 1985.

―――. *Protecting Soldiers and Mothers: The Political Origins of Social Policy in the United States*. Cambridge: Harvard University Press, Belknap Press, 1992.

―――. "Social Revolutions and Mass Military Mobilization." *World Politics* 40 (January 1988): 147–68.

―――. *Social Revolutions in the Modern World*. Cambridge: Cambridge University Press, 1994.

―――, ed. *Vision and Method in Historical Sociology*. Cambridge: Cambridge University Press, 1984.

Skocpol, Theda, and John Ikenberry. "The Political Formation of the American Welfare State in Historical and Comparative Perspective." *Comparative Social Research* 6 (1983): 87–148.

Smith, Anthony D. *The Ethnic Origins of Nations*. 1986. Reprint, Oxford: Blackwell, 1995.

Smooha, Sammy. *Israel: Pluralism and Conflict.* London: Routledge and Kegan Paul, 1978.

Soueif, Ahdaf. *In the Eye of the Sun.* London: Bloomsbury, 1992.

Spagnolo, John P., ed. *Problems of the Modern Middle East in Historical Perspective: Essays in Honour of Albert Hourani.* St. Antony's Middle East Monographs, no. 26. Reading: Ithaca Press, 1992.

Spears, Sir Edward. *Fulfilment of a Mission: Syria and Lebanon, 1941–1944.* Hamden, Conn.: Archon Books, 1977.

Spilerman, Seymour, and Jack Habib. "Development Towns in Israel: The Role of Community in Creating Ethnic Disparities in Labor Force Characteristics." In *Studies of Israeli Society.* Vol. 1: *Migration, Ethnicity and Community,* ed. Ernest Krausz. New Brunswick: Transaction Books, 1980.

Sprinzak, Ehud. *The Ascendance of Israel's Radical Right.* New York: Oxford University Press, 1991.

Spruyt, Hendrik. *The Sovereign State and Its Competitors.* Princeton: Princeton University Press, 1994.

Starr, Joyce. "Lebanon's Economy: The Cost of Protracted Violence." In *The Emergence of a New Lebanon: Fantasy or Reality,* ed. Edward Azar. New York: Praeger, 1984.

Steinmo, Sven, Kathleen Thelen, and Frank Longstreth, eds. *Structuring Politics: Historical Institutionalism in Comparative Perspective.* New York: Cambridge University Press, 1992.

Stevenson, William. *Strike Zion!* New York: Bantam Books, 1967.

Stone, Russell A., and Walter P. Zenner, eds. *Critical Essays on Israeli Social Issues and Scholarship: Books on Israel.* Vol. 3. Albany: State University of New York Press, 1994.

Strang, David. "British and French Political Institutions and the Patterning of Decolonization." In *The Comparative Political Economy of the Welfare State,* ed. Thomas Janoski and Alexander M. Hicks. New York: Cambridge University Press, 1994.

Stubbs, Richard. "War and Economic Development: Export-Oriented Industrialization in East and Southeast Asia." *Comparative Politics* 31, no. 3 (April 1999): 337–55.

Swift, Jeremy. "Why Are Rural People Vulnerable to Famine?" *Institute for Development Studies Bulletin* 20, no. 2 (1989): 8–15.

Swirski, Shlomo. *Israel: The Oriental Majority.* New Jersey: Zed Books, 1989.

Tamari, Salim. "Soul of the Nation: The Fallah in the Eyes of the Urban Intelligentsia." *Review of Middle East Studies* 5 (1992): 74–83.

Tarrow, Sidney. *Power in Movement: Social Movements, Collective Action, and Politics.* Cambridge: Cambridge University Press, 1994.

———. "States and Opportunities: The Political Structuring of Social Movements." In *Comparative Perspectives on Social Movements: Political Opportunities, Mobilizing Structures, and Cultural Framings,* ed. Doug McAdam, John D. McCarthy, and Mayer N. Zald. Cambridge: Cambridge University Press, 1996

Tauber, Eleazar. *The Arab Movements in World War I.* London: Frank Cass, 1993.

Tessler, Mark, ed., with Jodi Nachtwey and Anne Banda. *Area Studies and Social Science: Strategies for Understanding Middle East Politics.* Bloomington: Indiana University Press, 1999.

Therborn, Goran. "The Rule of Capital and the Rise of Democracy." *New Left Review* 103 (May-June): 3–41.

Thomas, George M., John W. Meyer, Francisco Ramircz, and John Boli, cds. *Institutional Structure: Constituting State, Society, and the Individual.* Neubury Park, Calif.: Sage Press, 1987.

Thompson, Elizabeth. *Colonial Citizens: Republican Rights, Paternal Privilege, and Gender in French Syria and Lebanon.* New York: Columbia University Press, 2000.

Tibawi, Abdul Latif. *A Modern History of Syria, including Lebanon and Palestine.* New York: Macmillan and St. Martin's Press, 1969.

Tibi, Bassam. *Arab Nationalism: A Critical Inquiry.* Trans. Peter Sluglett and Marion Farouk Sluglett. London: Macmillan, 1971.

Tignor, Robert L. *Egyptian Textiles and British Capital, 1930–1956.* Cairo: American University in Cairo Press, 1989.

———. "The Suez Crisis of 1956 and Egypt's Foreign Private Sector." *Journal of Imperial and Commonwealth History* 20 (May 1992): 274–97.

Tilly, Charles. *As Sociology Meets History.* New York: Academic Press, 1981.

———. *Coercion, Capital, and European States, AD 900–1990.* Cambridge, Mass.: Basil Blackwell, 1990.

———. "Reflections on the History of European State-Making." In *The Formation of National States in Western Europe.* Princeton: Princeton University Press, 1975.

———. "War Making and State Making as Organized Crime." In *Bringing the State Back In,* ed. Peter Evans, Dietrich Rueschemeyer, and Theda Skocpol. Cambridge: Cambridge University Press, 1985.

———, ed. *The Formation of National States in Western Europe.* Princeton: Princeton University Press, 1975.

Timmerman, Kenneth R. *The Death Lobby: How the West Armed Iraq.* London: Bantam Books, 1992.

Trimberger, Ellen Kay. *Revolution from Above: Military Bureaucrats and Development in Japan, Turkey, Egypt, and Peru.* New Brunswick, N.J.: Transaction Books, 1978.

'Ubayd, Makram. *Al-kitab al-aswad.* Cairo: Al-Markaz al-'Arabiyya lil Buhuth wa al-Nashr, 1984.

'Umar, Mahjub. "The Palestinian Ramadan War: Position and Results" (in Arabic). *Shu'un Filastiniyya* (Beirut), no. 119 (n.d.).

United Nations. *Statistical Yearbook, 1948.* New York: United Nations, 1949.

Vandervalle, Dirk. *Libya since Independence: Oil and State Building.* Ithaca: Cornell, 1998.

Verba, Sidney. "Some Dilemmas in Comparative Research." *World Politics* 20, no. 1 (October 1967): 111–27.

Vitalis, Robert. "The End of Third Worldism in Egypt Studies." *Arab Studies Journal* 4, no. 1 (spring 1996): 13–33.

———. "The New Deal in Egypt: The Rise of Anglo-American Commercial Rivalry in World War II and the Fall of Neocolonialism." *Diplomatic History* 20, no. 2 (spring 1996): 211–40.

———. *When Capitalists Collide: Business Conflict and the End of Empire in Egypt.* Berkeley and Los Angeles: University of California Press, 1995.

Waddell, Brian. "Economic Mobilization for World War II and the Transformation of the U.S. State." *Politics and Society* 22, no. 2 (June 1994): 165–94.

Waisman, Carlos. *Reversal of Development in Argentina: Postwar Counterrevolutionary Policies and Their Structural Consequences.* Princeton: Princeton University Press, 1987.

Wasserstein, Bernard. *The British in Palestine: The Mandatory Government and Arab-Jewish Conflict, 1917–1929.* Cambridge, Mass.: Blackwell, 1991.

Waterbury, John. *The Egypt of Nasser and Sadat: The Political Economy of Two Regimes.* Princeton: Princeton University Press, 1983.

al-Wazir, Khalil. *Fateh: Genesis, Rise, Evolution, Legitimate Representative—Beginnings* (in Arabic). Pt. 1. N.p., 1986.

Wedeen, Lisa. *Ambiguities of Domination: Politics, Rhetoric, and Symbols in Contemporary Syria.* University of Chicago Press, 1999.

Weir, Margaret, and Theda Skocpol. "State Structures and the Possibilities for 'Keynesian' Responses to the Great Depression in Sweden, Britain, and the United States." In *Bringing the State Back In,* ed. Peter Evans, Dietrich Rueschemeyer and Theda Skocpol. Cambridge: Cambridge University Press, 1985.

Weisburd, David. *Jewish Settler Violence: Deviance as Social Reaction.* University Park: Pennsylvania State University Press, 1989.

White, Hayden. *The Content of the Form.* Baltimore: Johns Hopkins University Press, 1987.

———. "The Question of Narrative in Contemporary Historical Theory." In *The Content of the Form.* Baltimore: Johns Hopkins University Press, 1987.

———. "The Value of Narrativity in the Representation of Reality." In *The Content of the Form.* Baltimore: Johns Hopkins University Press, 1987.

Wickes, George, ed. *Lawrence Durrell, Henry Miller: A Private Correspondence.* New York: Dutton, 1963.

Wilmington, Martin W. *The Middle East Supply Centre.* Albany: State University of New York Press, 1971.

Wilson, Jeremy. *Lawrence of Arabia: The Authorised Biography of T. E. Lawrence.* London: Minerva, 1990.

Wilson, Mary. "The Hashemites, the Arab Revolt and Arab Nationalism." In *The Origins of Arab Nationalism,* ed. Rashid Khalidi et al. New York: Columbia University Press, 1991.

Wolf, Eric R. *Peasant Wars of the Twentieth Century.* New York: Harper Row, 1969; New York: Harper Collins, 1973.

Wolfsfeld, Gadi. *The Politics of Provocation: Participation and Protest in Israel.* Albany: State University of New York Press, 1988.

Woloch, Isser. *The New Regime: Transformations of the French Civic Order, 1789–1820s.* New York: W. W. Norton and Co., 1994.

Yiftachel, Oren. "The Internal Frontier: Territorial Control and Ethnic Relations in Israel." In *Ethnic Frontiers and Peripheries: Landscapes of Development and Inequality in Israel,* ed. Oren Yiftachel and Avinoam Meir. Boulder, Colo.: Westview Press, 1998.

Yiftachel, Oren, and Avinoam Meir, eds. *Ethnic Frontiers and Peripheries: Landscapes of Development and Inequality in Israel.* Boulder, Colo.: Westview Press, 1998.

Young, Nigel. "War Resistance, State and Society." In *War, State and Society,* ed. Martin Shaw. New York: St. Martin's Press, 1984.

Yusif, Shihada. *Palestinian Reality and the Union Movement* (in Arabic). Beirut: PLO Research Center, 1973.

Al-Zaidi, Ahmad. *Al-Bina'a al-ma'nawi li al-quwwat al-musallaha al-'Iraqiyya.* Beirut: Dar al-Rawdha, 1990.

Zartman, I. William. "Opposition as Support of the State." In *Beyond Coercion: The Durability of the Arab State,* ed. Adeed Dawisha and I. William Zartman. London: Croom Helm, 1988.

————. "State-Building and the Military in Arab Africa." In *The Many Faces of National Security in the Arab World,* ed. Bahgat Korany, Paul Noble, and Rex Brynen. London: Macmillan, 1993.

Zeine, Zeine N. *Arab-Turkish Relations and the Emergence of Arab Nationalism.* Beirut: Khayyats, 1958.

CONTRIBUTORS

Steven Heydemann is associate professor of political science at Columbia University. He previously worked as program director at the Social Science Research Council in New York. He is the author of *Authoritarianism in Syria, 1946–1970: Institutions and Social Conflict* (1999).

Isam al-Khafaji is an Iraqi social scientist and writer. He teaches in the Department of Political Science, the Amsterdam School of International Relations and the International School of Humanities and Social Sciences, University of Amsterdam, and is a fellow of the Research Center for International Political Economy at the same university. Al-Khafaji is also a contributing editor of *Middle East Reports* and program director at the Transnational Institute in Amsterdam.

Joel S. Migdal is the Robert F. Philip Professor of International Studies at the University of Washington's Henry M. Jackson School of International Studies. His latest books are the Hebrew edition of *Palestinians: The Making of a People* (coauthored with Baruch Kimmerling, 1999) and the Chinese edition of *Peasants, Politics, and Revolution: Pressures Towards Political and Social Change in the Third World* (1996). Professor Migdal is also a former chair of the Joint Committee on the Near and Middle East of the Social Science Research Council. He is preparing two volumes of his essays, one on an approach to studying state-in-society, and one on state-society relations in Israel. His current research focuses on nonstate authority in public space.

Roger Owen is A. J. Meyer Professor of Middle East History, Harvard University. Before coming to Harvard in 1993 he taught Middle East economic history at Oxford University. He is the author of *Cotton and the Egyptian Economy* (1969), *The Middle East in the World Economy* (1981), and *State, Power, and Politics in the Making of the Modern Middle East* (1992); and he coauthored (with Sevket Pamuk) *A History of the Middle East Economies* (1998). Professor Owen is a former chair of the Joint Committee on the Near and Middle East of the Social Science Research Council and a past president of the Middle East Studies Association of North America.

Volker Perthes directs the Middle East/Mediterranean Programme at the Stiftung Wissenschaft und Politik, Research Institute for International Affairs, in Ebenhausen and Berlin, Germany. He previously was assistant professor at the American University of Beirut. He is the author of *The Political Economy of Syria under Asad* (1995) and *Vom Krieg zur Konkurrenz: Regionale Politik und die Suche nach einem neuen arabisch-nahoestlichen System* (1999).

Elizabeth Picard, an Arabist and political scientist, is a senior researcher at the Centre National de la Recherche Scientifique (Aix-en-Provence, France). She is currently the director of the Centre d'Etudes et de Recherches sur le Moyen-Orient Contemporain attached to the French Ministry of Foreign Affairs in Beirut and Amman. She is the editor of *La question kurde* (1993) and *La nouvelle dynamique au Moyen-Orient* (1993) and the author of *Lebanon, the Shattered Country* (1996) and *The Demobilisation of the Lebanese Militias* (1999).

Reem Saad is a social anthropologist with research interests in rural Egypt, issues of public culture, and ethnographic film. She is the author of a monograph entitled "Social History of an Agrarian Reform Community in Egypt," as well as a number of articles on village and peasant in contemporary Egypt. She was the Ioma Evans-Pritchard Junior Research Fellow at St. Anne's College, Oxford, and is presently working for the Social Research Center at the American University in Cairo.

Yezid Sayigh is assistant director at the Centre for International Studies at the University of Cambridge and was previously a research fellow at St. Antony's College, Oxford. His books include *The Third World beyond the Cold War* (coedited with Louise Fawcett, 1999); *Armed Struggle and the Search for State: The Palestinian National Movement, 1949–1993* (1997); *The Cold War and the Middle East* (coedited with Avi Shlaim, 1997); *Arab Military Industry: Capability, Performance, and Impact* (1992); and *Confronting the 1990s: Security in the Developing Countries* (1990).

Tariq Tell is an associate researcher at the Centre d'Etudes et de Recherches sur le Moyen-Orient Contemporain (CERMOC); he coordinated the Jordan program of CERMOC-Amman between 1995 and 1998. A Jordanian national, he was educated at the London School of Economics and Oxford

University. He has worked at the International Institute of Strategic Studies in London and was a permanent researcher at the Economic Research Department of the Royal Scientific Society in Amman between 1982 and 1991. He is the coeditor (with Eugene Rogan) of *Village, Steppe, and State: The Social Origins of Modern Jordan* (1994)and has written on the political economy of liberalization in Jordan after 1989 and on the historical evolution of rural policy and hydropolitics in Jordan.

Elizabeth Thompson is assistant professor of history at the University of Virginia and author of the recently published *Colonial Citizens: Republican Rights, Paternal Privilege, and Gender in French Syria and Lebanon* (2000). She is currently working on a comparative study of citizenship in Middle Eastern, African, and Asian territories of the late French empire.

Robert Vitalis is associate professor in the Department of Political Science at the University of Pennsylvania and director of the university's Center for Middle East Studies. He is the author of *When Capitalists Collide: Business Conflict and the End of Empire* (1995). He is currently involved in research on the oil industry and Saudi Arabia, and on race and international relations.

INDEX